Central Works of Philosophy

Central Works of Philosophy is a multi-volume set of essays on the core texts of the Western philosophical tradition. From Plato's *Republic* to the present day, the volumes range over 2,500 years of philosophical writing, covering the best, most representative, and most influential work of some of our greatest philosophers. Each essay has been specially commissioned and provides an overview of the work and clear and authoritative exposition of its central ideas. Together these essays introduce the masterpieces of the Western philosophical canon and provide an unrivalled companion for reading and studying philosophy.

Central Works of Philosophy
Edited by John Shand

Volume 1: Ancient and Medieval

Volume 2: The Seventeenth and Eighteenth Centuries

Volume 3: The Nineteenth Century

Volume 4: The Twentieth Century: Moore to Popper

Volume 5: The Twentieth Century: Quine and After

Central Works of Philosophy Volume 4

The Twentieth Century: Moore to Popper

Edited by John Shand

McGill-Queen's University Press
Montreal & Kingston • Ithaca

In memory of my parents, Alexander Hesketh Shand and Muriel Olive Shand

© Editorial matter and selection, 2006 John Shand. Individual contributions, the contributors.

ISBN 0-7735-3080-0 (hardcover)
ISBN 0-7735-3081-9 (paperback)

Legal deposit first quarter 2006
Bibliothèque nationale du Québec

Published simultaneously outside North America
by Acumen Publishing Limited

McGill-Queen's University Press acknowledges the financial support of the Government of Canada through the Book Publishing Development Program (BPIDP) for its activities.

Library and Archives Canada Cataloguing in Publication

Central works of philosophy / edited by John Shand.

Includes bibliographical references and indexes.
Contents: v. 1. Ancient and medieval -- v. 2. The seventeenth
    and eighteenth centuries -- v. 3. The nineteenth century --
    v. 4. The twentieth century : Moore to Popper.
ISBN 0-7735-3015-0 (v. 1 : bound).--ISBN 0-7735-3016-9 (v. 1 : pbk.).--
ISBN 0-7735-3017-7 (v. 2 : bound).--ISBN 0-7735-3018-5 (v. 2 : pbk.).--
ISBN 0-7735-3052-5 (v. 3 : bound).--ISBN 0-7735-3053-3 (v. 3 : pbk.).--
ISBN 0-7735-3080-0 (v. 4 : bound).--ISBN 0-7735-3081-9 (v. 4 : pbk.)

1. Philosophy--Introductions. I. Shand, John, 1956-

B21.C45 2006   100   C2005-902037-7

Designed and typeset by Kate Williams, Swansea.
Printed and bound in Malta by Gutenberg Press.

Contents

CONTENTS

Contributors

Robert L. Arrington is Professor Emeritus of Philosophy at Georgia State University, Atlanta. He is the author of *Rationalism, Realism, and Relativism* and *Western Ethics*, and the editor of *A Companion to the Philosophers* and *The World's Great Philosophers*. He is also the coeditor of three collections of essays on Wittgenstein.

Pascal Engel is Professor of Philosophy at Université de Paris IV–Sorbonne. He has written on philosophy of logic, of language and of mind. He is the author of *The Norm of Truth* and *Truth* (Acumen), *Ramsey, Truth and Success* (with J. Dokic) and editor of *New Inquiries into Meaning and Truth*.

Hans-Johann Glock is Professor of Philosophy at the University of Reading. He is the author of *A Wittgenstein Dictionary* and *Quine and Davidson*. He has edited *The Rise of Analytic Philosophy* and *Wittgenstein: A Critical Reader*, and coedited *Wittgenstein's Philosophical Investigations* and *Wittgenstein and Quine*.

Barry Gower was formerly Professor of Philosophy at the University of Durham. His current research interests are in how probabilistic reasoning has been used in science, and in the relations between metaphysical thinking and scientific theorizing.

Charles Guignon is Professor of Philosophy at the University of South Florida. He is the author of *Heidegger and the Problem of Knowledge* and *On Being Authentic*, and editor of *The Cambridge Companion to Heidegger* and *Existentialism: Basic Writings*.

Rom Harré began his academic career in mathematics and physics, being drawn into philosophy and psychology under the influence of Gilbert Ryle and John Austin. He is currently Emeritus Fellow of Linacre College, Oxford, and Distinguished Research Professor at Georgetown University, Washington DC. His most recent books include *One Thousand Years of Philosophy* and *Cognitive Science: A Philosophical Introduction*.

Christopher Hookway is Professor of Philosophy at the University of Sheffield. His research interests lie in epistemology, the philosophy of language and the study of American Pragmatism, and his books include *Peirce* in the Arguments of the Philosophers series, *Scepticism* and *Truth, Rationality, and Pragmatism: Themes from Peirce*.

Eric Matthews studied philosophy at Oxford with Grice, Ayer and Ryle, and taught philosophy for almost forty years at the University of Aberdeen, apart from two visiting appointments at US universities. Currently, he is Emeritus Professor of Philosophy at the University of Aberdeen, but continues to write, mainly on the philosophy of psychiatry.

William R. Schroeder currently teaches post-Kantian continental philosophy at the University of Illinois, Urbana-Champaign. His books include *Sartre and His Predecessors: The Self and the Other* and *Continental Philosophy: A Critical Approach*. He coedited the *Blackwell Companion to Continental Philosophy*.

John Shand studied philosophy at the University of Manchester and King's College, Cambridge. He is an Associate Lecturer in Philosophy at The Open University and is the author of *Arguing Well* and *Philosophy and Philosophers: An Introduction to Western Philosophy* (second edition, Acumen) and editor of *Fundamentals of Philosophy*.

Jeremy Shearmur studied at the London School of Economics, and subsequently worked there as assistant to Karl Popper. He later taught philosophy at the University of Edinburgh, political theory at the University of Manchester and was Research Associate Professor at George Mason University, Virginia. He currently teaches philosophy at the Australian National University.

A. D. Smith is Professor of Philosophy at the University of Sussex. He is the author of *The Problem of Perception* and *Husserl and the Cartesian Meditations* as well as several articles in the areas of the history of philosophy, the philosophy of mind and action and the philosophy of language.

Philip Stratton-Lake is Professor of Philosophy at the University of Reading. He is the author of *Kant, Duty and Moral Worth* and editor of *Ethical Intuitionism: Re-evaluations*, the revised edition of W. D. Ross's *The Right and the Good* and *On What We Owe To Each Other*.

Thomas Uebel is Reader in Philosophy at the University of Manchester. His research interests centre around topics in epistemology and philosophy of social science and history of analytical philosophy and history of philosophy of science. He has authored and edited five books on logical empiricism and has published widely in journals and the specialist literature.

Preface

The works in the *Central Works of Philosophy* volumes have been chosen because of their fundamental importance in the history of philosophy and for the development of human thought. Other works might have been chosen; however, the underlying idea is that if any works should be chosen, then these certainly should be. In the cases where the work is a philosopher's *magnum opus* the essay on it gives an excellent overview of the philosopher's thought.

Chapter 1 is Philip Stratton-Lake on G. E. Moore's *Principia Ethica*. Moore's book had a revolutionary impact on moral philosophy. Moore argues for moral realism – the doctrine that ethical judgements can be true or false – but against all forms of natural reductionism – the view that *good* can be defined in non-moral, natural, terms. The latter claim is the "naturalistic fallacy", and the fallacy is exposed by directed attention to positions such as hedonistic utilitarianism where "good" is defined in terms of pleasure. Moore uses the "open question" argument to refute all such reductions to some natural property x as giving the definitional *meaning* of good. If they really gave the definition of "good", then it would not make sense to ask "Is x good?", for one would be asking "Is good good?". But the question always does make sense. Moore defends a form of consequentialism according to which we should, morally speaking, aim at things that are good. There is a variety of things that are good, although none of these defines it; principal among these is the appreciation of beauty, love and friendship.

Chapter 2 is A. D. Smith on Edmund Husserl's *The Idea of Phenomenology*. In this work Husserl sets out a new path for philosophy, one in which it has a pure subject matter that makes no presuppositions whatsoever about the world. Philosophy should be "transcendental", and philosophy proper is transcendental phenomenology. Transcendental phenomenology comes about by adopting a certain unnatural attitude to our experience. It notes that all thoughts have "intentionality" or "aboutness", in that they are always thoughts *of* something, and thus have an object. This realm of intentional objects (say, the mouse that I am searching for in the room, regardless of whether there is a mouse existing in the room) grants an autonomous presuppositionless subject matter to philosophy. Instead of taking as read all the things that experience supposedly tells us about the nature of the world, and indeed that such a world exists, the correct philosophical perspective involves a "bracketing" (*epochē*) of these matters, and does not go beyond the certainty that we have particular sorts of experiences. The subject matter of philosophy as a "rigorous science" is quite distinct from natural science let alone common sense; philosophy's subject matter is the structure and content of experiences themselves, considered as universal *kinds*, rather than as individual instances. This structure and content is given in the intuition of the essence of experiences; that is, what it is that makes an experience the sort of experience that it is and not another sort of experience. The truths about essences are so, regardless of the nature or existence of the world. Phenomenology is concerned with experiences in their universal aspect, as sorts of experience, not with their particularity.

Chapter 3 is Christopher Hookway on William James's *Pragmatism: A New Name for Some Old Ways of Thinking*. An overarching aim of the book is to reconcile scientific and religious outlooks; the former tend to be associated with "tough-minded" empiricists and the latter with "tender-minded" rationalists. Pragmatism is seen by James not as a body of philosophical doctrine, but as a *method*, which when applied to various recalcitrant philosophical problems shows that really there is nothing vital in dispute between proposed opposing solutions, since adopting or failing to adopt one solution or the other has no practical import for our dealings with the world; such disputes are "idle". Concepts and theories are primarily tools and, as with mundane tools proper, they have value only if they have a job to do and do the job they are designed for well; otherwise disputes over such concepts and theories are mere castles in the air. Truth is seen by James as having primarily a pragmatic function: a belief should be considered true in so far as it has a practical utility for our coping with the world, for example, predicting our experience. The meaning of truth on this view is explained as being instrumental and regulative. From this explanation, content can be given to what is meant by a belief "agreeing with reality" and, thus, being "true".

Chapter 4 is Hans-Johann Glock on Ludwig Wittgenstein's *Tractatus Logico-Philosophicus*. In this work Wittgenstein thought that he had globally resolved all the problems of philosophy, and he thus abandoned philosophy for some years. The problems of philosophy are quashed globally by showing that there are no genuine philosophical propositions or questions at all. This is shown by giving an account of the essence of the proposition: the way that any genuine proposition – that is, a linguistic expression capable of being determinately true or false – has its sense. Propositions have a sense because they represent a possible state of affairs, a possible combination of objects. True propositions represent actual states of affairs, that is, facts. What a proposition represents is its sense, and it comes to have that sense by picturing a possible state of affairs. Although on the surface propositions may not look like pictures, the underlying logical structure of fully analysed elementary propositions must be made up of atomic names that go proxy for atomic objects in the world, and the proposition is true when the relations of those atomic names mirror the relation of the atomic objects in the world. The sentences employed in philosophy generally, and in metaphysics in particular, are literal nonsense, that is, not cognitively significant, for they cannot represent any possible state of affairs. The concepts occurring in putative philosophical propositions cannot occur in genuine propositions. The propositions of logic are senseless tautologies, which show by always being true whatever facts obtain that they say nothing about the world. The case is the same with contradictions, as they are always false. Therefore, there is no realm of meaningful *a priori* propositions in which philosophy may express truths or falsehoods about reality or anything else. The truths of metaphysics, ethics, aesthetics and religion are ineffable. The attempt to *say* – as opposed to *show* – things about these matters only distorts and trivializes their subject matter. The *Tractatus* itself attempts to say what cannot be said, but once we climb the ladder to get the correct logical point of view, we can discard it. The function of philosophy is then only to guard against transgressions of the bounds of what can significantly be said. It turns into an activity, that of logical analysis, which displays the underlying logical structure of meaningful propositions (the empirical propositions which present a possible state of affairs) and reveals the pronouncements of traditional philosophy to be bereft of sense.

Chapter 5 is Charles Guignon on Martin Heidegger's *Being and Time*. The central purpose of this book is to answer the question of what we mean when we talk about the *Being* of anything; what is meant when we say of something that *it is*. Heidegger runs deeply against the grain of the Western philosophical tradition that identifies existence with some kind of enduring stuff or substance: matter, for example. Many things that clearly seem to exist – that have Being – such as symphonies, love, truth, human beings and the Second World War, do not appear to be material objects or any kinds of enduring substantial objects. Nor is talk about such things plausibly reducible to talk about enduring objects, their attributes and relations. Heidegger undercuts these prevailing assumptions and raises the question of Being in such a way as to ask: how is it that certain kinds of things show up *as existing for us*? The answer is that things show up as existing for us because of our having a certain way of "human being-in-the-world" (*Dasein*). Things show up as existing because some things matter to us more than others; this mattering itself depends on our practical comportment to the world as engaged active creatures, beings who exist in time, not as disinterested, disembodied "objective" consciousnesses. The idea that the standpoint of disinterested, disembodied "objective" consciousnesses gives us the true view of reality has, since Descartes and even Plato, been the view that forms the basis of science and mainstream philosophy. Heidegger rejects the claimed logical primacy and epistemic privilege of this standpoint and gives a detailed phenomenological description of our primary pre-theoretical encounter with reality and how it arises.

Chapter 6 is Thomas Uebel on Rudolf Carnap's *The Logical Structure of the World*. In this book Carnap pursues the aim of the Vienna Circle: to construct an appropriate language representing how scientific theories properly relate to the empirical base. Carnap is not concerned with actual scientific language, but with a logical construction that grounds scientific language, in general, empirically. There can be no *a priori* knowledge of the world, only of pure mathematics. On one view, Carnap is showing that meaningful talk of physical objects must be reducible to phenomenal talk concerning the experience of individual consciousnesses; otherwise, statements concerning the physical world could not be verified. However, another view suggests that his chief aim is not this reduction itself, but rather to give a clear sense of objectivity in science. He is concerned with the logical and epistemic structure of how our experiences relate to scientific statements, not to their psychological relations or their qualitative phenomenal content. The sole structural starting-point is remembered similarity between experiences. In this way, the limit of objective knowledge, by which is meant scientific knowledge, and indeed the limit of meaningful discourse, is bounded by the possibility of verifiability or refutation by experience. Science as objective knowledge concerns itself only with the structural aspects of reality as they show up in our experience.

Chapter 7 is Pascal Engel on Bertrand Russell's *An Inquiry into Meaning and Truth*. Russell's subject is epistemology, or the theory of knowledge; in particular, he is concerned with the order of justification in empirical knowledge, through which we come to know facts about the world. Russell's approach in this relatively late work sustains features that run consistently throughout his thinking: realism; the separation of the subjective and objective; taking truth as primary and dependent only on a relation to facts that are independent of what we may be able to verify and thus come to know; empiricism, according to which knowledge of the world may come, basically, only through the verification or refutation of statements that stand in some direct relation to experience. The caveat is that although there can be no pure *a priori* knowledge of the world – *a priori* knowledge is possible only in logic and mathematics – we may in empirical knowledge have to rely on some non-demonstrative principles or postulates that cannot be based on empirical evidence. Russell is concerned to establish what is meant by empirical evidence for the truth of a proposition, and what we are entitled to infer from such evidence. Russell's empiricism is in the spirit of Hume. Russell, however, uses the latest tools in philosophical logic to tackle this issue linguistically and he makes distinctions within the various ways we talk about the world in order to show that there are "basic propositions" that depend for their truth or falsity on a relation to experience, and not, as in the case of higher-level assertions – which are ultimately justified by being derived from basic propositions – on their relation to other propositions. Thus, Russell aims to determine the epistemic order of our knowledge – the circumstances under which we are entitled to assert that we know propositions about the world to be true – as distinct from its logical or psychological order. Empirical knowledge cannot attain absolute certainty, but we can show how it may be derived based on the fewest and least doubtful set of assumptions. The threads of Russell's ideas in epistemology are brought together in an account of meaning and reference; the theory of knowledge is inseparable from an enquiry into the meaning of words.

Chapter 8 is William R. Schroeder on Jean-Paul Sartre's *Being and Nothingness*. This is a work of existential phenomenology. By "phenomenology" is meant the systematic study of the structure of consciousness and its objects. Sartre's phenomenology is "existential" because it takes as primary the way we encounter objects that show up as a consequence of our mode of being as humans who are practically engaged in the world. The essential intentionality of consciousness points to its objects being something other than modes of consciousness. The concrete situation has a meaning and structure that cannot be grasped in abstract speculation. This opposes the view that a true, supposedly objective view of reality is that gained only from a detached, disinterested, disembodied point of view – a position found in Husserl's transcendental phenomenology. This epistemic elevation of disinterested abstraction is a legacy of Cartesianism, which assumes that the seat of consciousness is an indubitable ego that can give us a "view from nowhere", with the distorting contingencies of our perspective removed, which supposedly reveals a more fundamental ontology than appears in our everyday lives. Sartre argues that this makes the mistake of thinking that the ego, or self, is a thing. Rather the self is nothing – literally nothing – and the self emerges only in reflection in the course of our engagement with a world that is ontologically other than the self. The self is made, and may be remade, through what we do. Sartre's philosophy, like Heidegger's, undercuts the "subjective" and "objective" dichotomy, because one side of the dichotomy cannot be considered intelligibly without the other. The ontological structure of reality – the kinds of things we encounter as objects in the world – only shows up as it does because of our engaged purposeful lives; the world does not present itself as "flat", with all parts having our equal attention and interest. Our consciousness, and who we are, is not a pure ego, but only emerges in reflection in the course of our purposeful engagement with the world. Self and world are inextricably linked. Sartre's book aims to give a systematic description of the relationship between the various objects as they appear in our lived experience with certain meanings and significances. This includes the significance of others; indeed our view of the world is shaped fundamentally intersubjectively, and strongly involves an awareness of how others see us.

Chapter 9 is Eric Matthews on Maurice Merleau-Ponty's *Phenomenology of Perception*. The purpose of the book is to give a pre-theoretical description of our experience without any metaphysical or scientific presuppositions. The way we experience the world prior to theorizing is the primary way in which we encounter the world, the way in which the world has any meaning or significance it has for us, and out of which any theoretical views are constructed. This undermines the legitimacy of two supposed philosophical starting-points: intellectual idealism and empiricism. They are both in fact laden with theoretical assumptions, and bring with them insoluble, but unnecessary, philosophical problems. Intellectual idealism reduces the world to a construct out of our experience; but this imperils the objectivity of the world and threatens to turn the mind in on itself because there is no genuine object of the experience. Empiricism posits the world as objective and utterly detached from experience; but this attempt to eliminate subjectivity has the consequence that many features we ascribe to the world, such as meaning and value, but also possibly scientifically essential notions such as causality, are mere subjective projects and not part of reality at all. Merleau-Ponty argues that both positions illegitimately impose a theory that gives a place to experience before examining experience itself. The world cannot in any case be detached from experience, nor can it be constructed out of a transcendental subjective perspective. Rather the world shows up in our experience as it does because of the kind of experiencers we are: embodied, engaged, purposeful creatures. Thus, "subject" and "object" mark an artificial distinction, a construct posterior to the two being such that necessarily talk of one must involve talk of the other.

Chapter 10 is Barry Gower on A. J. Ayer's *Language, Truth and Logic*. Ayer's book is one of those philosophical works that attempts to clear away once and for all the vast intractable jumble of disputes characteristic of philosophy. At the outset Ayer's logical positivism attempts to eliminate metaphysics. This may be seen as just part of an attempt to eliminate philosophy itself in so far as the subject is concerned with substantive "philosophical problems"; when properly looked at philosophical problems turn out to be pseudo-problems. Ayer goes about this by looking at the language in which philosophy expresses its ideas, and discovers that such ideas, which purport to concern matters that can be true or false, are expressed in language that conforms to neither of the two ways in which, exhaustively, statements can be literally meaningful. A genuine proposition (a linguistic form that can be literally either true or false) is either analytic and necessary, and true or false just because of the meaning of the terms making it up – in which case it tells us nothing about the world – or it is synthetic and contingent, and true or false because of facts about the world that may in principle be verified by experience. Otherwise, a putative proposition is a pseudo-proposition and literal nonsense. The putative propositions of metaphysics, and propositions in other areas of philosophy, fit neither category of meaningfulness, and so they do not express anything that can be true or false.

Chapter 11 is Rom Harré on Gilbert Ryle's *The Concept of Mind*. Ryle's overriding concern is to define the nature and function of philosophy itself. Central to his delineation is the systematic removal of conceptual confusions: showing that certain expressions do not refer to the states of affairs we think they do, and showing the states of affairs they do refer to. The first, negative, part of this Ryle called identifying "category mistakes". Category mistakes involve erring about the meaning and reference of concepts. Thus, for example, we see a brass band playing in perfect unison, but we still ask where the *esprit de corps* is that we have been told they have; or, having been shown all the Oxford colleges, we still ask where the University of Oxford is. Ryle applies this to what he sees as a perniciously misleading theory of mind, which has its origins in Cartesian dualism. If we take certain mental terms such as "knowing", "intelligence", "belief" and "sad", we are tempted to think of them as flickering events "in the head", predicated of a ghostly inner *thing* that has these states. Properly understood they should be seen as referring to dispositions to behave in certain ways under certain circumstances. Mind is not any kind of *thing*. Thus, "He believes Victoria is still Queen of England" refers to the disposition to answer "Victoria" if asked who the present monarch is. A vast array of so-called philosophical problems is shown to arise because of such confusions and not through their being genuine problems; a proper detailed analysis dissolves away such problems once and for all.

Chapter 12 is Robert L. Arrington on Ludwig Wittgenstein's *Philosophical Investigations*. Wittgenstein is the only philosopher to appear twice in these volumes;

this is owing to his having two, many would argue quite distinctive, philosophical positions. These philosophies share a common focus on language and meaning, both as a problem in itself, but also as the means to solve or eliminate a range of deep philosophical problems. However, the approaches are significantly different. In the earlier *Tractatus Logico-Philosophicus*, Wittgenstein grounds meaning in a certain sort of picturing of the world by language, albeit a picturing that takes place below the surface appearance of language. In the *Philosophical Investigations* there is said to be nothing outside language that determines meaning; not a metaphysical connection between language and the world, nor a connection between language and ideas in our minds, nor adherence to inviolable rules determined beyond language, nor reference. Indeed, no linguistically external facts at all give meaning to language. Rather, language is self-contained; meaning depends entirely on its autonomous *use*. There is nothing standing behind our use of linguistic expressions that is their true meaning; "nothing is hidden". In the end the justification for saying that an expression has a certain meaning stops at the "bedrock" of: this is how we use the expression. Wittgenstein solves (one should perhaps say dissolves) various fundamental philosophical problems by showing that their solution lies in an examination of how we actually use the language in which they are expressed; we discover then that really everything is in order and that there is no problem once we tie language to contexts where it has a genuine use and to what that usage, and thus meaning, is.

Chapter 13 is Jeremy Shearmur on Karl Popper's *The Logic of Scientific Discovery*. Popper's work is concerned with the rationality of scientific method. Such a method should give a way of rationally preferring one scientific theory to another on empirical grounds. Popper is clear that whether we adopt this method is a matter of choice. A consequence of defining this method is to distinguish science from pseudo-science. From the point of view of the logic of theory choice, the source of a scientific theory, or mode of discovery, is irrelevant; scientific theories may be, and often are, merely bold conjectures. While holding that only empirical evidence can make theory choice rational, he rejects the view that the justification of scientific theories is a process of building up to the theory from neutral non-theory-laden observations conjoined with inductive inference. Rather, all empirical statements are theoretical and fallible and may be subject to further analysis. What matters for giving grounds for rational theory choice is not the attempt to confirm theories, but the rigorous attempt to test them; that is, the attempt to refute, or falsify, them by deducing from them observations that would show them to be false. We should rationally choose the boldest, the most falsifiable, theory that has not been shown to be false and has been best tested. In this manner we may approach the truth.

John Shand

The Twentieth Century: Moore to Popper

Introduction

John Shand

The turn of the century, from the nineteenth to the twentieth, marked a significant change in how philosophy was done. There was the desire to bring about, even if not for the first time, a radical fresh start in philosophy, one that included a proper definition of the philosophical enterprise. There was the hope of pulling free from what many philosophers saw as the quagmire of philosophical ideas bequeathed by the nineteenth century. There was indeed the expectation that philosophy would at last definitively get off on the right foot, and, through the harnessing of new tools and methods, solve or eliminate philosophical problems that had been intractable for millennia.

Various notable factors in both the background and foreground contributed to the complex nature of philosophy in the early twentieth century. Foremost was the history of philosophy itself and major new developments within it. Before turning to this, it is perhaps enlightening to consider the cultural milieu external to the subject of philosophy that formed a background to changes within it, and that may, more or less directly, have influenced those changes. The opening of the twentieth century brought with it a slackening of social and personal bonds. There were increasing demands for complete political emancipation, as well as calls for the introduction of more state welfare. The nature of personal fulfilment and of how one may attain it, breaking free of social templates that would preordain one's life, was a central subject of writers and other thinkers. The beginning of the century was a period of huge intellectual and artistic experimentation, innovation and fecundity. In the arts, there were profound challenges to the accepted way of doing things. In music, literature and painting, old ways were overthrown, or changed out of all recognition. Artworks appeared that lacked anything close to what might be their expected content or form. Their content dealt with matters regarded previously as outside the ambit of art, to the point of being downright scandalous. Works with novel forms were castigated as formless. Many new artworks were based on principles that made a sharp break with anything that had been seen before, which included an acuter self-reflexive tendency to consider, through the medium of the artwork itself, the nature and possibility of art. In science the conception of the very large, the cosmos, was revolutionized by Einstein's theory of relativity, and the understanding of the very small, the atomic and subatomic, was shifted in the direction that would eventually lead to quantum mechanics. Both overturned the Newtonian view of the universe that had dominated science since the eighteenth century: the universe, along with being atomistic and strictly causally deterministic, was infinite in time and space, and space was a mere nothingness in which events occurred and material objects existed, which itself took no part in determining the laws of nature. All this was rejected or fundamentally modified. Scientifically literate philosophers felt the need to incorporate and recognize these developments, ones that lead us to think about the universe in a radically new way. In biology, Darwin, at the end of the nineteenth century, had already changed the conception of what human beings are, and placed them in the natural world among other animals with no requirement for a divine spark to explain their nature or existence. The theory of evolution by natural selection was seized upon – often in a manner that was theoretically unjustifiable – and used to support sometimes dubious new social theories and ideas of progress, as exemplified by the affirmations of the value of human eugenics and a reinvigorated belief in various forms of utopianism. In psychology, Freud further revolutionized the way we think about ourselves, pointing to "unconscious" psychological factors that act upon our outlook and behaviour and that are open to conscious scrutiny only with difficulty, if at all. Finally, for many of the most original philosophers, especially English-language philosophers, the last ties with religion were cut, and religion ceased to be a central concern, or even something for which intellectual room had to be made. Among the anxiety that such innovation created, there was also a sense of liberation from the most suffocating and restrictive aspects of nineteenth-century mores. Just how all these matters affected philosophy it is probably impossible to say in detail; nevertheless in considering them one is, at least, made aware of the sympathetic concomitant climate in which earlier ideas are shed like some subfusc brocaded old raiments, to be replaced by bright clean-lined new ones; philosophy did not stand aloof from the casting off of the old and the donning of the new, and the cultural background was both cause and consequence of the changes in philosophy.

Two features of the philosophical landscape stand out at the beginning of the twentieth century,[1] and they have both had a huge influence on philosophy right up to the present day: the rejection of idealism, in both its absolute and its transcendental forms, and the development of a powerful new logic. During the first third of the nineteenth century Hegelian absolute idealism had dominated philosophy. After that, absolute idealism waned in dominance until a revival at the end of the century. In the intervening period, the chief battle as a matter of fact, if not the one of profoundest philosophical significance viewed by the light of philosophical posterity, was that between neo-Kantian transcendentalism and naturalism. The chief tenet of naturalism is to subsume all explanations, and indeed philosophy itself, under empirically known physical and causal scientific theories. There is no autonomous realm of *a priori* truths outside science that might form the subject matter of philosophy. The rejection of absolute and transcendental idealism in the early twentieth century did not however mark a return of naturalism, but rather, an affirmation of realism: the independence of the world from the mind of a knowing subject. In case this is confusing, look back at the beginning of philosophy and consider Plato. Plato is a realist; the Platonic Forms are what they are independently of mind; the Forms subsist in a mind-independent transcendent realm; but Plato is not a naturalist, for the Forms are known *a priori* and are not subsumed under *a posteriori* causal physical explanations. The realism that appeared at the beginning of the twentieth century did indeed include a form of Platonism, but it was far from the only way it manifested itself. So, for the purposes of considering the philosophers in this volume, it is best to consider realism in its generality, characterized as the view that the world is what it is in some sense independently of whatever influences or distortions the mind brings to the act of apprehending it. Realism affirms that the nature and existence of the world is independent of the knowing subject. The rejection of idealism included both Kantian transcendental idealism and Hegelian absolute idealism. The intellectual counterpart to this rejection was an affirmation of realism.[2]

Before proceeding to look at the philosophical trends that the major philosophers in this volume personify, there is a need to pause and look at a thinker whose influence on many philosophers of the last century, especially those in the analytic tradition, is so profound that it must seem puzzling that there is not a chapter devoted to him. His name is Gottlob Frege (1848–1925).[3] There is no chapter on him for two connected reasons. Frege's immediate concern was with the foundations of mathematics and consequently his work is of a forbiddingly technical nature. It was for others to draw out explicitly and fully the philosophical implications of his ideas, and put to use in philosophy the powerful new logical tools he had developed as a consequence of his work in mathematics. The philosophers considered in this volume who were either influenced by Frege, or who made significant use of the new logic he developed, are Moore, Husserl, Wittgenstein, Carnap, Ayer and Popper; but perhaps most of all it was Russell who brought to fruition the philosophical value of Frege's ideas.

Logic had been in stasis since Aristotle. Indeed, Kant states unequivocally at the beginning of his *Critique of Pure Reason*[4] that logic had not taken – with the implication that it could not take – one step beyond the basic form it had in Aristotelian syllogistic term or categorical logic. The premises and conclusion in this logic are expressed in categorical propositions, and these may be analysed as being about how classes of things are, or are not, included in other classes of things, in whole or in part. The supposed truth of the finality of logic is a linch-pin in Kant's philosophy. The initial factual claim was not quite true, although true enough for Kant's purposes and ours of highlighting the monumental importance of Frege. There had in fact been significant work done in logic in the medieval period,[5] including the extending of basic logic into modal and tense logic. However, the basis of logic had not been fundamentally rethought. Kant himself had extended Aristotelian logic with a simple theory of disjunctive and hypothetical propositions. But again, the starting-point of logic remained unchanged. The building blocks, or units, of Aristotelian logic are terms or categories that refer to particular objects or classes of objects, which are then combined according to certain rules of inference to make arguments. It is the introduction of radically new units of logical computation that is Frege's initial contribution, and that meant that the once seemingly all-encompassing Aristotelian logic became but a minor subset of a vastly more powerful new logic. The use of Aristotelian logic alone meant that there were certain expressions and basic features of ordinary language that simply could not be represented in logical notation.

Frege's contribution was the development of propositional logic and predicate logic. He was not, to give credit where it is due, without precursors, notably the mathematician George Boole (1815–64) and the philosopher C. S. Peirce (1839–1914). However, it was Frege who took the logic far beyond these initial ideas and sought to repair their deficiencies. The main setting out of Frege's ideas is to be found in his *Begriffsschrift* [*Conceptual Notation*] (1879)[6] and *Die Grundlagen der Arithmetik* [*The Foundations of Arithmetic*] (1884).[7]

Frege's propositional logic allows the formal symbolic expression of the logic of inferences between whole propositions; the inferences could then be strictly tested for validity. In Aristotelian syllogistic term logic, this could not be done. Propositions are linguistic forms that are capable of being determinately true or false. They are connected into complexes of propositions by logical connectives or operators, such as "not", "and", "or", "if … then …" and so on, and the truth or falsity (truth-value) of the whole complex is determined by assigning truth-values to the constituent propositions; by a process of mechanical computation

4

one reads truth-values off truth-tables, until one comes to the truth-value for the whole complex. Tautologies always come out as true; contradictions always come out as false; all other propositions are contingent, and come out with some true, and some false, truth-value assignments. Brackets allow the "nesting" of expressions within other expressions. Thus one may symbolize "if, philosophers love a good time and goblins love a good time, then the world is a fine place" as $(p \ \& \ q) \rightarrow r$.[8] From this, logicians were able to build up new, powerful, valid deductive systems of inference, based on a set of valid argument-forms, and prove complex theorems. Deductively valid arguments are such that if the premises are true the conclusion must be true. This is because, in such cases, to assert the premises but deny the conclusion would be a contradiction. If all the steps in a logical deduction are valid, then so is the deduction as a whole.

This was far from the end of the logical innovations. Although Frege's primary concern, as has been said, in devising new logical tools was the understanding of the basis of mathematical reasoning, an innovation yet more powerful in its capacity to express the nuances of ordinary language was predicate logic, whose central feature was quantification. This involved an apparatus of terms denoting individual objects, terms used as individual variables (for which terms denoting individual objects may be substituted), terms denoting predicates that ascribe properties to objects, and logical constants that quantify over objects and bind variables, all built on the basic apparatus of propositional logic. Predicate logic allowed one to look within propositions and schematize their internal structure, thus allowing for the differentiation of propositions – ones that would be elided in propositional logic – that are not either identical or totally different, but partially different. So, we may symbolize "All philosophers love a good time" as $(\forall x)(Px \rightarrow Gx)$, and "Some philosophers love a good time" as $(\exists x)(Px \ \& \ Gx)$.[9] The new logic reveals concealed logical relations in ordinary language, and systematizes valid logical relations and valid modes of inference. Such logical tools allowed for the foundation of philosophical logic,[10] which enabled the sharp expression of philosophical problems in a way that some would argue was not possible before, and so aided their solution, or their dissolution as pseudo-problems.

Frege was not interested in logic for its own sake, but rather in using it to show that mathematics (but not, it should perhaps be said, geometry) was derivable entirely from logic. The aim of this logicist project was to show that mathematics could be derived from purely logical axioms and deduction without the use of any non-logical notions or axioms.

It was Bertrand Russell who fully realized the philosophical implications of Frege's logic. He also applied it to the foundations of mathematics in his works *The Principles of Mathematics* (1903)[11] and (written with A. N. Whitehead)

Principia Mathematica (1910–13).[12] A technical contribution in these works was the replacement of Frege's aesthetically appealing, but difficult to print, notation with that of a more practical one derived from Giuseppe Peano (1858–1932), and it is this notation that forms the basis of that used in most modern logic.

The logicist project aims to grant to mathematics a firm, absolute objectivity and certainty, and to rescue it from those who would in various ways undermine this. One such way, opposed by logicism, is the psychologizing of mathematics (and logic) according to which mathematics is based on facts about the way we think; logic and mathematics are manifestations of certain "laws of thought". Logicism opposes also the view that mathematical truths are synthetic, empirical *a posteriori* propositions – a view found in J. S. Mill – and the view that mathematical truths are synthetic *a priori* propositions based on sensible intuitions – a view found in Kant. Mathematical truths are not synthetic at all according to the logicist. They are rather *a priori* truths based on pure logic, and they concern an autonomous mathematical realm that stands as it is independently of psychological facts or facts about the world. For Frege numbers are self-subsistent, re-identifiable objects. A statement ascribing a number to something is a statement about a concept, but numbers themselves are objects, not concepts. The underlying idea here is to indicate the mind-independence of numbers and that considered either individually or collectively numbers are not properties of anything else. The motivation here is undoubtedly neo-Platonic.

Another piece of technical apparatus was needed to give the required purely logical foundation to mathematics and in Frege's work, specifically, a foundation to arithmetic: that of naive set theory. This, however, had a worm in the bud that was to prove the downfall of the logicist project, as we shall see. In order to reduce arithmetic to logic, it must be possible to refer to numbers in a way that does not mention the notion of number. This is done by introducing classes and positing their real existence, then replacing numbers by classes by defining numbers in terms of classes. A given number is the class of all classes that have the same number of members as that given number. The number three is the class of all classes that have three members. Surprisingly this is not circular, for one can say that one class has the same number of members as another without counting them by pairing off each member with a member in the other class, and so showing they are equinumerous. One then only needs the notion of an empty class to define zero, and the notion of a successor to develop the series of natural numbers.

Frege's far-reaching innovation was a new way of thinking about language, one that enabled Russell, and later on Wittgenstein and Carnap, to give an account of the way in which language can say something true or false about the world. Frege replaces the traditional grammatical analysis of a sentence, such as "William defeated Harold", into subject ("William") and predicate ("defeated Harold"), with one into *argument* and *function*, respectively. This is analogous to algebra where 6 is the value of the function $x \times 3$, for the argument $x = 2$. Thus, a function alone is incomplete. By analogy, the expression "[ ] defeated Harold" has the value *true* when the argument-blank is "William".

This may seem esoteric, but such logical considerations pointed the way to defining and actually constructing a fully respectable scientific language, a possibility fully explored by the philosophers who followed Frege. It would be one in which every term has a reference and every sentence a determinate truth-value. This in turn opens up the possibility of giving a proper foundation to what is meant by the verification of scientific theories: the entire content of the theory must in principle be reducible to talk about the content of the intersubjectively accessible elements of immediate experience.

In his famous paper "*Uber Sinn und Bedeutung*" ["On Sense and Reference"] (1892),[13] Frege identified and elucidated a significant ambiguity connected with the notion of meaning that had plagued the clarification and solution of philosophical problems. He distinguished between sense (*Sinn*) and reference (*Bedeutung*). Thus, the names in the expression "Hesperus is Phosphorus" have the same reference, namely the planet Venus, but a different sense, through their having different "modes of presentation" as, respectively, the evening star and the morning star. Sense determines reference, and not vice versa. The sense of an expression is an abstract object, thereby ensuring that the sense is neither something merely formal nor a subjective idea.

Frege's, and indeed Russell's and Whitehead's, logicist reduction of mathematics to logic came to a disastrous end. Russell conveyed the news of "Russell's Paradox" to Frege in a letter that sent Frege spinning. Naive set theory with Frege's axioms allowed for a logical contradiction or paradox to be generated, and so it could not be a sound logical foundation for mathematics. The problem arose because it allowed the formation of the class of all classes that are not members of themselves and a paradox then appears. If such a class is a member of itself, then it is not a member of itself; if such a class is not a member of itself, then it is a member of itself. Russell tried to circumvent this by the theory of types, which would prohibit, through a hierarchy of classes, such damaging self-reference. But few were convinced by such an arbitrary stricture, one that also ruled out perfectly benign self-reference. Another serious blow to logicism occurred in 1931 when Kurt Gödel (1906-78) proved that any consistent formal system at least as complex as arithmetic was "incomplete": it would always contain true theorems that could not be proved from its axioms. Adding more axioms to facilitate such proofs simply generated more unprovable true theorems.

The philosophical import of Frege's ideas, and the extensive use made of the logical machinery he developed in philosophy (and elsewhere, such as computing), would be hard to exaggerate. Not everyone, of course, thought that his ideas could be used profitably to generate a bright new beginning for philosophy, and some turned against the supposed value of logical analysis that his formal apparatus provided. Indeed, we find in one person, Wittgenstein, a philosopher who embraced as rigorously as one could ever expect the application of the new logic to the problems of philosophy, only in his later work to reject such an approach as fundamentally misconceived. In his later work, the messy web of meanings arising from the actual use of ordinary language is ineliminable, and the purity of formal logical systems, far from clearing up philosophical problems, actually contributes to the generation of further ones, sending us off yet again in the wrong philosophical direction. Other philosophers in this volume simply paid no attention to Frege's work; oddly, one might suppose, those who here represent an important strand in the philosophical tradition of continental Europe, namely, Heidegger, Sartre and Merleau-Ponty; the exception to this among the continental philosophers is Husserl.

Within the analytic tradition, Frege's logic provided the machinery to articulate and attempt to solve age-old problems in epistemology and metaphysics in a way that did not require reference to subjective ideas, as had been the case among the seventeenth- and eighteenth-century rationalist and empiricist philosophers. This ushered in the ascendancy of language as a focus for philosophy. This involved giving a proper understanding of public language through its logical analysis and thereby enabling the solution of philosophical problems. This contrasted with previous approaches that had courted the difficulties of dealing with such problems through an examination of mysterious mental entities in the form of ideas or representation, often seen as some kind of images. The new philosophy takes seriously the notion that language is the vehicle of thought, and that there is no need to refer to shadowy mental occurrences in order to examine the ways in which it is and is not proper to talk about the world. The aim of the new linguistic way was to create a philosophy that had rigorous objectivity.

We return now to look in more detail at the claim that one of the dominant strands in philosophy was, at the outset, and well into the twentieth century, non-naturalist realism. Realism should be understood in the broadest sense here: the existence and nature of the world is as it is independently of mind; the world is not ontologically mental, nor is epistemic access to the world mediated by a necessary, transcendental *a priori* valid mental framework.

With this in mind, we may take some of the philosophers considered in this volume and put them into two groups, each group corresponding to how realism and the rejection of idealism manifested itself in the analytic and continental traditions respectively. In the analytic realist group one may put together Moore, Russell, Carnap and Popper. In the continental realist group one may put together

Heidegger, Sartre and Merleau-Ponty. Of course, not only are there significant differences between these groups in the way that realism manifests itself, there are also differences within the groups that have to be elided and glossed over for what they have in common to become clear. The common realist philosophical trend found in both groups is sufficiently profound that we may, for the purposes of this account, temporarily set aside differences between and within the groups.

In Russell's case, realism can be seen initially in his acceptance of Frege's position that there are real immutable and eternal objects to which the certain *a priori* truths of mathematics refer. His conviction in this matter did not survive his acquaintance with Wittgenstein, who persuaded him that the *a priori* truths of mathematics did not describe or require a beautiful autonomous realm above the mess and uncertainty of the empirical world, but rather were one and all mere empty tautologies, and it was being so that explained their certainty and necessity. In either case, however, Russell rejected the Kantian notion, which as we have seen suggests that somehow the truths of mathematics (and geometry) consist of synthetic *a priori* statements that arise as the formal aspect of the determination of the mind in respect of our experience of time and space, so that such truths neither referred to a transcendent realm nor were *a priori* analytic truths. With Russell, as with Frege, whatever mathematical truths are, they are *a priori*, but not synthetic. Russell's realism with respect to the world, however, stayed with him all his life. He never gave up on the humbling notion that states of affairs in the world are what they are in utter independence of the determinations of the human mind, and, moreover, such states of affairs are logically independent of each other. This view Russell inherited from Hume. As Russell says, "It may be true that an earwig is in my room, even if neither I nor the earwig nor any one else is aware of this truth; for the truth concerns only the earwig and the room, and does not depend on anything else."[14] Russell never budged from this realist contention, and in this one sentence he denies both absolute and transcendental idealism. Russell hoped to give an exact and exhaustive analysis, using the pure and tight language of Frege's logic, of the meaning of empirical scientific statements by exhibiting them as statements about the content of actual experience (sense-data) and possible experience (sensibilia), and in so doing show how verification was possible. Again, Russell came to doubt whether this could be accomplished. He came also to believe that the determined sceptic concerning our knowledge generally could not, as Descartes thought, be defeated. There was no way to refute the sceptic's claim that in truth the world began five minutes ago, and that all that we take as evidence otherwise is an illusion. What Russell persisted in was the project to remove as much doubt as possible from our knowledge claims, and base the things we claim to know on the least contentious and fewest number of assumptions. This was a lifelong preoccupation of applying Ockham's razor wherever possible. The application of logical analysis was often the means to this.[15] In the end, however, such crucial notions as causality were postulates that we just had to accept if scientific knowledge was to be possible, and such postulates were neither *a priori* valid, nor demonstrable by experience.[16] The motive for idealism of any sort goes once one has a non-mentalistic (non-psychologistic) explanation of the *a priori* – one that rejects its being based on how we, supposedly, must think – and once one takes the view that occurrences in the world, perceived *a posteriori*, do not depend in any manner for the way they are on the mind that apprehends them or on mind in any other sense.[17]

In G. E. Moore, Russell's colleague and close friend at Cambridge, we find a similar adherence to an anti-idealist realism, but a rejection of naturalism. This comes to the fore in his ethics, where he contends that ethical statements are determinately true or false, that "good" is logically primary in ethics, and that good cannot be defined in terms of anything else, in particular not by any of the natural properties of things.

In Carnap, we find an attempt, similar to that in Russell's work, to exhibit fully the content of scientific theories in terms of experience so that a rigorous notion of objective verification can be defined. This is done in a manner that is not committed to reducing the world ontologically to experience; the concern is epistemic, not metaphysical. The chief purpose of Carnap's work is to give an objective foundation to science.

Popper is a realist too. He holds that the way the world is is independent of mind. However, this is complicated by his being a "critical realist". He holds that there is no possibility of accessing, or articulating an account of, reality in a manner unmediated by theory. Unlike Russell or Carnap, at least in some of their pronouncements, he sees no possibility of finding ultimate, non-theoretical basic statements that refer to immediate experience, to which the meaning of any theoretical statements might be reduced in a way that would count as their verification. Rather, there are statements about the world that have higher and lower levels of theoretical complexity, but no ultimate statements that are immune to further theoretical analysis and empirical testing. There are only relative basic statements. All our statements and theories about the world are fallible hypotheses, and may be overthrown by further testing and revision. Being rational in one's choice of theory about reality does not require foundational certainty – which is unattainable anyway – but rather the choosing of the best-tested theory, and in so doing one will approach the truth about reality. Popper's position, although it talks of the impossibility of untheoretically mediated access to the world, is not a return to Kantian transcendental idealism, for none of the mediating theories are *a priori* valid, although some may be psychologically *a priori* preconceptions.

In the case of the continental philosophers listed earlier – Heidegger, Sartre, Merleau-Ponty – the route to rejecting idealism, in particular Kantian transcendental idealism, is rather different. The Kantian contention is that what appear to be certain fundamental aspects of the world as a phenomenon – that is, how in any manner it can appear to us in our experiences – are in fact not in the world, but rather formal modes of the way in which we apprehend the world, modes that are contributed by our minds. Among these formal modes are those of space, time and causality. These modes of apprehension are transcendental in being valid for all human beings, and point to there being a transcendental self common to all human beings that underpins differences that arise naturally between various empirical selves; the common denominator of the transcendental self encapsulates the necessary ways we *have* to view and think about the world. Indeed such a transcendental self may be claimed as valid for all rational creatures in certain respects, although it is difficult to see how we could ever know this is true. The step taken by Heidegger, and later Sartre and Merleau-Ponty, is to deny the existence of any such transcendental self, a self that would somehow invest our knowledge of the world with a grand objectivity. The claim that such absolute objectivity is possible is found in Descartes, but in him the claim to objective knowledge derives not from the *a priori* validity of universal mental structures, but from the removal of all distorting preconceptions that would define a view as one from any particular perspective. The aim is the attainment of a disinterested, detached, contemplative objective conception, or "view from nowhere". Because of the unwanted intermediary contribution of the physical senses, it is also one where the self is essentially disembodied. Only in this way, it is argued, is it possible to see what reality is like in itself. The group of continental philosophers referred to hold that our view can only be non-transcendental, and deny that there are *a priori* valid necessary objective structures mediating our experience of the world; but nor can we strip away our point of view, our perspective, to leave a pure objective view of reality, as if at last we were holding up a flat true mirror to the world.

Husserl carried into the twentieth century the view that there is a transcendental self or ego, a view that could, if it took up an "unnatural" disinterested stance on the world, deliver things as they really are in themselves as part of a programme of pure phenomenology. He held that thought always has *intentionality*, thus, it always has an object; it is a thought *of* something.[18] In pure phenomenology these intentional objects provide a pre-theoretical, autonomous realm of study for philosophy. In his last works he came to doubt that the matter was as simple as this, and he moved closer to the position found in Heidegger, Sartre and Merleau-Ponty, so that the general object of phenomenological analysis is what he came to call the "life-world" (*Lebenswelt*).[19] However, Husserl's earlier position was that we should try to attain a presuppositionless philosophy – indeed this alone was philosophy proper – one that "bracketed off" any theoretical assumptions or inferences that take us beyond the pure content of our experiences. His concern then is not with the particular phenomenology of experiences, but with their universal essences in respect of both structure and content; such essences may be, he claimed, intuited, and in such a way that we may come to a definition of what it is to have an experience of a certain kind.

The key to our continental group of philosophers is a denial that such a disinterested, disembodied, contemplative view of the world is possible, or that there are necessary *a priori* structures that the mind as a transcendental self contributes to any possible experience. They came to think that the supposed presuppositionless intentional objects of pure phenomenology were in fact parasitic on the rich ontology that only arises from our *interested*, engaged, embodied perspective. If, *per impossibile*, such a disinterested, disembodied, contemplative stance were possible, then no world would arise in our awareness at all. This is because for a world to arise or exist it must involve some notion of Being – being a hammer, being in love, being out of reach – and for a disinterested, disembodied, contemplative consciousness, there would be neither need nor requirement for such Being. Such Being arises only because of our interests and our having interests. To put it crudely, things "show up" for us because when we try to do things we "bump into" them. Without interests and projects, the world would at best be a totally flat homogenous thing without definition or form. The world as we know it, indeed any world, only arises and comes into Being because we ascribe significances and meanings as a result of our engaging in interested activities in the world, activities that are themselves contingent upon the kind of psychological and embodied creatures we are: our particular form of being-in-the-world. We cannot separate ourselves from the world, as talk of one must always refer to the other. As has been said, there is, for one thing, the intentionality of our thoughts, in that they are always *of* something; it is a betrayal of this insight to suppose what the thought is of in another aspect of mind; rather it must be of something non-mental. The claim that science gives the true picture of reality through being objective is in fact spurious. The picture science gives of reality, one that is supposedly objective because it is disinterested, is in fact an extension of the logically primary way in which any world arises for us at all, that is, through our engaged activity in it. Science is not epistemically privileged. Thus, presuppositionless pure phenomenology becomes existential phenomenology. Pure phenomenology was in fact always impossible, for when examined the phenomenological experiences were already pervaded with meanings and significances that could only arise for engaged embodied creatures, not transcendental egos. The new task of existential phenomenology is to examine the structure and relations of things as they show up in our everyday existence as human beings.

It may be contended that such a position is realist, in that the primary things taken to exist – hammers, love, objects out of reach – are what we commonly take to be real constituents of the world. Moreover, they are not on this view thought of as somehow ontologically inferior or secondary, so that they might be "thought away", leaving us with a picture of the world as it "really is" in the sense of how it would look from a necessary *a priori* perspective or disinterested standpoint. Science, for all its supposed objectivity and capacity to reveal reality, seems to regard as illusory much that we take to be real, such as love and beauty, or secondary and not fundamental in the case of our mundane everyday objects. Existential phenomenology counters this, and puts our everyday world back at the centre of reality. This is not necessarily anti-science; it is just not to grant science total epistemic hegemony; science develops as it does for its own purposes and for good reasons. The background of the practical lived-world, our pre-theoretical conception of the world, has logical priority however, and is essentially prior to the theoretical view. It may also be said that such a position is anti-idealist, in that existential phenomenology involves the positing of things that are non-mental as the intentional objects of thoughts.

The remaining philosophers considered in this volume – James, Wittgenstein, Ayer, Ryle – fall into a different type from those so far considered – Moore, Husserl, Heidegger, Carnap, Russell, Sartre, Merleau-Ponty, Popper. The distinction is rather crude and impure, but still illuminating. Whereas the latter group might best be called problem *solvers*, the former group might with some accuracy be called problem *dissolvers*. The solvers tend to suppose that most philosophical problems are genuinely problems. They then use whatever techniques – such as the new developments in logic, or a new metaphysics – to tackle head-on philosophical problems: here is a problem, and here is its solution. Among these problems is the central issue of idealism versus realism. The dissolvers on the other hand tend to suppose that most philosophical problems (including the idealism versus realism issue) should not be tackled at their face value; they are at the least not the problems they seem to be, and at the most only have the appearance of problems; considered properly they are not "problems" at all. Finding a pair of socks to wear is a problem for a man with feet, one that requires he find socks as a solution. Finding a pair of socks to wear is not a genuine problem for a man without feet; it is not solved by finding socks to wear; it is dissolved as a "problem" by reminding him that he has no problem about finding socks, because he has no feet. Of course, a man without feet would need no reminding that he does not have feet, and thus has no sock-finding problem. In philosophy, however, the situation is quite other, and we need constant reminding; we need it pointed out to us, and indeed explained, that what we thought were problems are not genuinely so. We need this elaborate process of reminders and explanations, because our main way of thinking about things, language, the very tool we use to think, can betray us. Depending on the philosopher – or in Wittgenstein's case within the work of a single philosopher – language is seen as betraying us in ways either systematic and global, or *ad hoc* and piecemeal. The underlying point is the same however. We have before us a linguistic expression that apparently expresses a "philosophical problem" – it looks like any other mundane problem, such as "How do you stop a tap dripping?" – but in fact in philosophy, as Wittgenstein put it, "language has gone on holiday"; it has been taken from the areas where genuine problems arise and are articulated, and transferred to an area where the expressions *look* like they articulate problems in just the same way, but where no genuine "problems" exist to be articulated. All we have to do to free ourselves from philosophical debates that have no prospect of resolution is to reflect carefully on the language we use to express putative philosophical problems; we will then see that they are pseudo-problems that do not in fact require solutions; what we need to see is why they are not problems at all.

As has been suggested, the approaches of the dissolvers vary. We should perhaps begin with James. In a way he does not quite fully fit the descriptions I have given. But I think his inclusion among the dissolvers is justified. The reason for his not quite clearly sitting with the other dissolvers as just described is twofold. First, his work predates the powerful new logical tools that enabled the solvers to solve (or seem to solve) philosophical problems and the dissolvers to show up putative philosophical problems as not requiring a solution. Secondly, he does leave more outstanding genuine philosophical problems than the others listed as fellow dissolvers. Nevertheless, James's pragmatism involves a reflection on many philosophical problems in such a manner as to conclude that if "solving" them one way or another – say, opting for a metaphysical idealism over realism – makes no difference to, let alone is an improvement on, our capacity to cope with experience, then there is in fact nothing of substance at stake in believing one view rather than another.

This pragmatist connection between philosophical problems and what they might entail, or simply fail to entail, for our experience was deeply influential on Ayer. Unlike James, however, Ayer is able to call on the full resources of the new logic, and these resources enable him to systematically classify propositions in such a way as to show that there is simply no available sort of proposition in which philosophical problems or their solutions can be expressed. Exhaustive of genuine propositions are empty tautologies (which encompass the whole of logic and mathematics) and empirical statements that have the possibility of being verified or refuted by experience. All other putative propositions are, taken literally, meaningless nonsense, and "philosophical propositions" fall into that class. "Philosophical propositions" are to genuine propositions as window mannequins

14

are to real human beings, but the difference is harder to spot and explain. They can fool you into thinking they are genuine; but in fact they only look like the genuine article and are really nothing like what they appear to be at all.

Wittgenstein presents us with a more complex case of a dissolver, for he presents not one, but two, methods as to how most of the strenuous effort to solve philosophical problems might cease, and how the torrid philosophical debates of centuries might at long last be laid to rest. The first account he gives is in the *Tractatus* – so-called "early Wittgenstein". The second account is articulated in the *Philosophical Investigations* – so-called "later Wittgenstein" – although in the case of his later thought his ideas are spread across several other works. It is, one should note, a contentious issue to what extent there is continuity or discontinuity, sometimes it is argued on the latter view amounting to actual refutation, between the earlier and later positions. The commonality at least extends to our confusion about language misleading us to attempt to solve philosophical problems, which, when the language is properly understood, can be seen as pseudo-problems.

The philosophy of early Wittgenstein presents a single global view of the way language acquires its meaning, and it is one that when fully understood, and the proper logical stance thus taken up, excludes philosophical propositions as being genuinely matters of truth or falsity. They may serve another function for us – to edify, to express deep desires, and such like – but their truth or falsity is not what their value or significance hinges on. Indeed, it is to belittle philosophical propositions, and indeed a whole further class of religious, ethical and artistic expressions, to approach them so that their literal truth is what their values lie in. But it does mean that the attempt to solve the problems expressed by putative philosophical propositions by determining their truth or falsity is, if tackled directly, impossible. If anything, they concern matters about which one should be silent if all one can do as an alternative is to engage in the uncouth attempt to articulate what is literally true or false with respect to such matters. Setting aside mere tautologies, which are in any case literally senseless, Wittgenstein's position arises from the view that *genuine* propositions acquire their meaning from picturing a possible reality, and have any meaning at all if and only if they do so; if the reality is actual they are true, if it is not actual they are false. Philosophical propositions may look as though they picture a possible reality, but according to Wittgenstein, when fully analysed, we find that the terms that occur as an indispensable part of philosophical propositions cannot occur in genuine propositions – such terms disappear in genuine propositions.

The philosophy of the later Wittgenstein presents a different view of language. This denies that there is anything whatsoever external to language, including his own notion of a picturing relation to the world, that does or could determine the meaning of linguistic expressions. Rather, language is entirely autonomous. "The question 'What is a word really?' is analogous to 'What is a piece in chess?'"[20] Language acquires its meaning through its *use*; nothing more and nothing less; the meaning of linguistic expression *is* its proper use. There are many uses, not just that of describing reality. A useful analogy here is with money.[21] No external guarantor is needed to make something money; bottle-tops, cigarettes and matches, have all, often in times of war, been money, and they have been money simply by the way they are used. If I know that someone will accept bottle-tops in payment for the horse I want, I can sell my pig to someone else for bottle-tops, who can then of course buy what he wants. Monarchs soon discovered that they did not have to make money out of anything intrinsically valuable. In a comparable way, something becomes language and has a particular meaning through the way it is used. There is nothing further "hidden" behind the way it is used that is a linguistic expression's "real" meaning. Everything, as Wittgenstein says, is open to view. So where does this leave most philosophical problems? It leaves them as cases where the language in which they are expressed has no genuine use, and thus no meaning. Again, they look like expressions that have a genuine use because they have the grammar of expressions with a genuine use – but really they are taken out of context, a "language-game" – which is itself a manifestation of a "form of life" – in which we truly do have jobs (work) for language to do. "Only in the stream of thought and life do words have meaning."[22] But in the case of philosophy, and philosophical systems, the linguistic parts are like a spurious machine that has cogs and wheels that turn, but none of them is connected and the machine has no true function. "What is your aim in philosophy? – To show the fly the way out of the fly-bottle."[23]

Ryle, the final philosopher in our set of dissolvers, takes a similar view to the later Wittgenstein. He applies it particularly to age-old debates about the nature of mind. His view is that the conundrums that arise over what kind of thing mind is arise from our language misleadingly reifying mind – leading us to think that mind must be some kind of *thing*, whereas it is no kind of thing at all. The mistake we make Ryle calls a "category mistake": broadly we get into the way of thinking and speaking about something that is appropriate, and then applying that way to something where it is simply out of place. We might watch the animated marching band that passes, look at all its members, note how well and enthusiastically they play together, and yet wonder how we missed the band's *esprit de corps* we had heard about. We might then set this up as a serious problem, one needing a solution – here are the players, here are the instruments, here is the music produced, but where is the *esprit de corps*? – whereas really it is not a problem at all. In the same way, we might suppose that there is something going on in the world, which we have missed, that reifies the belief we ascribe to someone; we might then suppose that there are certain events, enacted in some kind of substance, be it of a material or unextended Cartesian kind, that constitute the belief. To do this throws up all sorts of "philosophical problems". How can unextended substance causally interact with matter to determine behaviour? How can mere matter have the property of thought? But really our problems are spurious. We only have them if we think of belief in the wrong way, as something that needs to be instantiated as a *thing*. But a belief is no kind of thing; rather it is a disposition to behave in certain ways. If I say, "Sarah thinks Queen Victoria was French", I mean just that if Sarah is asked the nationality of Queen Victoria, she will answer "French". I do not, in so doing, ascribe to Sarah any event, no matter how flickering and ghostly, going on in her head that *is* the belief; having the belief is the disposition. So too, Ryle outlines in tremendous detail, for other mental terms and ascriptions, how similar errors occur and pseudo-problems are generated.

The first half of the twentieth century, the time covered by this volume, was a period of enormous fecundity, ambition and range in philosophy. In some cases, there was the attempt to align philosophy with science by establishing it on a similarly rigorous foundation. Other philosophers saw science as the problem in the sense that philosophy was exactly *not* like science, but autonomous. Others still sought to undermine terminally the whole enterprise of philosophy, which, for something that claimed to be genuine intellectual endeavour of reasoned understanding, had implausibly made no progress over its history nor come to any settled body of knowledge. By no means all of the ideas generated in this period led to conclusions that have survived criticisms unscathed; in some cases indeed they resulted in heroic philosophical dead-ends. But the philosophical outlooks and ideas articulated in the works of the philosophers in this volume continue to be of tremendous importance and value in our deepest thinking.[24]

Notes

1. The flavour and detail of the *fin de siècle* transformation in philosophy, at least with respect to English-language philosophy, is well captured in John Skorupski, *English-Language Philosophy 1750–1945* (Oxford: Oxford University Press, 1993). Those wishing to trace the corresponding changes in continental European philosophy would do well to read David E. Cooper, *Existentialism* (Oxford: Blackwell, 1990).
2. Looking beyond the nineteenth century, it is worth noting that both naturalism and idealism have undergone something of a revival in the second half of the twentieth century. This is especially true of naturalism, which through the work of W. V. Quine has become in some quarters something of a philosophical orthodoxy.
3. Those wishing to explore Frege in detail might fruitfully start by going to the study by Anthony Kenny, *Frege* (Harmondsworth: Penguin, 1995).
4. Immanuel Kant, *Critique of Pure Reason* [*Kritik der reinen Vernunft*], Norman Kemp Smith (trans.) (London: Macmillan, 1929 [1st edn, 1781; 2nd edn, 1787]), 17, B viii.

5. See, Desmond P. Henry, *Medieval Logic and Metaphysics* (London: Hutchinson, 1972).

6. Gottlob Frege, *Conceptual Notation and Related Articles* [*Begriffsschrift*], T. W. Bynum (trans.) (Oxford: Clarendon Press, 1972 [1879]).

7. Gottlob Frege, *The Foundations of Arithmetic* [*Die Grundlagen der Arithmetik*], J. L. Austin (trans.) (Oxford: Blackwell and Mott, 1950 [1884]).

8. Here, p = "philosophers love a good time"; q = "goblins love a good time"; r = "the world is a fine place"; $\rightarrow$ is the operator of material implication, "if ... then ..."; & is the operator "and".

9. $(\forall x)$ is used to assert that *all* entities have a certain property, $(\exists x)$ is used to assert that *some* (at least one) entities have a certain property; "x" is an individual variable; P = "philosophers" and G = "love a good time". There are many excellent books on logic to which one may turn. Examples are, Howard Kahane, *Logic and Philosophy*, 6th edn (Belmont, CA: Wadsworth, 1990) and E. J. Lemmon, *Beginning Logic* (London: Chapman & Hall, 1990).

10. On this see, Mark Sainsbury, *Logical Forms: An Introduction to Philosophical Logic*, 2nd edn (Oxford: Blackwell, 2000).

11. Bertrand Russell, *The Principles of Mathematics* (Cambridge: Cambridge University Press, 1903).

12. Bertrand Russell & A. N. Whitehead, *Principia Mathematica*, 3 vols (Cambridge: Cambridge University Press, 1910–13).

13. Gottlob Frege, "On Sense and Reference" ["*Uber Sinn und Bedeutung*"], in *Translations from the Philosophical Writings of Gottlob Frege*, P. Geach & M. Black (eds and trans.) (Oxford: Blackwell, 1980 [1892]).

14. Bertrand Russell, *The Problem of Knowledge* (Oxford: Oxford University Press, 1978 [1912]), 51.

15. A classic instance of this is Russell's "theory of definite descriptions". See "On Denoting", *Mind* **14** (October 1905), 479–93. Widely reprinted, as in Bertrand Russell, *Logic and Knowledge*, R. C. Marsh (ed.) (London: Unwin Hyman, 1956), 39–56.

16. See, Bertrand Russell, *Human Knowledge: Its Scope and Limits* (London: Allen & Unwin, 1948).

17. Those wishing for a synoptic view of Russell would do well to read Bertrand Russell, *My Philosophical Development* (London: Allen & Unwin, 1959).

18. This is a view found in the ideas of Franz Brentano (1838–1917), who was a major proximate influence on phenomenology. He indeed took intentionality to be the defining feature of the mental. The notion of intentionality and intentional states is far older than this however, and it has a long and complex history that may be traced back though the medieval scholastics and ultimately to Aristotle.

19. Husserl's later thoughts are in the (unfinished), Edmund Husserl, *The Crisis of European Sciences and Transcendental Phenomenology*, David Carr (trans.) (Evanston, IL: Northwestern University Press, 1970 [1934]).

20. Ludwig Wittgenstein, *Philosophical Investigations*, G. E. M. Anscombe (trans.) (Oxford: Blackwell, 1974), §108.

21. Cf. Ludwig Wittgenstein, *Remarks on the Foundations of Mathematics*, G. H. von Wright and R. Rhees (eds), G. E. M. Anscombe (trans.) (Oxford: Blackwell, 1983), I, §153; and *Philosophical Investigations*, §268.

22. Ludwig Wittgenstein, *Zettel*, G. E. M. Anscombe and G. H. von Wright (eds), G. E. M. Anscombe (trans.) (Oxford: Blackwell, 1967), §173.

23. Wittgenstein, *Philosophical Investigations*, §309.
24. I am grateful to Adrian Moore for helpful and corrective comments on the Introduction, particularly with respect to Frege. I should also like to thank Charles Guignon for his improving suggestions on the Preface.

1

G. E. Moore
Principia Ethica

Philip Stratton-Lake

G. E. Moore's *Principia Ethica* was published in 1903. In the book Moore defends four theses. The first two are meta-ethical, about the nature of good, whereas the third and fourth express his first-order evaluative views about which acts are right and which things are good.

The first thesis is that goodness is the fundamental ethical notion. The fundamental nature of good for ethics means that it cannot be defined with reference to other ethical notions. Moore thus rejects the dominant intuitionist view that good can be defined in terms of ought, and maintains the contrary thesis that ought can be defined in terms of good – that "ought" means "maximizes good".

The second thesis is that the term "good" refers to a non-natural property, and so cannot be defined in wholly naturalistic (non-moral) terms. If good could be defined in naturalistic terms, then ethics could be subsumed under the relevant natural science. So if good could be defined in wholly psychological terms, ethics would be subsumed under psychology; and if it could be defined in evolutionary terms, then ethics would be subsumed under biology, and so on. Since good cannot be defined in moral terms either – this follows from his first thesis – Moore concludes that the term "good" must be indefinable, and the property it refers to must be simple.

The third thesis is that there is an irreducible plurality of good things. Moore defends this thesis by rejecting the dominant monistic views according to which the only good thing is pleasure, or what is desired, or what is more evolved. Moore maintains that such views are plausible only if "good" could be defined in

terms of pleasure, desire or evolution, for then monism would follow by definition. Once these definitions are rejected there is no good reason to endorse a
monism about the good.

Moore's fourth and final thesis is a form of consequentialism, which Rashdall
later termed "ideal utilitarianism" (Rashdall 1907). Moore agrees with classical
utilitarianism that morally we ought always to produce the best possible state of
affairs in the world. He thus agrees that all other obligations are to be subsumed
under the general obligation to promote the good. Where he departs from
classical utilitarians is in his rejection of their view that pleasure, or happiness
(which amounts to the same thing for some utilitarians) is the only thing that is
good, and is thus the only thing that we ought to promote. Moore maintains that
there is a plurality of intrinsic goods, the highest of which is a love of beauty and
the pleasures of friendship and other personal relations. Moore ends up, then,
with a pluralism about the good and a monistic theory of moral obligation.

Principia had a dramatic impact both within the philosophical world and
outside it, and it is now regarded as a classic text of analytic ethical theory. Its
importance cannot, however, be explained by its originality. *Principia* is not an
especially original book, and many contemporary reviewers criticized Moore on
this account (see Hurka 2003). Moore's claim that ethics cannot be subsumed
under some natural science had been a common theme among intuitionists since
the eighteenth century, and it was not uncommon for these intuitionists to claim
that goodness is simple and indefinable. His pluralism about the good was also
not new, nor was his combination of this pluralism with consequentialism. The
doctrine of organic unities (the view that the value of a complex thing need not
be equal to the sum of the value of its parts) can be found in Bradley, and Moore's
argument for the view that goodness is a non-natural property (the open question
argument) can be found in Sidgwick.

Furthermore, Moore is not always as clear and precise as he claims to be. He
gives us different accounts of key terms, such as the naturalistic fallacy and the
notion of a natural property, and there are at least two versions of the open
question argument (see Stratton-Lake & Hooker 2006).

What was distinctive about Moore's *Principia* was not its originality or clarity,
but a combination of the innovative way in which he brought these views
together, the sense that he was providing a new start for philosophical ethics, and
the youthful vigour with which he expressed many of his views, especially in
Chapter 6 where he lists what he regards as the highest goods. Furthermore,
although the naturalistic fallacy (the fallacy of supposing that goodness is a natural property) can be found in Sidgwick, he does not regard it as having a particularly important role. For Moore, however, it is the cardinal error that he claims
to find (not always very convincingly) in nearly all previous moral philosophy.

And although the doctrine of organic unities can be found in Bradley, Moore separates this doctrine from Bradley's Hegelian metaphysics. Thomas Baldwin (1990: 127) thinks that the doctrine makes no sense once it is separated in this way, but Moore's combination of this doctrine with the seemingly incompatible thesis that things with identical intrinsic natures must have the same intrinsic value was quite ingenious, and often quite plausible.

In this chapter I aim to give an outline of the four theses of Moore's *Principia* and of the basic notions that figure in these theses. Although I have tried to cover as much of the book as possible, I say nothing about Chapter 4 on metaphysical ethics. This is because the arguments in this chapter are largely aimed at the British idealists of the late-nineteenth century whose influence on subsequent moral philosophy has been quite minimal. The result is that many of the arguments of Chapter 4 seem directed at quite esoteric and bizarre views. This is not to claim that what Moore says there is without worth. It is just that including a discussion of that chapter would mean that my discussion of other aspects of *Principia* would have to be severely curtailed, and I do not think the benefit of comprehensiveness would outweigh this cost.

What is it for something to be good?

Good is, Moore insists, the fundamental ethical notion. All ethical judgements are, he maintains, fundamentally evaluative judgements – that is, they are judgements that something or other has the property of being good or best. Consequently, the fundamental task for a philosophical ethics is to define what it is for something to be good, or as Moore more often puts it, to define good. It is only once this is done, he maintains, that we will be in a position to offer some account of which things are good (or best).

We must start with a definition of goodness (or the term we use to denote this property), partly because we need to be clear what we are asking when we ask what things are good, and partly because certain definitions of good would settle the question of what things are good. If, for instance, being good is defined as being pleasant, as many naturalists have maintained, then we can know straight away that all and only pleasant things are good. Similarly, if the property of being good is defined as being desired (by someone or some community) we can know that all and only those things that are desired are good. We could know this because such judgements would be true by definition.

What, then, is it to *define* good? The question of how to define good is, for Moore, both a semantic and a metaphysical question. It is primarily a question of what we *mean*, what quality we have in mind, when we say or judge that something is good. To define good is, then, primarily to offer an analysis of the term "good". This is the semantic aspect of definitions, as Moore understands them. But definitions are metaphysical as well as semantic, for Moore. By telling us what we have in mind when we use certain predicates definitions tell us the nature of the properties we aim to pick out with those predicates. So if the predicate "is good" means "is pleasant", then the property of being good will be the property of being pleasant.

This link between semantics and metaphysics was strongly challenged by later philosophers (Kripke 1972; Putnam 1975). They deny that we can learn about the nature of things in the world through *a priori* reflection. We did not discover that water is H$_2$O, or that heat is molecular kinetic energy, by reflecting on what we mean by "water" and "heat", and we could not have discovered the nature of these things in this way. These identity claims were, and had to be, empirical discoveries, based on empirical research.

But if Moore is right that the concept of goodness is the concept of a non-natural property, then we have no reason to think that the empirical sciences are better equipped to tell us the nature of this property than *a priori* reflection. On the contrary, we have good reason to think that empirical science is rather poorly equipped to do this job. In this respect the concept of goodness would, for better or for worse, be like the concept of God. The only way in which we could know what it is that we are thinking about when we think about God is through *a priori* reflection on the concept of God. Similarly, if the concept of good is the concept of a non-natural property, then the only way in which we could know what it is that we are thinking of when we think of something as good is by *a priori* reflection on the concept of goodness. But why should we agree with Moore that the concept of good is the concept of a non-natural property?

The naturalistic fallacy

One of the central theses of *Principia* is that all naturalistic definitions of good commit what Moore calls the "naturalistic fallacy". What then is the naturalistic fallacy? For the most part Moore talks as if one commits this fallacy if one thinks that "good" is definable. But although Moore was convinced that "good" is indefinable, I do not think he thought one committed the naturalistic fallacy if one denied this (PE: 5, 19). The mistake is not to think that "good" is definable, but to think that it is definable in wholly naturalistic or metaphysical terms. If this is right, then one does not commit the naturalistic fallacy if one defines "good" in non-naturalistic or non-metaphysical terms. For example, Sidgwick defines "good" as what we ought to desire, but I do not think Moore would regard this as an instance of the naturalistic fallacy, because "ought" is not a naturalistic term.

Indeed, at one point Moore himself comes very close to endorsing such a definition (PE: 118).

What, then, is a naturalistic and metaphysical term? Naturalistic terms denote natural properties or things. In *Principia* Moore defines a natural property as one that can exist by itself in time and not merely as a property of some natural object (PE: 93). The idea is, then, that natural properties, such as the pleasantness or squareness of an object, can exist independently of that object, whereas the goodness of a good thing cannot exist independently of that thing.

But this definition is both obscure and fails to distinguish natural from nonnatural properties. It does not seem that the *particular* redness of some particular red object could exist apart from that object any more than the particular goodness of some good thing could. A particular instance of any property is a way in which something is, and the way in which some particular thing is cannot be separated from the particular thing that is in that way. One could not, for instance, take a particular snooker ball, remove its redness, roundness and impenetrableness, and lay these alongside it, as one could lay out the parts of an engine.

One might think that although particular instances of properties, the particular ways in which particular things are, cannot be separated from the things that are in those ways, the properties themselves as *universals* rather than as particular instances of those universals can and do exist by themselves apart from the things that instantiate them. But if this Platonic view about properties is true, then it would be true not only of properties such as pleasantness and squareness, but also of goodness. So if we are talking of property tokens, or instances, no properties can be separated from the things that instantiate them, and if we are talking of property types (properties as universals), then all of them can be separated.

Moore himself later abandoned this definition of the distinction between natural and non-natural properties. Indeed, he went so far as to describe his account of a natural property in *Principia* as "utterly silly and preposterous" (1942: 582). In the Preface to the second edition of *Principia* Moore offers an alternative definition that is suggested in Chapter 2 of *Principia*. According to this definition, a natural property is one "with which it is the business of the natural sciences or of Psychology to deal" (PE: 13). Since the term to be defined ("natural") appears in the definition, this definition may not seem very informative. But we can replace the term "natural sciences" with "empirical sciences" (understood to include psychology and sociology) to get a useful and workable epistemological definition of a natural property. On this account, then, natural properties can be known by empirical means, whereas non-natural properties cannot. Non-natural properties can be known only *a priori*.

What, then, is a metaphysical term? Metaphysical terms refer to supersensible things and their properties (PE: 163). An example of a metaphysical definition of goodness would be one that identified goodness with what is willed or desired by God or by some ideal rational will that exists outside space and time. Although Moore held that one commits the naturalistic fallacy if one defines "good" in metaphysical terms, for the sake of brevity I shall focus solely on naturalistic definitions of good.

Why should we believe that it is a fallacy, or, more precisely, a mistake, to define good in naturalistic terms? We may be willing to accept that no plausible naturalistic definition of goodness has so far been provided, but why should we think that no naturalistic definition *could* succeed? Moore supports his view that all naturalistic definitions of "good" are mistaken with his "open question argument". The open question argument runs as follows:

(P1) If "good" could be defined in terms of some natural property, then one could not meaningfully ask whether something that has that property is good.

(P2) For any natural property one can always meaningfully ask whether something that has that property is good.

(C)   "Good" cannot be defined in terms of some natural property (PE: 67).

Now this is a valid argument, with the naturalistic fallacy as its conclusion. So if the naturalistic fallacy is false, then either P1 or P2 is false.

Given how Moore understands definitions, P1 seems true. To define some term, in the sense Moore is concerned with, is to offer an analysis of that term – that is, to tell us what we mean when we use this term. So if being good is defined as being pleasant, then when we say or think "X is good" we mean "X is pleasant". It would follow from this definition that the question:

(Q1) "Is an X that is pleasant good?"

means

(Q2) "Is an X that is pleasant pleasant?"

Q1 is an open question in the sense that one could intelligibly answer either "yes" or "no". Even if I believe that all things that are pleasant are good, I would not think that anyone who doubted this must have misunderstood the question. Q2, however, is not an open question. Someone who understands the question could not think the answer might be "no". Since Q1 is an open question while Q2 is not, Q1 cannot mean Q2. So "good" cannot mean "pleasant".

Since P1 is true, if the naturalistic fallacy is false, then P2 must be false. It might be an open question whether something that is pleasant is good, or whether something that is desired is good, or whether something that we desire to desire is good, but what reason do we have to assume that such a question will be open no matter what natural property we ask about? Moore does not tell us, and this makes it look as though P2 simply begs the question against the naturalist (see Frankena 1952). For naturalists maintain that "good" can be defined in naturalistic terms, and so maintain that there is some property that is such that the question of whether something that has that property is good is not open. It looks then as if the open question argument would not provide the ground for rejecting all naturalistic analyses of "good" prior to an assessment of those analyses.

But even if the open question argument cannot be used to reject *all* naturalistic analyses of "good" in advance, the first premise of this argument indicates a useful procedure for assessing individual naturalistic analyses. For one could try the open question test as a way of assessing any proposed naturalistic analysis, and if all of the most plausible naturalistic analyses fail this test, we could plausibly conclude than none will succeed (see Ross 2002: 93).

The rejection of monism

Having established to his own satisfaction that the term "good" refers to a simple, indefinable, non-natural property, Moore proceeds in Chapters 2 and 3 to consider various answers to the question of what things have this property. The theories he considers are monistic theories. They all claim that there is only one type of thing that is good in itself. Moore insists that the monistic theories he considers all rest on the naturalistic fallacy. Monists come to believe that only one type of thing is good because they *define* goodness in terms of that thing. So in Chapters 2 and 3 Moore aims to show the significance of the naturalistic fallacy. Acceptance of some naturalistic definition of goodness will leave one with an impoverished view about which things are good.

Moore first considers the doctrine that only the natural is good, which he takes to mean either that the sole good is the *normal* state of the organism (PE: 94), or that the sole good is whatever is necessary to life. Moore maintains that neither the normal nor the necessary can seriously be held always to be good, or to be the sole good. Neither view can be forced through as true by definition. It is clearly an open question whether something that is normal or is necessary to life is (intrinsically) good. But once we reject the claim that either view is true by definition, there seems little reason to suppose that either is true at all. On the contrary, it seems that certain abnormal states are generally better than the normal, such as the excellence of Socrates or Shakespeare (PE: 94). And the same seems to be true of what is necessary to life. Certain actions may be *excused* as necessary for life, but they need not be praised on that account (PE: 96), and many things that are not necessary to life seem to have great value.

Evolutionary accounts of the good fair little better, in Moore's view. According to evolutionary ethics, evolution not only shows us how we have evolved but also how we should evolve. Moore takes Herbert Spencer as an example of such a view. Once again Moore denies that Spencer's view can seriously be regarded as true by definition. "Better" does not *mean* "more evolved", for it is an open question whether something that is more evolved is better. But if the evolutionary view is not true by definition, what grounds can be offered in its defence?

Spencer's only argument seems to be that the more evolved is better because it is more pleasant. But this argument seems to negate what is distinctive of evolutionary ethics, for it makes Spencer look like a hedonist. Ultimately his view seems not to be that certain things are better because they are more evolved, but that certain things, including the more evolved, are better because they produce more pleasure. If this is right, then Spencer's evolutionary ethics would stand or fall with hedonism, and Moore presents what he regards as decisive arguments against hedonism in Chapter 3.

Moore considers J. S. Mill's and Henry Sidgwick's hedonism. Once again, Moore maintains that hedonism owes most of its plausibility to the naturalistic fallacy, although he acknowledges that Sidgwick does not make this mistake. Mill seems to commit the naturalistic fallacy when he claims that "To think of an object as desirable (unless for the sake of its consequences) and to think of it as pleasant are one and the same thing" (PE: 116). As we noted earlier this naturalistic definition of good provides a very quick route to hedonism, but cannot be correct, as it is an open question whether something that is pleasant is good.

Moore also claims to detect a different instance of the naturalistic fallacy in Mill: this time he does not identify "good" with "pleasant", but with "desirable", where "desirable" is understood to mean "desired" (PE: 119). Mill did seem to use "desirable" as a synonym for "good", but this is unobjectionable unless he goes on to identify being desirable with being desired, and it is unclear whether Mill seriously proposed such an identification. Moore's evidence that he did is that Mill claims that "the sole evidence it is possible to produce that anything is desirable, is that people do actually desire it" (PE: 118). But it is one thing to regard what people actually desire as a test of what is desirable, and quite another to believe that being desirable and being desired are the same thing. Moore himself notes this difference with the distinction he often makes between a criterion of good and a definition. The passage Moore cites suggests that Mill regarded what people desire as a criterion or test of what is desirable, rather than as a definition of what it is to be desirable.

The analogy Mill draws between being desirable, on the one hand, and being visible and audible, on the other, may suggest that he understood desirable to mean "able to be desired". For to be visible is to be able to be seen, and to be audible is to be able to be heard. But this definition is clearly mistaken. We are able to desire many things that nobody could sensibly maintain are good. As Moore was quick to point out, "desirable" does not mean "able to be desired", but "ought to be desired", and the fact that people desire certain things does not support the belief that they ought to desire those things.

But Mill need not define "good" in this way to argue for his hedonism. If it is true that the only thing we desire for its own sake is pleasure, as Mill claims, this would support the view that we regard pleasure as the sole good. Moore does not deny that there is some very close relation between desire and pleasure. What he does deny is that pleasure is the sole *object* of desire – that is, he denies that it is *what* we desire.

Moore proposes that when we come to desire something we first have a thought of that thing, and this thought causes a feeling of pleasure. This feeling of pleasure in turn produces a desire for that thing (PE: 121). The idea here is that pleasure is bound up with the very nature of desire, not as its object but as its cause or ground. We do not always desire pleasure, but desire other things because the thought of those things is pleasant.

Moore illustrates this idea with a desire for a glass of wine. Mill would say that we do not desire the glass of wine for its own sake, but only for the sake of the pleasure we will get from drinking it. It is this future pleasure that is the real object of our desire, not the glass of wine. On Moore's view, however, the object of our desire is the glass of wine. Here we do not desire some future pleasure, but desire something else (the glass of wine) because the thought of it is pleasant. This desire is not aimed at future pleasure, but is caused by a present pleasure.

Moore argues further that pleasure cannot be the only thing we desire, for without the inclusion of what it is that we will get pleasure from, our desires will be indeterminate.

> If the desire were directed *solely* towards the pleasure, it could not lead me to take the wine; if it is to take a definite direction, it is absolutely necessary that the idea of the object, from which the pleasure is expected, should also be present and should control my activity.
>
> (PE: 122)

So Moore rejects both Mill's psychological claim that the only thing we desire is pleasure, and his meta-ethical claim that goodness is one and the same thing as pleasantness.

Moore treats Sidgwick (one of Moore's teachers) with a lot more respect than he does Mill. Sidgwick is clear that good does not mean pleasant, but nonetheless thinks that pleasure is the only thing that is good, and maintains that reflection reveals this to us. According to Sidgwick, then, other things, such as beauty, are only instrumentally good – they are good in so far as they produce pleasure in us (PE: 123). If something does not produce any pleasure then it can have no value at all.

Moore's response is to deny that reflection will lead us to hedonism. Rather, on reflection, the view that pleasure is the sole good turns out to be quite implausible. Acceptance of the view that pleasure is the sole good would commit one to the view that a life of pleasure, and nothing else, would be the best life, no matter what one got pleasure from. But no one could seriously accept this consequence. A life filled with base pleasures and nothing else might be fun, but could hardly be thought of as the pinnacle of human achievement.

Moore thought that we could come to see the falsity of hedonism by a thought experiment. Moore gets us to imagine two uninhabited worlds, one exceedingly beautiful, and the other "simply one heap of filth, containing everything that is most disgusting to us" (PE: 135). Moore is convinced that it would be better if the beautiful world existed and assumes we will share his intuition (PE: 135). If the beautiful world is better than the ugly one, then pleasure cannot be the only good. Since there is no one to get pleasure from the beautiful world, the value it has cannot be derived from pleasure.

Moore then turns to the two forms hedonism can take: egoism and utilitarianism. According to hedonistic egoism each of us ought to pursue our own greatest happiness as the highest good. Happiness here is to be understood in hedonistic terms. So greatest happiness means greatest amount of pleasure, or balance of pleasure over pain. Moore thinks that egoism, so understood, is based upon confusion (PE: 149). The chief confusion is involved in the very distinction between my own good and the good of others. First, he rejects the view that the only way to promote my good is by maximizing the amount of pleasure in my life (PE: 149). Secondly, and more fundamentally, Moore thinks that the very idea of an individual's own good is nonsense. Goodness is not something that an individual can possess. An individual might possess certain good things, say a great work of art, but what the individual possesses is the thing that is good (here, the work of art), not its goodness (PE: 150). Since the idea on which egoism rests is senseless, according to Moore, egoism itself must be rejected. The only reason I can have for aiming at "my own good" is that it is good absolutely, that is, non-relatively. But then, everyone else has as much reason to aim at my having it as I do. So if something is a rational end for me, it must be a rational end for everyone, and if it is not a rational end for everyone, then it will not be a rational end for me (PE: 151).

Having rejected hedonistic egoism Moore turns to utilitarianism. According to utilitarianism (a) we ought always to bring about the best state of affairs possible, and (b) the best state of affairs is determined solely by the amount of pleasure, or balance of pleasure over pain. Moore thinks that the first element of utilitarianism is correct (PE: 157). Where utilitarians go wrong is that they think that the only thing that is good in itself is pleasure.

Moore's analytic consequentialism

Moore not only thinks that we ought morally to produce the greatest possible amount of good in the universe, but maintains that this is true by definition: "the assertion 'I am morally bound to perform this action' is identical with the assertion 'This action will produce the greatest possible amount of good in the universe'" (PE: 197). In §89 Moore claims to have shown this identity in §17, although no argument to that effect can be found there. All Moore does in §17 is assert that judgements about what we ought morally to do are judgements about what is the means to the best outcome (77). This is not an argument. He does, however, offer the following argument for his view in §89:

> It is plain that when we assert that a certain action is our absolute duty, we are asserting that the performance of that action at that time is unique in respect of value. But no dutiful action can possibly have unique value in the sense that it is the sole thing of value in the world; since, in that case, *every* such action would be the *sole* good thing, which is a manifest contradiction. And for the same reason its value cannot be unique in the sense that it has more intrinsic value than anything else in the world; since *every* act of duty would then be the *best* thing in the world, which is also a contradiction. It can, therefore, be unique only in the sense that the whole world will be better, if it be performed, than if any possible alternative were taken.   (PE: 197)

If judgements about what we should do are judgements that some act is unique in respect of value, then the most plausible construal of this uniqueness is as producing the most good. But deontologists such as Prichard (2002), and Ross (2002) would deny the antecedent of this argument. They argue that there is *no* necessary connection between right acts and good acts, so judgements about which act is obligatory cannot be judgements about which act is unique in respect of value. By simply assuming that they are wrong Moore comes close to begging the question at issue between deontologists and consequentialists.

In any case, Moore himself has provided good reason to suppose that "ought morally to be done" does not mean "will produce the best possible state of affairs" with his open question argument. For it is an open question whether some act that will produce the best possible state of affairs is the one we ought morally to do. Deontologists maintain that sometimes the act that will produce the best possible state of affairs is not the one that we are morally bound to do. If Moore's analysis of moral obligation is correct, however, this deontological claim would be nonsense. For if his analysis is correct, then what deontologists assert is that sometimes the act that will produce the best possible state of affairs will not be the act that will produce the best possible state of affairs. This is not what deontologists claim when they claim that consequentialism is false. Those who question the truth of consequentialism may be mistaken, but such questioning makes sense.

Moore himself later came to see this (1966: 29–30; 1968: 558–9). He never abandoned the view that the right act is always the one that will produce the best outcome, but he did deny that this is true by definition. So he later came to abandon the analytical consequentialism he proposed in *Principia*. His later view seems to be that being productive of the best possible outcome is not *what it is* for an act to be obligatory, but is what *makes* certain acts obligatory.

Because of his consequentialism, Moore was sceptical that we could ever know that a certain act is our duty. We cannot know this because we cannot possibly know all of the consequences of our actions, or what consequences other actions would have had. "Ethics, therefore, is quite unable to give a list of duties" (PE: 199). What ethics can do, however, is show which among the alternatives *likely to occur to any one* will generally produce the best sum of good (PE: 201); that is, ethics can come up with a set of rules that we have reason to believe will on the whole produce good outcomes.

This view may make Moore seem like he is proposing a form of rule-consequentialism, but he is not. Rule-consequentialists maintain that the right act is determined by whether it accords with a set of rules for the general regulation of society that would produce the best outcome if generally accepted. Moore does not accept this. His view is that the right act is determined not by a set of rules, but by the fact that the actual consequences of that action are better than those of any alternative action. This is act consequentialism. What makes him look like a rule consequentialist is that he thinks that because of our ignorance, the best chance we have of doing what is right is by acting in accordance with a certain set of rules. But rightness is not determined by the rules, but in each and every case by the consequences of the particular act.

Moore thinks that the set of rules that are most likely to lead to the right action are the commonly accepted rules of morality, for example, rules forbidding murder, theft, deceit and so on. Moore thinks we should conform to these rules even when we think they recommend the wrong action (PE: 211). This is for two reasons. First, our ignorance is so great that we are far more likely to do the right act if we conform to the general rule than if we transgress it (PE: 211). Secondly, our act of transgression will tend to weaken the general observance of the rule, and thus will contribute to a general transgression that is disadvantageous (PE: 212). Of course if the rule is a bad one then the example one sets in transgressing it may be for the general good. But, Moore maintains, clear examples of where a certain rule would be better than the generally observed ones will be rare (PE: 214).

The ideal

So far we have seen that Moore held that the right act is always the one that will produce as much intrinsic value as is possible. To fill out the details of his account we need to turn to what he thinks has intrinsic value. Moore addresses this question in the final chapter of *Principia*.

We have seen that Moore is a pluralist about the good – he believes that there is an irreducible plurality of intrinsically good things. In Chapter 6 he does not attempt to list all of these, but mentions only those he regards as the most significant goods. He maintains that there is a plurality of intrinsic goods and evils, and that (with the exception of consciousness of pain) the most simple of them are complex wholes made up of parts that themselves have little or no intrinsic value.

This view rests on what he calls his principle of organic wholes, or what he sometimes calls the principle of organic relations, or unities. According to this principle, the intrinsic value of a complex whole bears no regular proportion to the sum of the intrinsic values of its parts (PE: 79). The idea is that the things that have the most intrinsic value are complex things that typically involve some consciousness of an object (e.g. of a beautiful thing, or of someone else's happiness) and some emotional attitude towards that object, such as aesthetic pleasure, or satisfaction.

Moore offers consciousness of a beautiful object as an example of an organic whole. Such consciousness, he maintains, is something of great intrinsic value (PE: 79), but it is made up of parts that have very little intrinsic value in themselves. Consciousness of a beautiful object is a complex that is composed of (a) the beautiful object and (b) being conscious, according to Moore. The beautiful object itself has some intrinsic value, but no great worth. Being conscious also has little intrinsic value in itself. So here we have something of great intrinsic value that is composed of parts that have very little intrinsic value.

This is not a very plausible example of an organic whole. As W. D. Ross later pointed out, consciousness of a beautiful object is not a complex whole consisting of the beautiful thing plus consciousness as such. Rather such consciousness consists in the beautiful object plus the consciousness *of it*, and one might think (as Ross did) that any intrinsic value this whole has stems solely from the latter element (Ross 2002: 70–71).

Moore provides a better illustration of his principle with the value of punishment. To punish someone is (roughly) to inflict some evil on him because he has inflicted some evil on someone else. Although the suffering of the criminal is intrinsically bad, just as the suffering of his victim is, the fact that he is made to suffer may make things better, rather than worse (PE: 262). So here the addition of something intrinsically bad (the criminal's suffering) makes the whole of which it is a part better.

But once again we may doubt whether Moore offers an accurate account of punishment. It seems that in cases where punishing someone does make things better, this is because the evil inflicted on the criminal is deserved and proportional to the evil he inflicted on his victim. But these relations (desert and proportionality) get left out of Moore's analysis of punishment, and this omission highlights a general failure in his principle of organic wholes.

Moore always talks of complexes as made up of various parts. The relations in which those parts stand to each other never seem to be mentioned. It cannot be that Moore thought of the relation of the parts as further parts of the whole, for if the notion of a unified whole is to be maintained these further parts would in turn have to be related to each other. But this clearly leads to an infinite regress (of relations being converted into parts that then need to be related). It seems then that he has to allow the relations of the parts in addition to the parts they relate in his account of any particular whole.

Once we add the relations between the parts to the parts so related we will often have a ready explanation of why the sum of the value of the parts may not be the same as the value of the whole. This discrepancy arises, we might argue, because some of the value (or disvalue) of the whole stems from the value of the relations in which the parts stand to each other. For example, the relations of proportionality and deservedness certainly seem to be relevant to whether we think the criminal's punishment makes things better, and these relations may plausibly be thought of as things that have value. If this is right, then the value of the whole may always be equal to the value of its parts *and relations*, and we need not assume that the value emerges *ex nihilo* at the more complex level.

A further difficulty with Moore's principle of organic wholes is that it has the counter-intuitive consequence that it allows intrinsic value to be cut off from practical reasons. It seems that if something is intrinsically good, then we have reason to desire it and approve it, and the contrary is true of intrinsic disvalue. Moore wants to say that in the case of punishment, the criminal's suffering is both intrinsically bad and makes the whole of which it is a part better. Now in so far as his suffering makes things better we have reason to approve of his punishment. But what are the reasons associated with the intrinsic disvalue of his suffering? If his suffering is intrinsically bad, then we have reason to disapprove of it. But how could our approval and disapproval be justified by the very same feature of the situation, by the criminal's suffering? How could the very same instance of suffering be of a nature to be approved and at the same time be of a nature to be disapproved?

It may seem that the above point about relations could be used to help Moore out here. For if it is allowed that the whole is composed of the relations of proportionality and desert as well as the parts that are related in these ways, then Moore could respond that it is not the very same feature of the whole that justifies both approval and disapproval. He might say that what we have reason to approve of is not the criminal's suffering as such, but its being deserved and proportional to his crime, and what we have reason to disapprove or regret is not the deservedness and proportionality of his suffering, but simply his suffering. There is nothing paradoxical about that.

But the cost of reconnecting the link between value and reasons in this way is that it is likely that the principle of organic wholes may lose its significance. For once relations are brought into the picture, any discrepancy the principle allows between the value of the whole and of the parts may always be explained by the value of the relations in which the parts stand.

What then are the complex wholes Moore claims have great intrinsic value? Moore divides his account into unmixed goods, mixed evils and mixed goods. Unmixed goods are complex wholes of which the elements are all good, and of these the highest goods are the love of the beautiful and personal affection. Mixed evils contain both good and bad elements. He offers a love of the bad and of the ugly and a hatred of the good and of the beautiful as examples. Mixed goods, on the other hand are complexes of intrinsically bad elements, and include the hatred of what is ugly or of the first two evils, and a compassion for pain.

By far the most significant goods, in Moore's view, are a love of the beautiful and of friendship:

> By far the most valuable things, which we know or can imagine, are certain states of consciousness, which may be roughly described as the pleasures of human intercourse and the enjoyment of beautiful objects. No one, probably, who asked himself the question, has ever doubted that personal affection and the appreciation of what is beautiful in Art or Nature, are good in themselves; nor, if we consider strictly what

things are worth having *purely for their own sakes*, does it appear probable that any one will think that anything else has *nearly* so great a value as the things which are included under these two heads.   (PE: 237)

Appreciation of a beautiful object involves both a cognitive and an affective element. It is to be aware of the features that make the object beautiful, and to have an appropriate emotion directed at those qualities (PE: 238). The value of this whole is enhanced if it is accompanied by a true belief in the existence of the beautiful object (PE: 247), but, Moore maintains, true belief and knowledge by themselves have little or no intrinsic value.

Each of these three elements is also present in the pleasures of human intercourse, or of personal affection. But whereas the object of aesthetic appreciation has little intrinsic value, the object of personal affection "must be not only truly beautiful, but also truly good in a high degree" (PE: 251). But the object of such love can have great intrinsic value only in so far as its object includes some admirable mental quality or other, and one loves the other person in virtue of such qualities. Such admirable qualities will include the emotional contemplation of beautiful objects, and the emotional contemplation of other people's admirable qualities. The highest goods for Moore, then, are the higher-order goods of the admiring contemplation of the admiring contemplation of the beautiful and the admirable (PE: 252–3).

Moore here assumes that for any good, an appropriate pro-attitude towards that good will have more intrinsic value than its object. He assumes further than this principle is iterable. So if *A* is intrinsically good, then the appreciation of *A* will be better than *A*, and the appreciation of the appreciation of *A* will be better than the appreciation of *A*, and so on.

This view of the comparative value of higher-order goods is peculiar. It seems to recommend that we strive for an ever-higher order of appreciation. If the appreciation of the appreciation of beauty is better than the appreciation of beauty, then we should aim at this second-order appreciation. But if a third-order appreciation is better still, then we should aim at that, and so on for a fourth-order appreciation, and a fifth-order appreciation. But this just seems wrong. It seems far more plausible to suppose the opposite: that our attitudes have less value as we move away from the first-order good.

Conclusion

It is the meta-ethical claims in Moore's *Principia* that have had an enduring influence on philosophical debates. Not everyone is persuaded by his open question argument, or by his claim that goodness is a simple, non-natural property. It is, however, generally agreed that Moore articulates a serious challenge to any naturalistic meta-ethics. Even those who ultimately reject Moore's arguments still feel the need to engage with them.

But although the influence of Moore's *Principia* has been largely meta-ethical, what ultimately interested Moore was the question of what things are good. Moore spends so much time on the meta-ethical question of the nature of goodness because he thought that a particular, naturalistic account of goodness leads one to an impoverished conception of the good. Once we recognize that hedonism, or some desire-based theory, is not true by definition, and accept the principle of organic unities, the view that the sole good is pleasure or what is desired loses all plausibility. There are few arguments for his positive thesis about the good in Chapter 6, but this adds to the impact of the chapter on the reader. Whether or not Moore is right about the highest goods, he is surely right that there is a plurality of goods.

Bibliography

Baldwin, T. 1990. *G. E. Moore*. London: Routledge.

Frankena, W. K. 1952. "The Naturalistic Fallacy". In *Readings in Ethical Theory*, W. Sellars & J. Hospers (eds), 103–14. New York: Appleton-Century-Crofts.

Hurka, T. 2003. "Moore in the Middle". *Ethics* **113**, 599–628.

Kripke, S. 1972. *Naming and Necessity*. Cambridge, MA: Harvard University Press.

Moore, G. E. 1968 [1942]. "A Reply to My Critics". In *The Philosophy of G. E. Moore*, P. A. Schilpp, 535–677. La Salle, IL: Open Court.

Moore, G. E. 1966. *Ethics*. Oxford: Oxford University Press.

Moore, G. E. 1993 [1903]. *Principia Ethica* (PE), T. Baldwin (ed.). Cambridge: Cambridge University Press.

Prichard, H. A. 2002 [1912]. "Does Moral Philosophy Rest On A Mistake?". In *Moral Writings*, H. A. Pritchard, J. MacAdam (ed.), 7–20. Oxford: Clarendon Press.

Putnam, H. 1975. "The Meaning of Meaning". In *Language, Mind and Knowledge*, Minnesota Studies in the Philosophy of Science, VII, K. Gunderson (ed.), 131–93. Minneapolis, MN: University of Minnesota Press.

Rashdall, H. 1907. *The Theory of Good and Evil: A Treatise on Moral Philosophy*. Oxford: Oxford University Press.

Ross, W. D. 2002. *The Right and the Good*, P. Stratton-Lake (ed.). Oxford: Clarendon Press.

Stratton-Lake, P. & B. Hooker 2006. "Scanlon versus Moore on Goodness". In *Metaethics after Moore*, T. Horgan & M. Timmons (eds), 149–68. Oxford: Oxford University Press.

Further reading

Bradley, F. H. 1962 [1876]. *Ethical Studies*. Oxford: Clarendon Press.

Darwall, S., A. Gibbard, P. Railton 1992. "Towards *Fin de siecle* Ethics". *Philosophical Review* **101**, 115–89.

Hutchinson, B. 2001. *G. E. Moore's Ethical Theory: Resistance and Reconciliation*. Cambridge: Cambridge University Press.

Levy, P. 1980. *Moore: G. E. Moore and the Cambridge Apostles.* New York: Holt, Rinehart & Winston.

Regan, T. 1986. *Bloomsbury's Prophet*. Philadelphia, PA: Temple University Press.

Schilpp, P. A. (ed.) 1942. *The Philosophy of G. E. Moore*. La Salle, IL: Open Court.

Sidgwick, H. 1981 [1874]. *The Methods of Ethics*. Indianapolis, IN: Hackett.

Stratton-Lake, P. 2002. *Ethical Intuitionism: Re-evaluations*. Oxford: Clarendon Press.

See also two special journal editions marking the centenary of *Principia Ethica*: *Ethics* **113** and *The Journal of Value Inquiry* **37**.

2

Edmund Husserl
The Idea of Phenomenology

A. D. Smith

The Idea of Phenomenology, which consists of five lectures that Husserl delivered in Göttingen in 1907, comes from perhaps the most important period in his overall philosophical development. For although in 1912 Husserl could refer to his *Logical Investigations* of 1900–1901 as constituting the "breakthrough" of phenomenology, after the publication of this magisterial work Husserl entered the most profound philosophical crisis in his life, in which he felt, the astonishing achievement of the *Logical Investigations* notwithstanding, unable to provide a satisfactory account of the possibility of human knowledge. *The Idea of Phenomenology* is his first public presentation of his thoughts after having worked his way out of this crisis and into a position that he would hold for the rest of his life: a position that he would term *Transcendental Phenomenology*. If phenomenology as such had emerged in the *Logical Investigations*, the transcendental perspective, which alone can answer fundamental sceptical worries about human knowledge, had not. We need, therefore, to understand what it is, according to Husserl, for philosophy to be "transcendental", and why he deems it to be of such importance that it should be.

Transcendental phenomenology involves taking a novel, indeed unnatural, perspective on the world. It is, Husserl believed, the one truly philosophical perspective. However, because of its unnatural character, there is a problem in explaining why this perspective should be adopted at all. Hence, from *The Idea of Phenomenology* until his death Husserl repeatedly attempted to provide a convincing motive for adopting this perspective, writing numerous "introductions" to phenomenology. Husserl scholars speak in this connection of the various "ways" into phenomenology that Husserl presented.[1] One of them is called the "Cartesian way", and it is this way that *The Idea of Phenomenology* presents. What is distinctive of this way is that it presents transcendental phenomenology as the only philosophical position that can adequately respond to a fundamental *epistemological* demand: that we make clear to ourselves how genuine knowledge is a possibility. Although there are other "ways" of motivating phenomenology, this Cartesian way has a certain priority in Husserl's writings. For not only does he resort to it more often than any other way, it was, as *The Idea of Phenomenology* testifies, the way in which Husserl himself originally arrived at the transcendental perspective. In the pages of *The Idea of Phenomenology* we can occasionally sense the excitement of Husserl's recent discovery of a way of settling a fundamental sceptical worry concerning knowledge.

The sceptical worry that exercised Husserl was an absolutely fundamental one. It was how knowledge could be so much as even a possibility: how we can make sense of there being such a thing as knowledge at all. As Husserl himself says, "The riddle is *how* it is possible" (IP: 37).[2] This explains Husserl's repeated references to the *essence* of knowledge. For only if we understand this essence, understand the *nature* of knowledge, shall we be in a position to understand how knowledge is possible (if it is at all). Indeed, the fundamental sceptical worry that haunts Husserl is, in effect, that the essence of knowledge is itself such as to render actual knowledge an impossibility. Perhaps our very concept of knowledge places impossible demands upon us. This is what Husserl has in mind when he states that epistemology "must expose and reject the mistakes that natural reflection upon the relation of knowledge, its sense, and its object almost inevitably makes; and it must thereby refute the explicit or implicit skeptical theories concerning the essence of knowledge by demonstrating their absurdity" (IP: 22). As the word "implicit" intimates, Husserl does not see his task as simply that of refuting various sceptical arguments that philosophers have put forward, but as addressing a worry that is inexorably bound up with "natural reflection". For such reflection, in Husserl's view, *inevitably* leads to our forming mistaken views concerning the nature of knowledge: views on what knowledge *must* be, if there is any. Natural reflection is reflection that is carried on in what Husserl calls the "natural attitude". He opens his first lecture by stating that this attitude is not concerned with a critique of knowledge. This may seem surprising, since Husserl is also claiming that the reflection that is carried on in this attitude leads us to formulate theories about the nature or essence of knowledge: theories that inevitably lead to scepticism. This would seem precisely to involve a concern with a critique of knowledge. We can get a firmer handle on what Husserl has in mind if we attend to his initial positive characterization of the natural attitude: "In such an attitude, our attention is turned … to *things* given to us, and given self-evidently" (IP: 17, translation modified). Two things are important here. First, that we are concerned with *things*, by which Husserl means that we are concerned with things *rather than with our cognitive relation to things*. Secondly, that we take these things to be self-evidently, unproblematically there: "as a matter of course" (IP: 18). Both of these are in play when Husserl immediately goes on to say that all our judgements made in the natural attitude concern *the world*. As Husserl will put it in later writings, in the natural attitude we are "dedicated", or "given over" to the world. All everyday life is founded on an unquestioned belief in the *reality* of the world, and all our judgements are about this world. Indeed, "What else could they be about?" the natural attitude will ask. ("Transcendental consciousness" will be Husserl's answer.) Even when we reflect on ourselves, we are directing our attention to the world, because we unthinkingly take ourselves *to be part of the world*. Although, as I have said, natural reflection can lead to a critique of knowledge of sorts, it arrives at this on the basis of a fundamental orientation to and commitment to the world. The sceptical worries that arise here take the form of worries over how certain *worldly* facts can obtain. How can I, as one element in the world, be related knowingly to another element in that world? The essence of knowledge, on such a view, would be the essence of a certain worldly relation. It is this very general way of conceiving the issue – one that is inevitable for the natural attitude – that, Husserl believes, lands one in insuperable difficulties. Although the natural attitude can indeed, therefore, be concerned with knowledge, that concern always comes too late, since it arises as a result of reflections that themselves presuppose the existence of a world. Indeed, natural reflection's concern with knowledge is hardly a "critique" at all. It is, rather, simply a puzzle that arises when it brings to bear on the topic of knowledge its own uncriticized presuppositions. Husserl, by contrast, insists that philosophy should *begin* with a full-scale critique of knowledge, *without any presuppositions at all.* Philosophy distinguishes itself from all other enterprises precisely by engaging in such a radical "critique of positive knowledge" (IP: 22). Phenomenology therefore begins with what Husserl calls the "phenomenological reduction" (IP: 5), which excludes the very presupposition that there is a real world at all. In such a reduction we restrict ("reduce") our assertions to what is indubitable: to what must be recognized *even if there is no real world.* All reflection conducted in the wake of this reduction is carried out in the *phenomenological attitude*, which in later writings Husserl claims is the only genuinely distinct alternative to the natural attitude. In the present lectures Husserl simply contrasts the natural attitude with the "philosophical attitude" (IP: 18), for his considered view is that the phenomenological attitude is the only truly philosophical one. For any so-called philosophy that does not effect the phenomenological reduction shares the natural attitude's concern with the world, and so will be unable to escape the sceptical quandary that the latter necessarily involves. It will also fail to address the radical question of what it means to say that a world exists (or does not): it naively passes over what the *sense* of "world" might be. For Husserl, sense is grounded in knowledge. What we understand something to be is determined by what it is seen to be in genuine knowledge. So there must be knowledge if there is even thought or opinion at all. The problem is to understand, however, how any of this is possibly true.

But we are getting ahead of ourselves. For what, after all, is supposed to be the insuperable epistemological problem for the natural attitude in the first place? The problem arises from the *transcendence* that is essential to knowledge: "If we take a closer look at what is so enigmatic about knowledge, and what causes our predicament in our first reflections on the possibility of knowledge, we find that it is its transcendence" (IP: 34). Suppose that you know that this page of print is before you.[3] If you do, it would seem that this knowledge is a *state of you*, or of your mind. It is *your* (putative) knowledge that we are concerned with: so it is a *subjective* state. But this page, the supposed object of your knowledge, is not a state of you. It is a separate entity from you: a "transcendent" entity, simply in the sense that it is something *over and above*, distinct from, any state of you. But your state of knowledge, if it really is *knowledge of* this page, must, it would seem, have in some way to *make contact* with the page (IP: 3–4). So your state of knowledge, it would seem, has to *transcend itself*: it has, even though it is a state of you, somehow to reach out beyond itself to grasp a distinct entity. This, as I shall explain shortly, is really the heart of the problem of transcendence as Husserl sees it: to make sense of this *relation to an object* that is supposedly possessed by a subjective, psychological state. But Husserl, in his initial presentation of the problem, immediately goes on to pinpoint the supposedly central problem as being a matter of a state of knowledge itself *guaranteeing* that such contact has indeed been made: "In all of its manifestations, knowledge is a mental experience: knowledge belongs to a knowing subject. The known objects stand over against it. How, then, can knowledge *be sure of its agreement* with the known objects?" (IP: 20, emphasis added). Or again: "But how can knowledge go beyond itself to reach the object *and yet be sure of this relation with complete indubitability.* How can we understand that knowledge, without losing its immanence, can not only be correct but *can also demonstrate this correctness*?" (Addendum III, my emphasis). This, however, may appear both implausible and confused. If the real question is supposed to be how knowledge is *even possible*, Husserl might appear to be confused when he apparently starts demanding that we be *indubitably sure* that our purported knowledge really is what it purports to be. And if the suggestion is that all knowledge must be indubitable knowledge – that indubitability is the essence of knowledge – that appears implausible. I believe that what Husserl is actually getting at in this stretch of argument is that if there is to be any knowledge at all, there must be some knowledge that *acquaints* us with things. If there is to be knowledge, some objects must be *given* to consciousness in such a way that, in the wide sense that Husserl gives to this term, we simply *see* them. And, as Husserl repeatedly says, it makes no sense to doubt what we simply see (e.g. IP: 31), for this would be to doubt that anything even appears to us – that there are phenomena. Now, it is perception that would constitute our most basic knowledge of the world. If we perceived nothing, we would know nothing – at least nothing about the actual world. But natural reflection leads us to think that perception is "nothing more than an experience that belongs to me" (IP: 20). As such, it has lost its essential relation to an object. There are experiences in me, and a world out there. How is contact to be made? Within the natural attitude the only candidate for bridging the gap would be causality. But causality by itself cannot explain acquaintance. Let the world *cause* as many experiences in me as you like; if these experiences are still merely states of me, presenting only themselves to consciousness, we have made no progress. The whole situation is, therefore, deeply puzzling. We need a direct awareness of objects, but cannot understand how this is possible.

We can make progress with this problem only if we can be sure that, at least in some cases, *contact* is made with an object of supposed knowledge. Is there, however, any possible form of cognition that matches up to this demand for absolute clarity concerning our relatedness to an object? Initially it seems that there can certainly be none that would relate to transcendent objects, for these involve the very obscurity that we are trying to overcome. However, Descartes provides us with a more promising candidate: the immediate knowledge that we have of our own current mental states. Husserl agrees with Descartes that such knowledge is indeed indubitable – in the sense that its object must exist (its non-existence is inconceivable) and be the way it appears. So we have here an indisputable example of knowledge. However, we should not misunderstand how this is supposed to help us with our initial problem. For Husserl's thought is *not*: here is a case where knowledge is actual, therefore knowledge is possible. That is just the kind of inference that, valid as it is, Husserl explicitly rejects as irrelevant to his concerns (IP: 37). For recall, it is the *"how"* of knowledge that puzzles him. A sheer instance of knowledge, even a wholly undeniable one, does not of itself address this worry. It is, rather, the *source* of indubitability in this case that points the way forward. Immediate knowledge of your own mental states and processes is indubitable precisely because of the complete *clarity* that characterizes it. In particular, in such cases of knowledge we simply *see* the object in question. When we reflectively turn our attention to our own conscious mental lives, its contents are immediately *present to us*, and completely so. Husserl speaks in this connection of such objects being "adequately" or "absolutely" given. It is, therefore, this privileged mode of givenness, rather than the indubitability that it sustains, that will serve to point us forward in our enquiry. For it is this that meets the philosopher's demand that "the essence of this relation is somewhere given to him, so that he could see it, so that the unity of knowing and the known object, which is suggested by the phrase 'making contact with reality', would itself stand right before his eyes" (IP: 37). Husserl is demanding that we be able to "see" an essence, about which more later.

Although I have mentioned Descartes in the present connection, Husserl is not simply appropriating the Cartesian *cogito*, for he feels that this is far from indubitable. For Descartes's "mind or soul", the supposedly indubitable *res cogitans*, is arrived at by doubting everything else in the world. In other words, it is something *left over from the world* when other dubious elements have been set to one side. It is, as Husserl says towards the end of his philosophical career, in the *Cartesian Meditations*, a "little tag-end of the world". In particular, the Cartesian self is thought of as persisting in "world-time" (IP: 7) or "objective time" (IP: 44), the very same time as worldly objects would exist in. Again, for the Cartesian a possible external world is thought of as being "out there", so that a relation of the self to space is presupposed. The Cartesian ego is thought of as "in the world" (IP: 44); it is just that that world, apart from the ego, is perhaps empty. But another entity *could* exist *alongside* the ego. So the ego is located in the *world-framework*. All this is not just questionable, according to Husserl, but obscure, and in need of clarification: phenomenological clarification. This is the kind of thing that Husserl has in mind when he says that Descartes's conception of the self carries "transcendent freight" (IP: 7). Husserl's awareness of such presuppositions also lies behind his perhaps initially puzzling claim that we should not "confuse the evidence of the being of the *cogitatio* [thought, in the wide Cartesian sense] with the evidence for the existence of *my cogitatio*" (IP: 43). Such confusion does not make sense for Descartes, since there is for him no distinction here. After all, it might be said, whose indubitable thoughts could possibly be in question within a Cartesian perspective but one's own? Husserl's point is that Descartes is presupposing a certain conception of the self: as something that is already implicitly related to what is transcendent. Attributing thoughts to *such* a self will therefore be as questionable – that is, dubitable – as the existence of the self so conceived. So Descartes's famous "*cogito ergo sum*" is not indubitable, since it employs a questionable, because unclear, concept of the self and its "thoughts". Husserl therefore requires a "purer" concept of experience, one untainted with any reference to what is transcendent. Hence he can say that "the Cartesian *cogitatio* itself requires the phenomenological reduction" (IP: 7). We must reduce, or restrict, our attention to what is purely seen in reflection, and set ourselves free from any presupposition about how what we find there *must* in principle relate to other possible things should they exist. Not to do this would simply be to engage in *psychology*, which is a "positive science" arising out of the natural attitude, since it focuses on one particular aspect or stratum of the world. As Husserl says, transcendental phenomenology means that "we abandon once and for all the basis of psychology – even descriptive psychology" (IP: 7).[4] Phenomenology, unlike psychology, is the "science of *pure* phenomena" (IP: 43, emphasis added). Its phenomena are "pure" – and thereby alone indubitable – because they have been purified of any reference, even implicit, to a real world.

It is precisely at this point, however, where we may seem to have made a critical discovery, that we must beware of a possible "fatal mistake" (IP: 36). For it is easy to think that what confers a privilege on our awareness of our own mental states is that they are not transcendent to consciousness, but, rather, *immanent* in it. A pain, for example, of which you may have immediate reflective awareness, is a literal part of your stream of consciousness – the same individual consciousness that also contains your reflective act of awareness of the pain. Here your knowledge is adequate, it would seem, just because it does not seek problematically to find an object "outside" the mind, but encounters one "inside", in the mind itself. After all, was it not transcendence, being outside the mind or consciousness, that gave us our epistemological problems in the first place? So where else could we find our solution except by turning *inwards*, to the immanent elements that make up our own stream of consciousness? "The immanent is in me, the beginner will say at this point, and the transcendent is outside of me" (IP: 5). Indeed, the Cartesian turn inwards may seem only to reinforce the epistemological problem with which we started, since it seems to offer no more than a knowledge that is restricted to the contents of our own minds. This, however, is the fatal mistake. For we should not interpret this turn inwards as a turn to objects that are literally parts of our conscious life: that are contained in consciousness in, as Husserl puts it, a "real [*reell*]" manner. Although Husserl endorses the claim that we must restrict our attention to what is "immanent", and that we must, in some sense, turn "inwards", the notion of immanence now being offered is a "false sense" of immanence (IP: 57). Immanence is simply contrasted with transcendence; but "transcendence turns out to be ambiguous" (IP: 35). There are two notions attaching to each term, therefore, that it is essential for us to distinguish.

When we reflectively turn our attention on to our own current experiences, then, at least when such experiences have been purified, by the phenomenological reduction, of any even implicit reference to an objective world, we can be indubitably sure of what we find there. Here we simply "see" things in their immediate presence. Here, as Husserl puts it, we are dealing with "absolute givenness". This gives us one sense of what it is to be immanent: "immanent in the intentional sense", as he later terms it (IP: 55). For it is not unnatural to express such epistemological security by saying that the given items are not "external" to knowledge: "In the seeing of the pure phenomenon the object is not external to knowledge, or to 'consciousness'; rather, it is given in the sense of the absolute self-givenness of what is simply seen" (IP: 43). Husserl says of such objects that they are contained in consciousness in an "intentional" manner, for such immanence is defined *solely* in terms of indubitable "seeing". This is to be distinguished from a second sense of immanence, according to which something is immanent if it is literally a *constituent part* of the stream of consciousness – like a sensation or a process of thinking. Husserl speaks of these latter as being contained in consciousness in a *"reell"* manner. The crucial mistake of the "beginner" mentioned above is in supposing that something is immanent in the first sense – is epistemologically absolutely secure – only if it is immanent in the second sense – by being a mental item. Husserl gives a number of examples of how something can be the first without being the second.

His first example is that of essences or universals. Could there not, he asks, be cases of knowledge where "a universal would come to self-evident givenness in an act of seeing and any doubt concerning it would be absurd?" (IP: 50). If there could be, this would mean that in such knowledge an essence would be immanent in the first ("intentional") way. And Husserl strongly affirms this possibility, writing of the possibility of our "seeing" and "intuiting" essences. Husserl's thought here is this. Suppose that you are seeing something red. Now perform the phenomenological reduction, discounting anything that could conceivably be false in this situation. What is left over is not just a bare *"cogito"* or "I am conscious", but a determinate form of consciousness: that of redness. This redness may not really exist in the "transcendent" world; but that you are given an instance of redness, rather than, say, greenness, is as indubitable as that you are being "given" anything at all. Now, and this is the important step, you know perfectly well, with absolute indubitability, that you could possibly be "given" this very colour in a visual experience on some other occasion. This *possibility* is self-evident. It is absolutely "given" to you, for you cannot possibly doubt it. But what is thus given is not any concrete element in your current experience. For you are not saying that this very experience could be had again; or that this particular instance of redness could be an object of awareness on another occasion. Both of these claims are, arguably, necessarily false. What you are claiming is that this *type* of experience could be had again, or that this *shade* of redness could be experienced again. But types and shades are not concrete particulars, but universals. Hence they are not *"reell"* parts of your experience. So here we have a whole range of objects that can be absolutely given to us, but that yet escape the confines of "immanence" as it was initially understood. Because we are dealing with a new sort of object, the experiences in which they are given will be different too. Here

45

we are not concerned with simple reflective awareness of our experiences, but with a species of *thinking*. Husserl does not, in *The Idea of Phenomenology*, say much about the nature of the acts in which such universal objects are given. He merely says that they involve "universalising" or "ideating" a concrete appearance by means of "abstraction". Since Husserl does not say much about this process in *The Idea of Phenomenology*, neither shall I. For the real interest in this work lies in the other examples that he offers of givenness that exceed the bounds of the "really immanent". I should point out, however, that the possibility of "seeing" essences was extremely important for Husserl. It is because of this that he can characterize phenomenology as an *eidetic* discipline: one that is concerned with essences. It is also of importance, of course, for the specific problem addressed in these lectures, which concerns, it will be recalled, how the *essence* of knowledge can be brought to clarity.

Although we may have avoided a "fatal mistake", we may not seem to have progressed very far, for we still seem to be restricted to our own mental states and recognizing the kinds that they fall into. This hardly takes us beyond the sceptical predicament of Descartes's first two *Meditations*. The way forward lies in recognizing types of object other than *kinds* that may be absolutely given to us while yet not being immanent in consciousness in the "real" sense. This is the decisive point in the development of phenomenology as we find it in *The Idea of Phenomenology*. For even certain non-abstract, "concrete" objects can be absolutely given to us, and yet not be immanent in the *reell* sense. Husserl gives the example of the experience of hearing a tone. Suppose that you are now hearing a high-pitched whistle. After the phenomenological reduction you concern yourself only with what is indubitable in this situation: your acoustic experience and its object – the whistle, whether it be real or not. Now, many philosophers have held that if this whistling tone is really indubitable, it can only be because it is a part of your stream of consciousness. It is, as it is often put, an "acoustic sensation". So, in this "reduced" situation, there is not really a distinction to be drawn between the sound and your awareness of it – any more than, it is commonly held, there is a distinction between a pain and your awareness of it. But this is where Husserl crucially disagrees. For suppose you are in the middle of hearing the whistling tone. Suppose you have been hearing it for three seconds. At this point in time the object of your awareness is not just the whistling sound of the instant, but of a sound that is the *continuation* of an extended tone. Your present act of awareness indubitably embraces, as part of its object, a temporal phase of the object that is *not present*. Hence, it is not a *reell* part of your present act of awareness. But surely, it may be retorted, Husserl is not claiming that we can have indubitable knowledge of the past? That is precisely what he is claiming. The only question, for Husserl, is how far into the past such indubitable knowledge extends. Perhaps the whistling tone was not experienced by you for a full three seconds. But could you have been experiencing it only for a millisecond? The claim that indubitable knowledge is *strictly* restricted to the present is incoherent, since it is incompatible with the essentially extended, "flowing" nature of experience. A literally instantaneous, punctiform experience makes no sense. Every instant of our conscious lives is experienced as a continuation of a past phase of it. And this is possible only if the present moment in some way *holds the immediate past in its grasp.* Husserl's term for this holding-in-grasp is "retention", and he says that it is "necessarily bound up with every perception" (IP: 67). A number of philosophers around this time had recognized that something like this must be true. Hence the popularity of the term "specious present" to denote this *stretch* of consciousness to which we have indubitable access. But Husserl realizes that this means that we must make a distinction between experience and its object even within the sphere of "immanence": that we must distinguish between the appearing (in the present moment, say) and that which appears (at least part of which must not be of the present moment). This seems to have come as a startling discovery to Husserl: "If we look closer and notice how … even after the phenomenological reduction *the appearance and that which appears stand over against one another*, and do so *in the midst of pure immanence*, that is within genuine immanence, then we are astounded" (IP: 11, translation modified). Elsewhere he speaks of this fact as a "miracle" (IP: 72). It certainly constitutes a dramatic rejection of the accounts of the mind that dominated the period before Husserl. For such accounts, at least where they are concerned with the most fundamental level of consciousness – where, if at all, indubitability is to be found – held that there is no distinction to be made between an object and the awareness of that object. "Ideas" (in the Cartesian sense), "sensations", "impressions" and so forth were taken to be both the immediate, indubitable objects of awareness and themselves episodes of awareness. According to Husserl, such an identity of object and awareness is an impossibility. There is *always* a distinction to be drawn here, even when we are dealing with "inner" objects. For consciousness is a temporal flux – it constantly "flows"; whereas any object of awareness is a more or less stable unity. To be aware of an object, any object, is to be aware of such a unity in its unity. In his other writings Husserl often underlines this point by stressing that we can always "return" to an object of awareness, by becoming aware of it again. For example, a sensation that I am now experiencing is something that I can later recall. Here the *same* object is present to consciousness on two separate occasions. But, of course, it makes no sense to speak of us having the same act of awareness twice over.

Another example that Husserl provides of an object that is immanent in an intentional but not in a *reell* sense is an *imaginary* object (69–70). Imagine something: a bird standing on one leg, say. By "imagine" I mean "concretely visualize" (for that is what Husserl means by the term): so that it makes sense to ask whether you imagined a large bird or a small one, and whether the bird was imagined face-on, from the side or from the back, as being close up or far away and so forth. If you followed my instructions and visualized a bird, it does not make any sense for you to doubt, while you were visualizing it, that it was indeed a bird standing on one leg – rather than say a motor car – that you were visualizing. But, once again, this indubitably given, self-evident object was not a *reell* part of your experience of visualizing it. What makes this clear in such cases is that the experience was entirely real, but the bird was not.

Husserl's series of examples continues with one that may seem to bring us closest to the epistemological problems with which we started: our awareness of a transcendent physical object in perception. Suppose we see a house. We perform the phenomenological reduction and exclude from our description of the situation everything that is in any way dubitable. Even after this reduction, Husserl asks rhetorically, "is it not … evident that a house appears in the house-phenomenon, thus giving us a reason to call it a house-perception?" (IP: 72). Here, as elsewhere, it is impossible to dissociate the object from the experience. That an experience is of one sort of object rather than another is an "inner characteristic" of it (IP: 46), intentionally immanent in it. But, once again, we cannot identify this object with anything immanent in the experience in a *reell* fashion: not only because of the temporal factors that we recognized in relation to the tone, but also because, in this case, it makes sense to raise the question concerning the object, concerning *what* appears, whether it is real or not – something that makes no sense (since the answer is self-evident) in relation to real constituents of an experience itself. Moreover, if I move in relation to the house while keeping my eye on it, the real components of my visual experience will change, but the house itself, even as reduced, pure phenomenon, does not: the house does not even *appear* to change, but only my relation to it. Here Husserl is rejecting a very common, almost universal, move in philosophy. When it is recognized that some claim to have made cognitive contact with a real object is dubitable – you may be mistaken in believing in the physical existence of this page – and yet also recognized that there is *something* indubitable in this situation – it is quite clear that at least you *seem* to see such a page – the conclusion is almost universally drawn that what you are indubitably aware of is something of a different nature from the dubitable entity, at least in the cases where the latter actually does not exist. If you are not now visually aware of a real page of print (because you are hallucinating), then, given the indubitable character of your subjective state, it must be that you are aware of *something else*: a visual sensation, or impression, or an "idea". It is precisely this switching of subject matter that Husserl rejects. Even if you are now hallucinating, it remains the case that what you are aware of has the character – the phenomenological character – *page of print.* To deny this would be to doubt the intrinsic, descriptive character of the mental state in question. For a hallucinated object is not, subjectively, at all like a sensation. Sensations do not appear to be located in three-dimensional space, they do not appear to have undisclosed rear sides, and we cannot even attempt to move closer to or further away from them. All of this, by contrast, applies to a hallucinated object. The difference between veridical perception and hallucination is not, for Husserl, a difference between different kinds of objects; it is, rather, a difference between a certain kind of object being in the one case real, and in the other, unreal. The common, alternative view stems ultimately from the conviction that *awareness* is a relation in which we must stand to *real objects,* or *entities.* If the object is not a real physical object, it must be a real *mental* object. This, however, is just a presumption, and one that Husserl rejects as flying in the face of the facts of lived experience. When we hallucinate, there certainly are, according to Husserl, real mental items present – *reell* elements of consciousness. (He is even happy to speak of perceptual "sensations".) These, however, are not the *objects* of which we are aware in such situations. Rather, they go to make up our *awareness* of an object.

Although in our last discussion we have returned to the issue of external perception of a "transcendent" object, we do not find a resolution of the episte-mological worries with which we started. For although Husserl has been stress-ing that, in the examples just considered, objects that are not *reell* constituents of experience are evidently given, he now makes clear that it is not the case that such objects are "given in the genuine sense of actual givenness" (IP: 73) – by which he means that he is not supposing that what we are given are necessarily *real* objects in the actual world. It still fails to be the case that the sorts of objects we take ourselves to be aware of in our daily lives are "given with evidence". And it is here, more or less, that Husserl stops. So, given that the initial epistemological concerns have clearly not been answered, what could Husserl think he had actu-ally achieved in these lectures? A reader may even wonder, perhaps, whether even the *possibility* of the kind of knowledge that was initially discussed has been clearly secured.

If the question that began *The Idea of Phenomenology* is taken to be "How is knowledge of what is transcendent to consciousness possible?", then in one sense Husserl has answered it. For since the notion of transcendence is, as we have seen, ambiguous, one sense of this question is: "How is knowledge of what is not a *reell* constituent of consciousness possible?" And Husserl has given us a number of examples where indubitably certain knowledge is not of objects that are really contained in experience. The "How?" is answered by the evident "seeing" that is involved in his examples. A reader is likely to be dissatisfied with this, however. For Husserl's initial laying out of the epistemological problem will almost certainly instil a desire in the reader to know how any knowledge *of the real world* is possible. Not only has this problem not been solved, it may even seem that it has been excluded in principle in virtue of the phenomenological reduction.

I think it is clear that Husserl did not think that he had answered *this* question in these lectures. For he indicates that there is a prior, fundamental issue to be addressed before the question of our relation to a real world can be adequately discussed:

> The original problem was the relation between subjective psychological experience and the reality in itself apprehended in this experience … But first we need the insight that the radical problem is rather the relation between knowledge and object, but in the *reduced* sense … without any relation to existential co-positings, be they of the empirical ego or of a real world. We need the insight that the truly significant problem is the problem of the *ultimate sense-bestowal of knowledge*, and thus of what it is to be an object in general.
>
> (75–6, translation modified)

In other words, the *primary* problem for Husserl in this work is consciousness's relation to an object as such – whether that object be real or not. Husserl's primary concern in these lectures is with *intentionality*: the essential object-directedness of consciousness. The fundamental step that needs to be made in any epistemological investigation is to understand how consciousness relates to objects as such. And Husserl's insight is that this is *never*, not even in "introspection", a matter of identity between object and experience. We should not misread Husserl's list of cases where an intentionally immanent object fails to be really immanent in consciousness. This is not a list of special cases that go against the rule. It is *always* the case that states of consciousness, in virtue of their internal (*reell*) constituents, involve an awareness of an object that is not itself part of the *reell* make-up of that state. This is something that Husserl's discussion of hearing a tone should teach us: for the temporal distinctions unearthed there between object and awareness apply to *every* conscious state. Whenever we are aware of an object, there is a complex of elements really inherent in consciousness that so function as to allow an object to appear. An object, writes Husserl, "is not something that in knowing is like something is in a sack, as if knowing were a completely empty form – one and the same empty sack – into which one thing is put, and then another" (IP: 74–5). Awareness is not "a featureless mental look, always one and the same, bearing no distinctions within itself" (IP: 11), Rather, as Husserl puts it, consciousness *constitutes* objects:

"Constitution" means that things given immanently are not, as it first appeared, in consciousness as things are in a box [i.e. in a *reell* manner], but rather that they present themselves in something like "appearances", in appearances that are not themselves the objects, and do not really [*reell*] contain the objects, appearances that in a certain sense create objects for the ego in their changing and highly peculiar structure – "create" insofar as it is appearances of precisely such a sort and structure that belong to what we have been calling "givenness".

(IP: 71)

This concept of constitution allows us to understand what Husserl means by "transcendental". To say that consciousness is transcendental is simply to say that consciousness constitutes objects. Hence we can only understand the possibility of objects being given to consciousness if we understand how it is that consciousness is transcendental.

Husserl thinks it is so important to get the character of intentionality clear because the only alternative to his account is one that conceives us to be mentally *self-contained* beings, in the sense that the immediately given objects of awareness are just elements in our own stream of consciousness – so that we can never attain epistemological contact with a real world, but at best be causally related to one. On such a view the world can at best prod us into an awareness of aspects of ourselves. But then a solution to the epistemological problem is foreclosed in principle. Husserl's account of intentionality shows how consciousness can be understood as opened out to something other than itself.

When all is said and done, however, the reader may well still be concerned that Husserl has not properly squared up to the question of our possible cognitive relation to objects in a real world. I shall end this investigation with a few words on this topic. Husserl only intimates the line he will take on this issue in his subsequent writings. Yet intimate it he does, as in the following passage:

Since I have to strike out the pregivenness of anything transcendent to which I might refer, where else could I examine not only the sense of this referring that reaches out beyond itself but also its possible *validity*, or the sense of such validity, except where this sense is absolutely given and where the sense of validity comes to givenness within the pure phenomenon of relation, confirmation and justification.

(IP: 46–7)

It is in the reference to "validity" that we find Husserl broaching the question of our relation to a real world. Our perceptual experiences ostensibly present us with elements in the world. They can, however, actually fail to present us with any such thing, as when we hallucinate. Such a perceptual experience lacks "validity", Husserl will say. So, what would it be for a perception to attain validity, to give us genuine perceptual acquaintance with something in the real world? Note how Husserl is setting up the question. He is distinguishing between a "referring that reaches out beyond itself" and the question of the validity of this reference. Even in an "invalid" perception – a complete hallucination, for example – consciousness has already reached out beyond itself. The object of a hallucination is, say, a house, and not some mere constituent of consciousness. If we are concerned with the validity of our perception, it is the *object*, not our subjective state, that we are concerned with. For we want to know if *it* is real or not. Now, here, as elsewhere, before addressing such a question, Husserl insists that we attain clarity concerning the *sense* of what we are discussing. And we attain such clarity only when the sense of reality is brought to "givenness": that is, when we "see" its essence. What Husserl is saying is that, if we can make sense of a notion of reality, we must be absolutely acquainted with a sense of reality, attaching to objects, in our experience. And in the passage just quoted Husserl tells us where we are to find such givenness: in our experience of *confirmation*. Suppose I take myself to see a chair across the room. I walk up to it and grab it. If things proceed normally, as I walk up to the chair, while keeping it in view, it will come to occupy a larger and larger portion of my visual field; and when I touch it, I will feel its solidity. Both of these experiences confirm – not absolutely and indefeasibly, of course, but they do confirm – that it is a *real* chair that I initially espied: for the first will typically not happen if I am hallucinating, and the second will not happen if what I saw was a hologram. In such experiences of confirmation we experience "reality" or "truth". Since, as I have just said, such experiences do not confirm indefeasibly (because what they indicate can itself be undermined by future experience), the notion of the unqualified reality of any worldly object emerges as what Husserl calls an "Idea in the Kantian sense": an ideal conception of that which is indicated by an inexhaustible course of experience that *harmonizes* with itself (and with the experiences of all other sentient beings) in such a way that each part of it confirms each other.[5] For such an object, as appearance, so to chime in with the totality of possible experience is what it is for that object to be real.

Notes

1. See Kern (1977).
2. I quote from Lee Hardy's translation of *The Idea of Phenomenology* (IP) (Husserl 1999). However, I follow the pagination of the German *Husserliana* edition, which is indicated in square brackets in this English translation. (The German pagination is also indicated

in the margins of the earlier English translation of *The Idea of Phenomenology* by Alston and Nakhnikian.)

3. Husserl believes that there is also a problem of transcendence even with logical and mathematical thoughts, and with introspective knowledge. The issue is most easily introduced, however, in relation to "external" objects.

4. "Descriptive psychology" refers both to the work of Brentano, and also to Husserl's own procedure in *Logical Investigations*, which latter Husserl is in the process of modifying.

5. This is a brief sketch of a complex issue. For a fuller treatment of Husserl's understanding of reality, see Smith (2003: ch. 4).

Bibliography

De Boer, T. 1978. *Development of Husserl's Thought.* Dordrecht: Kluwer.

Bernet, R., I. Kern & E. Marbach 1993. *An Introduction to Husserlian Phenomenology.* Evanston, IL: Northwestern University Press.

Husserl, E. 1999. *The Idea of Phenomenology*, L. Hardy (trans.). Dordrecht: Kluwer.

Kern, I. 1977. "The Three Ways to the Transcendental Phenomenological Reduction in the Philosophy of Edmund Husserl". In *Husserl Expositions and Appraisals*, F. Elliston & P. McCormick (eds), 126–49. Notre Dame, IN: University of Notre Dame Press.

Mohanty, J. N. & W. R. McKenna 1989. *Husserl's Phenomenology: A Textbook*. Lanham, MD: University Press of America.

Smith, A. D. 2003. *Husserl and the Cartesian Meditations*. London: Routledge.

Sokolowski, R. 1970. *The Formation of Husserl's Concept of Constitution*. The Hague: Martinus Nijhoff.

Zahavi, D. 2003. *Husserl's Phenomenology*. Stanford, CA: Stanford University Press.

3

William James

Pragmatism: A New Name for Some Old Ways of Thinking

Christopher Hookway

Introduction

Pragmatism: A New Name for Some Old Ways of Thinking was first published in 1907, only three years before the end of James's life. It contains the text of a series of lectures that he had delivered in Boston in late 1906 and then at Columbia University in New York early the following year. The book represents James's attempt to give a general account of the "pragmatist movement". Pragmatism, as we shall see, emerged more than thirty years earlier, but it had very little impact until shortly before James's lectures. When it "rather suddenly precipitated itself out of the air" it rapidly encountered controversy and even scorn. The book reflects James's sense that "much futile controversy might have been avoided … if our critics had been willing to wait until we got our message fairly out". In an attempt to "get the message out" (P: 5),[1] James promised to "unify the picture as it presents itself to my own eyes, dealing in broad strokes and avoiding minute controversy". As this suggests, the book is lively and enthusiastic, with James's passionate commitment to his position making the lectures a delight to read. But the lack of rigour in formulating positions and defending them meant that controversy (futile or otherwise) increased rather than diminished. The lectures require a sympathetic reader, but, as is evidenced by the writings of G. E. Moore (1907–8) and Bertrand Russell (1908), it did not find one: they responded with impatient refutations of his positions and their interpretations helped to give currency to a crude caricature of what pragmatism is to which a more careful reading of the lectures gives the lie.

The lectures provide a fascinating and, in many ways, delightful introduction to James's pragmatism. Before exploring the arguments of the individual lectures, we should set pragmatism into its intellectual context. Although the name "pragmatism" does not seem to have been used in print until James delivered a lecture called "Philosophic Conceptions and Practical Realities" in 1898, the views associated with this "movement" were acknowledged to have been born in an ironically named "Metaphysical Club", which met in Cambridge, Massachusetts in 1871. This group of lively young scholars, all educated at Harvard, included both James and his colleague in pragmatism, Charles Sanders Peirce. Indeed many pragmatist themes first appeared in Peirce's publications on logic in the 1870s. Other members included Chauncey Wright, an avid defender of the views of Charles Darwin, and some young lawyers, most notably Oliver Wendell Holmes.[2]

Many critics of pragmatism perceived it as distinctively American: as a crude, unsophisticated form of "frontier philosophy". The subtitle of James's book suggests to us that this is a mistake. "Pragmatism" is a "new name for some old ways of thinking". Where Peirce identified Berkeley, Spinoza and (especially) Kant as forerunners of pragmatism, James tells us that he learned "pragmatic openness of mind" from the English empiricist and utilitarian John Stuart Mill. Harvard was a major intellectual centre, and pragmatism emerged from the attempt to unify "a number of tendencies that have always existed in philosophy". What may be the source of a distinctively American character to pragmatism was that the young philosophers in the Metaphysical Club had a much more extensive knowledge of science than many European philosophers. We have already noted that Wright was an early disciple of Charles Darwin. In addition, Peirce was a skilled mathematician who worked for the Coast Survey and did important experimental work; and James was a professor of first medicine and then psychology at Harvard before joining the Department of Philosophy. His most famous book, *Principles of Psychology*, is recognized as a classic text in that discipline, and it contains an "instrumentalist" account of beliefs and concepts that was an essential foundation for his pragmatism.

The introduction: the present dilemma in philosophy

In this chapter, my main focus will be on James's account of what pragmatism is in the second lecture and then some of its applications. His pragmatist account of truth was the most detailed, best-known and most controversial view associated with his pragmatism, and we shall explore that in some detail before turning to his novel and exciting applications of pragmatism to religious belief and to our understanding of freedom of the will. An important clue in understanding

pragmatism is provided by the first lecture, in which James identifies the fundamental challenge faced by philosophy at the beginning of the twentieth century,
and introduces pragmatism as the philosophical outlook that is uniquely qualified to meet this challenge. When we come to examine how pragmatism enables
us to do this, it will be very important to bear in mind that, for James at least,
pragmatism is not a substantive philosophical theory, a metaphysical or epistemological position. Rather, it is a way of approaching problems, a way of understanding apparently irresoluble questions that, he hopes, will disarm the problems and
enable us to leave them behind.

James's dilemma is a familiar one: it is related to the question of how we can
reconcile the claims of science, on the one hand, with those of religion and
morality on the other. However this is not how he initially introduces it. Instead,
in an interesting instance of the fact that important ideas surface independently
in the work of different thinkers in different places, he announces, like Nietzsche,
that "The history of philosophy is to a great extent that of a certain clash of
human temperaments" (P: 11). Indeed, although a professional philosopher holds
that temperament provides no "conventionally recognized reason" for accepting
a position, and tries to defend his views on the basis of "impersonal reasons", still
"his temperament really gives him a stronger bias than any of his more strictly
objective premises". Philosophers *trust* their temperaments, allowing them to
shape how they weigh different kinds of evidence, "making for a more sentimental or a more hard-hearted view of the universe". So the dilemma derives from this
clash of temperaments (tender-minded versus tough-minded), and it issues in
views of the universe that are (in turn) sentimental and hard-hearted. Religious
and moral outlooks are more sentimental; the scientific outlook is more hard-
hearted; and it is a measure of the irresoluble character of the dilemma that we line
up on the side that best suits our temperaments.

Early in the lecture, James identifies some of the traits that go with these
different temperaments (P: 13). The tender-minded are, typically, rationalist,
defending views by reference to *a priori* principles; the tough-minded are empiricist, "going by the facts". Where the tender-minded trust the intellect, the tough-
minded trust the senses. One is idealistic, optimistic and religious, and the other
is materialistic, pessimistic and irreligious. The tender-minded are "free-willist"
and dogmatic, and the tough-minded "fatalistic" and sceptical. And so on. Here
we see the familiar dilemma emerging: the empiricist approach is pessimistic and
materialist, allowing no place for religion or for human freedom; and optimistic,
religious-minded philosophers are idealists who choose to ground their opinions
in *a priori* reflection. It is easy to see that "objective reasons" will not settle the
matter between the tender-minded and the tough-minded. Their differences
extend to their views about what sorts of reasons there are, about how knowledge

WILLIAM JAMES: *PRAGMATISM*

is to be obtained. Each will reject the other's view about what sorts of "objective reasons" there are: one appeals to principles, the other to experiential facts. It is no wonder that temperament thus determines on which side we settle. The tough-minded view of the world is bleak and deterministic, providing no place for human freedom or religion; and the tough-minded view of knowledge is strongly empiri-cist and cannot allow for our obtaining knowledge of religious matters or of moral truth.

We can now identify a major driving force behind James's thought (P: 14–15). By the early twentieth century, "never were so many men of a decidedly empiri-cist proclivity": "our children … are almost born scientific". But this has not weak-ened religious belief. People need a philosophy that is both empiricist in its adherence to facts yet finds room for religious belief. But all that is on offer is "an empirical philosophy that is not religious enough and a religious philosophy that is not empirical enough for your purpose". The challenge is to show how to reconcile "the scientific loyalty to facts" with "the old confidence in human values and the resultant spontaneity, whether of the religious or the romantic type". We must reconcile empiricist epistemic responsibility with moral and religious optimism. Pragmatism is presented as the "mediating philosophy" that enables us to overcome the distinction between the tender-minded and the tough-minded: we need to show how adherence to tough-minded epistemic standards does not prevent our adopting the kind of worldview to which the tender-minded aspire.

James had confronted these issues nearly ten years earlier in his paper "The Will to Believe".[3] He was responding to the empiricist W. K. Clifford, whose work on the "ethics of belief" (1879) led him to claim that it is always wrong to believe anything for which one does not have sufficient evidence. From this ethical principle, he concluded that religious belief contravened the principles of the ethics of belief: we had a moral obligation to be agnostic. James responded that it could be rational to believe things for which we do not have adequate evidence, albeit only in certain special circumstances. Sometimes believing a proposition contributes to making it true: if I am anxious that someone likes me but lack evidence to establish whether they do, it may be rational to hold the belief because this will make it more likely that I shall be likeable in my dealings with them. Further evidence may then confirm the belief I form (in advance of the evidence). In the case of religious belief, James considered the possibility that evidence may be available that only someone who already held the belief could appreciate. Even before his pragmatism was fully articulated, James was arguing that beliefs can be formed in advance of the evidence without compromising empiricism.

We can now set the scene for the following lectures. In Lecture II, James's pragmatism is introduced as a technique for clarifying questions and propositions that is in harmony with the ways in which scientific theories are understood and tested. Many of these questions concern doctrines that are attractive to the tender-minded: questions of free will and substance in Lecture III; metaphysical questions about monism and pluralism in Lecture IV, issues about truth in Lectures II and, especially, V; issues about religious belief in Lecture VIII. In subsequent lectures he addresses a range of problems from a pragmatist perspective. In this chapter we shall discuss just a few of these.

Pragmatism

As we have seen, James presents his pragmatism as a *method*. It is a "method of settling metaphysical disputes that otherwise might be interminable", and it exploits the idea that "Whenever a dispute is serious, we ought to be able to show some practical difference that must follow from one side or the other's being right" (P: 28). If no such difference can be found, then the dispute is "idle". And if such a difference can be found, this enables us to see what the dispute is actually about.

So what are "practical differences"? One clue to this is provided when James discusses the origins of his pragmatism in the rule for "clarifying ideas", which Peirce presented in his famous 1878 paper "How to Make our Ideas Clear", although James does not discuss Peirce's rule in any detail. He does tell us that the practical effects involved in our conception of an object are a matter of the "sensations we are to expect from it" and the "reactions we must prepare": for a dispute not to be idle, which side we adopt must make a difference to one or other of these. This is supported by James's approving reference to Ostwald's claim that we should settle disputes in chemistry by asking "what particular experimental fact could have been different by one or the other view being correct" (P: 29). Indeed, we can see why James thinks of this as an empiricist outlook, and one thing we have to explore is why he thinks it presents its empiricism "in a more radical and in a less objectionable form than it has ever yet assumed", turning away from many of the sins of earlier kinds of empiricism (P: 31).

How he does this is not made very clear. However several points are stressed later in the lecture that appear relevant to what makes James's kind of "empiricism" distinctive. First, as he admits, James never really explains what will count as a "practical consequence", and most readers have gained the impression that he allows for a much more varied range of "practical consequences" than traditional empiricists and "laboratory" philosophers would. This is clearest from his concrete illustrations of pragmatism at work and we shall examine some of these below.

Another clue to how the method works is provided by a famous "trivial anecdote" that is discussed at the very beginning of the lecture. After walking in the mountains, James returned to camp to find his fellows engaged in a "ferocious metaphysical dispute" about a squirrel that was hanging on to one side of a tree trunk while a human observer was standing on the other side:

> This human witness tries to get sight of the squirrel by moving rapidly round the tree, but no matter how fast he goes, the squirrel moves as fast in the opposite direction, and always keeps the tree between himself and the man, so that never a glimpse of him is caught. The resultant metaphysical problem is this: *Does the man go round the squirrel or not?* (P: 27)

Roughly equal numbers of his friends passionately defended each answer and they appealed to James for help. His solution, which must surely have tried the patience of his companions, was that which answer is correct depends on what you "practically mean" by "going round". If you mean passing from north of him to east, then south, then west, then the answer to the question is "yes". If, on the other hand, you mean first in front of him, then to his right, then behind him, and then to his left, before returning to being in front of him again, then the answer is "no". Pragmatic clarification disambiguates the question, and once that is done, all dispute comes to an end. The pragmatic method anticipates that all apparently irresoluble metaphysical disputes can be resolved in like manner.

But why should we adopt this method? What reason is there to think that all metaphysical problems can be resolved in this fashion? Why should we expect serious metaphysical disputes to be analogous to the "trivial anecdote" about the squirrel? James does not provide much of an argument for his pragmatism when he first introduces it. However at this point it is important to remember that James describes his pragmatism as a *method*. Perhaps we should see him as proposing his method and urging us to give it a try, recognizing that the true test of the method is how well it performs in practice. If, in the course of his series of lectures, he can convince us that the method does indeed enable us to dismiss apparently irresoluble metaphysical problems in a satisfying way, then the "practical effects" of employing it will vindicate our decision to do so. James describes his pragmatism and invites us to try it out; and the test of the method is how far it works in practice.

But James is able to say more than this. He links pragmatism to an idea that is fundamental to his psychology: concepts and theories are primarily instruments. We can see this from his comparison of pragmatism and rationalism. As well as confronting particular facts and undergoing particular experiences, we formulate theories and categories that enable us to classify and explain these particulars. James's examples include categories such as matter, reason, God, energy. Rationalists think that we can grasp these categories and concepts through a kind of intellectual intuition: our grasp of them is clearer and more certain than our grasp of the mass of confusing particulars we encounter. Pragmatists, by contrast, treat these abstract categories (and also scientific theories) as instruments that get their meanings from the way in which they enable us to organize particular experiences. Rationalists think we understand particulars by linking them to these clearer and abstract ideas; pragmatists think we only understand the abstractions because we understand how they are reflected in experience, because we understand how they have practical consequences. This leads to a further characterization of pragmatism: it is an "attitude of orientation": "*The attitude of looking away from first things, principles, 'categories', supposed necessities; and of looking towards last things, fruits, consequences, facts*" (P: 32). Such claims help us to see how pragmatism is a form of "anti-intellectualism", but James seems anxious to avoid telling us exactly what it is for consequences to be "practical".

The final third of this lecture begins James's exploration of the most important and most interesting of these applications: the investigation of the concept of *truth*: he returns to this topic in Lecture VI. It is no surprise that this particular application is introduced in explaining what pragmatism means. First, as James ruefully admits, pragmatism was already primarily associated with a controversial account of truth rather than with a method for dealing with metaphysical problems. Indeed he is sometimes happy himself to accept that pragmatism is a theory of truth. But it is important that the search for a pragmatic clarification of truth is more than just one application of pragmatism among others. We can see this by noting that the debate between James's climbing companions concerned whether it was *true* that the man went round the squirrel, so the use of the pragmatic method must rest on the belief that the practical effects of something are an indication of the truth of descriptions of it. The pragmatic method, a distinctive theory of truth, and the instrumentalist account of concepts, beliefs and theories form a set of three mutually supporting views. So the pragmatic account of truth is both an application of the pragmatic method but also a requirement for the method to be a good one.

The meaning of truth

Most of James's book is concerned with illustrations of pragmatism in practice. The most famous of these occupies both the final third of Lecture II and the whole of Lecture VI. This is the search for a pragmatist clarification of the concept of *truth*. Indeed, this example is more fundamental to pragmatism than some of the others, for this account of truth reflects the instrumentalist view of beliefs and theories that is used to support pragmatism. Its centrality may be reflected in a fact that James acknowledges: when the lectures appeared, the word "pragmatism" was already used as the name of an account of truth, more readily than as the name of a method for making progress with metaphysical issues. This is not surprising. Truth is itself a philosophically troubling concept that pragmatism should be expected to clarify; we might expect that different views of what truth involves would be adopted by the tough-minded and the tender-minded. The former may insist that true propositions must correspond to the empirical facts, and that experience provides us with a way of identifying these facts. Some tender-minded thinkers, who are often sympathetic to philosophical idealism, might urge that so long as a proposition contributes to the coherence of an overall satisfactory system of beliefs, then it is true. Getting clear about *truth* is clearly important.

However when James says that pragmatism *is* a theory of truth, he has something else in mind. When I believe something, I believe it to be true; when I am puzzled by some proposition, I want to know whether it is true. So a clarification of what I mean by the proposition that God exists – or that I possess freedom of the will – may well be a clarification of what I think would be required for it to be *true* that God exists, or that I am capable of free action. Equally, to clarify what I mean when I say something is true, may be to clarify what is required for it to be *true* that it is true! So *true* is not just one concept among others that can be clarified or investigated in a pragmatic way. Rather, every application of pragmatism, it appears, is an attempt to understand the meaning of some potential *truth*. The pragmatic technique for clarifying concepts seems to require some distinctive assumptions about truth. Hence applying the technique to the understanding of *truth* is the best way of getting a better grasp of just what pragmatism involves in its other applications too, and of seeing what sorts of practical effects are relevant to meaning. A practical effect can be relevant to the meaning of an idea, we might think, only if it is relevant to the truth of the idea. In that case it is unsurprising that James discusses truth throughout the lectures: after a preliminary discussion in Lecture II, he devotes the whole of Lecture VI to further discussion of truth. The sequel to *Pragmatism* that he published in 1909 was called *The Meaning of Truth*; it was a collection of papers that responded to the many misunderstandings and indignant criticisms that the earlier book had encountered.

James often makes claims about truth that make it easy to understand why his views were treated with such scorn by philosophers such as G. E. Moore and Bertrand Russell. For example, he said that "the true is the name of whatever proves itself to be good in the way of belief" (P: 42). In subsequent writings, he urged that the true was what it was "expedient" for us to believe and added that it can be expedient "in any way at all" (P: 106). It is no surprise that he has been widely accused of encouraging wishful thinking: if it contributes to their happiness for a cancer sufferer and her friends to deny that she has cancer, then, it seems, it is true that she lacks the disease. If it contributes to our success in the practical concerns of life for us to believe something, then it is true. James's discussion of religious belief at the end of Lecture II appears to support this interpretation. He says that if religious ideas "have a value for concrete life, they will be true for pragmatism" (P: 40), so long as they do not conflict with other valuable ideas. And for religious belief to have such value, it is enough that they provide "religious comfort, a sense that finite evil has been 'overruled'" (P: 41). The confirmation of religious belief seems to depend upon the fact that it makes us feel good, and that we are no longer burdened by a sense of responsibility or anxiety for all the evils of the world. The common reaction was that, although this may explain why it may be good for us to hold the religious belief, it is not relevant to the question of whether it is true. It may make me feel good to believe that my friend is in good health, but that is irrelevant to whether it is true. If self-deception makes us happy and helps us to deal with our lives effectively, then, it seems, it is not deception at all because the things we believe are thereby true.

It is in reading James's discussion of truth that it is most important to remember that he is dealing in broad strokes. For example the claim that the truth is what it is expedient to believe is qualified "to put it very briefly" (P: 106), but his critics clearly viewed the claim as a candidate for "minute controversy". The standard criticisms suggest that James has lost sight of the considerations that lead us to say that true propositions "correspond to the facts". But on several occasions he insists that the pragmatist *accepts* that true propositions agree with reality and is offering a distinctive pragmatic clarification of just what this means in practice. Indeed, when we examine what he says more carefully, the position is more qualified and less wild. Even when he says that the true is what it is good to believe, he qualifies this by saying "on the whole and in the long run, of course". The value for life that comes from religious belief is relevant to the truth of that belief only if it does not conflict with other valuable ideas. It seems likely that some of the most obvious counterexamples to James's view will face difficulties when we take account of these qualifications.

In fact, many of James's accounts of his views on truth are rather different from those cited above. He emphasizes that he is exploiting the way that the concept of *truth* is used in the sciences, and he is presumably drawing on his views about how beliefs, concepts and theories function as instruments. He tells us that scientific ideas are "true just in so far as they help us to get into a satisfactory relation with other parts of our experience" (P: 34). They do this when they guide us in moving from one part of our experience to another, "linking things satisfactorily, working securely, simplifying, saving labour":

> Any idea upon which we can ride, so to speak; any idea that will carry
> us prosperously from one part of our experience to another, linking

things satisfactorily, working securely, simplifying, saving labor; is true for just so much, true in so far forth, true *instrumentally*.   (P: 34)

This suggests an empiricist story: a theory or proposition agrees with reality when it helps us to make coherent sense of all our varied experience of the world, yielding reliable predictions and avoiding surprising experiences. Thus he tells us that "True ideas are those we can assimilate, validate, corroborate and verify". This is supported by what he says about how we find new truths. Questions about the truth of propositions arise when some surprising new experience exposes tensions in our stable stock of "old opinions": we no longer know what sorts of experiences to anticipate. A new proposition or theory is described as *true* when it enables us to make sense of the new experience while disrupting the old certainties as little as possible.

These remarks are puzzling. We expect a theory of truth to tell us what truth consists in, *what it is* for something to be true, but James here appears to be concerned with a different *epistemological* issue: in what circumstances do we (or should we) accept something as true? This gains support when, in Lecture VI, James presents these ideas about truth by introducing the idea of "absolute truth", by which he means "what no further experience will ever alter". This is identified with "that ideal vanishing-point toward which we imagine that all our temporary truths will some day converge", and, although James may be sceptical that we ever will reach this point, he gives regulative value to the idea that our current theories are likely to be left behind and recognized as "relatively true" within distinctive "borders of experience". Since absolute truth is rarely available to us, we should "live to-day by what truth we can get to-day, and be ready to call it falsehood" (P: 106–7). Absolute truth is a genuine candidate for a "constitutive account of what truth is"; and James is sometimes more concerned with how people live with "truths", such as those of Ptolemaic astronomy, that ("absolutely") are falsehoods. He is clarifying how we use the word "true", when we say things are true and when we say they are not. And since he thinks we are rarely concerned with "absolute truth", his claims sit uneasily on the boundary between an account of what truth is and an epistemological account of when and how we take things to be true.

These views of truth engage nicely with the instrumentalist story of beliefs, concepts and propositions. James exploits a view about the function of scientific beliefs, he gives an account of how we enquire when our current beliefs fail to carry out that function, and propositions are endorsed as new truths when they enable our corpus of opinions to serve their ordained function once again. A new experience prevents our instrument working, and we strive to amend the instrument so it works for us once again. A major difficulty is to see how this can be reconciled with what he says about religious belief. Is he rejecting the more empiricist story here? Or does he think that the comfort provided by religious belief should be seen as "corroboration" of it? Does he think that religious belief has a distinctive function, a distinctive instrumental value, which may not be the same function as ordinary scientific belief? And do the standard counterexamples divorce a belief being expedient from a belief's serving its function? These exegetical issues are hard to settle on the basis of the text, and this may be unsurprising given James's goal of painting with a broad brush.

We saw earlier that the pragmatist account of truth is more than an *application* of the pragmatic method. It also provides support for that method itself: the method assumes that the only things that are relevant to whether some claim about an object is correct are "the sensations we are to expect from it" and "the reactions we must prepare". The empiricist sounding formulations of James's ideas about truth are clearly in harmony with this. But what of the claims he makes about the truth of religious claims? These seem to focus on the kinds of actions that will be undertaken if we hold religious views. It does indeed appear that the account does what is required of it: the pragmatist clarifies a proposition by identifying the "practical consequences of its being right"; and James is now asserting that these consequences are all that is relevant to the proposition's truth.

In an invaluable paper, "James's Theory of Truth", Hilary Putnam observes that "much of what James wanted to deny should be denied" (Putnam 1997: 183). We cannot explain truth in terms of a *mysterious* relation of "agreement with reality", or see what is required for individual beliefs to be "copies" of reality. But it is a platitude that beliefs can "agree with reality" and the pragmatist strategy should be to apply the pragmatic method to work out just what this familiar phrase comes down to in practice. What practical difference does it make if a belief agrees with reality? James's answers are suggestive and intriguing: a belief agrees with reality when it enables us to enter into satisfactory relations with our experience; to remove anomalies that face our existing beliefs and to solve the concrete problems of life. But the fact that James kept returning to the task of clarifying his positive position, for example in the papers collected in his *Meaning of Truth*, suggests that we should not expect to find a clearly formulated positive view in these lectures.

The meaning of freedom of the will

Much of Lecture III is devoted to showing how James's pragmatism enables him to dismiss philosophical problems that have seemed both deep and unanswerable. A number of these involve issues about *substance*, about material substance and spiritual substance, and so on. However I shall concentrate on just one of these discussions, his intriguing discussion of what we mean when we say that the will is free, and whether it is true that human beings possess freedom of the will. This provides an excellent illustration of pragmatism at work, and it also has valuable connections with James's contributions to our understanding of religious belief. Human freedom is one of the phenomena that tender-minded philosophers want to make sense of, and that the tough-minded dismiss as a non-scientific myth. It is one of those cases where pragmatism is supposed to show us how we can have it both ways. The tender-minded are, the reader will recall, typically "free-willist" and view human freedom as "a principle, a positive faculty or virtue added to man, by which his dignity is enigmatically augmented" (P: 59). And they think that tough-minded empiricists are likely to be determinists who deny our dignity, diminish us, by saying that we can "originate nothing": we merely "transmit to the future the whole push of the past cosmos". The reason that the issue is deep is that it addresses this fundamental concern with whether we possess this distinctive "dignity" that distinguishes us from non-human creatures. But why should this dignity matter?

According to James, the most common answer to this question emphasizes the role of *blame* or "accountability" (P: 59): if my actions are determined by my history and by the history of the universe before I was born, then how can I be held responsible for the actions these forces cause me to perform? But, as the determinist typically responds, if my acts are just spontaneous free choices that do not reflect my values and the character I have acquired through my education, it seems equally absurd to hold me responsible for them. As with the other metaphysical debates that James describes in his first lecture, this focus on dignity and accountability promises an unending and unsatisfying philosophical debate. If we place questions of accountability at the centre of the stage, it is likely that we shall make very little progress.

So, James's pragmatist asks, why should we really care about freedom of the will: what is the use of this concept in our lives? He thinks that there is something shameful in this obsession with dignity and accountability. Questions about praise and blame concern how best to organize various social institutions: they do not raise deep metaphysical issues. James seems to be defending a consequentialist view of accountability here: the people we should blame are the people whose punishment or castigation may yield benefits. The question of blame is a practical one, not a metaphysical one. So what other explanation can be found of why we should value freedom? James's suggestion is that free will is important because it holds out the optimistic hope that things can get better: if we are free, then we are in a position to change things for the better. It is a doctrine of "*novelties in the world*" (P: 60). We can overcome our vices and redeem our sins: freedom of the will "holds up improvement as at least possible" (P: 61). The proper attitude towards our sins is not to dwell on our guilt and responsibilities; that is shameful. Rather, we require the optimistic sense that we can make things better. Once the pragmatist shows that questions about praise and blame can be separated from issues about the grounds for optimism that we can overcome our pasts and our characters, once we abandon the notion of "dignity" that seems to tie them together, the question no longer seems unanswerable. The issue about blame turns into one about social arrangements, and the second issue, which James calls "religious", is seen for what it is: it requires us to approach the future in an optimistic spirit, and it is not obvious at all that scientific determinism and the results of responsible enquiry need challenge our readiness to exclaim: "God's in his heaven: all's right with the world" (P: 62). And it is this claim that is "the heart of [our] theology".

At the end of Lecture III, James draws a moral from such examples. Pragmatism produces a change in the "centre of gravity of philosophy" (P: 62). Traditional philosophy displayed an abstract concern with principles and foundations: we look for the metaphysical faculty of free will, which is tied to notions like dignity, and to *principles* that concern, for example, accountability. Instead, he says "we look forward to the facts themselves". The most important questions concern: "What is this world going to be?"; "What is life eventually to make of itself?" We can understand this by reminding ourselves that ideas, concepts and theories are *instruments* that are to be assessed by how well they put us into a satisfactory relation to our experience. There are issues about the most satisfactory social arrangements for the distribution of praise and blame; there are issues about the attitudes towards the future, towards the possibilities that it offers, that are required for an optimistic and improving life. "Religious" beliefs such as free will are vindicated by their role in nurturing this form of optimism; practices of praise and blame are vindicated by their value in enabling us to live well. So we turn our back on the idea that religious attitudes and our habits of accountability must be grounded in something *metaphysical*: in principles and facts about the source of our dignity or about the nature of God. One virtue of pragmatism lies in its role in enabling us to turn our backs on this intellectualist heritage. Belief in free will is made true by its role in improving our lives; and we explain what it means by showing what this role is.

Monism and pluralism

The remaining lectures in the book explore the case for this reshaping of philosophy. Lecture VII, on pragmatism and humanism, deplores the "great single-word answers to the world's riddle, such as God, the One, Reason, Law, Spirit, Matter" and challenges the assumption that "In everything, in science, art, morals and religion there *must* be one system that is right and *every* other wrong" (P: 115). The "humanistic" side of pragmatism is shown in its "pluralism"; where rationalists see a reality that is "ready-made and complete from all eternity" (P: 123), our task being to arrive at an accurate cognitive "copy" of it, James talks about a world that is "still in the making" (P: 123). We confront a "malleable" world that develops as we live in it and think about it, being shaped in accordance with our needs and interests. This section contains some of James's most cryptic and allusive language. The talk of humanism and of our "making reality" can be irritatingly unclear and we miss the vividly worked out examples that are found in James's best work.

This "pluralism" is one of the most difficult themes in James's thought, and has also been one that makes it attractive to contemporary philosophers. So just what is this pluralism? And how does it feed into his pragmatist views about religion? Monists hold that "the world is one"; pluralists deny this. But that does not yet make the issue very clear. In Lecture IV, he identifies a number of different ways of taking the slogan that "the world is one" (P: 66ff.), most of which are perfectly acceptable. To take just one example of these, the different parts of the world stand in complex patterns of causal relation; we can travel continuously from one part of the world to another; there are no parts of the world that are wholly cut off from each other so that we cannot travel from one to the other. But philosophical monists seek a deeper unity than this: somehow they find the universe understood as a unity to be more "illustrious" (P: 65) than it is when grasped in its great variety. They think of the world as a single substance, or as manifested in the consciousness of a unique "instantaneous eternal" knower, the reality of individual things depending upon their place in this absolute mind, and so on. James has no sympathy for such ideas. Where his Harvard colleague Josiah Royce held that our human knowledge was but a fragment of the knowledge of this absolute mind, James held, by contrast, that the "trail of the human serpent is … over everything" (P: 37): that all knowledge is shaped by our human interests and capacities.

We classify things into sorts: cats and dogs, rivers and lakes, planets and stars and so on. Common sense naturally holds that there are many overlapping kinds of things in the world, these kinds becoming more or less important according to our needs and interests. One monist view holds that there is a fundamental classification that classifies things according to how they *really* are. Perhaps there is just one fundamental *kind* of thing in the universe: scientific realists may tell us that there are just fundamental particles; other metaphysicians may say that there are *substances* or *beings*. Another form of monism arises when we ask about the purpose or meaning of the universe *as a whole* rather than asking different questions about the importance to different people of things of different kinds. The monist seeks a single, extremely general or abstract, story of *everything*: a story that finds room for everything and that can explain everything; one that tells us the story of the universe and enables us to understand our place in it. This is what is grasped by the absolute mind.[4]

James is struck by the role of this monistic picture in philosophy and in much thought about morality and religion. His pluralism leads him to reject it: he wants to celebrate the variety of our classifications and our cognitive and emotional needs, and the variety of the beliefs, concepts and theories that enable us to deal with them. Most importantly, religious belief is not the keystone of the overarching story that tells us the principles that hold this entire system of things together; it is not a rival to the scientific story or a metaphysical framework that finds a place for the scientific account of things. It is one way of thinking among others, a set of cognitive and emotional instruments that meet particular needs, which can be appreciated for the ways in which they enable us to live well. In the final lecture we learn that "On pragmatistic principles, if the hypothesis of God works satisfactorily in the widest sense of the word, it is true" (P: 143). And, he concludes, experience shows that it *does* work: "pragmatism can be called religious, if you allow that religion can be pluralistic or melioristic [improving] in type" (P: 144). If we are optimistic that it is possible for our ideals to be satisfied as our lives develop, then we are optimistic about the world's salvation. Religion thus consists in a distinctive kind of optimism towards the future: the dogmatic beliefs associated with, for example, religious fundamentalism have no place in this view of religion. And the doctrinal differences between different sects and "religions" emerge as superficial surface features that can distract attention from the common patterns of religious "experience" that they share. These views are more fully set out in another series of lectures, *Varieties of Religious Experience*.

When *Pragmatism* first appeared, James's views were widely dismissed as a crude and unsophisticated philosophical position. Bertrand Russell was a great admirer of James's radical empiricism but was scornful in his criticisms of pragmatism; Wittgenstein responded to *Varieties of Religious Experience* as a model of philosophical sensitivity, but had no time for *Pragmatism* (see Goodman 2002). The book had its admirers and its influence was considerable, but its lively style and aversion to "minute controversy" made it very easy for readers to approach it without the care and sympathetic exegesis that it requires. This is unfortunate for it is a rich and exciting work, one that contributed to challenging intellectualist *a priorism* in philosophy, and that developed a body of ideas that reflected James's wide knowledge of psychology, and that emphasized the richness of our experience and the variety of the ways in which we deal with our surroundings. It is interesting that contemporary philosophers sympathetic to pragmatism – for example Richard Rorty and (especially) Hilary Putnam – have been able to respond to the insights James has to offer, especially in his complex reflections on truth and his emphasis on the human dimension of knowledge.

Notes

1. Reference to James's *Pragmatism* (P) uses the pagination of the volumes in *The Works of William James* (see the section "Primary text" in the Bibliography).
2. The story of this group is told in Louis Menand's fascinating *The Metaphysical Club: A Story of Ideas in America* (New York: Farrar, Straus & Giroux, 2001). More information about the background to pragmatism can be found in Bruce Kuklick's *The Rise of American Philosophy: Cambridge Massachusetts, 1860–1930* (New Haven, CT: Yale University Press, 1977). Chapter VI of Thomas Baldwin (ed.) *The Cambridge History of Philosophy 1870–1945* (Cambridge: Cambridge University Press, 2003) provides a more general perspective on the pragmatist tradition as a whole.
3. This paper is in James's book *The Will to Believe and Other Essays in Popular Philosophy*, available in *The Works of William James* edition from Harvard University Press.
4. A classical example of monism is found in the work of Spinoza; James would probably have been more familiar with the version defended by his Harvard colleague Josiah Royce.

Bibliography

Primary text

William James, *Pragmatism: A New Name for Some Old Ways of Thinking* (New York: Longmans, Green, 1907). This book is available as a volume in *The Works of William James* (Cambridge, MA: Harvard University Press, 1975). Page references in the text are to this edition. Other books by James mentioned in the text are also available in this scholarly edition. There are many inexpensive paperback editions of *Pragmatism. Pragmatism and The Meaning of Truth* (with an introduction by A. J. Ayer) (Cambridge MA: Harvard University Press, 1978) uses the texts and the pagination employed in *The Works of William James*, and also contains *The Meaning of Truth: A Sequel to Pragmatism*, which was published in 1909 and contains James's replies to his many critics.

Secondary reading

Ayer, A. J. 1968. *The Origins of Pragmatism: Studies in the Philosophy of Charles Sanders Peirce and William James.* London: Macmillan.

Baldwin, T. (ed.) 2003. *The Cambridge History of Philosophy 1870–1945.* Cambridge: Cambridge University Press.

Bird, G. 1986. *William James* (The Arguments of the Philosophers series). London: Routledge & Kegan Paul.

Clifford, W. K. 1879. "The Ethics of Belief". In *Lectures and Essays*, vol. 2. London: Macmillan.

Gale, R. M. 1999. *The Divided Self of William James.* New York: Cambridge University Press.

Goodman, R. B. 2002. *Wittgenstein and William James.* Cambridge: Cambridge University Press.

Hookway, C. 1997. "Logical Principles and Philosophical Attitudes: Peirce's Response to James's Pragmatism". In *The Cambridge Companion to William James*, R. A. Putnam (ed.), 145–65. Cambridge: Cambridge University Press.

Kuklick, B. 1977. *The Rise of American Philosophy: Cambridge Massachusetts, 1860–1930*. New Haven, CT: Yale University Press.

Menand, L. 2001. *The Metaphysical Club: A Story of Ideas in America*. New York: Farrar, Straus & Giroux.

Meyers, R. G. 1971. "Meaning and Metaphysics in James". *Philosophy and Phenomenological Research* **31**, 369–80.

Moore, G. E. 1907–8. "Professor James's 'Pragmatism'". *Proceedings of the Aristotelian Society* **8**, 33–77.

Myers, G. E. 1986. *William James: His Life and Thought*. New Haven, CT: Yale University Press.

Pratt, J. Bisett 1907. "Truth and Verification". *Journal of Philosophy* **4**, 320–24.

Putnam, H. 1997. "James's Theory of Truth". In *The Cambridge Companion to William James*, R. A. Putnam (ed.), 166–85. Cambridge: Cambridge University Press.

Putnam, R. A. (ed.) 1997. *The Cambridge Companion to William James*. Cambridge: Cambridge University Press.

Russell, B. 1908. "Transatlantic 'Truth'". *Albany Review* **2**, 393–410. This paper is reprinted under the title "William James's Conception of Truth", in B. Russell, *Philosophical Essays* (London: Allen & Unwin, 1966), 112–30.

Suckiel, E. K. 1982. *The Pragmatic Philosophy of William James*. Notre Dame, IN: University of Notre Dame Press.

4

Ludwig Wittgenstein
Tractatus Logico-Philosophicus

Hans-Johann Glock

Introduction

Ludwig Wittgenstein (1889–1951) came from a wealthy and cultured Jewish family in Vienna. It provided Ludwig with what he later called his "good intellectual nursery-training". This included Karl Kraus's brilliant polemics against the abuse of language in the late Habsburg Empire, the scientific and philosophical writings of the physicists Heinrich Hertz and Friedrich Boltzmann and the transcendental idealism of Arthur Schopenhauer. From 1906 Wittgenstein studied engineering in Berlin and Manchester. He developed an interest in the foundations of mathematics that led him to the writings of Frege and Russell. In 1911 he went to Cambridge to work with Russell. The *Tractatus* is the eventual result of this supremely fruitful yet equally fraught intellectual encounter. It was finished in 1918, while Wittgenstein served in the Austrian army, and it remained the only philosophical book he published during his lifetime. He always referred to it as *Logisch-Philosophische Abhandlung*. Nevertheless, the title G. E. Moore suggested for the English edition, *Tractatus Logico-Philosophicus*, has carried the day and has become an academic household name. Alas, the work itself has remained obscure. Exegetical controversies rage not just about matters of detail but about the very nature of the book.

It is clear, however, that the *Tractatus* revolves around the relation between *thought* and *language* on the one hand, *reality* on the other. But its interest in that relation differs fundamentally from the epistemological concerns that dominated

Western philosophy after Descartes. Instead, the focus is on logical or semantic questions that are in some respects prior to those of epistemology and metaphysics. The issue is not: do we possess knowledge of reality? How can we represent reality accurately, that is, arrive at beliefs that are true and justified? It is rather: how can we represent reality *at all*, whether truly or falsely? What gives content to our beliefs and meaning to our sentences? What enables them to be about something?

The *Tractatus* is devoted to two major themes, the essence of *representation* or *intentionality* on the one hand, the nature of *logic* and *philosophy* on the other. The two are interrelated, since for Wittgenstein logic constitutes the most general preconditions for the possibility of representation. We represent reality through thought. But the *Tractatus* breaks with the traditional view that language is merely a medium for transmitting a pre-linguistic process of thought. Thought is intrinsically linked to the linguistic expression of thought. Wittgenstein's first masterpiece features a striking account of the essence of symbolic or linguistic representation – the famous picture theory of the proposition – that at the same time furnishes a novel understanding of logic, a metaphysical account of the basic constituents of reality, pregnant remarks about the mystical and a revolutionary if hugely controversial conception of the proper task and method of philosophy itself.

Part of the difficulty of the *Tractatus*, and of its appeal, lies in the fact that it combines the formal with the romantic and mystical. "The work is strictly philosophical and at the same time literary, but there is no babbling in it", as he wrote to von Ficker (FL Oct. 1919). Furthermore, because of his literary aspirations Wittgenstein often condensed his insights to the point of impenetrability, and failed to spell out the arguments in their support. Doing so would "spoil their beauty", he maintained in 1913, to which Russell trenchantly replied that he should acquire a slave to take over this task. The marmoreal remarks are not unconnected aphorisms, since they are rigidly fitted into a tight structure. But in his attempt to avoid babbling Wittgenstein adopted a laconic tone and compressed his remarks into what C. D. Broad later called "syncopated pipings" (1925: vii).

Wittgenstein himself acknowledged the justice of that remark, admitting that every sentence in the *Tractatus* should be read as the heading of a chapter, needing further exposition. Some of that exposition can be garnered from the *Notebooks 1914–1916*. The famous numbering system (used in my subsequent references) is supposed to indicate the importance and place of individual remarks: "The propositions $n.1, n.2, n.3$ etc. are comments on proposition no. n; the propositions $n.m1, n.m2$, etc. are comments on proposition no. $n.m$; and so on", as he explains in a footnote to remark number 1. Wittgenstein considered this system essential to the book (FL 5 Dec. 1919), but it has struck many as misleading. He first used it in the so-called *Prototractatus*, a typescript that he composed from his *Notebooks* in 1917–18. It originally served as an aid for composition, but later turned into a system of signposting. Wittgenstein does not apply it consistently. What he called his "basic thought" is tucked away as 4.0312, and proposition 4 is elucidated not by what follows but by what precedes it.

Wittgenstein had great difficulties finding a publisher for the *Tractatus*. It eventually appeared in 1921 in Oswald's *Annalen der Naturphilosophie*, and a year later in an English–German parallel edition. To ensure publication, Russell wrote an Introduction, which Wittgenstein condemned as superficial and misleading, with partial justification. In 1923 Wittgenstein made handwritten corrections to Ramsey's copy of the book. A second edition incorporating some of these corrections appeared in 1933, followed by a critical edition (which includes the *Prototractatus*) in 1989.

Frege and Russell

Frege and Russell pioneered logicism: the project of providing mathematics with secure foundations by deriving it from purely logical concepts and principles. To this end, they replaced the old syllogistic logic by a more powerful one based in mathematical function theory. Unlike grammar and syllogistic logic, they analysed propositions not into subject and predicate, but into *function* and *argument*. The expression "$x^2 + 1$" represents a function of the variable x, because its value depends solely on the argument we substitute for x; it has the value 2 for the argument 1, 5 for the argument 2 and so on. Frege extended this mathematical notion so that functions do not just take numbers as arguments, but objects of *any* kind. Thus the expression "the capital of x" denotes a function that has the value Berlin for the argument Germany. Equally, the sentence "Caesar conquered Gaul" is analysed not into the subject "Caesar" and the predicate "conquered Gaul", but into the name of a two-place function, "x conquered y", and the names of its two arguments, "Caesar" and "Gaul". In Frege's mature work the value of this kind of function is either one or other of two "logical objects", "the True" and "the False". The value of the function x *conquered* y is the True for the arguments Caesar and Gaul and the False for Alexander and Russia.

Frege further extended this idea of a truth-function to propositional connectives and expressions of generality. Negation, for instance, is a function that maps one truth-value onto the converse truth-value: "p" is true if and only if "$\sim p$" is false. Similarly, "All electrons are negative" is analysed not into a subject "all electrons" and a predicate "are negative", but into a complex one-place function-name "if x is an electron, then x is negative" and a universal quantifier ("For all x, …")

73

that binds the variable occurring in the function-name. "All electrons are negative" does not claim of the class of electrons that it is negative; it claims of every thing in the universe that *if* it is an electron, it is also negative. Existential propositions ("Some electrons are negative") are expressed through the universal quantifier and negation ("Not for all x, if x is an electron, then x is not negative"). This quantifier-variable notation is capable of formalizing propositions involving multiple generality (propositions with more than one quantifier), which are essential to mathematics. It captures, for example, the difference between the true proposition "For every number, there is a greater number" ("$(x)(\exists y)\, y > x$") and the false proposition "There is a number that is greater than all other numbers" ("$(\exists y)(x)\, y > x$").

Frege distinguished between two aspects of the content of signs: their "meaning", which is the object they refer to, and their "sense", the "mode of presentation" of that referent. The meaning of a sentence is its truth-value; the sense of a sentence is the thought it expresses (what is asserted). The meaning of a proper name is what it stands for; its sense the descriptions through which we identify that bearer. For instance, for some the sense of "Aristotle" is given by the description "the pupil of Plato", for others by "the teacher of Alexander".

Frege's logical system is the first complete axiomatization of first-order logic (propositional and predicate calculus) and exhibits the basic operation of arithmetic – mathematical induction – as the application of a purely logical principle. Frege defined numbers – the basic concept of arithmetic – as sets of sets with the same number of members. The number two is the set of all pairs, the number three the set of all trios and so on. Unfortunately, this ingenious procedure made unrestricted use of the notion of a set, and therefore led to the paradox of the set of all sets that are not members of themselves. Russell, who had devised the paradox, developed a logical system closely resembling Frege's. He endeavoured to protect logicism from the paradox by means of his "theory of types", which prohibits as nonsensical formulae that predicate of sets properties that can only significantly be predicated of their members (as in "The class of lions is a member of the class of lions").

Russell's system differed from Frege's in other notable respects. The value of a function such as *x conquered y* is not a truth-value, but a proposition; for example, its value for the arguments Bush and Iraq is the proposition that Bush conquered Iraq. As a consequence, Russell denied that sentences are names of truth-values, and he repudiated Frege's sense–meaning distinction. For Frege, in natural languages a sentence of the form "The *F* is *G*" – for example "The king of France is bald" – expresses a thought but lacks a truth-value if nothing that is *F* exists. Russell's seminal "theory of descriptions" analysed such sentences into a quantified conjunction, namely "There is one and only one thing that is *F*, and that thing is *G*". If there is no unique thing that is *F*, this proposition is simply false rather than neither true nor false.

Like Frege, Russell thought of his formal system as an *ideal language*, one that avoids the logical defects (indeterminacy, ambiguity, referential failure, type-confusions, etc.) of natural languages. Unlike Frege, he used this language to advance a logical atomism. Following the recipe of the theory of descriptions, complex propositions from diverse areas of discourse are analysed into truth-functions of simple "atomic propositions". These in turn are further analysed into "logically proper names". Unlike ordinary proper names and definite descriptions, these *real* names are supposed to be proof against referential failure. According to Russell, the only expressions that satisfy this requirement are demonstratives that refer to "sense-data". By this token, atomic propositions are statements like "This is red"; they refer to a mental experience with which the speaker is presently acquainted, and the existence of which is therefore immune to sceptical doubt.

Logic , thought and language

Wittgenstein's ambition was not to develop the formal aspects of the new logic, to provide new proofs or tools, but to elucidate its philosophical implications. First and foremost among these was the question "What is logic?" It was in this area that he soon became Russell's equal and his remorseless critic. Russell was forced to acknowledge that *Principia* had left the nature of logic obscure. He decided to leave this job to Wittgenstein; but he got more than he bargained for. Wittgenstein took over and transformed important elements of Frege's and Russell's logical systems, notably the idea that a proposition is a function of its constituents and that it is composed of function and argument. Moreover, he followed Russell in identifying philosophy with the logical analysis of propositions. But his "philosophy of logic" departed radically from his predecessors. With considerable chutzpah, he included their work under the label "the old logic", and castigated them for having failed to clarify the nature of logic (4.003–4.0031, 4.1121, 4.126).

At the turn of the century, there were four accounts of the nature of logic. According to Mill's radical empiricism, it consists of well-corroborated inductive generalizations. According to psychologism, logical truths or "laws of thought" describe how human beings (by and large) think, their basic mental operations, and are determined by the nature of the human mind. Against both positions Platonists like Frege protested that logical truths are both necessary and objective, and that this special status can only be secured by assuming that their subject matter – logical objects and thoughts – are abstract entities inhabiting a "third realm" beyond space and time, rather than material objects or private ideas in the minds of individuals. Finally, Russell held that the propositions of logic are supremely general truths about the most pervasive traits of reality.

Wittgenstein eschews all four alternatives, by exploiting a Kantian idea that he may have picked up from Schopenhauer or Hertz. Necessary propositions are neither inductive generalizations about the world nor statements about the way people actually think. Nor are they about a Platonist *hinterworld*, or about the most pervasive features of reality. Philosophy *qua* logic is a second order discipline. "Logic is transcendental" (6.13). Unlike science, it does not itself represent any kind of reality. Instead, it reflects on the preconditions of representing reality, just as Kant's philosophy reflects on the transcendental preconditions of experiencing reality. Philosophy is the "logical clarification of thought". It investigates the nature and limits of *thought*, because it is in thought that we represent reality. Echoing Kant's critical philosophy, the *Tractatus* aims to draw the bounds between legitimate discourse, which represents reality, and illegitimate speculation – notably metaphysics (4.11ff.). At the same time, it gives a *linguistic twist* to the Kantian tale.

> Thus the aim of the book is to draw a limit to thought, or rather – not to thought but to the expression of thoughts: for in order to be able to draw the limits of thought, we should have to find both sides of the limit thinkable (i.e. we should have to be able to think what cannot be thought). It will therefore only be in language that the limit can be drawn, and what lies on the other side of the limit will simply be nonsense.
> (Preface)

Language is not just a secondary manifestation of something non-linguistic. For thoughts are neither mental processes nor abstract entities, but themselves propositions, sentences that have been projected onto reality (3.5–4). Thoughts can be completely expressed in language, and philosophy can establish the limits and preconditions of thought by establishing the limits and preconditions of the *linguistic expression of thought*.

Indeed, these limits *must* be drawn in language. They cannot be drawn by propositions talking about both sides of the limit. By definition, such propositions would have to be about things that cannot be thought about and thereby transcend the bounds of sense. The limits of thought can only be drawn *from the inside*, namely by delineating the "rules of logical grammar" or "logical syntax" (3.32–3.325). These rules determine whether a combination of signs is meaningful, that is, capable of representing reality either truly or falsely. What lies beyond these limits is not unknowable things in themselves, as in Kant, but only nonsensical combinations of signs, for example, "The concert-tone A is red". The special status of necessary propositions is due not to the fact that they describe a peculiar reality, but to the fact that they reflect "rules of symbolism" (6.12ff.). Logical syntax *antecedes* questions of truth and falsity. It cannot be overturned by empirical propositions, since nothing contravening it counts as a meaningful proposition.

Wittgenstein's "logic of representation" (4.015) comprises the most general *preconditions for the possibility of symbolic representation*. Consequently, there is no such thing as a logically defective language. Any language, any sign-system capable of representing reality, must conform to the rules of logical syntax. Natural languages are capable of "expressing every sense". Therefore their propositions must be "in perfect logical order" just as they are; "they are not in any way logically *less correct* or less exact or *more confused* than propositions written down ... in Russell's symbolism or any other 'Begriffsschrift'. (Only it is easier for us to gather their logical form when they are expressed in an appropriate symbolism.)" (OL 10 May 1922; see 4.002; 5.5563). Ordinary language allows the formulation of nonsensical pseudo-propositions because it conceals the logical form of propositions: quantifiers look like proper names ("nobody") or predicates ("exists"), ambiguities lead to philosophical confusions ("is" functions as copula, sign of identity and existential quantifier), and formal concepts such as "object" look like legitimate genuine concepts. To guard against such deception, however, we require not an *ideal language* capable of expressing things natural languages cannot express, but an *ideal notation* (*Zeichensprache*). Such a notation is "governed by *logical* grammar – by logical syntax" (3.325); it displays the hidden logical form that ordinary propositions possessed all along.

> The idea is to express in an appropriate symbolism what in ordinary language leads to endless misunderstandings ... where ordinary language disguises logical structure, where it allows the formation of pseudo-propositions, where it uses one term in an infinity of different meanings, we must replace it by a symbolism which gives a clear picture of the logical structure, excludes pseudo-propositions, and uses its terms unambiguously.
>
> (RLF: 163)

Russell's Introduction went wrong, therefore, in treating the *Tractatus* as a contribution to ideal language philosophy. The mistake was already pointed out by Ramsey, yet this has not deterred subsequent commentators from repeating it.

The focus on the preconditions of representation also resolves another exegetical problem. According to "ontological" interpretations (Pears 1987; Hacker

1998 [1986], 2001; Malcolm 1986), the *Tractatus* is the climax of a metaphysical tradition for which the structure of thought and language has to mirror the essence of a mind-independent reality. According to "linguistic" interpretations (Anscombe 1959; McGuinness 2002; Ishiguro 2001), the *Tractatus* anticipates Wittgenstein's later work in regarding language as autonomous, and the so-called essence of reality as a mere projection of the structure of language. In fact, however, the emphasis is neither on language nor on reality, but on *the relation of representation between them*. Wittgenstein's central idea is that there must be an *isomorphism* – a structural identity – between language and reality, if the former is to be capable of representing the latter. The essential logical form of language is identical with the essential metaphysical form of reality, because it comprises those structural features that language and reality must share if the former is to be capable of depicting the latter: "To state the essence of the proposition is to state the essence of all description, and thus the essence of the world" (5.4711; see NB: 22.1.15, 2.8.16 and p. 106).

The linguistic interpretation is right, therefore, in that Wittgenstein's ontology is a fallout of his account of language. At the same time, the ontological interpretation is right in that language is prior only with respect to the *ordo cognescendi*, not the *ordo essendi*. Language provides a guideline to ontology precisely because it has to *mirror* reality.[1] The rules of logical syntax are not linguistic conventions (as the logical positivists later held, partly under Wittgenstein's influence). Logic is a "mirror image of the world" and represents its "scaffolding". Whereas the superficial features of language, those that distinguish various sign-systems, are arbitrary, there is only one "all-embracing logic which mirrors the world" (6.13; 6.124, see 5.511, 3.34ff.). It embraces those essential features that *every* sign-system must possess in order to be capable of picturing reality and hence of being meaningful.

Logical atomism and the picture theory of the proposition

The *Tractatus* starts out with an ontological discussion according to which the world is the totality of facts (1–2.063), and then proceeds to investigate a subset of that totality, namely pictures, in particular propositions, that is facts that are capable of representing other facts (2.1–3.5). "The world is everything that is the case. The world is the totality of facts, not of objects" (1–1.1). The ontology of the *Tractatus* forms part of a theory of *symbolic representation*. The world is primarily what is being represented in language. And in order to *represent* the world we have to represent facts, how things are. Furthermore, the actual world cannot consist of, that is, be identified with, its ultimate constituents, the "objects" (*Gegenstände*), since the latter are common to all *possible* worlds. These objects are essentially *simple*, while *complexes*, notably ordinary material objects, are combinations of simples. They form the fixed "substance of the world": all change is the combination or separation of objects, consequently the objects themselves are *unchanging* and *indestructible*; what can vary is only the way they are combined (2.02–2.027).

Objects have both "internal properties" (or "form") and "external properties" (2.01–2.0141). The internal properties of an object *A* determine what other objects it *can* combine with; by contrast, the external properties of *A* are determined by what other objects it is *actually* combined with. It is an internal property of a visual object *not* to have a pitch, but to have *some* colour (and *vice versa* for a note), an external property to have, for example, the colour red.

A possible combination of objects is a "state of affairs" (*Sachverhalt*); the obtaining of such a combination is a "fact".[2] The representation of a state of affairs is a model or picture. It must be isomorphic with what it represents, that is, it must have the same "logical form": logical multiplicity and structure. Propositions or thoughts are "logical pictures": maximally abstract pictures that do not rely on a particular medium, by contrast to speech, writing, painting or sculpture, for instance (2.18ff., 3, 4.032ff., 5.474ff.).

The logical analysis of propositions yields "elementary propositions", which are logically independent of each other because their truth or falsehood depends solely on the obtaining or non-obtaining of the state of affairs they depict. The ultimate constituents of elementary propositions are unanalysable "names" or "simple signs". These are the equivalent of Russell's logically proper names. They stand for the indecomposable objects that are their meaning (3.144–3.26). Their logico-syntactical form (combinatorial possibilities) mirrors the metaphysical essence of the objects they stand for (2.012–2.0272), this being one salient respect in which language pays heed to reality rather than the other way around.

Like Frege, Wittgenstein distinguished between sense (*Sinn*) and meaning (*Bedeutung*). Unlike Frege, he recognized that there is a crucial difference between names (and words more generally) on the one hand, propositions on the other. Propositions are not names; they do not stand for either a truth-value (Frege) or a fact (Moore, Russell). Conversely, simple names go proxy for objects directly, without the mediation of a sense (description). As a result, the *Tractatus* maintains that names have a *meaning but no sense*, while propositions have a *sense but no meaning* (3.142, 3.203, 3.3). The sense of an elementary proposition is the state of affairs it depicts, and it is a function of the meanings of its constituent names, this being one reason why the logical structure of language has to pay heed to the metaphysical constitution of reality.

The picture theory is an attempt to explain the nature of intentionality. How can a thought or proposition depict the world? More specifically, it addresses two interrelated puzzles. One is the venerable problem of how a proposition can be *meaningful yet false*. How can one *think what is not the case*? For if it is not the case, then it does not exist, and what does not exist is nothing. But to think nothing, is not to think anything at all, as Plato averred (*Theaetetus* 189A; see PI: §518).

Russell's *dual-relation theory of judgement* fell into this trap, by treating the content of a belief as a fact. Othello's belief that Desdemona loves Cassio cannot be a relation between Othello and the fact that Desdemona loves Cassio, since there is no such fact. Russell's *multiple-relation theory* avoided the problem by holding that Othello is related to – "acquainted with" – the *constituents* of the fact – Desdemona, Cassio and the relation of loving – rather than a whole fact (a complex of things). Wittgenstein pointed out, however, that this no longer guarantees that these constituents are combined in a meaningful way and would hence allow one to judge a nonsense, for example, that the table penholders the book (5.5422; NB: 95, 103).

The other puzzle was discovered by Wittgenstein. How can a proposition "reach right up to reality" (2.151ff.)? If "*p*" is true, it depicts a fact, that is, what it says *must be* what is the case, namely that *p*. But if "*p*" is false, it does not depict a fact, that is, what it says *cannot* be what is the case. Yet it not only remains meaningful; the content of "*p*", what it says, must be the *same* in both cases, irrespective of whether it is true or false. This puzzle defies not just Russell's suggestion that the content of a proposition is a fact, but also Frege's proposal that it is a thought, an abstract entity that *stands between* the proposition and the fact that verifies it if it is true. The content of a true proposition "*p*" is that *p*, and this is not an intermediary between the true proposition and the fact that *p*, but rather the fact that *p* itself.

By contrast, the picture theory explains how a proposition can reach right up to reality by holding that its sense is a potentiality. Whether or not my thought is true, its content is one and the same *possibility*, a possibility that is actualized in the first case but not in the second. *What I think* is the "sense of the proposition", the state of affairs depicted, a possible combination of objects (3.11, 4.021). The possibility of that combination is guaranteed by the proposition making sense (2.203, 3.02). The world – how things are – only decides whether or not the place in logical space determined by the proposition is filled. Propositions are not just bivalent, as Russell had it, that is, either true or false, but *bipolar*. That is to say that they are *capable of being true* but also capable of being false. In this they reflect what they represent (yet another respect in which language mirrors reality). A state of affairs (combination of objects) either does or does not obtain; but, being a potentiality, it cannot obtain necessarily.

For a proposition to depict, no fact need correspond to it as a whole. But two things are required. First, something must correspond to its *elements*. There must be a one-to-one correlation between these elements – its constituent names – and the elements of the situation it depicts – the objects. Second, it must be determined what relationships between the names depict what relationship between things. If both "pictorial relation" and "structure" are in place, the *fact* that the elements of the picture are related to each other in a determinate way represents that the corresponding things are related to each other in the same way, whether or not they actually are. To depict falsely is to depict a *non-existing combination of existing elements*. "In a proposition a situation is, as it were, assembled by way of experiment" (4.031, see 2.1–2.15, 4.01–4.1).

In the *Notebooks* leading up to the *Tractatus*, Wittgenstein wavered between assigning the role of objects to physical atoms on the one hand, and minimal objects of perception like points in the visual field and unanalysable perceptual qualities on the other. But in the *Tractatus* he is reticent on the issue of what the objects, names and elementary propositions postulated by his logical atomism look like. His main concern there is to insist "on purely logical grounds" that there *must be* such elements of reality on the one hand, of language on the other, if the latter is to represent the former (5.55ff., 4.221; NB: 14.–17.6.15). According to the picture theory, an elementary proposition can only depict a possible state of affairs because each of its ultimate constituents – each simple name – stands for an object. If these objects could fail to exist, however, the capacity of the elementary proposition to depict a possible state of affairs would be contingent on the truth of another proposition, namely one that asserts the existence of the objects to which the names of the first proposition refer. This would run counter to Wittgenstein's conviction that the sense of a proposition must antecede all matters of fact. Consequently, the objects for which names stand must be indestructible.

The *Tractatus* is standardly credited with a sophisticated *correspondence theory* of truth, one according to which a proposition is true if and only if it is isomorphic with reality. But a structural identity or isomorphism holds between an elementary sentence and its sense, the *possible state of affairs* – a possible combination of objects – it depicts (2.202–2.221, 4.031). It does not just hold between a *true* elementary sentence and an *actual fact*. Moreover, Wittgenstein declares that "a proposition is true if things are as we say they are by using it" (4.062; see NB: 9, 113). This suggests a deflationary account, one that shuns the idea of a truth-making relation between language and reality and explains truth by reference to a trivial logical equivalence between what is said and what is the case. At the same time, we also find: "A picture agrees with reality or fails to agree; it is correct or incorrect, true or false. … The agreement (*Übereinstimmung*) or disagreement of its sense with reality constitutes its truth or falsity" (2.21–2.222). Here an agreement with reality does not give sense to pictures/propositions, but distinguishes *true* from false ones.

The pieces of this jigsaw fall into place once one realizes that the agreement between a proposition and reality involves two components (Glock 2005). First, the proposition has a sense, that is, it *depicts a state of affairs*: a possible combination of objects. Secondly, that sense agrees with reality in that this possible combination of objects *actually obtains*, that is, it is a *fact*: "if an elementary proposition is true, the state of affairs [it depicts] obtains (*besteht*): if an elementary proposition is false, the state of affairs does not obtain" (4.25; see 4.21). The *Tractatus* explains *depiction* by reference to an isomorphism between proposition and a possible state of affairs; it explains *truth* by reference to the obtainment of the depicted state of affairs. There is no genuine truth-making relation: isomorphism accounts for the sense of a proposition rather than its truth and the agreement between that sense and reality is simply the logical equivalence between what a true proposition says and what is actually the case. Nevertheless, the account gives substance to passages in Moore and Russell that are generally treated as evincing a correspondence theory: a proposition is true if and only if *there is* a fact to which it corresponds, that is, one that it depicts or has as its content.

The nature of logic and the essence of propositions

The picture theory of elementary propositions is only one part of the "theory of symbolism" (CL 22.6–26.12.12), the account of representation through which Wittgenstein sought to elucidate the nature of logic. The other part is his explanation of how elementary propositions combine to form molecular propositions. This explanation is shaped by what he calls his "fundamental thought" (4.0312). The logical constants (propositional connectives and quantifiers) are not *names* of logical objects or functions, as Frege and Russell had it, but express the truth-functional *operations* through which complex propositions are constructed out of simple ones. The truth-value and the sense of the result of such operations *is* a function of the truth-values and senses of their bases. But the operators do not name relations between propositions, they express *what has to be done* to one proposition to turn it into another, for example, that "$p \lor q$" has to be negated to obtain "$\sim p \bullet \sim q$" (5.21–5, 5.3). In contrast to genuine function-signs such as "x is red", *nothing in reality* corresponds, for example, to "$\sim$". A false proposition does not correspond to a negative fact that includes an object called "negation"; there is *no* fact that corresponds to it. The only effect of "$\sim$" is to reverse both the truth-value of a proposition and its sense. Both "p" and "$\sim p$" are about the same configuration of the same objects (4.0621); they have opposite senses because the former says that this configuration obtains, the latter that it does not. Furthermore the symbols "$\sim$", "$\supset$", "$\bullet$" "(x)", "$(\exists x)$" and so on are interdefinable; hence they are neither "primitive signs", as Frege and Russell assumed, nor do they denote distinct entities (5.42, 5.441).

All possible forms of truth-functional combination can be generated out of a single operation (joint negation). This operation is a generalized version of the diadic truth-operator "$\sim (p \vee q)$", one that operates on an arbitrary number of propositions to yield a *single* proposition, the joint denial of them all. Furthermore, Wittgenstein insists that all meaningful propositions are the result of truth-functional operations on the set of elementary propositions. Just as the sense of an elementary proposition is given by the possible combination of objects that it depicts, the sense of a molecular proposition is given by its "truth-conditions", that is, the combinations of truth-values among its constituent propositions under which it comes out as true in a truth-table: for instance, "$p \bullet q$" is true if and only if both "p" and "q" are true (4.431).

As a result, *all* meaningful propositions share with elementary propositions the feature of saying how things are, of depicting situations that may or may not obtain. The "general propositional form" is to say "Things are thus-and-so" (4.5–5.01, 5.54). Various types of propositions differ in their logical forms, which are to be discovered by the "application of logic", a process of piecemeal analysis that the *Tractatus* advocates without practising it (5.557). But the *Tractatus* lays down *ab initio* that these possible forms must share the general propositional form. It is the *essence of all propositions*, the necessary and sufficient conditions for something to be a proposition in any sign-language.

A central part of the doctrine of the general propositional form is the *thesis of extensionality*: the truth of any proposition is dependent solely upon the elementary propositions into which it can be analysed. Consequently, Wittgenstein has to explain away the numerous *intensional contexts* of natural languages, such as the embedding of a proposition in the scope of an intentional verb (in indirect speech or ascriptions of propositional attitudes), causal explanations, scientific laws and modal propositions. He does so with varying degrees of implausibility, by either reducing these occurrences to extensional ones – as in the case of causal explanations and ascriptions of belief – or denying that they constitute genuine propositions – as in the case of scientific laws and modal propositions.

The general propositional form is also the only logical constant: "the one and only general primitive sign in logic". For all logical operations, and hence the whole of logic, are given with the very idea of a bipolar elementary proposition (5.47ff., 4.001; NB: 22.1./5.5.15, 2.8.16). All logical relations (relations of entailment or inconsistency) between propositions are due to the fact that they are the result of such truth-functional combination.

There are two limiting cases of truth-functional combination, namely "tautologies", which are unconditionally true, and "contradictions", which are unconditionally false. They constitute the propositions of logic. Just as the *signs* of logic (the logical constants) do not name logical objects, the *propositions* of logic do not describe such objects. The necessity of tautologies simply reflects the fact that they combine bipolar propositions in such a way that all information cancels out. They exclude and hence *say nothing*, which means that they are senseless, that is have zero sense. "It is raining" says something true or false, and so does "It is not raining". By contrast, "Either it is raining or it is not raining" says nothing about the weather. The hallmark of such logical propositions is not their supreme generality, as traditionally assumed. For this specific statement is strictly necessary, while general principles like the law of induction are merely contingent (4.46ff., 6.123ff.). At the same time, the fact that a certain combination of bipolar propositions says nothing about the world *shows* something. Thus, that "$\sim(p \bullet \sim p)$" and "$((p \supset q) \bullet p) \supset q$" are tautologies shows, respectively, that "p" and "$\sim p$" contradict each other and that "q" follows from "$p \supset q$" and "p".

Logic is a fall-out from the essence of representation in general, and of elementary propositions in particular. Both logical propositions and logical inferences arise out of the truth-functional complexity of propositions, which in turn is the result of applying truth-operations to bipolar elementary propositions (4.31–4.461, 5.47ff., 6.1–6.13). Contrary to the axiomatic systems of Frege and Russell, all logical truths are on the same level, and there is no need to appeal to rules of inference. That one proposition entails another will be evident, once the two are properly analysed.

Saying and showing

By contrast to logical propositions, which are limiting cases of propositions with a sense, the pronouncements of metaphysics are nonsensical "pseudo-propositions". They try to say what could not be otherwise, for example, that red is a colour, or 1 a number. What they seem to exclude – for example, red being a sound – contravenes logic, and is hence nonsensical. But the attempt to refer to something nonsensical, if only to exclude it (as in Russell's theory of types), is itself nonsensical. For we cannot refer to something illogical like the class of lions being a lion by means of a meaningful expression. What such philosophical pseudo-propositions try to *say* is *shown* by the structure of genuine propositions (e.g. that "red" can combine only with names of points in the visual field, not with names of musical tones). The only necessary propositions that can be expressed are tautologies and hence analytic.

The *Tractatus* combines reflections on the nature of representation with mystical themes, which were inspired by Wittgenstein's experiences during the First World

War and influenced by Schopenhauer. Indeed, Wittgenstein seems to have adopted a linguistic version of transcendental idealism: what projects sentences onto reality are acts of meaning or thinking something, acts that, by the lights of the *Tractatus*, could only be performed by a metaphysical self (see 3.11; NB: 26.11.14, 22.6.15). Like the eye of the visual field, this subject of representation is not itself part of experience, it cannot be represented through meaningful propositions (5.6ff.). The metaphysical self is ineffable, and so is what Wittgenstein calls "the higher", the realm of ethical, aesthetic and religious value (6.42, 6.432).

The distinction between what can be said by meaningful propositions and what can only be shown pervades the *Tractatus* from the Preface to the famous final admonition "Whereof one cannot speak, thereof one must remain silent". In a letter to Russell, Wittgenstein referred to it as "the main point of the book". Part of its importance lies in the fact that it holds together the two parts of the book, the logico-semantic reflections on the essence of symbolic representation and the mystical pronouncements about ethics, aesthetics, the self and death. What unites them is the contrast with the bipolar propositions of science. While the latter make factual statements, depict combinations of objects that may or may not obtain, the former attempt to say things that could not be otherwise. The pronouncements of the *Tractatus* itself are in the end condemned as nonsensical, because they concern the essence of representation rather than contingent facts.

> My propositions serve as elucidations in the following way: anyone who understands me eventually recognizes them as nonsensical, when he has used them – as steps – to climb up beyond them. (He must, so to speak, throw away the ladder after he has climbed up it.) He must transcend these propositions, and then he will see the world aright.
>
> (6.54)

The propositions of the *Tractatus* are repudiated because they try to express metaphysical truths about the essence of language that, by Wittgenstein's own lights, cannot be expressed in philosophical propositions, but that manifest themselves in non-philosophical propositions properly analysed. This paradoxical conclusion provoked Russell into observing that "after all, Mr Wittgenstein manages to say a good deal about what cannot be said" (Introduction). Similarly, it invites Ramsey's complaint that if you cannot say it you cannot say it, but then you cannot whistle it either. If philosophy is nonsense, we should simply refrain from it.

Recent commentators including Diamond (1991; see also Crary & Read 2000) have repudiated such criticism. According to them, Wittgenstein was not trying to whistle it. Instead of "chickening out" we should acknowledge that the *auto-*

da-fé at the end must be taken literally. The *Tractatus* is meant to consist not of illuminating nonsense, nonsense that vainly tries to hint at ineffable truths, but of "plain nonsense", nonsense in the same drastic sense as gibberish such as "ab sur ah" or "piggly tiggle wiggle". The purpose of the exercise is therapeutic. By producing such sheer nonsense, Wittgenstein tries to unmask the idea of metaphysical truths (effable or ineffable) as absurd and to wean us off the temptation to engage in philosophy.

The "plain nonsense" interpretation promises to rescue the *Tractatus* from the charge of being self-defeating. Alas, it has several fatal drawbacks. First, it is at odds with the external evidence, numerous writings and conversations before and after the *Tractatus* in which Wittgenstein professed his allegiance to the idea of ineffable truths. Secondly, it employs hermeneutical double standards. On the one hand, it must reject as deliberate nonsense remarks that insist that philosophical pseudo-propositions are attempts to say something that can only be shown, and that the proper method of philosophy is to "signify what cannot be said by clearly delineating what can be said" (4.115; see 4.122, 5.535, 6.522). On the other hand, it must accept as genuine those remarks that provide the rationale for declaring philosophical pronouncements to be illegitimate, notably the claim that any well-formed sentence with a sense must be bipolar and that "formal concepts" such as "proposition", "object" and "fact" cannot be employed in meaningful propositions. Yet these two types of remarks are inextricably interwoven. Furthermore, any concession that some parts of the book furnish the standards by which the *Tractatus* in particular and metaphysics in general qualify as nonsense reintroduces a distinction between illuminating and non-illuminating nonsense that the plain nonsense condemns with such fervour. The only consistent interpretation of the text is therefore that it condones the idea of truths that language, by its very nature, cannot express (Hacker 2001: ch. 4; Schroeder 2005: ch. 2.5).

Thirdly, if the pronouncements of the *Tractatus* were meant to be mere nonsense, Wittgenstein would have to be neutral between, for example, Frege's and Russell's idea that propositions are names of objects and the idea that they differ from names in saying something, or between the claim that the propositions of logic describe abstract objects and the claim that they are tautologies. This is obviously not the case. On the contrary, Wittgenstein continued to defend the latter ideas even after abandoning much of the *Tractatus*. Finally, the idea that metaphysical pronouncements are nonsense in the same way as gibberish is untenable and at odds with important strands in the *Tractatus*, not to mention Wittgenstein's later work (Glock 2004). The "plain nonsense" interpretation demeans the book by sweeping aside both its hard-won insights and its illuminating errors, and assimilating it to an existentialist gesture or a protracted nonsense poem with a numbering system.

At the same time, we need not rest content with lumbering the text with the idea of ineffable truths. It is crucial to take seriously the *propadeutic* nature of the *Tractatus* explicit in 6.53. The book *is* self-defeating, because, in delineating the essential preconditions of representation it violates its own restrictions on what it makes sense to say. This is a pitfall for any attempt to draw the bounds of knowledge or sense in such a way as to exclude metaphysics or philosophy; witness Kant or the logical positivists. Wittgenstein heroically tried to overcome it by violating his self-imposed prohibitions solely to attain a "correct logical point of view" (4.1213), an insight into the essence and structure of language that would allow one to engage in critical logical analysis *without* committing any further violations. Once we have achieved an ideal notation that displays the logical structure of meaningful propositions, we can throw away the ladder on which we have climbed up, namely the pronouncements on the essence of meaningful propositions that we needed to construct the ideal notation.

From this perspective, Russell's aspiration to introduce scientific method into philosophy is misguided. Proper philosophy cannot be a doctrine, since there are no philosophical propositions. It is an *activity*, not of deliberately uttering nonsense with the aim of debunking it, however, but of *logical analysis*. Without propounding any propositions of its own, it clarifies the logical form of the meaningful propositions of science by translating them into the ideal notation. This positive task is complemented by the negative task of demonstrating that the propositions of metaphysics violate the rules of logical syntax since they resist such translation.

The impact of the *Tractatus*

Wittgenstein later realized that such critical analysis cannot and need not push away the ladder. It cannot assume a *once-and-for-all vision* of the essence of language. Instead of wielding a ready-made ideal notation for the algorithmic resolution of philosophical problems, philosophy turns into a dialectic process, namely of showing in a piecemeal fashion that metaphysicians create conceptual confusions by using words according to conflicting rules. This process must involve continuous reminders of how philosophically relevant words are actually used. The attempt to capture the essence of representation is misguided, since "formal concepts" such as "thought", "proposition" and "language" are *family-resemblance concepts* that cover diverse cases. Thus "proposition" applies not just to the bipolar propositions of science, but also to "grammatical propositions" that express rules for the use of words. In criticizing philosophical mistakes we can and must rely on grammatical propositions concerning terms such as "meaning", "nonsense" and "proposition", contrary to the saying–showing distinction.

In this respect, as in many others, the *Philosophical Investigations* builds on the *Tractatus* both by way of continuation and by way of self-criticism. It further develops what Wittgenstein once called "the transition from the question of truth to the question of meaning". Philosophy is not a cognitive discipline, but an activity that aims at clarity. But the ineffable metaphysics is dropped, and the mere promise of critical analysis is replaced by a dialectic-cum-therapeutic practice: philosophy dissolves the conceptual confusions to which philosophical problems are alleged to owe their existence.

As a result of practising the dialectical method the *Tractatus* had preached, the *Philosophical Investigations* jettison several cornerstones of the earlier book (see Malcolm 1986; Glock 1996: 19–27). Wittgenstein abandoned the idea of logically independent elementary propositions and the resulting restriction of logical syntax or, as Wittgenstein later preferred to call it, grammar to rules for their truth-functional combination. Logical atomism is a chimera. The distinction between simple and complex is not absolute. Standards of complexity must be laid down separately for each kind of thing, analytical tool and purpose. The collapse of logical atomism also undermines the picture theory of the proposition (although there is a continuing debate as to the extent; see Kenny 1973: ch. 12). The picture theory provided a partially correct account of the intentionality of thought and language. It was right to insist that the relation between a proposition and the fact that verifies it if it is true is a logical rather than contingent one, which is to say that it could not fail to obtain. But it went wrong in explaining that internal relation by holding that proposition and fact share a logical form, or that a shadowy entity (a possible state of affairs) mediates between them.

If there are no ultimate constituents of facts – objects – that are simple in an absolute metaphysical sense, then there are no corresponding constituents of propositions that are simple in an absolute semantic sense. Wittgenstein also realized that "the word 'meaning' is being used illicitly if it is used to signify the thing that 'corresponds' to the word". Frege, Russell and the *Tractatus* were guilty of assimilating all expressions to names, and even the meaning of those expressions that *do* refer to something must not be confused with their meaning. Instead, the meaning of a word is its role or "use in the language" (PI: §§40–42). This suggestion runs counter to *Tractatus* 3.203, while at the same time extending the idea that a word without "logico-syntactic employment" is meaningless and that we can learn the meaning of a name from its use in propositions (3.326ff.).

Wittgenstein also retained and developed the idea that philosophy and logic are rooted in language. At the same time he recognized that language is not a self-sufficient abstract system, but part of human practice, part of a "form of life". In particular, language is not governed by a calculus of hidden rules that must be unearthed by logical analysis. Ironically, it was precisely this picture through which Wittgenstein has exerted his strongest – if often indirect – influence on contemporary linguistics and philosophy of language, in particular on the complementary projects of unearthing the underlying syntax of natural languages (Chomsky) and of constructing a theory of meaning for them (Davidson). Within this second context, the thesis of extensionality inspired a more specific research programme stretching from Carnap through Quine to Davidson, which aims to analyse all meaningful propositions with the help of purely extensional languages, preferably the predicate calculus.

By way of interpretation and misinterpretation alike, the *Tractatus* was the major inspiration behind logical positivism, which in turn became the most influential philosophical movement of the twentieth century. It provided them with their key weapon against Kant's synthetic *a priori* truths, namely the idea that all *a priori* propositions are ultimately tautologies that say nothing about the world. Through its linguistic conception of thought, its explanation of logic by reference to rules for the combination of signs and its conception of philosophy as the critical analysis of language (*Sprachkritik*; 4.0031), the *Tractatus* initiated the *linguistic turn* of analytical philosophy. Even those analytic philosophers that are going back on this turn are in its debt, however, because it placed the nature of representation or intentionality at the centre of the subject, and thereby set the agenda for current theories of meaning and content. Furthermore, its enigmatic yet beautiful style and its sibylline pronouncements have inspired analytic philosophers, continental philosophers and artists alike. Last but not least, the *Tractatus* remained the starting-point for Wittgenstein's later work, which has had an equally profound impact on contemporary thought.

Notes

1. The first point runs parallel to Kant, whose metaphysics is derived from an account of experience; the second point runs counter to Kant's "Copernican revolution", which treats the preconditions of representation as imposed by the subject rather than the objects of representation. One caveat: *if* the *Tractatus* also propounds a form of transcendental idealism or solipsism (see below), then the reality that logic mirrors in some way depends on the mind. But an idealist conception of reality is no less an ontology than a realist one.
2. There is a terminological unclarity here (see H. J. Glock, *A Wittgenstein Dictionary* (Oxford: Blackwell, 1996), 115–20). In a letter to Russell dated August 1919, Wittgenstein stated that a *Sachverhalt* is what corresponds to a true *elementary* proposition, for example, *p*, whereas a *Tatsache* is what corresponds to a true *molecular* proposition, for example "*p* • *q* • *r*" (CL 125); and he approved of Ogden's translation of *Sachverhalt* as *atomic fact*. Nevertheless, "state of affairs" is the literal translation and does not beg exegetical questions. For there is also evidence that the difference is also one

between what is *possibly* and what is *actually* the case (see below), with states of affairs being possible combinations of objects depicted by elementary propositions and situations (*Sachlage*) being potentialities depicted by molecular propositions. The sense of a proposition, what it depicts, is a state of affairs or situation. A state of affairs is a *possible* combination of objects that obtains if the proposition is *true*, and does not if it is *false*. By contrast, a fact is something *that is actually the case* (1ff.; 2.201ff., 4.02ff.; NB: 2.10./ 2.11.14).

Works by Wittgenstein

Tractatus Logico-Philosophicus, D. F. Pears & B. F. McGuinness (trans.) (London: Routledge & Kegan Paul, 1961).

Logisch-Philosophische Abhandlung, Kritische Edition, B. McGuinness & J. Schulte (eds) (Frankfurt: Suhrkamp, 1989). [Also contains a preliminary version from 1917, the "Prototractatus".]

Notebooks 1914–16 [NB], rev. edn, G. E. M. Anscombe & G. H. von Wright (eds), G. E. M. Anscombe (trans.) (Oxford: Blackwell, 1979). [These contain not just the Notebooks on which Wittgenstein worked during the war, but also two pre-war dictations, *Notes on Logic* and *Notes dictated to Moore in Norway*.]

Ludwig Wittgenstein: Cambridge Letters [CL], B. McGuinness & G. H. von Wright (eds) (Oxford: Blackwell, 1995). [The letters to Russell, Moore and Ramsey shed light on the genesis of the *Tractatus* and on matters of exegetical detail.]

"Letters to L. von Ficker" [FL], G. H. von Wright (ed.), B. Gillette (trans.), in *Wittgenstein: Sources and Perspectives*, C. G. Luckhardt (ed.) (Hassocks: Harvester Press, 1979).

Letters to C. K. Ogden [OL], G. H. von Wright (ed.) (Oxford: Blackwell, 1973).

"Some Remarks on Logical Form" [RLF], *Proceedings of the Aristotelian Society*, suppl. vol. ix (1929), 162–71.

Philosophical Investigations [PI], G. E. M. Anscombe & R. Rhees (eds) (Oxford: Blackwell, 1958 [1st edn 1953]). [The definitive statement of Wittgenstein's later thought, including his criticisms of the Tractatus (§§1–88).]

Further reading

Anscombe, G. E. M. 1959. *An Introduction to Wittgenstein's "Tractatus"*. London: Hutchinson.

Black, M. 1964. *A Companion to Wittgenstein's "Tractatus"*. Cambridge: Cambridge University Press.

Broad, C. D. 1925. *Mind and its Place in Nature*. London: Routledge & Kegan Paul.

Copi, I. M. & R. W. Beard (eds) 1966. *Essays on Wittgenstein's Tractatus*. London: Routledge.

Crary, A. & R. Read (eds) 2000. *The New Wittgenstein*. London: Routledge.

Diamond, C. 1991. *The Realistic Spirit*. Cambridge, MA: MIT Press.

Fogelin, R. F. 1987. *Wittgenstein*. London: Routledge.

Glock, H. J. 1996. *A Wittgenstein Dictionary*. Oxford: Blackwell.

Glock, H. J. (ed.) 2001. *Wittgenstein: A Critical Reader*. Oxford: Blackwell.

Glock, H. J. 2004. "All Kinds of Nonsense". In *Wittgenstein at Work*, E. Ammereller & E. Fischer (eds), 221–45. London: Routledge.

Glock, H. J. 2006 forthcoming. "Truth in the *Tractatus*". *Synthese*.

Hacker, P. M. S. 1986. *Insight and Illusion*. Oxford: Clarendon Press.

Hacker, P. M. S. 1996. *Wittgenstein's Place in Twentieth Century Analytical Philosophy*. Oxford: Blackwell.

Hacker, P. M. S. 2001. *Wittgenstein: Connections and Controversies*. Oxford: Oxford University Press.

Ishiguro, H. 2001. "The So-called Picture Theory: Language and the World in Tractatus Logico-Philosophicus". In Glock (ed.) (2001), 26–46.

Kenny, A. J. P. 1973. *Wittgenstein*. Harmondsworth: Penguin.

McGuinness, B. 2002. *Approaches to Wittgenstein*. London: Routledge.

Malcolm, N. 1986. *Nothing is Hidden*. Oxford: Blackwell.

Mounce, H. O. 1981. *Wittgenstein's Tractatus: An Introduction*. Oxford: Blackwell.

Pears, D. 1987. *The False Prison, Vol. I*. Oxford: Clarendon Press.

Schroeder, S. 2005. *Wittgenstein: The Way out of the Fly-Bottle*. Cambridge: Polity.

Schulte, J. 1992. *Wittgenstein: An Introduction*. New York: SUNY Press.

5

Martin Heidegger
Being and Time

Charles Guignon

There seems to be agreement even among people who do not read Heidegger that *Being and Time* is one of the most important philosophical works of the twentieth century. Published in 1927 when Heidegger was thirty-six years old, the book represents an intensive effort to bring together a number of seemingly conflicting intellectual traditions, including, among others, those of Aristotle, St Paul, St Augustine, Luther, Kant, Hegel, Kierkegaard, Nietzsche, Bergson and Husserl. *Being and Time* can be read as a response to the domination of the theory of knowledge in modern philosophy since Descartes (Guignon 1983). While the most influential thinkers in Germany at the time, the neo-Kantians and positivists, were trying to give an account of how we come to know the world, Heidegger set aside questions about knowledge and turned directly to an examination of the Being of entities.

Moreover, as the title of the book shows, the account of Being presented there stands in stark opposition to one of the central assumptions of mainstream Western philosophy: the assumption that Being must be thought of as something permanent and unchanging. Whereas most philosophers since Plato have assumed that the Being of anything must be understood in terms of what is eternal and fixed (Forms, essences, scientific laws, etc.), Heidegger suggests that Being is temporal unfolding; indeed, it is time itself. As Heidegger only finished half of *Being and Time*, we cannot be sure how he envisaged the final connection between Being and time. But the parts of the book that were published contain some of the most careful, insightful and original reflections on human existence and our understanding of Being ever written.

The question of Being

Being and Time begins with a question that sounds very strange to our ears: what is the meaning of Being? Heidegger tells us that this is an ancient and venerable question in the history of philosophy, the leading question of that branch of metaphysics called *ontology*. It is the question that provided the stimulus for the work of Plato and Aristotle, and, in Heidegger's view, it remains central to the thought of all philosophers whether they recognize that or not. What does this "question of Being" mean?

To answer this, we shall need to get clear about some of the technical terminology Heidegger employs. The first word to clarify is the term typically translated as "beings" or "entities".[1] As the German word *Seiende* indicates, this term refers to anything of which we can say that "it is" in any sense; for example, there *are* rocks and squirrels, and Sherlock Holmes *is* a fictional character, as *is* Santa Claus. Symphonies, landscapes, thoughts, numbers, people, love, historical events: all of these *are* in some sense. The aim of this book is to find out in *what* sense we can say that they *are*. It is helpful to know that *Seiende*, although translated as "beings" or "entities", is singular, not plural; it is probably best translated as "what-is". Heidegger holds that, in addition to examining beings to discern their properties, we can consider in what respect these entities *are* what they are. In what sense are they "real" or existent? What is it to say *that* they exist (their "existence") and in *what* does their being consist (their "essence")? Heidegger constantly reminds us that Being is always the Being of what-is; it is not something different from beings, floating above them or underlying them (as God or Plato's Forms are supposed to do), but is rather that *in* beings that determines *that* they are and *what* they are. Using this terminology, then, we can ask: what *is it to be* a rock (or a hammer or Sherlock Holmes or the number 7 or the Battle of Little Big Horn or justice or the Easter Bunny)? What is the *Being* of such things? And what is the Being of *anything*? To ask these questions is to engage in ontology.

It might seem at first that such questions will be easy to answer. We today tend to assume that everything that exists must be a material substance that is continuously present in space through time. So rocks and hammers are *real*, we think, because they are tangible and visible and clearly endure through time, whereas Sherlock Holmes is *not* real because he has none of these features. But Heidegger suspects that it is precisely the aura of *self-evidence* surrounding such a response that shows that we in the modern world have arrived at an uncritical set of assumptions about Being, presuppositions we do not even recognize as such. When we look at the views about Being that have arisen at various times in history, we find that they generally have been variations on a particular conception of the Being of entities that arose around the time of Plato: the assumption that Being is defined by enduring presence. This assumption continues to be taken as self-evident throughout the history of mainstream Western thought, as we can see in Descartes's claim in his second *Meditation* that what defines the essential being of a piece of wax is that which remains constant through change. Such an assumption is the source of the modern idea that the Being of a human being must consist in something that remains constant through change: initially identified as the mind, where mind is understood as the immortal soul, and more recently pictured as the physical being of humans regarded as organisms in a natural environment. Because what endures through change is called "substance" in the Western tradition (that which stands under, what underlies), we can say that Western thinkers have generally supposed that Being must be understood in terms of substances with attributes.

But how evident is this assumption about the Being of what-is? It seems to make sense for rocks and other physical objects, but for other things it is not at all helpful. How does the substantialist conception of Being help us understand a historical event such as the First World War? Does that war continue to exist? What was its substance? Consider such beings as justice, love, beauty and hatred. Do these have a substance? Do they occupy space? Yet surely love exists! And what are fictional beings on this view? What are numbers? Symphonies? Even humans do not seem to be adequately captured by identifying some *substance* that makes them up. We can see the tendency to suppose that anything that exists must be a substance in "reductionist" characterizations of things; think, for example, of the claim that music is "just" vibrations in the air or that love is "nothing but" hormones and neural discharges. Such claims show that when it is hard to find a substance referred to by a noun, it is tempting to suppose that talk about beings of a non-substantial sort must be reduced to talk about physical objects and their causal interactions. But reductionisms of this sort can begin to look very contrived. Moreover, when we look back to some pre-Platonic philosophers (e.g. Heraclitus) or at non-Western thinkers (e.g. Buddhists), we find that the substance ontology simply has no role to play in their thought. On reflection, the substance ontology we have inherited from the tradition comes to appear as an ungrounded assumption of "Platonism", the one-sided and distortive outlook peculiar to mainstream Western thought.

So Heidegger's project is to rethink the question of Being, asking once again: what do we mean when we talk about the "Being" of anything? But note how, in this formulation of the question, *we* have become implicated in the content of the question. Put this way, the question is about *our* sense of reality, that is, it asks about how things show up as existing or not existing *for us*. What Heidegger has done is to shift the questioning from ontology *per se* (What is it to be?) to a question about how *we* encounter or gain access to entities in their Being (How do we come to take things *as* being such-and-such?). The shift in questioning indicates that we need to see how entities enter into our intelligibility: how they are accessed by us. This more basic enquiry into the conditions for the possibility of intelligibility is called *fundamental ontology*, and it makes up the core project of *Being and Time* (see Carman 2003). What it asks are two related questions: what must entities be like such that they can enter into our understanding in the ways they do; and what must we be like such that we can understand what entities of various types are? This second question, obviously, requires a full account of what we are – an account of the *Being of humans* (or *Dasein*, as Heidegger calls human being) – in so far as we can access, encounter and comprehend entities *as* Being such and such. In other words, the project of fundamental ontology must start with an analysis of human existence, an "analytic of *Dasein*" or "existential analytic", aimed at showing those essential structures of human existence that make it possible for us to grasp beings *as* what they are. Only when we have clarified our own Being as entities who can understand anything, Heidegger claims, will we have a frame of reference or "horizon" for thinking about the Being of entities in general.

In the first sections of *Being and Time*, Heidegger gives us reasons to think that we *can* undertake the project of fundamental ontology. Our attempt to answer the question of Being is made possible by the fact that, as agents in an everyday practical lifeworld, we *always already* have at least some "vague average understanding of Being". Through our dealings with furniture, for example, we already know what a chair *is*, even though we would be hard put to give a precise definition of the word "chair". Our sense of reality, as well as our sense of who and what we are, is familiar to us because it is embodied in our practical *comportments* towards things as we move around in the world. *Being and Time* will attempt to make this tacit background of understanding explicit through careful description (or *phenomenology*) of how things show up in our pre-theoretical experience. Because the attempt to articulate our ordinary "pre-understanding" of Being is interpretive, the method will also be interpretive or *hermeneutic*, that is, it involves interpreting the meaning of Being of particular entities in the light of a prior grasp of what it is to be and then revising the initial understanding of Being in the light of the findings of that interpretation. Due to the interpretive and open-ended hermeneutic nature of the enquiry, Heidegger tells us, addressing the question of Being will be a dynamic, ongoing process rather than the presentation of a systematic theory imparted in a set of propositions.

Being-in-the-world

In order to avoid unreflectively slipping into the standard, most widely accepted ways of thinking about humans – for example, as "minds" or "bodies" or some combination of the two – Heidegger sets out to describe human existence as it shows up in the midst of such pre-theoretical everyday activities as making something in a workshop. Activities of this sort have the character of what Heidegger calls "being-in-the-world". The expression "being-in-the-world" is hyphenated (it is one word in German) because it expresses a "unitary concept" that cannot be understood in terms of a relationship between a self and the constituents of the physical world. Heidegger says that the word "in" in this expression is used not in the spatial sense of being *contained in* (as a knife is in a sheath), but in the existential sense of being *involved* in …, the sense implied in such expressions as being "in the army" or being "in love". And the word "world" should be understood not as the totality of what is on the planet earth, but in the existential sense implied by such expressions as "the world of theatre" or being a "man of the world" (see Dreyfus 1991). For the most part in our everyday practical lives, our Being is characterized by being-in-the-world in the sense that we are absorbed or engrossed in handling familiar equipment in such a way that there is no way to drive in a wedge between a "self" component and the entities we find around us.

Heidegger supports this conception of everydayness by presenting a description of ordinary activity in a workshop. When everything is running smoothly in dealing with some project – Heidegger considers nailing boards together as part of a woodworking project – we do not usually experience a clear separation of self and things. On the contrary, as I hammer away in the workshop, my skilful comportment flows into and through the equipment at hand – workbench, tools, lighting and so forth – while the equipment shows up as meaningful and in motion in relation to my project. What is given in such cases is a totality of meaningful equipment as it comes alive and melds into my activity. As Heidegger says, "there 'is' no such thing as *an* equipment. To the Being of any equipment there always belongs a totality of equipment" (BT: 97). The Being of equipment in such a workshop is called "ready-to-hand" or "handy" in relation to certain purposes. On Heidegger's account, it would be wrong to suppose that the equipmental character of the ready-to-hand should be thought of in terms of a "subjective colouring" superimposed over antecedently given objects. On the contrary, we have every reason to assert, and no reason to deny, that this holistic and dynamic way of Being of equipment in use is the way things really *are* in concrete life-situations.

If reality at the deepest level is ready-to-hand, then we should ask: why does the philosophical tradition tend to assume that reality should be understood as a collection of objects that just occur in space and time – what Heidegger calls the "present-at-hand"? The answer is that, because philosophy starts in the kind of "wonder" that makes one step back and objectively look at things, philosophers have always tended to focus on how entities show up when one adopts the detached standpoint of cool and disinterested observation and reflection. The objective standpoint emerges when there has been a "changeover" in one's being-in-the-world. It can occur, for example, when there is a breakdown in the equipment that is used in the workshop: when for example, the head falls off the hammer or a nail gets bent. When such a changeover occurs, things are momentarily frozen; they show up as mere things "on hand", occurrent objects, with no inbuilt meanings or function. Forced to step back from our activities, we look around to see how to fix the problem. If the problem cannot be fixed, then we find ourselves just staring at things that present themselves to us as meaningless, only contingently related objects in a space–time coordinate system. Heidegger's interesting suggestion is that philosophy traditionally has started from a condition of changeover and breakdown in which things show up in a specialized way that does not reflect their most "primordial" way of Being. In other words, theoretical reflection distorts. To back up the claim that the ready-to-hand is more primordial than the present-at-hand, Heidegger tries to show that present-at-hand things (e.g. pieces of metal and wood) are discovered only derivatively through the breakdown of ready-to-hand equipment (e.g. the hammer that was hammering). It follows, if Heidegger is right, that what philosophers and scientists have taken as the most fundamental way of Being of things – namely, brute objectivity – is in fact derivative from a more fundamental way of Being they never notice.

Heidegger's account of being-in-the-world places special emphasis on the way things in the world generally show up as part of a shared "we-world". The world presents itself as a world we have in common, and this is the case because we, in the very core of our Being, are what Heidegger calls "co-being" or "being-with". To be human is to be initiated into a familiar cultural context in such a way that one initially and almost always encounters things as "one" or "anyone" does. "We take pleasure and enjoy ourselves as *one* takes pleasure; we read, see and judge about literature as *they* see and judge; likewise … we find 'shocking' what *one* finds shocking" (BT: 164). Humans are, in John Haugeland's words, "censorious conformists" (Haugeland 1982). They can *be* human in a recognizable sense only if they are initiated into the norms and conventions that regulate the practices of a social group. And because such attunement to shared practices makes human existence possible, people tend to censor each other in their attuned activities, constantly nudging each other so that no one gets out of line. Heidegger describes this behaviour as the "dictatorship of the they", a characterization that indicates the role of social involvement in levelling down all possibilities of existence to the lowest common denominator. At the same time, however, Heidegger emphasizes that there is no exit from the all-pervasive "being-with" of communal existence. The they or anyone, he says, is an *existentiale* or essential structure of human existence, and so it *"belongs to Dasein's essential constitution"* (BT: 167). For this reason, Dasein initially and generally *is* the they. As the ultimate source of all possibilities of self-interpretation and self-evaluation, "the they itself articulates the referential context of significance" that makes up the worldhood of the world. Even authentic existence, as a possible way of Being for *Dasein*, must be understood as a specialized *"modification of the they – of the they as an essential existentiale"* (BT: 167–8).

The description of being-in-the-world shows that *Dasein* should be regarded not as one item among others *in* a world, but rather as the Being of a *there* (the word *"Dasein"* literally means "being-there") or a "clearing" through which entities can show up in determinate ways as ready-to-hand *or* as present-at-hand. This is surely one of the most fundamental and potentially confusing claims in all Heidegger's writing. His claim is that instead of thinking of humans as individuals, persons, selves or subjects, or even as collectives, we should think of human existence as the emergence of an open "space of meaning" (Crowell 2001) in virtue of which anything, including persons and social systems, can show up *as* counting or mattering in some way. The human, then, is a *disclosure* or *disclosedness* in the light of which anything, including "selves" and "persons", can be *discovered* as entities of a particular sort.

In the attempt to identify the essential structures that make such a "disclosedness" possible, Heidegger points out three constitutive structures of the "there". First, to be human is always to have a dimension of *thrownness* pervading one's Being; to be human is to be thrown into the midst of a world in such a way that one is always already underway in undertaking projects and being part of a wider context of meaning. This thrownness or situatedness defines one's *facticity* and it becomes manifest in one's *moods*. Secondly, to be human is to have some *understanding*, where this refers to the ongoing activity of projecting outwards into an open range of possibilities for action. The specific possibilities we have before us are made accessible by our thrownness into a specific cultural and historical context and are called "possibilities" in the sense that humans can and always do *choose* the roles and lifestyles they adopt, even when they do so in the "privative" mode of just going along with the crowd. Thirdly, Heidegger says that *Dasein* is always *discursive* in the sense of articulating the world in terms of the schema (or *logos*) of a shared, public language. The discursive ordering of things lays out the pattern of synthesis and differentiation characteristic of the public world. This pattern provides the resources of intelligibility for the social agent and is sustained by the concrete ways of "addressing" things that make up our utterances and dealings with things.

Heidegger concludes his discussion of being-in-the-world by claiming that these three constitutive dimensions of disclosedness make up the unified tripartite structure that is definitive of *Dasein*'s Being. As thrown, *Dasein* is *already in* a meaningful context that shapes its possibilities in advance. As understanding, *Dasein* projects possibilities into the future and so is, *as* these possibilities, always *ahead of itself*. And as discursivity, *Dasein* is caught up *in the midst of beings*, always articulating and engaging them in various ways. This tripartite structure makes up the phenomenon Heidegger calls "care", and care turns out to be the Being of *Dasein*. This is what Heidegger means when he says that the Being of *Dasein* is "ahead-of-itself-Being-already-in-(the-world) as Being-amidst (entities encountered within-the-world)" (BT: 237, translation modified; the hyphens show that this is a unitary phenomenon with three dimensions).

The definition of the Being of *Dasein* as care confirms the formal provisional suggestion Heidegger proposes concerning *Dasein*'s Being in Section 4 of the Introduction to *Being and Time* (BT: 32–5). There he says that *Dasein* is the entity whose Being is *in question* or *at issue* for it. *Dasein cares* about what it is; it cares about how its life is going and how it will go right up to the end. Because it cares about its Being, it has always taken some *stand* on itself; it takes up possibilities of Being and enacts them in undertaking its life as a whole. This stand is called "understanding". The term "existence", Heidegger tells us, will be used in the technical sense to refer to *Dasein*'s *being towards* as a projection towards the fulfilment of its life: "The Being towards which Dasein can comport itself in one way or another, and always does comport itself one way or another, we call '*existence*' [*Existenz*]" (BT: 32). In contrast, the term "essence" will be used to refer to the *task Dasein* has as an entity that cares about itself: that "it has its Being as its own to be" (BT: 32–3, translation modified). We can now see that the characterization of *Dasein* as care developed in the first division of *Being and Time* fills out the initial characterization of *Dasein* in the Introduction. What defines our Being as humans is a "relationship-of-Being" in which we undertake projects in terms of the context into which we are thrown by acting in the present. As we shall see, this tripartite structure of *Dasein*'s Being paves the way for seeing human existence as temporality.

Falling, anxiety, death and authenticity

Before turning to the treatment of temporality in the second division of *Being and Time*, however, we need to explicate Heidegger's conception of authenticity. At the end of his discussion of being-in-the-world, Heidegger points out that our absorption in mundane affairs has a tendency to cover over or conceal an aspect of life that is just as crucial to who we are as is being-in-the-world. As we have seen, it is characteristic of the "dictatorship of the they" that we have an inveterate tendency to fall into step with the crowd, doing what one does according to the norms and standards of the social world. This falling prey to the anyone's concerns is coupled with a pervasive temptation to let ourselves be totally engrossed in the chores and preoccupations we find around us. We get sucked into what Heidegger calls the "movement of falling" (BT: 221). Getting entangled in the busy-ness of everyday affairs, we plunge into the turbulence of constant frenzied activity, we are benumbed by the demands of the day, while at the same time we are tranquillized by the assumption that we are living well because we are "doing what one does" (BT: 222–3). In all this, we become *alienated* from our own selves; we are adrift, lacking any coherent focus or steadfastness, caught up in what Erich Fromm calls "automaton conformism" (1994).

Heidegger suggests that the very intensity of the "falling" that is characteristic of everydayness suggests that it is motivated by an unconscious desire to avoid facing up to something, something we find deeply unsettling and threatening. Certainly it is true that falling into everyday busy-ness is unavoidable if we are to be able to function in the world. But in its extreme forms, it seems that it amounts to a sort of *fleeing* or *evasion*; we are using the demands of everydayness as an excuse to run away from something we find threatening and do not want to face. How do we find out what it is we find so threatening? The answer is given by a "basic mood" that underlies all life and is always just below the surface: the mood of *anxiety*. When we experience anxiety, Heidegger claims, we are gaining access to something that is fundamental to the human condition. In the experience of anxiety, all the daily rituals I cling to for assurance that my life "adds up" now seem insignificant; my possessions no longer assure me that I am living well and my social connections no longer buoy me up and guarantee that I am a success. What I encounter in anxiety is the fact that worldly things cannot provide a ground for my existence and, as a result, I am brought face to face with my own being-in-the-world as something I have to realize and ground by myself. In other words, in anxiety I come to see that this is my life to live, and that nothing outside me can prove that I am doing it well. In anxiety, Heidegger says, *Dasein* encounters itself as "*individualized, pure, and thrown*" (BT: 233).

The experience of anxiety is tied into a recognition of one's "being-towards-death". When Heidegger says that anxiety is always anxious in the face of one's own death, his point is not that we have a fear of growing old or getting hit by a bus. On the contrary, the point is that, in confronting death, we discover that our lives have the structure of a forward-moving unfolding that, as finite, is constantly pervaded by the possibility of no more possibilities. Experiencing one's relationship to death pulls one back from the swirl of involvements in the world and forces one to confront the fact that one's life is going somewhere and will not go on forever.

The recognition of one's own being-towards-death can transform the way a person lives. If you face up to your mortality with courage and clear-sightedness, you can undertake the project of living your life as a whole in a way that is focused and coherent. You then realize your life by "coming into your own", that is, by truly *being* the finite entity you always already are. Such a life, Heidegger says, is *authentic*. To understand what this word means, we need to see that "authenticity" is a translation of the German word *Eigentlichkeit*, which comes from the stem meaning "own". To say that one is authentic, then, is to say that one is *owning up to* one's Being in the sense of actually and fully *being* the unified thrown projection one actually is. To say that one is *inauthentic*, on the other hand, is to say that one is turned away from one's true Being as an instance of *Dasein*; that one's Being is getting covered up and concealed; that one is, in short, *unowned* or *disowned*.

Heidegger develops this conception of authenticity further by examining what he refers to as the "call of conscience". We know what it is like to feel the pangs of conscience when we have done something wrong. This is the source of familiar guilt feelings, and the experience generally impels us to make amends for what we have done. But in talking about the call of conscience, Heidegger is talking about something deeper, more "primordial", than this familiar phenomenon. What he has in mind is what might be called *existential* conscience and guilt. As an existential phenomenon, the call of conscience does not tell us about any particular wrongdoing we need to remedy. Instead, it tells us *nothing*. That is to say, the call tells us that there is nothing at the source or ground of our Being that could guarantee us that we are on the right track, and nothing at the end of the journey of our lives that can assure us that we have lived properly. "Existential guilt" here means that our Being is bordered on all sides by *nothingness*. The basic message imparted by the "silent call" of conscience and the experience of guilt is that, although we are indebted to the world for all our possibilities of Being, nothing in those worldly possibilities can ground our existence. When we grasp the call of conscience, we see that we have to face up to our responsibility for our own lives. As in the case of anxiety, we find ourselves alone, thrown on to ourselves, with no external supports or justifications.

To live authentically, then, is to (i) direct oneself towards the fulfilment of one's own life story with clarity, integrity and steadfastness, and (ii) to take responsibility for what one's own life is adding up to, resolutely holding to one's own chosen life-defining commitments by carrying forwards (or "repeating") what one has been in one's undertakings. Such a life fulfils the distinctive possibility of Being of *Dasein*, namely, that it is a temporal unfolding that can be characterized by continuity, wholeness and coherence. Such a life realizes what

Heidegger calls "authentic temporality". It is on the basis of this conception of original temporality that Heidegger will work out his account of temporality as the underlying meaning and ground of human existence.

Temporality and historicity

The account of "primordial temporality" is one of the most innovative parts of *Being and Time*. Its claim is that both the time of physics (that is, the conception of time as an endless series of "nows" following one after another) and the everyday experience of time as a time of works and days are derived from a more fundamental sort of human temporality that has for the most part been unnoticed in the history of philosophy. Yet for all its originality and suggestiveness, the discussion of time remains one of the most difficult parts of *Being and Time*. The topic of time is introduced after the completion of the characterization of *Dasein*'s "potentiality-for-being" as an authentic individual. Heidegger asks, "What makes this authentic being-a-whole of Dasein possible with regard to the unity of its articulated structural whole?" (BT: 372). The answer to this question is given in terms of what he calls the "ecstasies" of *Dasein*'s Being (the word "ecstasy" comes from the Latin *ex* and *stasis*, meaning "standing outside [oneself]" or "being outside"). In other words, the fact that *Dasein* has the potentiality to be authentic – the fact that *Dasein can* live a life characterized by the constancy, steadfastness and coherence that constitutes wholeness – shows that *Dasein* is, at the deepest level, a unified temporal "happening" or "movement" with three temporal "ecstasies".

This means, first, that as being-towards-death, "Dasein *can, indeed,* come towards itself in its ownmost possibility" (BT: 372). For example, as a teacher I am coming towards the realization or definition of my life as *being* a teacher, and in doing so I am defining one aspect of my Being as a whole. *Dasein* has "coming towards" (*zu-kommen*) as an essential ex-stasis ("standing outward") of its Being, and this coming towards makes up the essential structure of *futurity* (-*Zukünftigkeit*) that is definitive of *Dasein* as a forward-directed happening. Secondly, to be human is to be *thrown* on to one's lack of a basis and one's "*being ... as [one] already was*" (BT: 373). The ex-stasis of *having-been* is opened up and given meaning by the life-defining projects one takes over as being-towards the future. In my own case, this means that nothing has determined that I *ought* to be a teacher and no worldly approbation ensures that I was right to have chosen this possibility. Only my resolute carrying forwards of the possibility gives it whatever ground it has. Finally, one's futural having-been makes it possible to address oneself to the matters that arise in the present. *Dasein*'s Being is characterized by the *making-present* of "taking action" in the concrete situation. So my

interactions with students and colleagues and my comportment towards class-
rooms and books make concrete my being as a thrown projection.

What makes the account of temporality difficult to grasp is that Heidegger
insists that these temporal ecstasies should not be thought of as attributes of
Dasein, as if *Dasein* were a thing that happened to have temporal properties. All
one can say is that "temporality temporalizes itself": temporality "is not",
Heidegger says, that is, it is not a thing about which one can say that it is. Instead,
it *temporalizes* itself (the German words literally mean it "brings itself to fruition") (BT: 377). The implication seems to be that *primordial time* (in a special
sense often marked by the Latinate word *Temporalität*) is in some sense prior to
and definitive of human existence: humans *are* only by virtue of the temporalizing
of original temporality. Needless to say, such an idea goes beyond what most
people can comprehend. Towards the end of *Being and Time*, Heidegger tries to
show that the lived time of everyday life ("now", "earlier", "later", etc.) is derived
from this primordial time, and that the time of physics (the so-called "arrow of
time") is in turn derived from lived time. Recently, William Blattner (1999) has
presented a convincing argument to show that this attempt to derive familiar
forms of time from a "primordial time" is incoherent, since primordial time has
no succession (i.e. futurity is not "after" having-been and making-present, and
having-been is not "earlier than" or "prior to" futurity). So it seems that "primordial temporality" can never account for the obvious fact that lived time and physical time have sequence and succession.

Although the jury is still out on Heidegger's claims about temporality, there
is no doubt that his accounts of historicity and history in general are extremely
insightful and fertile. The discussion of historicity is introduced with the assertion that historicity "is just a more concrete working out of [*Dasein*'s] temporality" (BT: 434). The implication is that the earlier account of temporality was
rather formal and empty to the extent that it did not show us how our concrete
ways of taking over possibilities of Being and making something of them take
place. The description of historicity spells out how a life "happening" (*Geschehen*)
comes to have the form of a coherent life story or history (the German word
Geschichte, which Heidegger sees as cognate with *Geschehen*, can mean either
"story" or "history"). To show how life is knitted together into a meaningful
story, Heidegger examines the historicity (*Geschichtlichkeit*) of life.

The discussion of historicity is introduced with the observation that up to this
point in the book all the emphasis has been on authentic *Dasein*'s futural mode
of being-towards-death. If *Dasein* is a happening that is "stretched out between
birth and death", however, then we need to account for *Dasein*'s *birth*, where this
refers to the *origins* of the possibilities of self-understanding that provide the
content for a life story. In considering the origin of possibilities, Heidegger once

again reminds us that all of *Dasein*'s possibilities come from the "they" or "anyone": "for the most part the self is lost in the 'they'", he writes; "It understands itself in terms of those possibilities of existence which 'circulate' in the 'average' public way of interpreting Dasein today" (BT: 435). As representatives of the they, we absorb the "tradition" and pick up whatever fads and outlooks are popular today. We are, for the most part, censorious conformists.

But the discussion of historicity marks a shift in the characterization of the reservoir of possibilities into which *Dasein* first grows. We are now told that there is a distinctive way that *Dasein* can absorb the interpretations that have been handed down in its historical culture. Instead of merely drifting along with the crowd, *Dasein* can encounter its historical context as a *heritage*. What this means is that a person can stop just doing what everyone else is doing and can come to grasp his or her historical inheritance as containing deep, meaningful projects that define what is truly worthwhile in life. In authentic historicity, Heidegger says, "every accidental and 'provisional' possibility [is] driven out" (BT: 435), and one becomes focused and "simplified" in one's wholehearted commitment to a "goal" that defines one's Being.

In being simplified, clear-sighted and focused, one comes to have a defining content for one's life, a coherent direction drawn from the aims of one's historical context. A focused life story has the form of what is called *fate*. But fate is not a private affair. On the contrary, to live one's life as a fate is also to see that one's life is inextricably bound up with the lives of others, the unfolding story of "a community, of a people" (BT: 436). Authentic historicity, in living out a shared *destiny* with others, is lived "in communicating and struggling" with the defining issues of one's "world-historical … Situation" (BT: 442) as those issues present themselves to one's "generation". To achieve authentic historicity, according to this account, is to adopt exemplary role models from the past and to carry forwards what they set out to accomplish: it is to "choose [one's] hero" and follow in the footsteps of that which can be repeated (BT: 437). It involves "loyalty" and "reverence" for "the sole authority which a free existing can have … the repeatable possibilities of existence" (BT: 443). As should be evident from these lines from the text, Heidegger's *Being and Time* culminates with a stirring exhortation to solidarity and activism on behalf of one's community.

Truth and reality

Two of the most thought-provoking ideas in *Being and Time* are Heidegger's distinctive construal of the notion of truth and his position on the realism–anti-realism debate. As we have seen, Heidegger characterizes human existence or *Dasein* as *care*: to be human is to be a being for whom things matter in some way or other, for whom things show up *as* such and such (as hammers or beautiful sunsets or threats) because their lives are *at issue*. Because care is definitive of human existence, *Dasein* is said to be a *clearing* or *disclosedness*, that is, a "there" or space of meaning in virtue of which entities of various sorts can come to show up *as* the beings they are. In so far as the "*as*-structure" of entities defines the *Being* of those entities, it is evident that Heidegger holds that human agency (the clearing or *Lichtung* that humans are) determines the Being of the entities that show up in a world. So, for example, the Being of a hammer is defined by the uses to which hammers are put by agents engaged in workshops and work sites. Here, the Being is the *use* to which the equipment is (or can be) put in relation to human forms of life. And, in the same way, a brute, meaningless thing found in one's backyard has the mode of Being of the present-at-hand precisely because there is (presently, at least) no context of intelligibility or frame of reference that lets it show up as significant in our world. On this view, even our own identities as students, teachers, home craftsmen and so forth are defined by the background of intelligibility that is opened up by the shared practices definitive of a particular historical community. In a preliterate culture, for instance, there could be neither books nor readers, and I could not exist *as* the bookish educator I am.

As we saw earlier, this conception of *Dasein* as a clearing makes it possible for Heidegger to distinguish between *disclosedness*, which refers to the opening up or illuminating of things in general, and *discovering* or *uncovering*, which is the concrete way some entities come to show up within a pregiven context of intelligibility. So, for example, a simple piece of equipment such as a needle-threader can present itself as something to be used for threading needles only in a world in which there are practices of sewing with needles that are not easy to thread. This context of intelligibility making possible the practice of sewing defines the realm of *disclosedness* in which seamstresses, needles, cloth, thread and so forth can show up *as* equipment for sewing. In contrast, *discovering* refers to the process by which particular entities of some sort comes to show up *as* such and such in a world, for example, the way this strangely shaped item becomes manifest as a needle-threader by being used to thread a needle.

Heidegger's conception of disclosedness leads to his view of *truth*. In §44 of *Being and Time*, he reflects on the traditional conception of truth as a correspondence between our thoughts, beliefs or propositional states generally (e.g. thinking or saying, "The picture in the other room is askew") and a fact or state of affairs in the world (e.g. the slightly tilted picture in the other room). According to this traditional account of truth, the assertion "The picture on the wall is askew" is true just in case the picture actually is askew. Such a correspondence view of truth is not wrong, in Heidegger's view. But to fully grasp what it means, he claims, we must look at what is needed for such true assertions to be possible. Making a true assertion is a matter of discovering or uncovering some entity or entities as being such and such. True assertion lets something show forth *as* what it is. But in order for that to happen, we must live in a world where there are established practices for uttering assertions, forming beliefs, knowing how to confirm claims, knowing what counts as a "picture" and being "askew" and so forth. In other words, truth in the traditional sense of correspondence is possible as a human mode of comportment only if there is a background of intelligibility in which identifications, ascertainments and communication are possible.

It is this background of intelligibility Heidegger calls "disclosedness". The claim is that any *discovering* of entities, including the specific form of discovering characteristic of true assertion-making, depends on a prior *disclosure* of a space of intelligibility or clearing that lets things appear in some determinate way or other. Such a disclosure can be thought of as an *unconcealing*, in the sense that it lets things come out of concealment and into the light. So understood, the notion of disclosedness has the same connotation as the ancient Greek word for truth, *alethēia*, which comes from the stems *a-* (meaning "not") and *lētheia* (as in the river *Lethe*, meaning "forgetfulness" or "concealment"). It appears, then, that the ancient and original understanding of truth as "unconcealment" or "disclosedness" should be taken as truth in its most basic and originative sense. Given this conception of truth, truth is an event – the lighting of a world out of darkness and concealment – which makes it possible for things to show up so that any propositions can count as true. *Dasein*, as the "being of a there", is the condition for anything making sense or counting as real.

In the light of this conception of truth as a space of intelligibility, we can see why Heidegger says that:

> Newton's laws, the principle of contradiction, any truth whatsoever – these are true only as long as Dasein *is*. Before there was any Dasein, there was no truth; nor will there be any after Dasein is no more. … Before Newton's laws were discovered, they were not "true;" it does not follow that they were false. (BT: 269)

This surprising claim (one is tempted to say "You mean there were no dinosaurs before there were humans?") has to be understood in the entire context of Heidegger's thought. The claim is not that human thinking brings entities into existence, but that it is only where things can matter in some way or other, where there are capacities for discernment, inference, differentiation and synthesis, that anything can stand out as counting as, say, a dinosaur. The fact that something can show up for us as a dinosaur means that identifying and talking about something as a dinosaur depends on the prior opening of a space of intelligibility in which such identifications and talk make sense. From this it follows that we have no way to gain access to things as they *really* are *in themselves*, independent of human ways of taking things.

Heidegger's conception of the priority of disclosedness over any discovery of entities also has consequences for the traditional debate about realism and anti-realism. In approaching this issue, Heidegger asks about the assumptions underlying the debate. Given the traditional conception of our human predicament we have inherited from Descartes, it is natural to assume that, at a most basic level, humans are subjects or minds collecting bits of data and forming beliefs about the world. Set over against us and existing outside our minds is a world of medium-sized material objects with properties of various sorts. The traditional *realist* view holds that: (i) those objects and properties really do have a determinate Being independent of our thought and practices; and (ii) we can know those objects and their properties as they are *in themselves*. The traditional alternative to realism, called "idealism", holds that what we encounter as real, independently existing objects are actually products of our own minds, with no mind-independent features that can be encountered or known. Idealism therefore claims that: (i) objects and their properties have no determinate Being independent of our thought and practices; and/or (ii) we can never know reality as it is in itself, since reality is always in some crucial sense mind-dependent.

Heidegger's way of dealing with the realism–anti-realism debate is to challenge the assumption it rests on, namely, the assumption that our most basic condition as humans is to be minds or fields of consciousness set over against and distinct from a collection of objects. As we have seen, Heidegger describes *Dasein* as a being that is already *outside* itself, *ex-sisting* in the sense of being always already engaged with things and ahead of itself in projecting an open range of possibilities of Being. In this "being already outside", *Dasein* is a clearing or open space through which anything can show up. Thus, it is only because modern Western humanity exists in the mode of scientific research, taking what shows up *as* physical objects in causal interactions, that entities can appear on the scene as the entities they are interpreted as being in scientific research. If there were no human interest and practices of the sort that make up science, or if there were no humans at all, then there would be no entities of the sort projected by modern science. What this account of the reality of entities shows is that the *Being* of entities is inseparable from the practices and ways of taking things of *Dasein*. In other words, the Being of entities is a function of their being understood in some way or other.

Does this mean that Heidegger is an idealist or anti-realist? Well, that depends on how one defines these terms. If idealism is the view that reality exists only in the mind, or that entities as they are in themselves are unknowable to us, then

Heidegger is not an idealist, for his claim is that entities *are* and that *Dasein* it-self *is* only when thrown into the midst of entities and world. So entities as we encounter them are, so to speak, as real as anything can get. But if Heidegger is not exactly an idealist or anti-realist, neither is he a realist in the ordinary sense. For his claim is that anything at all can show up *as* existing in some way only if there is a world or disclosedness in which things can show up, a world that is inseparable from *Dasein*. So the idea of "what things are really like in themselves, independent of any *Dasein*" is in fact an incoherent notion, like the idea of the colour things would be if there could never be light in the universe.

These observations help explain what Heidegger means when he says: "Of course only as long as Dasein *is* (that is, as long as [there is] an understanding of Being ...), 'is there' Being. When Dasein does not exist, 'independence' 'is' not either, nor 'is' the 'in-itself'" (BT: 255). Ontological characteristics of things such as "independence" and "is-ness" are possible only if there is the frame of reference or understanding of Being in terms of which such traits can show up at all. For this reason, Heidegger can say that "Being (not entities) is dependent upon the under-standing of Being; that is to say, Reality (not the real) is dependent upon care" (BT: 255). Only where there are beings for whom it makes a difference that things are can we make sense of the idea of an "ontological difference" between Being and entities.

Critical assessments of *Being and Time*

Being and Time immediately came under attack after it appeared, and Heidegger constantly revised his views over the next forty-nine years of his life. Some lines of criticism seem to be deep and insightful. For example, one might claim that the attempt to undercut the realism–anti-realism debate is a "nice dodge" (as they say of politicians today), but not totally convincing. Heidegger seems to want to have it both ways. He wants to talk about *Dasein* as always already out there in the midst of beings in such a way that its own Being as human is unavoidably bound up with its relation to those beings. Yet he also wants to say that nothing can be said about those beings aside from references to how they happen to be taken *as* such and such by *Dasein*. But it seems that questions about the reality of those entities can still be asked. One might ask, for example: what is it about the enti-ties that exist independently of *Dasein* that allows them to be taken *as* the beings they are found to be? Are there any limits, for example, on the things we *call* quarks that justify us in taking them *as* quarks? And if the answer to this is "yes", then what are the features and traits of these entities that enable them to show up in our (scientific) world in the ways they do?

Many astute commentators, especially in France, have criticized Heidegger for not discussing the body, where "body" means not the physical thing Descartes called *res extensa*, but rather the spatially oriented and interactive centre of comportment we experience in our concrete dealings with the world. The claim is that by ignoring the body, Heidegger failed to provide a genuine alternative to Cartesianism's claim that the essence of human being consists in the mind. But it seems that Heidegger could respond to this objection by saying that any attempt to deny one term of a binary opposition just reasserts the validity of the binary opposition, so that any talk about either body or mind will sustain the dualism Heidegger hoped to undercut. It is for this reason that Heidegger attempts in *Being and Time* to characterize the human without bringing in any mentalistic or physicalistic language.

Needless to say, Heidegger's *Being and Time* can be criticized from a number of different angles. The fact that the book has stirred up such heated controversy is part of what makes it one of the most powerful and influential works of modern times. It already has had a huge impact on such intellectual movements as phenomenology, existentialism, hermeneutics and postmodernism, and it will continue to provide fresh ideas for future generations of thinkers who are dissatisfied with the traditional way of looking at things.

Notes

1. All references in parentheses are to *Being and Time* (BT), J. Macquarrie & E. Robinson (trans.) (New York: Harper & Row, 1962).

References

Blattner, W. D. 1999. *Heidegger's Temporal Idealism*. Cambridge: Cambridge University Press.
de Boer, K. 2000. *Thinking in the Light of Time: Heidegger's Encounter with Hegel*. Albany, NY: SUNY Press.
Carman, T. 2003. *Heidegger's Analytic: Interpretation, Discourse, and Authenticity in "Being and Time"*. Cambridge: Cambridge University Press.
Cooper, D. 1996. *Heidegger*. London: Claridge Press.
Crowell, S. G. 2001. *Husserl, Heidegger, and the Space of Meaning: Paths towards Transcendental Phenomenology*. Evanston, IL: Northwestern University Press.
Dreyfus, H. L. 1991. *Being-in-the-World: A Commentary on Heidegger's "Being and Time", Division I*. Cambridge, MA: MIT Press.
Fromm, E. 1994. *Escape from Freedom*. New York: Owl Books.
Guignon, C. (ed.) 1993. *The Cambridge Companion to Heidegger*. Cambridge: Cambridge University Press.

Guignon, C. 1983. *Heidegger and the Problem of Knowledge*. Indianapolis, IN: Hackett.

Haugeland, J. 1982. "Heidegger on Being a Person". *Noûs* **16**: 15–26.

Inwood, M. 1997. *Heidegger*. Oxford: Oxford University Press.

Kisiel, T. 1993. *The Genesis of Heidegger's "Being and Time"*. Berkeley, CA: University of California Press.

Mulhall, S. 1996. *Routledge Philosophy Guidebook to Heidegger and "Being and Time"*. London: Routledge.

Polt, R. 1999. *Heidegger: An Introduction*. London: UCL Press.

Zimmerman, M. E. 1986. *Eclipse of the Self: The Development of Heidegger's Concept of Authenticity*, rev. edn. Athens, OH: Ohio University Press.

6

Rudolf Carnap

The Logical Structure of the World

Thomas Uebel

Rudolf Carnap's first major book, *The Logical Structure of the World* [*Der logische Aufbau der Welt*] (2003a [1928]; hereafter referred to as "*Aufbau*"), is a key work for the understanding of the philosophical movement called "logical positivism" or "logical empiricism". Like this movement it has suffered a protracted period of misinterpretation, but also profited from a recent renewal of interest. Once regarded as the explicitly phenomenalist completion of Wittgenstein's positivistically misunderstood *Tractatus*, it is now recognized as an extremely complex work in its own right that continues to be the focus of intense efforts of re-evaluation and reinterpretation. Here the aim is to abstract as much as possible from the wealth of logical details that make up the *Aufbau* and to uncover the philosophical point of this work and the interpretative debates about it.[1]

Carnap, language constructor: overview of the *Aufbau*

Carnap pursued the aim uncontroversially ascribed to the Vienna Circle – furnishing an account of the nature of scientific knowledge adequate to the then latest advances – and his own, more recently recognized aim – accounting for the possibility of objective knowledge – by developing constructed languages for scientific disciplines. Importantly, Carnap did not seek to defend the knowledge claim of science by analysing the languages that science actually used. Over the course of his long career, Carnap changed his mind about the nature of the languages appropriate to the representation of scientific theories, but not about the philosophical strategy of providing so-called rational reconstructions of the logico-linguistic frameworks of scientific theories (in place of analysing them in their historically given form). Their point lay in the clear exhibition of the meaning and empirical basis of scientific propositions.

The *Aufbau* provides one such partial "constructional" or "constitution system" (in Part IV), which is embedded in turn in a general theory of possible constructional systems (Parts I–III).[2] (Part V discusses the deflationary philosophical consequences of the project.) The title of Carnap's work is thus somewhat misleading. It is not concerned with ontological matters but with the reconstruction of the concepts with which we form knowledge claims about the world, their relation to each other and to the experientially given. Moreover, the aim of rational reconstruction was not to give an accurate picture of the actual cognitive processes of knowledge acquisition, nor even to provide new tools for the practice of science. As Carnap put it in the original Preface, laying a "rational foundation" for the exercise of scientific concepts must be distinguished from investigations of how these concepts have actually been arrived at. (Carnap here drew the methodological distinction later codified by Reichenbach as that between the "context of justification" and the "context of discovery", with philosophy proper being attentive only to the former.)

One leading thought of the theory of constructional systems was that showing that a proposition was meaningful consisted in showing that it stood in a certain logical relation to propositions about the content of an individual's consciousness. In the *Aufbau* Carnap opted for the relation of logical reducibility. According to its model, the scientific picture of the world could be generated by purely logical constructions out of the elements of immediate experience. Importantly, however, Carnap insisted that in this construction one had to proceed purely structurally. The delineation of the conditions of meaningfulness had to abstract from the experiential quality of states of consciousness and the intuitive meaning of the terms involved and only use scientific, that is, relational descriptions of objects and extensional predicates.

The philosophical ground plan of the *Aufbau* must therefore be distinguished from the scientific strategy by which the reconstruction of empirical knowledge was to be effected. Carnap's ground plan consisted in providing a "genealogy of concepts", which related them to a base in the phenomenal given. Once this phenomenalist setting was granted, however, knowledge became itself the object of scientific analysis: the given itself was to receive descriptions of its relational structure. Carnap's genealogy of concepts assigned to each concept a definite place in the hierarchy of the system wherein it was constituted. It is one measure of the complexity of Carnap's project – and one aspect that distinguished the *Aufbau* from Russell's *Our Knowledge of the External World* (1993 [1914]) project – that he sought to do with only one primitive predicate (see below) and held that even sense-data were objects to be constructed from unanalysable whole experiences with the help of logic and that one basic predicate.

Reconstructional choices: the mechanics of the *Aufbau*

Let us now focus on the four important choices that Carnap made in deciding on the form of his constitution system, that is, his constructional language. There is, first, the choice of its object domain, whether it be the physical or the psychological; secondly, the choice of the category of predicates to be used, whether these be relational structural or predicates expressing intrinsic properties; thirdly, the choice of basic predicates within the chosen category; fourthly, the choice of the criterion of adequacy for the reconstruction of empirical knowledge.

The phenomenalist choice of the object domain

In the *Aufbau*, the basic relation holds between experiences of an individual subject. The ultimate basis of scientific theories therefore consists of the experiences of individual investigators. Carnap opted for an "auto-psychological", phenomenalist basis (§64).[3]

What was the status of this option? Most important to Carnap's decision was his desire not only to reflect "the logico-constructional order of the objects [of science] but also their epistemic order" (§64). Carnap spoke explicitly of a "choice" here. Nothing in the "logico-constructional order of objects" forced him to adopt the phenomenalist basis; indeed, several constitution systems with physicalist bases could be devised (§59). Nevertheless, the phenomenalist base was the "natural starting point in the epistemic order of objects" (§66). This, then, was the position of "methodological solipsism": physical objects were constructed from phenomenal ones, other minds from physical objects, and, finally, cultural objects from other minds. Importantly again, this order of epistemic priority was held to be of reconstructive import only and abstracted from real cognitive processes (§54; cf. §50).

Methodological solipsism did not carry metaphysical import: the epistemological reduction was not intended to entail an ontological reduction and therewith idealism, indeed, real solipsism. Carnap's grounds for metaphysical abstinence were what could be called his "intertranslatability thesis" (§57). On pain of the meaninglessness of all physical object discourse, it followed that all physical objects had to be reducible to phenomenal ones, for only if statements about physical objects could be reduced to statements about phenomenal objects could they be verified. Reduction in the opposite direction, of the psychological to the physical domain, could in principle be achieved along two routes: once by considering the phenomenon of psycho-physical correlation, and once by considering the "expression relation" between bodily motions and psychological processes. The first of these routes depended on accepting psycho-physical parallelism as the working hypothesis of the empirical science of psychology, for then every statement about a psychological object became translatable into statements about physical objects (if only in principle because it could not yet be stated to just which physical objects psychological objects are to be reduced). The second way of reducing the psychological to the physical was less hypothetical. Every psychological state of another was held to be recognizable only on the basis of his expressive motions, or reports that served as "indicators" of that psychological state. Every statement about other minds could thus be translated into statements about their indicators, that is, behaviour, and thus all hetero-psychological objects became reducible to physical ones.

Given the intertranslatability thesis, Carnap thought it possible to construct a constitution system of concepts that reflected his conception of epistemic priority without prejudging the ontological issue of phenomenalism versus realism or materialism (§60). Moreover, the constitution system was so designed that scientific assertions concerning the reality or non-reality of objects were at first "bracketed" but later on could themselves be reconstructed within it. According to the conception of epistemic priority adopted in the *Aufbau*, the world of science was recoverable from the resources of individual epistemic subjects alone (§64). The consequent task to render objective what was ultimately subjective fell to the structural method of concept construction (§66).

The structuralist choices of language form

In his choices of language form Carnap took his cue from the perceived fact that science aims to use only relational predicates (§10). Relational descriptions, unlike intrinsic property descriptions, do not make assertions about their objects as isolated individuals, but instead make assertions about them in a network of relations to others. Carnap further narrowed the scientific preference for relational predicates to structure descriptions that "do not even specify the relations themselves which hold between these elements … only the structure of the relation is indicated … by formal properties … without reference to the meaning of the relation" (§11). Structure descriptions feature only logical terms and variables. (A simple example: in a universe containing just one family, consisting of the parents A and B and the children C and D, the relation "father of" can be given as the structure description "(A, C) & (A, D)".)

Carnap's use of structure descriptions represents a critical development of Hilbert's concept of implicit definitions. Following Hilbert's axiomatization of Euclidean geometry, Schlick had championed implicit definitions that laid down "the mutual relations of the primitive concepts [of a theory] as expressed in the axioms" (1985: 36) as fixing the meaning of scientific concepts without reliance on intuition, in terms of their formal relational properties alone. The novelty of Carnap's use of Hilbert's implicit definitions in the context of the *Aufbau* consisted in responding to Frege's criticism that implicit definitions only determined equivalence classes (not individual objects, but only types of objects functionally defined) and his development of definite structural descriptions: they designated one object uniquely, ultimately without any need to specify the domain they were meant to apply (§15).

The *Aufbau*'s constructional system contained only one basic descriptive predicate: the relation of remembered similarity. (Even that was thought to be treatable like an uninterpreted predicate so that it could appear in structure descriptions where only logical concepts figured essentially.) The relation of remembered similarity says that one experience is remembered to be similar in some unspecified respect to another, namely the present one (it is a non-symmetrical relation; §78). All the other descriptive predicates of empirical science were held to be reconstructable by logical operations on this one basic descriptive relation. Carnap's project of showing that "each scientific statement can in principle be so transformed that it is nothing but a structure statement" (§16) required renouncing all reference to the descriptive meaning of terms. For this to be possible, the basic elements of the constitution system also had to be carefully chosen. Carnap took as his "undefined basic objects" not objects, but "relation extensions", ordered pairs. As he explained, "basic relations take precedence over the basic elements which are their members; generally speaking, construction theory considers individual objects as secondary, relative to the network in which they stand" (§61). Carnap made this choice because the basic objects proper of the system were "elementary experiences" and he deemed such experiences unanalysable, holistic *Gestalten* (§68) Since it was, however, the very contents of these elementary experiences from which scientific concepts were to be built up in his system, Carnap devised the ingenious method of "quasi-analysis" of elementary experiences, which "analyses" indivisible units into quasi-constituents (§71). Fortunately, the details of quasi-analysis need not concern us here.[4] It suffices to note that it worked with the following idealizations: that a pair list of all the elementary experiences of an individual as ordered by the basic relation was assumed to be available to the theorist and that, accordingly, possession of an infinite memory was ascribed to the epistemic subject (§101). Objects of ascending orders of complexity (first sense-data, later objects) were then constructed from similarity classes of unanalysable experiences as determined in this basic extension list.

In its finished state then – Carnap repeatedly claimed to have provided only a sketch – a constitution system would allow the transformation of every empirical statement such that for each non-primitive non-logical concept its constitutional definiens is substituted:

> [E]ventually the sentence will have a form in which (outside of logical symbols) it contains only signs for basic relations ... the sentence ... has now been so transformed that it expresses a definite (formal and extensional) state of affairs relative to the basic relation.　　　(§180)

Every statement so transformed became in principle decidable. Due to the *Aufbau's* solipsistically reduced universe and the assumption of infinite memory, even universal empirical statements now were decidable in principle: Carnap stressed that the number of elements connected in his reduction chains was finite (*ibid*.). The method of definite structure descriptions thus allowed the verifiable meaning of all statements to be exhibited by their logical form relative to the given.

The same method also prescribed Carnap's choice of the criterion of the adequacy of the constitution system. Structures are individuated extensionally: two isomorphic structures are type-identical. Similarly, if two apparently different concepts were assigned the same place in the hierarchy, that is, if they received the same reductive definition, then they were considered type-identical, no matter what different connotations they ordinarily carried. That Carnap's constructional language only had to be extensionally adequate to the actually used scientific language that it reconstructed, meant that no attempt was made to explicate the ordinary meaning of the reconstructed concepts (§51). The *Aufbau* was "concerned exclusively with logical, not epistemic, value [of concepts]; it is purely logical, not psychological" (§50). Carnap was emboldened in this decision by his belief (here misleadingly stated as a fact) that all purportedly intensional statements could be translated into extensional ones (§45). Thus he could contend that no logically relevant meaning of an assertion could possibly be lost by the extensional reduction of empirical statements to the given.

The compatibility of ground plan and method

The *Aufbau* is enlivened by an internal tension that may be put as follows. Behind it stands a seemingly phenomenalist conception of justification: true to the strategy of the linguistic turn initiated by Frege and Wittgenstein (who held that thought contents could only be dealt with when expressed in language), thoughts were considered linguistically constituted, but their meaning was to be reduced to what is immediately given to the subject's consciousness (if the thoughts were true). At the same time, however, the treatment that such knowledge received at Carnap's hands was decidedly untraditional: it was the formal structure that mattered, not experiential quality or ideational content. Experience was treated by Carnap in the same way as all other objects of science, structurally. It can hardly be denied that there obtains an at least superficial contrast between experiential quality and content and meaning on the one hand, and relational structure and pure form, on the other. Consider now some objections to Carnap's project that turn on the purported incompatibility of his ground plan and his procedure.

One might wonder, first, whether the complete formalization of empirical knowledge envisaged by Carnap did not turn empirical knowledge into logico-mathematical and thus non-empirical knowledge.[5] Carnap divided the theorems of the constructional system into two kinds, analytic and synthetic. The analytic theorems (apart from those of logic and arithmetic, which were simply presupposed in the constitution system) were provided by the reductive definitions of the empirical concepts in the constructional language. The synthetic theorems concerned relations between constructed objects that were not definitionally fixed, but that could be ascertained through experience (§106). The synthetic theorems mirrored what a person actually knew, given what she experienced. Only the reductionist framework of scientific concepts was analytic; any factual, non-definitional claims depended on what was, in fact, given. Contrary to the objection envisaged, the empirical nature of the knowledge reconstructed was safeguarded by the synthetic theorems of the constitution system that translated empirical knowledge claims.

Carnap's safeguarding of the synthetic nature of empirical knowledge thus depended on having the correct dictionary, the right analytical framework. Here it may be wondered how the distinction between analytic and synthetic theorems came to be drawn in the first place: did this not compromise the full structuralization of knowledge claims? Carnap admitted that the reconstructive theorist (but not the individual whose knowledge was to be reconstructed) had to be familiar with the sense of the basic relation and know "all of reality" (§102): only against this prior knowledge was it possible for the theorist to determine "which constructional steps are appropriate for each level and to which entity each of them leads, even though he does not know of what nature A's experiences are" (*ibid.*). Two distinct steps, then, were involved in the reconstruction of empirical knowledge. The first step provided the reductive dictionary. For the purposes of this step the theorist needed only the general knowledge of reality, but not the previously mentioned inventory list of the extension of the basic relation extension of remembered similarity of any one epistemic subject. The dictionary was formulated "independently from the individual subject" (*ibid.*). Only the second step reconstructed any one individual's positive knowledge: the reductive definitions enabled the theorist to produce translations of an individual's knowledge claims and compare them with the remembered similarities stated in that individual's inventory list. Whatever the theorist must know, the claim to the full structuralization of empirical knowledge is not compromised by the distinction of analytic and synthetic theorems.

A different objection exploiting the tension in the *Aufbau* would hold that we do not experience the structure of our mental states but their content. Here Carnap would answer, of course, that he was only providing a rational reconstruction. A related kind of objection would hold that the concept of justification is a concept that imputes self-reflection and that cannot be shown to apply where no reference to the contents of an individual's experience is made. By contrast, Carnap's concept of justification consisted in the satisfaction of the necessary and sufficient conditions for the application of empirical concepts that were spelled out by their replacement by indicators for them in the constructional language, by reduction sentences (§47). This concept of justification was a formal logical one: reducibility of empirical content to the strictly verifiable given.[6] Against the objection Carnap would again stress that he aimed only for a rational reconstruction. It was sufficient that an individual's experience did, after all, figure in the reconstruction, albeit under a structuralist description.

As the rebuttal of these objections shows, Carnap's philosophical ground plan and his scientific method would seem to cohere: their tension appears to be resolved – given his conception of objectivity as intersubjective communicability (§64). Carnap's formalist structuralism became elevated to epistemological relevance and gave a new lease of life to empiricism.

The aim of the *Aufbau* project

What, then, was the point of Carnap's project? To start with, we can distinguish two prominent answers that correspond to two prominent perspectives on Vienna Circle philosophy. The insufficiency of either suggests a third interpretation.

The old reading: phenomenalist foundationalism
The traditional reading of the *Aufbau* takes its cue from Russell's "Wherever possible, logical constructions are to be substituted for inferred entitites" (1994: 149), adopted by Carnap as his guiding maxim (§1). Yet why develop such a substitutional reconstruction of empirical concepts? For Russell, the point of constructing "some logical function of less hypothetical entitites which has the

requisite properties" of the inferred entities was to "swe[ep] away … the useless menagerie of metaphysical monsters" (1994: 149–50). According to the traditional reading, Carnap followed Russell in this anti-metaphysical vein and sought to show that science was only committed to claims that could be justified by reference to sense experience.

This picture of Carnap as the fulfiller of the Russellian project fits nicely with the traditional picture of Vienna Circle philosophy and is widely endorsed.[7] Accordingly, the *Aufbau* represents the fulfilment of the old empiricist dream to establish conclusive knowledge of nature on the basis of the data of sense experience alone, albeit with the then new tools of mathematical logic (thereby going beyond Hume's associationism and Mach's neutral monism) and with some of the then new insights of Gestalt psychology (beyond Russell's psychological atomism).

Why would Carnap have wanted to undertake a project like this? One of Carnap's declared tasks was to demonstrate the possibility of constructing a unified system of all scientific concepts: therewith the thesis of the unity of science would be proven and the purported inevitability of the separation into unrelated special sciences or even science types would be refuted (§4). Following the linguistic turn, Carnap read the unity of science thesis as a thesis about the language of science and in this form returned to phenomenalist reductionism. All the concepts of empirical science were to be shown to be meaningful due to their relation to the given, and all scientific statements were thus to be shown to be justified. Science rested entirely on experiential foundations.

Given this reading, what posterity has come to learn of the *Aufbau* as the failure of Carnap's phenomenalist reduction is easily seen as disposing of what is of interest in his project. For example, Quine pointed out that Carnap's reconstruction failed at precisely the point where the step from reconstructed classes of sense qualities to spatiotemporal objects was to be taken: no explicit, eliminative definition was provided of the relation "is at", which locates objects not in a phenomenal but an intersubjectively accessible physical space (§126).[8] With the phenomenalistic reduction failed, the foundationalist project failed as well.

But was this really Carnap's main concern? There are weighty reasons to doubt the reading of Carnap as a merely logicistically reconstructed traditional foundationalist. One is that Carnap reconstructed empirical terms in accordance with their use in the empirical sciences (§106). As a result, Carnap's reductive definitions were themselves relative to a given state of scientific knowledge. Carnap thus from the start precluded the fulfilment of the traditional foundationalist ideal of certainty (due to the circularity incurred). Another reason for doubting that phenomenalist reductionism was the main concern of the *Aufbau* is provided by the recognition that the traditional reading cannot explain why Carnap

119

insisted on the structuralization of the content of knowledge claims and even the one basic relation had to be treated as uninterpreted.

The new reading: structuralist neo-Kantianism

The alternative neo-Kantian interpretation disputes the traditionalist reading (although not the diagnosis of the reductionist failure). It holds that Carnap was concerned not merely with the facts and limits of knowledge, but, first of all, with its possibility. What are of major interest in the *Aufbau* for this reading are Carnap's steps to effect the linguistic turn within a broadly Kantian perspective on the problem of knowledge: how is objectivity possible? Accordingly, the marriage of phenomenalism and structuralism was meant to improve what was perceived as Kant's flawed answer to the problem he had correctly identitified: it was not meant to discard the problem he had unearthed, as the traditional view implies.

The picture of Carnap as a neo-Kantian is best summarized in the words of Alberto Coffa:

> Hosts of philosophers had tried to develop the Kantian idea that experience and its objects are constituted through our categories ... In conformity with the ontological bent of traditional idealism, they agreed to compare constitution to construction, thus suggesting that what our mind does with the objects of experience is an activity comparable to what the engineer does with his bridges ... Carnap may have been the first among admirers of the idea of constitution to come up with a reasonable theory about the nature of that activity which grasps both the kernel of truth in the Kantian doctrine and excludes the ontological-idealist implication.   (Coffa 1985: 147–8)

Carnap was ultimately concerned not with the constitution of the objects of experience, but with "the constitution of meaning" (Coffa 1986: 59). Moreover, Carnap investigated the latter in order to reach "the articulation and defense of a radically new conception of objectivity" (Friedman 1999: 95).[9]

The essential idea of this new reading is that we must distinguish between the form and content of experience. Kant's answer to the question of the possibility of knowledge was that the content of experience was given through the senses, but that it was presented to us in particular forms that were imposed upon it by both the faculty of intuition and that of understanding, and that it was the particular synthetic *a priori* forms of intuition and understanding that made for the objectivity of knowledge. To reconstruct the *a priori* conditions of knowledge by contrast as purely formal, analytic conditions was one aspect of Carnap's project of improving on Kant.

Carnap shared with Kant the conviction that the possibility of objective knowledge could not reside in the content of experience. It is important to note what "content" means here. First of all, it means the "stuff" of experience, its "qualitative material". For Carnap, what militated against basing the objectivity of knowledge in the content of experience so understood was the fact that the stuff of experience is by definition private: we cannot intersubjectively compare the qualitative character of our sense experiences (§16). Secondly, Carnap thought not only the stuff of sensory intuition to be so private but the intuitive meaning of language as well. This intuitive meaning, after all, concerned precisely the "epistemic value" of expressions that was relevant only to psychological, but not logical investigations (§§50–51). Accordingly, Carnap's primary aim in the *Aufbau* was this:

> science wants to speak about what's objective and whatever does not belong to the structure but to the material (i.e. anything that can be pointed out in a concrete ostensive definition) is, in the final analysis subjective … The series of experiences is different for each subject. If we want to achieve, in spite of this, agreement in the names for the entities which are constructed on the basis of these experiences then this cannot be done by reference to the completely divergent content, but only through the formal description of the structure of these entities. (§16)

Carnap's method of reconstructing empirical knowledge by means of definite structure descriptions was not merely a convenient ploy to make phenomenalism work, but constituted the very heart of his enterprise. Carnap answered the question of the possibility of objectivity with reference to his choice of the predicate form of the constitution system. It was the requirement of "the achievement of objectivity" that pressed Carnap to assert that *"for science it is possible and at the same time necessary to restrict itself to structure statements"* (ibid., original emphasis). Carnap's choice of structure descriptions as the basic predicate form also determined his answer to the question whether, and just how, the objectivity of empirical science could be accounted for, if the meaning of empirical statements rested in subjective givens: first, all that was required were "intersubjectively valid assertions", that is, assertions that possess a "validity which also holds for other subjects" (§66); secondly, that such intersubjective validity was guaranteed by the objectivity bestowed by structural descriptions.

Carnap's neo-Kantianism asserted that the objectivity of knowledge rested in the form, not the content, of experience but this form was not determined by synthetic *a prioris*, as it was for Kant, but by analytic determinations that set out the framework of representations used in terms of formal logical relations between them. Carnap thus rested the objectivity of knowledge in the structures that his constitution analysis held basic to the analysis of experiences, the framework of reductive definitions: "all streams of experience agree in respect of certain structural properties" (*ibid.*, translation modified). Carnap thought the intersubjective validity of empirical science preserved because, unlike the qualities of different subjects' experiences, the formal structures of these experiences were in principle comparable: different subjects can share the form or logical structure of their experiences. In short, Carnap conceived of intersubjectivity as consisting in the relation of isomorphism between the logical structures of the objects that form the linguistically explicated givens of different subjects.

The two readings compared

The new reading of the *Aufbau* has the virtue of explaining what the traditional view cannot explain: Carnap's insistence on the radical structuralization, even formalization of empirical knowledge. Why did Carnap insist, first, on reconstructing the concepts of empirical science of just one predicate, and why did he even insist, secondly, that the intuitive meaning of the basic, last empirical predicate not be relied on, that it itself be treated as uninterpreted? The complete structuralization of empirical knowledge required the prior reduction of all descriptive predicates to just one. (How could two basic predicates of the same language be differentiated and yet be treated as uninterpreted?) The de-interpretation of the one basic predicate, in turn, followed from Carnap's neo-Kantian project: if only form makes for objectivity, then even this last basic descriptive predicate must be individuated in terms of its form alone; we cannot rely on its intuitive content. (Acquaintance with sense data was not fit to serve as the foundation of objectivity unless it could itself be constituted structurally.)

At the same time, of course, Carnap's answer to the question of the possibility of objectivity of knowledge brought a broadly Kantian response in line with the thesis of logicism and extended the rule of analytic forms to empirical science. But it also provided an alternative to Kant and the neo-Kantians in yet a further respect. Carnap agreed with Russell's remark that "a great deal of speculation in traditional philosophy which might have been avoided if the importance of structure, and the impossibility of getting behind it, had been realized" (1919: 61). Russell had concluded:

> every proposition having a communicable significance [due to its structure] must be true of both worlds [phenomena and things in themselves] or of neither: the only difference must lie in just that essence of individuality which always eludes words and baffles description, but which, for that very reason, is irrelevant to science.   (*Ibid.*)

Reading this passage through Carnap's eyes, we find the following meaning. If it is the form of the given, not its intuitive content, that makes for the objectivity of cognition, then only these formal properties pertain to reality (in so far as reality is scientifically comprehensible). By resting objectivity in the logico-linguistic form of cognition alone, all duplications of intersubjective reality by things in themselves become entirely unnecessary: objective reality is what is structurally comprehensible. Following through the implications of Carnap's structuralism, one can thus see that his anti-metaphysical conclusions, that is, that science is neutral *vis-à-vis* the question of realism or idealism (§177), was rooted not so much in his phenomenalist verificationism (which would, after all, tip the scales towards idealism), but in his structuralist revamping of Kant.

Is the traditional reading then to be abandoned in its entirety? Carnap sought both to prove the unity of science thesis by the thoroughgoing reduction of all scientific concepts to the given and at the same time establish the nature of the objectivity of science by the structuralization of knowledge. Carnap avowed both aims; the question whether it was Russell or Kant that were influences on the *Aufbau* is wrongly put: Russell also inspired the structuralization project. It is possible and advisable to endorse certain aspects of the traditional reading in addition to the new reading of the *Aufbau*.

The question arises therefore how closely the two aims were related. Could Carnap have pursued his structuralist Kantianism in a non-phenomenalist setting, had he so chosen? Within the terms of construction theory this is to ask whether the propositional content of a given consciousness could be structuralized if it were not phenomenalistically reducible. The answer would appear to be that, given the assumption of the epistemic priority of the auto-psychological, it required the phenomenalist reduction as the conduit for objectivity. So Carnap did require the phenomenalist reduction to make his structuralist Kantianism work, even though his Kantian concern superseded the foundationalism that typically motivates phenomenalist reductions. So the traditionalist claim to Carnap's foundationalism must be dropped, but neither can Carnap simply be turned into an analytic neo-Kantian.

The problem of the basic relation

The ecumenical construal above will not stand, however, for there was an important technical hitch to Carnap's project that requires us to take account also of still other motivations. The problem was that the method of definite structure descriptions required that all descriptive concepts be dealt with purely in terms of their form – and that the *Aufbau* failed to do so in the case of the single basic relation.

Three sections of the *Aufbau* (which, said Carnap, "may be omitted") sought to deal with the problem of "whether it is possible to complete this formalization by eliminating from the statements of science these basic relations as the last, non-logical objects" (§153). Yet Carnap was unable to define the basic relation structurally further than up to isomorphism. This meant, of course, that the envisaged method of defining the basic relation structurally did not single out one and only one such relation as a definite description should. (Carnap was unable fully to escape Frege's criticism of Hilbert.)

To complete the formalization of empirical concepts, Carnap had to delimit the conditions of applicability for the basic relation as structurally defined to just one. His proposed solution started from his recognition that, after the envisaged iso-morphism-preserving transformations, the inventory lists of the basic relation extension were "lists of pairs of basic elements without any (experienceable) con-nection" (*ibid.*). Carnap accordingly required that the structural descriptions should be restricted to "experienceable 'natural' relations", which he called "founded relations" (§154). To complete his structuralist project, Carnap required that the concept "founded relation extensions", a concept that made reference to empirical conditions, be counted a logical one. Carnap himself noted that this con-stituted "an unresolved problem" (§155). In defence he wrote:

> That this concept [foundedness] is concerned with the *application* to object domains is not a valid objection to introducing it as a basic con-cept of logic. The same is true for another basic concept of logic, namely, generality: "(x)fx" means that the propositional function of fx has the value true for every argument of an object domain in which it is meaningful. Logic is not really a domain at all, but contains those statements which (as tautologies) hold for the objects of any domain whatsoever. From this it follows that it must concern itself precisely with those concepts which are applicable to any domain whatever. And foundedness, after all belongs to these concepts.   (§154)

Carnap's idea was to save both the generality and the uniqueness of his recon-struction by insisting that the theory is true over every domain that is "founded" (presuming that there is only one such founded domain).

The question arises how much of a problem this was for Carnap. According to Friedman (Friedman 1999: 103), the original motivations of the programme to structuralize knowledge and disengage objective knowledge from subjective intuition "have been totally undermined by Carnap's final move". The concept of foundedness only refers us back to the stuff of intuition. Similarly, according to Küng (1967: 89–90), Carnap ended up relying on something like the intensional notion of intended interpretation and so undermined his extensionalism. Both objections turn on the contentious claim that foundedness is a formal logical notion.

To assess these criticisms we have to determine what conception of logic is operative in the *Aufbau* (a matter Carnap did not discuss). According to the Frege–Russell–Wittgenstein conception of logic as a universal language, logic provides specifications that hold for any object whatsoever, it establishes the ground rules for arranging the furniture of the universe, as it were; this is opposed by the conception of logic as calculus where logic functions as the specification, in a metalanguage, of specific frameworks within which certain aspects of the world are to be comprehended. Now, on the traditional conception of logic as a universal language Carnap's argument does not work, owing to its faulty analogy. "Foundedness" is not a concept of the same order of "concern with application to object domains" as the concept of generality, the universal quantifier. "Foundedness" topicalizes what the universal quantifier takes for granted and spells out and restricts what the universal quantifier presupposes, namely, application to an object domain. "Foundedness" restricts application to intended domains and rules out others: it is no longer a purely formal concept. On the conception of logic as a calculus, however, Carnap's argument gains in plausibility, for concerning such a calculus we may require a specification of the intended domain. Since Carnap's *Logical Syntax* of 1934 (2002) represents the clearest conception of logic as calculus to date, one can see these sections of the *Aufbau* as experimenting with the as yet not fully worked out (and for the fastidious Carnap therefore problematic) calculus conception.

So the question becomes whether the calculus conception of logic can shoulder the weight of the task of the structuralization of empiricial knowledge. Here the answer would seem to be that if indeed there existed as a matter of fact only one domain in which the basic relation was founded, then restricting the interpretation in this way would guarantee the success of the structuralization. Certainly extensionality would be preserved, but it cannot be denied that the notion of what is "formal" is stretched considerably here (as it is in *Logical Syntax* anyway). Even though Carnap's suggested method would help to safeguard the intended interpretation, calling the constraints he adopted "structural" appears to go too far.

In any case, that Carnap himself was worried here indicates once again that the traditional interpretation cannot be upheld. Without a complete formalization, that is, with residual reliance upon intuitive, ostensive meaning, a purely phenomenalistic programme would still have been fulfilled, but not the formalist-structuralist one. But the neo-Kantian interpretation is also endangered here, as Friedman's criticism indicates. The problem of the basic relation thus suggests the need to broaden the interpretive perspective on the *Aufbau* still further.[10]

Conventionalism and the point of rational reconstructions

Taken in their customary spirit, ascribing neo-Kantian ambitions to Carnap runs the risk of ascribing to him concern with a transcendental grounding of the objectivity of science: without structuralist determination all the way down, no objectivity would be possible. But did Carnap merely abandon empirical for transcendental foundationalism?

In the section "The Aims of Science" we read:

> [T]he formation of the constitution system is the first aim of science. It is the first aim … in a logical sense … it is followed by the second aim, namely, the investigation of the non-constituted properties of relations and objects. The first aim is reached through convention; the second, however, through experience. (In the view of constitution theory, there are no other components in cognition than these two, the conventional and the empirical; thus there is no synthetic a priori.)
>
> (§179)

So far, we have paid little attention to the conventional elements in the *Aufbau*. Yet conventionalism is widely recognized as one of the most consistent features of Carnap's life work. Is it absent in his first major work? This focus opens the way to regarding Carnap's structuralist strategy as indeed a rational reconstruction of the conditions of objectivity even though it remained incomplete.

Consider how conventions figure in the *Aufbau*. As noted, logic and mathematics were presupposed. "Logic (including mathematics) consists solely of conventions concerning the use of symbols, and of tautologies on the basis of these conventions." (§107) But conventions also figure in the execution of his project. As Carnap put it, "constitution takes place through definition" (§38). This definitional formation of a constitution system is what Carnap designated as "conventional". Conventions here figure in various ways. To start with, the relation sign-signified "always contains a conventional component; that is, it is somehow brought about voluntarily" (§21); moreover, the choice of the type of physical-state magnitudes in scientific theories was conventional (§136). But still more important for our purposes is how the analytic component of the constitution system is fixed. Fixing the reductive definitions of all empirical concepts required the theorist to be apprised of the sense of the basic relation and also know "all of reality" (§102). This meant that the ideally eliminative definitions of object-types were so formed as to make antecedently attained results of empirical science come out true in the reconstruction. That is to say, Carnap opted to choose from logically possible definitions of higher object-types those that were "the most convenient" given the point of his constitution system (§179). The conventionality of the constitution system was not unconstrained by empirical science, but neither was the constitution system determined by empirical science.

This pervasive conventionality points to what is perhaps the most distinctive feature of the *Aufbau* (a feature that links it both with the remainder of his life's work and the work of his closest colleagues in the Vienna Circle). As Carnap tells readers in the Preface, his concern was to render philosophy itself scientific. For him this did not mean the pursuit of traditional philosophical aims by science, but the integration of philosophy into science as its metatheory. Constitution theory undertook the logical investigations pertaining to scientific metatheory, it investigated the logico-linguistic frameworks of scientific theories. It is in this context that Carnap's rational reconstructions are to be understood (later he used the term "explications" for this). Rational reconstructions of concepts provided definitions that sought to render explicit the conditions of their correct or justified employment. Justification as such is little mentioned in the *Aufbau* itself, of course, yet Carnap's own index tellingly lists under "justification": "see rational reconstruction" (where in turn "rational justification" appears listed as a synonym). Rational reconstruction was to replace psychologistically and metaphysically loaded notions of justification and present an appropriate substitute.

That Carnap was concerned with what made scientific objectivity possible need not therefore mean that he was engaged in an inquiry into the transcendental ground of science, but rather means that he was concerned with the logico-linguistic presuppositions of scientific theorizing. Accordingly, Carnap did not endeavour to exhibit the very ground of the possibility of cognition but sought to show what concretely makes it possible to formulate scientific theories. Investigating this he was struck by the room that was left for conventional determinations in the construction of logico-linguistic framworks. (Already in the *Aufbau*, Carnap indicated other possible constitution systems, built on a different basis (§59).) In a word, although it has often been read this way, the *Aufbau* is not a work of general epistemology but a treatise in philosophy of science.

How then does the recognition of Carnap's conventionalism at least ameliorate the problem of the basic relation? Carnap was not concerned to explain the ground of the possibility of objectivity, what objectivity consists in (surely an "essence question" to be dismissed as "metaphysical" (§20)), but only to reconstruct what is required of descriptions in order for them to allow for rational decidability and intersubjective agreement. In that case the problem of the basic relation becomes a problem of the "explicative limit" of his method (Ryckman 1991: 156). The form or structure of scientific descriptions made the objectivity of scientific discourse possible, but it presupposed a particular embedding of the scientific symbol system. That embedding, however, cannot be reconstructed in structural terms in turn (and this Carnap was slow to appreciate). Accordingly, what the problem of the basic relation shows is that Carnap's conventionalist reconstruction of scientific knowledge represents a philosophical method of legitimising scientific knowledge claims that proceeds from within science – and does not proceed from without by providing indubitable foundations or transcendental groundings (as the traditional or the neo-Kantian intepretation would have it). Proceeding from within, Carnap's method has its explicative limits.

Carnap's conventionalist rational reconstructionism also allows us to defuse a residual worry about Carnap's choice of the phenomenalist basis. Why did Carnap not use the physical domain as basic instead of the phenomenal one with which it is intertranslatable? What spoke against this was Carnap's reasoning that "the further claim of behaviorism, namely, that this ordering of objects is also a correct reflection of the epistemic relations would still be problematic" (§59). Carnap's choice was epistemologically motivated (§60). His decision to adopt the auto-psychological as the basic object domain of his constitution system followed neither from formal considerations of constructional convenience nor from factual, strictly scientific considerations. Rather, it would seem to have followed from *a priori* considerations about what the epistemic order would look like, the autopsychological basis as "the natural starting point in the epistemic order of subjects" (§66). Constitution theory as scientific epistemology thus required that the traditional conception of epistemic priority be followed, if it was traditional epistemology that Carnap sought to render scientific. And here we reach the question of how traditional an epistemologist Carnap wanted to be in the *Aufbau*. As noted, for Carnap, rational reconstruction of logico-linguistic frameworks (explication) replaces traditional philosophy: for him, scientific philosophy laid bare the meaning and justification conditions of scientific knowledge claims, it did not seek for an ultimate reality beyond the reach of science. The *Aufbau* was dedicated to promoting this conception of philosophy (it provided, after all, but a sketch of a constitution theory, not a completed one). Now the first step in promoting this conception is to show fellow philosophers that explication is what they ought to be pursuing. Considering metaphysicians beyond redemption, Carnap addressed epistemologists. To convince them of the virtues of the method of explication, he thus assumed the "natural" conception of the epistemic order for his exemplary constitution system. But that, for him, was just a conventional choice, namely that of traditional epistemologists. When Carnap dropped that convention in 1932, he also dropped all foundationalist assumptions; by 1935 he had dropped all pretensions to be pursuing (traditional) epistemology.[11]

So one undeniable obstacle to the interpretation of the *Aufbau* as an in intention non-foundationalist exemplar of scientific philosophy can be overcome. While *prima facie* it appears as if his Cartesian presuppositions determined the setting of the epistemological problem that subsequently was to be solved by the resources of formal science, we can now recognize this appearance as an artefact of the dialectical situation of his beginning campaign for a truly scientific philosophy.

Summary

If the reconstruction of the *Aufbau* given above is correct, we must recognize three different major strands of philosophical concerns to be operative in it: phenomenalist empiricism as its basic epistemological perspective, a structuralist reconstruction of objectivity and a conventionalist approach to concept formation. The *Aufbau* must be distinguished from Russell's foundationalist programme, from neo-Kantian attempts to provide a transcendental grounding for objectivity, and from earlier conventionalisms that merely exploited instances of underdetermination. It is in reaching beyond these pioneers and combining their insights in a new conception of what scientific philosophy does that the originality of the *Aufbau* lies. It was with comparable boldness and in the same spirit that in his next major work, *The Logical Syntax of Language* (2002 [1934]), Carnap built on the pioneering works of logicism, formalism and intuitionism to reorient the quest for foundations in logic and mathematics towards conventionalist reconstructionism, complementing in formal science the approach taken to empirical science in his *Aufbau*.[12]

Notes

1. For extensive descriptions and discussions of the *Aufbau*, albeit from a traditional perspective, see V. Kraft, *The Vienna Circle*, A. Pap (trans.) (New York: Philosophical Library, 1953), J. Jørgenson, *The Development of Logical Empiricism* (International Encyclopedia of Unified Science 2(9)) (Chicago, IL: University of Chicago Press, 1951) and N. Goodman, *The Structure of Experience*, 3rd edn (Dordrecht: Reidel, 1978). For non-traditionalist interpretations of varying kinds see, for example: S. Haack, "Carnap's Aufbau: Some Kantian Reflections", *Ratio* **19** (1977), 170–76; R. Creath, "Carnap's Conventionalism", in S. Sarkar (ed.), *Carnap: A Centenary Reappraisal*, *Synthese* **93** (1992), 141–66; E. Rungaldier, *Carnap's Early Conventionalism: An Inquiry into the Background of the Vienna Circle* (Amsterdam: Rodopi, 1984); A. Coffa, "Idealism and the Aufbau", in *The Heritage of Logical Positivism*, N. Rescher (ed.), 133–56 (New York: University Press of America, 1985) and *The Semantic Tradition from Kant to Carnap: To the Vienna Station*, L. Wessels (ed.) (Cambridge: Cambridge University Press, 1991), ch. 12; J. Proust, *Questions of Form: Logic and the Analytic Proposition from Kant to Carnap*, A. A. Brenner (trans.) (Minneapolis, MN: University of Minnesota Press, 1989), ch. 4; M. Friedman, "Carnap's *Aufbau* Reconsidered", *Noûs* **21** (1987), 521–45 and "Epistemology in the

Aufbau", in Sarkar (ed.), *Carnap: A Centenary Reappraisal*, 15–58; W. Sauer, "On the Kantian Background of Neopositivism", *Topoi* **8** (1989), 111–19; A. Richardson, "How Not to Russell Carnap's *Aufbau*", in *PSA 1990*, vol. 1, A. Fine, M. Forbes & L. Wessel (eds), 3–14 (East Lansing, MI: Philosophy of Science Association, 1990) and *Carnap's Construction of the World* (Cambridge: Cambridge University Press, 1997); T. A. Ryckman, "Designation and Convention: A Chapter of Early Logical Empiricism", in *PSA 1990*, vol. 2, A. Fine, M. Forbes & L. Wessel (eds), 149–58 (East Lansing, MI: Philosophy of Science Association, 1991); V. E. Mayer, "Die Konstruktion der Erfahrungswelt: Carnap und Husserl", in *Hans Reichenbach, Rudolf Carnap: A Centenary*, W. Spohn (ed.), *Erkenntnis* **35** (1991), 287–304; C. U. Moulines, "Making Sense of Carnap's *Aufbau*", in *Hans Reichenbach, Rudolf Carnap*, Spohn (ed.) (1991); T. Uebel, *Overcoming Logical Positivism From Within* (Amsterdam: Rodopi, 1992), ch. 2 and "Conventions in the Aufbau", *British Journal for the History of Philosophy* **4** (1996), 381–97; T. Oberdan, *Protocols, Truth, Convention* (Amsterdam: Rodopi, 1993); R. G. Hudson, "Empirical Constraints in the Aufbau", *History of Philosophy Quarterly* **11** (1994), 237–51; C. Pincock, "Russell's Influence on Carnap's Aufbau", *Synthese* **131** (2002), 1–37 and "Carnap and the Unity of Science: 1921–1928", in *Language, Truth and Knowledge: Contributions to the Philosophy of Rudolf Carnap*, T. Bonk (ed.), 87–96 (Dordrecht: Kluwer, 2003); T. Mormann, "Synthetic Geometry and the Aufbau", in *Language, Truth and Knowledge: Contributions to the Philosophy of Rudolf Carnap*, T. Bonk (ed.), 45–64 and "A Quasi-analytical Constitution of Physical Space", in *Carnap Brought Home: The View From Jena*, S. Awodey & C. Klein (eds), 79–100 (Chicago, IL: Open Court, 2004); and C. W. Savage, "Carnap's Aufbau Rehabilitated", in *Language, Truth and Knowledge: Contributions to the Philosophy of Rudolf Carnap*, T. Bonk (ed.), 79–86.

2. Carnap's translator rendered "*Konstitutionssystem*" as "constructional system"; I shall use this and "constitution system" and so on interchangeably.

3. The basis was further delimited within the phenomenal domain. In general, Carnap counted into this realm both "acts of consciousness: perceptions, representations, feelings, thoughts, acts of will, and so on … [and] also unconscious processes to the extent to which they can be considered analogous to acts of consciousness, for example, unconscious representations" (§18). As a basis for the constructional system, however, no unconscious occurrences but only "conscious appearances (in the widest sense)" (§64) were permitted to serve; these Carnap called "the given". Since he also noted that "all experiences belong to [the basis of the constitution system] no matter whether or not we presently or afterward reflect upon them" (*ibid*.) it would appear that Carnap meant to include preconscious states but to exclude Freud's unconscious proper.

4. See Goodman, *The Structure of Experience*; J. Proust, "Quasi-Analyse et reconstruction du monde", *Fundamenta Scientiae* **5** (1984), 285–304; and Mormann, "Synthetic Geometry and the Aufbau".

5. See K. Popper, "The Demarcation Between Science and Metaphysics", in *The Philosophy of Rudolf Carnap*, P. A. Schilpp (ed.), 183–226 (LaSalle, IL: Open Court, 1963) and Friedman, "Carnap's *Aufbau* Reconsidered".

6. In *Pseudoproblems in Philosophy*, R. A. George (trans.) (Chicago, IL: Open Court, 2002), Carnap merely speaks of "implication" (§1), but there he no longer aims for strict verifiability (§7).

7. See, for example, Kraft, *The Vienna Circle*, §B1; A. J. Ayer, "Editor's Introduction", in *Logical Atomism*, A. J. Ayer (ed.), 3–28 (New York: Free Press, 1959), 3; W. V. O. Quine,

"Two Dogmas of Empiricism", *Philosophical Review* 60 (1951), 20–43 and "Epistemology Naturalized", in *Ontological Relativity and Other Essays*, W. V. O. Quine, 69–90 (New York: Columbia University Press, 1969); N. Goodman, "The Significance of *Der Logische Aufbau der Welt*", in *The Philosophy of Rudolf Carnap*, P. A. Schilpp (ed.), 545–58 (LaSalle, IL: Open Court, 1963). Carnap's retrospective comments in his "Preface to 2nd edition", *The Logical Structure of the World*, R. A. George (trans.) (Berkeley, CA: University of California Press, 1967), v–xi and "Comments and Replies", in *The Philosophy of Rudolf Carnap*, P. A. Schilpp (ed.), 859–1016 may seem to enforce this reading, but see Friedman, "Epistemology in the *Aufbau*".

8. See Kraft, *The Vienna Circle*, §B1; Quine, "Two Dogmas of Empiricism" and "Epistemology Naturalized"; for a defence of Carnap's project against this widely accepted criticism see Mormann, "A Quasi-analytical Constitution of Physical Space".

9. See also Friedman, "Epistemology in the *Aufbau*" and Richardson, *Carnap's Construction of the World*.

10. See, for example, G. Küng, *Ontology and the Logistical Analysis of Language*, rev. edn, E. C. M. Mays (trans.) (Dordrecht: Reidel, 1967); Friedman, "Carnap's *Aufbau* Reconsidered"; Ryckman, "Designation and Convention"; Uebel, "Conventions in the Aufbau"; Richardson, *Carnap's Construction of the World*. On the different conceptions of logic, see J. van Heijenoort, "Logic as Calculus and Logic as Language", *Synthese* 17 (1967), 324–30.

11. In "On Protocol Sentences", R. Creath & R. Nollan (trans.), *Noûs* 21 (1987) 457–70, esp. 467, any statement whatsoever may serve as a test statement for science and ever since "Testability and Meaning" it was a matter for science to determine what the class of observation statements should be ("Testability and Meaning", *Philosophy of Science* 3 (1936/37), 419–71, 4, 1–40, esp. 13). Epistemology was outright abandoned for logic of science in "Von der Erkenntnistheorie zur Wissenschaftslogik", *Actes du Congress Internationale de Philosophie Scientifique, Sorbonne, Paris 1935*, Facs. I "Philosophie Scientifique et Empirisme Logique" (Paris: Herman & Cie, 1936), 36–41.

12. I wish to thank the editor for helpful suggestions.

References

Ayer, A. J. 1959. "Editor's Introduction". In *Logical Positivism*, A. J. Ayer (ed.), 3–28. New York: Free Press.

Bonk, T. (ed.) 2003. *Language, Truth and Knowledge: Contributions to the Philosophy of Rudolf Carnap*. Dordrecht: Kluwer.

Carnap, R. 1936. "Von der Erkenntnistheorie zur Wissenschaftslogik", *Actes du Congress Internationale de Philosophie Scientifique, Sorbonne, Paris 1935*, Facs. I "Philosophie Scientifique et Empirisme Logique", Paris: Herman & Cie, 36–41.

Carnap, R. 1936/37. "Testability and Meaning". *Philosophy of Science* 3, 419–71, 4, 1–40. Reprinted with corrigenda and additions (New Haven, CT: Yale Graduate Philosophy Club, 1954).

Carnap, R. 1961. "Preface to 2nd edition", R. A. George (trans.). See Carnap (1967a), v–xi. Originally published as "Vorwort zur zweiten Auflage", *Der logische Aufbau der Welt. Scheinprobleme in der Philosophie* (Hamburg: Meiner, 1961).

Carnap, R. 1963. "Comments and Replies". In *The Philosophy of Rudolf Carnap*, P. A. Schilpp (ed.), 859–1016. LaSalle, IL: Open Court.

Carnap, R. 1987 [1932], "On Protocol Sentences", R. Creath & R. Nollan (trans.). *Noûs* **21**, 457–70. Originally published as "Über Protokollsätze", *Erkenntnis* **3** (1932), 215–28.

Carnap, R. 2002 [1934], *The Logical Syntax of Language*, rev. edn. A. Smeaton (trans.). Chicago, IL: Open Court. Originally published as *Logische Syntax der Sprache* (Vienna: Springer, 1934).

Carnap, R. 2003a [1928]. *The Logical Structure of the World*, R. A. George (trans.). Chicago, IL: Open Court. Originally published as *Der logische Aufbau der Welt* (Berlin: Bernary, 1928).

Carnap, R. 2003b [1928]. *Pseudoproblems in Philosophy*, R. A. George (trans.). Chicago, IL: Open Court. Originally published as *Scheinprobleme in der Philosophie* (Berlin: Bernary, 1928).

Coffa, A. 1985. "Idealism and the Aufbau". In *The Heritage of Logical Positivism*, N. Rescher (ed.), 133–56. New York: University Press of America.

Coffa, A. 1986. "From Geometry to Tolerance: Sources of Conventionalism in Nineteenth-Century Geometry". In *From Quarks to Quasars*, R. G. Colodny (ed.), 3–70. Pittsburgh, PA: University of Pittsburgh Press.

Coffa, A. 1991. *The Semantic Tradition from Kant to Carnap: To the Vienna Station*, L. Wessels (ed.). Cambridge: Cambridge University Press.

Creath, R. 1991. "Carnap's Conventionalism". In Sarkar (1992), 141–66.

Friedman, M. 1987. "Carnap's *Aufbau* Reconsidered". *Noûs* **21**, 521–45. Reprinted in Friedman (1999), 89–113.

Friedman, M. 1991. "Epistemology in the *Aufbau*". In Sarkar (1992), 15–58. Reprinted with a new Postscript in Friedman (1999), 114–62.

Friedman, M. 1999. *Reconsidering Logical Positivism*. Cambridge: Cambridge University Press.

Goodman, N. 1978. *The Structure of Experience*, 3rd edn. Dordrecht: Reidel.

Goodman, N. 1963. "The Significance of *Der Logische Aufbau der Welt*". In *The Philosophy of Rudolf Carnap*, P. A. Schilpp (ed.), 545–58. LaSalle, IL: Open Court.

Haack, S. 1977. "Carnap's Aufbau: Some Kantian Reflections". *Ratio* **19**, 170–76.

Hudson, R. G. 1994. "Empirical Constraints in the Aufbau". *History of Philosophy Quarterly* **11**, 237–51.

Jørgenson, J. 1951. *The Development of Logical Empiricism* (International Encyclopedia of Unified Science 2(9)). Chicago, IL: University of Chicago Press.

Kraft, V. 1953. *The Vienna Circle*, A. Pap (trans.). New York: Philosophical Library. Originally published as *Der Wiener Kreis* (Vienna: Springer, 1950), 2nd edn 1968.

Küng, G. 1967. *Ontology and the Logistical Analysis of Language*, rev. edn, E. C. M. Mays (trans.). Dordrecht: Reidel. Originally published as *Ontologie und logistische Analyse der Sprache* (Vienna: Springer, 1963).

Mayer, V. E. 1991. "Die Konstruktion der Erfahrungswelt: Carnap und Husserl". In *Hans Reichenbach, Rudolf Carnap: A Centenary*, W. Spohn (ed.). *Erkenntnis* **35**, 287–304.

Mormann, T. 2003. "Synthetic Geometry and the Aufbau". In *Language, Truth and Knowledge: Contributions to the Philosophy of Rudolf Carnap*, T. Bonk (ed.), 45–64.

Mormann, T. 2004. "A Quasi-analytical Constitution of Physical Space". In *Carnap Brought Home. The View From Jena*, S. Awodey & C. Klein (eds), 79–100. Chicago, IL: Open Court.

Moulines, C. U. 1991. "Making Sense of Carnap's *Aufbau*". In *Hans Reichenbach, Rudolf Carnap: A Centenary*, W. Spohn (ed.). *Erkenntnis* **35**, 263–86.

Oberdan, T. 1993. *Protocols, Truth, Convention*. Amsterdam: Rodopi.

Pincock, C. 2002. "Russell's Influence on Carnap's Aufbau". *Synthese* **131**, 1–37.

Pincock, C. 2003. "Carnap and the Unity of Science: 1921–1928". In *Language, Truth and Knowledge: Contributions to the Philosophy of Rudolf Carnap*, T. Bonk (ed.), 87–96.

Popper, K. 1963. "The Demarcation Between Science and Metaphysics". In *The Philosophy of Rudolf Carnap*, P. A. Schilpp (ed.), 183–226.

Proust, J. 1984. "Quasi-Analyse et reconstruction du monde". *Fundamenta Scientiae* **5**, 285–304.

Proust, J. 1989. *Questions of Form: Logic and the Analytic Proposition from Kant to Carnap*, A. A. Brenner (trans.). Minneapolis, MN: University of Minnesota Press. Originally published as *Questions de Forme* (Paris: Gallimard, 1986).

Quine, W. V. O. 1951. "Two Dogmas of Empiricism". *Philosophical Review* **60**, 20–43. Reprinted in Quine, *From a Logical Point of View*, rev. edn, 20–46 (Cambridge, MA: Harvard University Press, 1980 [1953]).

Quine, W. V. O. 1969. "Epistemology Naturalized". In *Ontological Relativity and Other Essays*, W. V. O. Quine, 69–90. New York: Columbia University Press.

Richardson, A. 1990. "How Not to Russell Carnap's *Aufbau*". In *PSA 1990*, vol. 1, A. Fine, M. Forbes & L. Wessel (eds), 3–14. East Lansing, MI: Philosophy of Science Association.

Richardson, A. 1997. *Carnap's Construction of the World*. Cambridge: Cambridge University Press.

Rungaldier, E. 1984. *Carnap's Early Conventionalism: An Inquiry into the Background of the Vienna Circle*. Amsterdam: Rodopi.

Russell, B. 1919. *Introduction to Mathematical Philosophy*. London: Allen & Unwin.

Russell, B. 1993 [1914]. *Our Knowledge of the External World*, 2nd edn. London Routledge.

Russell, B. 1994 [1914]. "The Relation of Sense Data to Physics". In *Mysticism and Logic*, rev. edn, 140–72. London: Routledge.

Ryckman, T. A. 1991. "Designation and Convention: A Chapter of Early Logical Empiricism". In *PSA 1990*, vol. 2, A. Fine, M. Forbes & L. Wessel (eds), 149–58.

Sarkar, S. (ed.) 1992. *Carnap: A Centenary Reappraisal*. *Synthese* **93**(1–2).

Sauer, W. 1989. "On the Kantian Background of Neopositivism". *Topoi* **8**, 111–19.

Savage, C. W. 2003. "Carnap's Aufbau Rehabilitated". In *Language, Truth and Knowledge: Contributions to the Philosophy of Rudolf Carnap*, T. Bonk (ed.), 79–86.

Schilpp, P. A. (ed.) 1963. *The Philosophy of Rudolf Carnap*. LaSalle, IL: Open Court.

Schlick, M. 1985 [1918]. *General Theory of Knowledge*, 2nd edn, A. E. Blumberg (trans.). LaSalle, IL: Open Court.

Spohn, W. (ed.) 1991. *Hans Reichenbach, Rudolf Carnap: A Centenary. Erkenntnis* **35**.

Uebel, T. 1992. *Overcoming Logical Positivism From Within*. Amsterdam: Rodopi.

Uebel, T. 1996. "Conventions in the Aufbau". *British Journal for the History of Philosophy* **4**, 381–97.

can Heijenoort, J. 1967. "Logic as Calculus and Logic as Language". *Synthese* **17**, 324–30.

7

Bertrand Russell

An Inquiry into Meaning and Truth

Pascal Engel

Introduction

In comparison with his early essays on analytic philosophy and with the writings of his logical atomist period, Bertrand Russell's *An Inquiry into Meaning and Truth* has received less attention and is often neglected by contemporary readers. There are, I think, two main reasons for this. The first is probably stylistic. In contrast to the sharpness of his earlier works such as "On Denoting" (1905) and *Problems of Philosophy* (1967 [1912]), the style of the *Inquiry* – which was originally presented as Russell's William James Lectures at Harvard in 1940 – is less polished and the views expressed less clear-cut than, for instance, those of *Our Knowledge of the External World* (1914) or "The Philosophy of Logical Atomism" (1918). The second reason owes more to the content and the atmosphere of the book. Whereas Russell's first philosophy is based on the logical analysis of language as a guide to the structure of the world and displays a sort of analytic purity, his second philosophy, especially in the *Inquiry*, is more epistemological and provides a mixture of considerations on knowledge, meaning and ontology that is sometimes disconcerting, in particular when it introduces psychological considerations in matters of logic. For those readers who have been accustomed to think of Russell, along with Frege and Moore, as the founder of analytic philosophy, and who consider that the distinctive mark of this kind of philosophy is a logical analysis of language free of all psychological considerations, it comes as a surprise to see Russell analysing meaning in terms of psychological concepts. When he

134

says, for instance, in Chapter 5 of the *Inquiry* that "psychologically, the logical connective 'or' corresponds to 'a state of hesitation'", the readers of early Russell raise their eyebrows. Moreover the psychology of the *Inquiry* is mostly behaviouristic and outdated. If you add to that the fact that a large part of the book is a discussion of the doctrines of logical positivism, with which Russell declares himself in the Preface to be "more in sympathy than with any other existing school", it is not completely surprising that today's readers, who in their majority are less in sympathy with logical positivism than with any other existing school, should be put off.

Although these reactions are understandable, they rest upon a misapprehension of Russell's real concerns and of the history of his views. During his Platonist period, in *The Principles of Mathematics* (1903), he believed that logic is the royal road to metaphysical truth about the world, and he eschewed considerations about the nature of knowledge, largely in reaction to his own early idealist apprenticeship. He was concerned with stating what is real, not with stating how we know what is real, and he believed that considerations about our knowledge of reality always lead to idealism. Epistemological questions, however, came quickly back into the picture. Even when he wrote "On Denoting" his interest in logical analysis of descriptions such as "The present King of France" was related to the distinction between two kinds of knowledge: knowledge by "acquaintance" and "knowledge by description". *Problems of Philosophy*, published in 1912, just after the publication of the first volume of *Principia Mathematica* (1910), as well as his unpublished *Theory of Knowledge* (1984 [written in 1913]), show clearly that his philosophy had taken an epistemological turn. A few years later, in *The Analysis of Mind* (1921) as well as in *An Outline of Philosophy* (1927) Russell had taken a psychological turn, and shown a strong interest in behaviourism and in scientific psychology in general. Two elements in his investigations led to these developments. The first one was his rejection, under the influence of Wittgenstein's criticisms, of his theory of judgement. In *Problems of Philosophy* Russell considered a judgement such as the one expressed by the sentence "Othello believes that Desdemona loves Cassio" as a "multiple relation" between Othello on the one hand, and the complex formed by the relation of belief and love between Desdemona and Cassio. But this analysis stumbles on the fact that the relation does not exist when the judgement is false (as in the present case) and that the relation between Othello and the complex in question is not of the same kind as that between the terms of the complex and the relation (love). This led Russell to reject the idea that judging is a relation between a subject and the elements of a judgement. In the meantime, Russell had adopted the view that we do not perceive objects directly, but are acquainted with *sense data*, which are the immediate objects of sensation. These doctrines led him progressively to be more favourable to a view about the relation of the mental and the physical world that he had earlier criticized when he discussed William James's philosophy, namely neutral monism, according to which mind and matter do not form opposing realms but are a single "stuff" that is neither mental nor physical. On this view the distinction between the subject and the objects of judgement disappears. Even though he rejected the Cartesian idea of a pure Ego or Subject standing in front of his objects, Russell has always been a Cartesian in the theory of knowledge. His problem has always been: how can we be justified in what we know, and how can we base our knowledge on a firm foundation? After the First World War, his version of this problem was: how can we reconcile our knowledge of the physical world with our immediate sensory knowledge? The *Inquiry* is the result of his re-evaluation of his answers to this question over thirty years.

The *Inquiry* is complex not only because it incorporates several layers of Russell's views, but also because it combines four strands: epistemological, semantic, psychological and metaphysical. The starting-point is epistemological: what is the nature of our empirical knowledge and what justifies our empirical beliefs? From *Problems of Philosophy* to the end of his philosophical career, Russell never ceases to ask this traditional question, which he formulates in *Human Knowledge* thus: "How comes it that human beings, whose contacts with the world are brief and personal and limited, are nevertheless able to know as much as they do know?" (1948: xi). In 1940, however, his method for answering this question is explicitly linguistic. He is concerned with the way in which our empirical beliefs are expressed in sentences, and his question is: "What justifies our empirical sentences?" Sentences, like beliefs, have a certain content or meaning. Russell distinguishes two components of meaning in the *Inquiry*: a psychological component and what we shall call a truth-conditional component. The psychological component is, in Russell's terminology, what a sentence *expresses*. The truth-conditional component is what the sentence *indicates*, which is in general a fact or a state of affairs in the world. For instance the sentence "There is food on the table", uttered by me at a certain time and place, expresses my belief that there is food on the table, and indicates the fact that there is food on the table. The truth-conditional component, in turn, is made of various entities in the world – things, their properties or relations and facts – that, combined in a certain way, make our sentences true. But how are these various dimensions – meaning, truth and knowledge – combined?

In order to understand Russell's conception of meaning and truth in the *Inquiry* it is useful to sort out the various kinds of possible relations between the two notions. It will enable us to locate Russell's view among those that have been prominent in the twentieth century.

Let us call, following a recent tradition,[1] a *theory of meaning* a philosophical account of meaning that would give us a specification – or explanation, or characterization – of meaning in terms of a certain property of sentences of a given language of the form

[M]   S means that *p* iff ...

(where "S" is a sentence of a given language and "*p*" the appropriate meaning-giving condition). The point of a theory of meaning is to find an appropriate concept, or set of concepts, susceptible to define, or at least to give a *substantial* characterization of, meaning.

Frege, the early Russell and the early Wittgenstein subscribed to a version of the view that "means that" in [M] can be explained in terms of the *truth-conditions* of the sentence *p*: what a sentence means consists in its truth-conditions.[2] On such a *truth-conditional conception of meaning*, the meaning of a given sentence S is spelled out with an appropriate specification of the schema

[T]   S is true iff *p*

(where "S" denotes a given sentence and "*p*" is a sentence describing the truth-conditions of S). An essential ingredient of truth-conditional theories is that the meaning of a sentence S should be determined by the meanings of its component parts, hence that the truth-conditions of the whole sentence be determined by the contribution of its parts to these truth-conditions. Russell's theory of descriptions (Russell 1905) was, with Frege's earlier analysis of quantified sentences (i.e. those sentences containing phrases such as "all", "some" and similar expressions), a major step in the analysis of the truth-conditional element in meaning.[3]

Now, will the replacement of "means that" by "is true" in [M] do? According to a familiar objection (Dummett 1975), the problem is that a speaker who would know a sentence of the form [T], for instance

[1]   "Lilac smells" is true iff Lilac smells

might well know that [1] is true without knowing what [1] means, that is without understanding this sentence. There is all the difference in the world between knowing what the sentence "Lilac smells" means or the proposition it expresses, and knowing that the *metalinguistic* sentence [1] is true. When we accept that sentences of the form [T] "give the meaning" of sentences of the object-language on their left-hand side, we tend to forget that this is so because we already know what these sentences mean. This remark often leads to the conclusion that the bare truth-conditional conception of meaning is insufficient, and that there must be something more to the meaning of a sentence than its truth-conditions. But what is this something more? The obvious candidate is knowledge of truth-conditions, or some epistemic state that constitutes the understanding that a speaker has of the sentence. According to an *epistemic conception of meaning*, the meaning of a given sentence consists in what the speaker knows, or is justified to believe, when he uses the sentence. An epistemic conception of meaning is often associated (but as we shall see it need not be) to the view according to which to know the meaning of a sentence is to know how to verify it. We can call this a *verificationist conception of meaning*. In rough form (for a declarative sentence), it can be formulated thus:

[EM]   S means that *p* iff one is justified in asserting *p*

A verificationist theory of meaning says that understanding a sentence is to grasp the information that would verify this sentence. It does not tell us what this information consists in. There are, however, two distinct versions of the theory, depending on how we conceive the information in question. On one version, it can be said that what the speaker knows are the truth-conditions of the sentence. But this leads to an obvious difficulty: for a large number of sentences (about infinite quantities, about the past, or about remote regions of space and time) we do not know their truth-conditions, even though we do understand these sentences. A verificationist about truth will find it much more plausible to say that what we know when we know the meaning of a sentence are its *verification* conditions. On this second reading, the epistemic conception of meaning is coupled to a verificationist conception of truth.

Both the truth-conditional and the verificationist conception of meaning share one presupposition: an account of what linguistic meaning is has to be formulated in terms of something that is necessarily extra-linguistic: namely states of affairs, objects or facts, or whatever there is in the world that accounts for the truth-conditions and the reference conditions of our sentences, or states of a speaker (presumably states of mind) or capacities that account for what the speaker knows when he knows what the sentences mean. But the objection to the truth-conditional conception suggests that it is impossible to account for what the sentences mean without invoking our knowledge of what they mean, hence without relying on our mastery of linguistic expressions. The same objection can be pressed against the verificationist conception of meaning: how can we account for what a speaker knows without looking at how he *uses* the sentence, that is without taking this knowledge to be, in large part, a knowledge of the rules of language use? But then how can this knowledge of rules be spelled out without presupposing that the speaker masters them, hence already follows these rules? Such an objection is familiar from Wittgenstein's reflections on language use and rules. A famous remark by Wittgenstein says that:

In a certain sense, the use of language is something that cannot be taught, i.e. I cannot use language to teach it in the way language could be used to teach someone to play the piano. – And that of course is just another way of saying I cannot use language to get outside language.

(Wittgenstein 1975: 54)

On such a view, any specification of what meaning is has to be formulated in terms of language rules, and hence must presuppose the speaker's mastery of these very rules. It follows that there is no language-independent account of meaning – be it in terms of truth-conditions or in terms of mental states, or epistemic states – which we could specify in language-free terms.[4] In other words we cannot explain understanding a linguistic expression as knowing what the expression means as if the meaning were an entity independent of language. We have to use our knowledge of meaning rules in order to account for them. Let us call this *the priority thesis*, following John Skorupski (1997). According to many versions of this thesis, no genuine theory of meaning can be given, if a "theory" of meaning is supposed to explain, or account for, meaning in terms of an independent concept. This is why a priority thesis is often called modest, or deflationary or non-substantive about the aim of giving a theory of meaning.[5] We can recapitulate these distinctions thus:

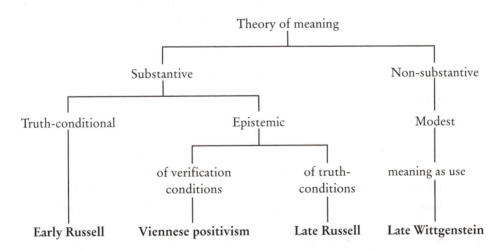

Now, where does Russell fit within this framework? The early Russell, as we have already remarked, defended a version of the truth-conditional view. But from 1919 onwards he adopted a version of the epistemic conception of meaning, according to which the propositions expressed by sentences are psychological entities (mostly made up of images) that are grasped by speakers, and correlated to their behaviour in the use of sentences. During the 1930s, Wittgenstein and the logical positivists also defended an epistemic conception of meaning, but their version was clearly associated to a *verificationist conception of truth*. According to the celebrated criterion of empirical meaning proposed by the positivists, a sentence is meaningful only if it is either analytic and true in virtue of meaning, or synthetic, in which case its meaning consists in its method of verification. Various members of the Vienna Circle had divergent views on the nature of this method: some, such as Schlick, held that the method of verification had to be based on knowledge of basic sentences, themselves based on sensory experiences; others, such as Neurath and Hempel, believed that the verification conditions had to be holistic, and based on the language of science as a whole. Other writers, such as Carnap, influenced by the methods proposed by Tarski (1933) for defining truth in formal language, developed conceptions of meaning in terms of the precise statement of meaning rules, understood as conventions tacitly accepted by speakers of a language. Wittgenstein himself became critical of these views.

Russell's *Inquiry* is obviously inspired by these debates, and much of the book is devoted to a dialogue with these views. Russell's late approach however, is genuine, and owes as much to his previous evolution and premises as to the positivist atmosphere of the 1930s. Most positivists defend a version of the verificationist or epistemic conception of meaning and a verificationist conception of truth, but the originality of Russell's views lies in his defence of an epistemic conception of meaning (meaning is a function of what a speaker knows) but a *non-verificationist*, truth-conditional or realist conception of truth.

In order to understand in what sense it is an epistemic conception of meaning, we must first place it in the context of Russell's general conception of knowledge. Russell presents his *Inquiry* as an investigation into the sources and justifications of our knowledge of empirical propositions. He tells us that he is not concerned, in this work, with propositions of logic or mathematics, but only with the relation of basic propositions to experiences. This sets apart his approach from that of the logical empiricists, who distinguished two kinds of meaningful sentences: those that are synthetic or true in virtue of their relation to experience (such as "This is hot") and those that are analytic or true purely in virtue of meaning (such as "An oculist is an eye doctor").[6] He also differs from the Viennese philosophers in his lack of interest in a general criterion of the meaningfulness of sentences, which would allow us to demarcate science from metaphysics. For him not only is there no such demarcation, but legitimate metaphysical issues arise in the theory of knowledge, which is not purely limited, as Carnap for instance had argued in his *Logical Syntax of Language* (1934), to knowledge of words.

Russell's conception of knowledge is twofold. On the one hand he defends a version of what we call today a "naturalized epistemology": knowledge is a natural phenomenon, which can be studied, like anything within nature, in causal terms. The general outlook is broadly speaking behaviouristic and physicalistic: organisms enter into causal contact with a physical environment that provides stimuli to which they react by forming appropriate habits. In this respect, however complex human organisms can be, there is not much difference, except of degree, between animal cognition and human cognition. Russell's conception of belief is also causal. A belief is the mental state intermediary between environmental inputs and output actions of the organism. This can be understood in a purely behaviourist way, but Russell is not a straight behaviourist. He considers belief to be a genuine psychological state, which together with sensory inputs and with other mental states, such as desires, leads to actions. In this respect, this conception is very close to what today is called a *functionalist* conception of belief.[7] On the other hand, Russell considers that it is impossible to reduce an account of knowledge to an account of the causal relations between an organism and a physical or biological environment. The physicalist point of view is also in need of justification, when it presupposes the naive realism of common sense. But scientific realism cannot be simply presupposed. As Russell says in what may be one of the most well-known *modus ponens* of contemporary philosophy: "Naïve realism leads to physics, and physics, if true, shows that naïve realism is false. Therefore naïve realism, if true, is false, hence it is false" (1970: 13). Epistemology is concerned not merely with the causal question of why and how our beliefs can become knowledge, but with the normative question of why we *should* believe this or that. The kind of answer that Russell gives to the latter question is a version of what is traditionally called a form of foundationalism: all our beliefs are ultimately based on some basic or foundational beliefs that are beyond doubt. And his version of foundationalism is empiricist: ultimately our beliefs are based on experiences. Or, to put it into the linguistic terms adopted by Russell, our knowledge rests upon basic propositions that in turn owe their truth to basic experiences.

Much of the originality of Russell's approach in the *Inquiry* lies in this two-fold conception of knowledge, both causal and foundationalist, descriptive and normative. But there is also a potential tension between these two points of view, since there is no necessary coincidence between the propositions that come first in the causal order, and those that come first in the logical order. Another source of tension is due to the double character of experiences and of beliefs based on them: on the one hand they are defined by their causal connections and can be studied objectively; on the other hand they involve an irreducible subjective element.

Another doctrine that lies in the background of Russell's *Inquiry* is logical atomism. Logical atomism is the view, which Russell borrowed initially from

Wittgenstein's *Tractatus*, that all complex propositions can be decomposed into simpler elements until we reach ultimate "simples". Another part of the doctrine is that the structure of propositions mirrors the structure of the world, and that all propositions correspond to facts, which can in turn be analysed into complex facts and atomic facts. In the version of the doctrine that he defended in "The Philosophy of Logical Atomism" (1918), Russell admitted both positive facts corresponding to positive propositions such as "The chair is blue" and negative facts corresponding to negative propositions such as "The chair is not blue". He also accepted that the ultimate simple entities that compose atomic facts are particulars that are denoted by demonstrative words such as "this" or "that", which he called "logically proper names". He held that we are directly acquainted to these entities in sensation. Although in 1940 Russell rejects a number of these views, he keeps the basic structure of logical atomism. In the first place, as we have already noted, he continues to hold that propositions correspond to facts and he still accepts these as genuine entities in his ontology, over and above things and their properties or relations. In his 1940 terminology, facts are the "verifiers" of sentences. This terminology is potentially misleading, because it suggests that the semantic dimension of sentences is constituted by their verification-conditions, in the manner of the verificationist theory of meaning and of truth held by the positivists. But it would be wrong to take the verifiers as indicating epistemic conditions. On the contrary Russell's verifiers are more properly conceived as those entities *in the world* that *make true* our sentences, or, to use a terminology made popular today by contemporary ontologists, such as David Armstrong, their "truthmakers".[8] In other words, they are the truth-conditions of our sentences in the substantive sense required by a correspondence theory of truth.

That our sentences are made true by facts is one thing. Our knowledge of these facts is another thing, which we have to account for. According to Russell's empiricist outlook, all sentences are made true ultimately by entities that are known through basic experiences. Now sentences are made up of words, such as names, demonstratives, predicates and verbs, which themselves get their meaning and truth-conditions through certain basic experiences. In order to achieve this foundationalist strategy, Russell supposes that there exists a basic level of language, "the object-language", which contains only words – "object-words" – which get their meaning through our direct contact with the world. For instance natural kind terms such as "dog", or names of sensible qualities, such as "yellow", names of actions, such as "walk", or adverbs referring to events, such as "quick" and "slow", belong to this object-language and are learnt by "ostension". He has two distinct arguments for postulating such a "primary language". The first is a classical foundationalist move: if we did not posit a basic level of learning of words, we would get into a regress and language could not be learnt. The second is modelled after

Tarski's theory of truth, which is based on the schema [T] above, which rests upon a distinction between an object-language and a metalanguage: semantic words such as "true" or "refers", but also logical words such as "or", "and" or "some" presuppose the existence of the basic language but cannot belong to it. Hence Russell distinguishes the first-level object-language from a second-order language introducing logical words and semantic words. Russell's recognition of the existence of a hierarchy of languages was, as he says at the beginning of Chapter 4, implicit in his own theory of types, according to which we have to postulate a hierarchy of expressions of different types in order to avoid the famous paradoxes of set theory. Here the hierarchy of languages is mostly devised for epistemological and ontological purposes, and both the ontology and epistemology of his classification of facts have undergone important changes since his logical atomist period.

In "The Philosophy of Logical Atomism", Russell accepts that the kinds of facts that make true propositions more or less parallel the structure of the kinds of propositions. Thus he accepts, somewhat reluctantly, the existence of negative facts, corresponding to negative sentences such as "The pen is not on the table" and general facts, corresponding to existential sentences such as "Some men are bald" or universal sentences such as "All emeralds are green".[9] But he accepts neither the existence of conjunctive facts such as "Paul is bald and Mary is blonde", because they can be reduced to singular atomic facts, nor the existence of disjunctive facts such as "Paul or Mary came". In the *Inquiry*, he rejects conjunctive, disjunctive and negative facts, and he admits that the relation between general sentences (existential or universal) and the facts that make them true is less straightforward than it might seem on a simple correspondence conception of truth.[10] Although he is sceptical about the panoply of facts that the first version of logical atomism implied, Russell accepts the epistemic counterpart of the various kinds of propositions. In his terminology, the fact that not all sentences *indicate* a certain kind of entity does not imply that sentences do not *express* a certain kind of belief. In this respect there are negative, conjunctive, disjunctive and general beliefs, which express certain kinds of psychological states. Thus a disjunctive belief such as "John is in town or abroad" expresses a state of hesitation. Russell also accepts that there are negative basic propositions that express experiences of absence, such as those that are expressed by our answering "No" to the question "Do you hear something?" Most of the time, however, complex beliefs of the disjunctive or general form are inferred from basic beliefs, and for this reason Russell concentrates upon these.

The most basic propositions are those that are of "atomic form" Fa or aRb, where a and b are proper names, and F and R denote properties or relations. During his logical atomist period, Russell held the view that to such atomic propositions corresponded atomic facts, made up of simple particulars and of properties and relations, conceived as genuine universal entities. He also held the famous view that the proper names of ordinary language (such as "George W. Bush" or "Texas") are actually "truncated" or disguised descriptions such as "The 43rd President of the USA", which can in turn be analysed according to Russell's theory of descriptions into sentences of the form "There is a unique x that is 43rd President of the USA". Ordinary proper names, on this view, do not directly denote their objects. In Russell's early works, only demonstratives such as "this", personal pronouns such as "I", or adverbs of time or place such as "now" or "here" denote directly particulars with which we are acquainted, and for this reason he called them "logically proper names". The particulars denoted by these "genuine" names are individual substances, distinct from universals denoted by common nouns such as "man" or "horse". In a famous paper (Russell 1912), Russell had argued for a strong dualism of particulars and universals and rejected the nominalistic view that universals are only resemblances between particulars. In the *Inquiry*, however, especially in Chapters 6 and 7, he adopts a quite different conception.

He first defines a name syntactically, as the kind of expression that can occur in an atomic sentence of the form $R(a)$, or $R(a, b, ...)$ where "R" is a predicate or a relation, and "a", "b" and so on are names, and semantically as an entity that occupies a continuous portion of spacetime. Names in this sense can be of two sorts: either ordinary names, such as "Donald Rumsfeld" and "Iraq", or demonstratives and expressions that he calls "egocentric particulars", such as "this", "I", "here" or "now", including words such as "past", "present" and "future" and tense in verbs. Russell's account of egocentric particulars deserves to be considered, together with Hans Reichenbach's,[11] as one of the pioneering accounts of indexical and other context-sensitive expressions, which has become one of the main issues in contemporary philosophy of language. Russell rightly points out that, semantically, demonstratives such as "this" and other expressions cannot be paraphrased in terms of general concepts and definite descriptions, unlike ordinary proper names according to his official strategy in his theory of descriptions. Whatever number of descriptions we try to put in the place of "this" – such as "what I am now noticing" – the uniqueness of the demonstrative will not be accounted for.[12] On the ontological side, however, Russell's account of proper names and egocentric particulars is squarely eliminativist. He defends the view that particulars denoted by "this" or "I" are not needed in an objective physical description of the world. According to him, a statement reporting the content of a perception of the form

(1) This is red

is actually of the form

(2) Redness is here now

which in turn is considered as a bundle of coexisting qualities. More precisely, let a given red patch in the visual field be denoted "C". Let the angular coordinates of this patch be (θ, φ). Let the patch be also present at another place (θ', φ'). So the bundle (C, θ, φ) coexists with the distinct bundle (C, θ', φ'). There are no more particulars or substances, since they are replaced by "compresent" or co-instantiated qualities such as redness, hardness and so on, instantiated at a particular place and time. Substances are eliminated in favour of bundles of qualities, and the dualism of universals and particulars is abolished. This is often known as a "bundle theory" of individuals. An ontology of substances has, according to Russell, two disadvantages. In the first place, a substance is an unknowable entity, considered as irreducible to the sum of its predicates. On the other hand the principle of the identity of indiscernibles is a synthetic proposition: two substances can share all their predicates without being identical, for the predicates do not exhaust the nature of the substance (spatial and temporal differences can account for this diversity). On the bundle theory, on the contrary, a particular, being replaced by a set of compresent qualities, becomes entirely knowable. The set of properties to which a thing is identical is given in experience, and its experience can be described in purely causal terms. Moreover a thing being defined by the set of its qualities, and space and time being among these qualities, the principle of the identity of indiscernibles becomes analytic: by definition two things are different if they do not share their spatiotemporal properties.

This procedure of elimination of proper names and of egocentric particulars, and hence of the substances that they denote, is an echo of Russell's famous motto: "Wherever possible replace inferred entities by logical constructions" (1914: 115). But it also involves a rejection of some of the main tenets of Russell's logical atomism. One of Russell's targets, in his rejection of Hegelian idealism, was a form of ontological monism that prevents the analysis of a thing into its simple elements, and that takes space and time as irreducible to properties of things. This was in large part the meaning of the principle of "external relations", which the early Russell defended against Bradley: spatial and temporal relations are not internal to things and they imply diversity (see Russell 1910). Atomism was the very foundation of analysis. To a large extent, as he explains in Chapter 24, Russell rejects this atomism. Judgements of perception give us a global pattern, which we may call "this", that we can analyse into properties and relations without this analysis coming down to ultimate elements. Names in the primary or object-language are names of totalities or continuous spatiotemporal regions that belong to a given whole (here the influence of *Gestalt* psychology is obvious). These perceived totalities are in turn internal to a physical object, that is, the brain of the observer.

Russell's analysis encounters difficulties at both the ontological and the epistemological level. The bundle theory of individuals tells us that an individual

145

thing is a set of properties that are united by the relation of co-instantiation ("compresence" in Russell's terminology), which ensures that the properties are all possessed by the same individual. But if we say that it is the same individual that possesses these properties are we not reintroducing the idea of a substance lying behind the set of properties? And if a thing is a set of properties, how can anything ever change its properties? In order to answer this question it is crucial that the relation of co-instantiation be contingent: if two or more properties are co-instantiated it is not necessary that it is so. On this view redness is co-instantiated with roundness in a ripe tomato, but the two properties might not have been instantiated at all. It is not clear that Russell escapes these difficulties. The fact that the principle of the identity of indiscernibles becomes analytic on his view means that if two things (sets of properties) are distinct, they are necessarily so. This seems, as we have noted, to reintroduce a principle similar to Leibniz's principle that an individual has all his properties essentially. Russell is aware of this difficulty, for he wants to say that if a given name, say "T", is the name of a bundle of qualities, we do not have to know, when we give the name, *what* qualities constitute the totality T. It is not clear, however, that this does not reintroduce the difficulties of the notion of substance: for if we know a bundle of properties without knowing which are its elements, does a bundle not look like a "I do not know what"? On the epistemological side, Russell's analysis of singular judgements of the form "this is red" is meant to eliminate all elements of subjectivity that affect demonstrative and other indexical beliefs. The bundles of qualities are supposed to coexist without a perceiver. But is it certain that we can dispense with the subjective point of view of the perceiver? This question has figured prominently in all theories of perception and indexical beliefs.[13]

Atomic sentences of the form "Fa" where "a" is a proper name or a demonstrative form the basis of our experiential knowledge. There verifiers (or truth-makers) are ultimately, as we have seen, bundles of properties. What about general sentences? These are of two kinds: existential sentences such as "There is a fox" of the form "There is an x such that Fx", and universal sentences such as "All foxes run" of the form "For all x if Fx then Rx". The verifiers of existential sentences are individual facts of the form "Fa" (at least one such fact). But the correspondence between "There is an x such that Fx" and its verifier Fa, or Fb, or ... cannot be the same as for atomic sentences. The correspondence, Russell tells us, is causal, and it is known through an inductive generalization, which is an inference. Consider, next, universal sentences of the form "For all x Fx". What are their verifiers? In his *Logical Atomism* lectures, Russell held that the existence of general facts should be granted as much as the existence of particular atomic facts. In other words, when we have listed all the particular facts, Fa, Fb, Fc, ... there is a further fact in the world, the fact that all x are F. In the *Inquiry*, Russell rejects this view, and takes the verifier to be simply the collection of particular facts. He further tells us that what we know when we know the meaning of such sentences cannot be based on our experience, but on induction. Both the ontological view and the epistemological view, however, raise one of the most difficult problems for any empiricist epistemology.

The problem is this: if the collection of facts that are "indicated" by universal sentences is infinite, how can we know their meaning if all meanings have to be based on basic beliefs? How can their meaning consist in their truth-conditions if these conditions are unfathomable? The Viennese positivists, who subscribed both to the verificationist theory of truth and to the verificationist theory of knowledge, concluded that the meaning of these sentences could not consist in their truth-conditions. They also held that truth could not be interpreted in the realist way, as a form of correspondence with facts. In Chapter 21 of the *Inquiry*, Russell examines these views, and related ones, such as Dewey's and Reichenbach's, who attempted to reduce truth to warranted assertibility or to some epistemic notion, such as probability. He refuses to assimilate the meaning and truth-conditions of general sentences and of sentences about unknowable facts to their assertion conditions. In this respect, he refuses to question classical logical principles such as the law of excluded middle (a proposition is either true or false), which is rejected by mathematical intuitionism and the strong versions of verificationism or anti-realism. He sides, both in mathematics and in natural science, with an uncompromising realism. Truth, for him, transcends knowledge and cannot be reduced to an epistemic notion.[14] But how can this be reconciled with an empiricist epistemology? At this point, Russell bites the bullet: he accepts that pure empiricism, the view that all true propositions are verifiable, is false, and that there are principles of inference and propositions that are neither demonstrative nor derivable from experience. He will return to these themes in his last great philosophical book, *Human Knowledge*, in 1948. There he admits that our knowledge of such principles as the principle of induction is distinct from our knowledge of particular facts: it is known "solely in the sense that we generalize in accordance with them when we use experience to persuade us of the truth of a general proposition".[15]

The originality of Russell's views is obvious if one compares them to the other versions of empiricism that he discusses in the course of his William James Lectures. He rejects the verificationist and pragmatist theories of meaning and truth, and defends a realist conception of truth. Although he manifests a strong attraction for the linguistic turn in epistemology introduced by the logical positivists, he refuses to accept that the justification of empirical knowledge rests upon the choice of a language and his ontological and metaphysical perspectives are very far from Carnap's neutralism or Hempel's holism. But in spite of their originality, what is the legacy of Russell's ideas?

Actually, if the *Inquiry* has had a legacy, it seems to have been, in the first two decades that followed its publication, mostly negative. At the time when Russell was delivering his William James Lectures, Wittgenstein was writing the work that led to his *Philosophical Investigations*. One of his main targets is "the myth of pure ostensive definition": the view that the very basis of meaning resides in primitive acts of "ostension". Basically, the gist of Wittgenstein's remarks is similar to his objection to the idea that we could account for our mastery of language rules and linguistic meaning from outside language, which led to what we called above the priority thesis: there can be no such ostensive acts of definition without presupposing a great deal of mastery of language.[16] The very idea of an object-language that could form the basis of knowledge is also one of the ideas that was fought by Wittgenstein. It threw doubt on empiricist theories of meaning for at least a generation of British philosophers.

Within the empiricist tradition, the main heritage of Russell's *Inquiry* is to be found in Quine's analysis of meaning in *Word and Object* (1960) and in the *Roots of Reference* (1973). Quine starts, like Russell, from the question: how is an empirical theory of meaning possible? And his account, like Russell's, is strongly influenced by behaviourism. Like Russell, Quine takes a naturalistic starting-point. Quine is also very interested in giving an ontogeny of reference, proceeding from the earlier stages of infant life, where quantification is not yet in place, according to him, to its later stages, where individuation, reference and identity in objects come in. But apart from these similarities, Quine's and Russell's perspectives are diametrically opposed. Quine starts from sentences, which he takes to be the immediate object of assent and the main unit of meaning, where Russell starts from words. Quine's epistemology is explicitly holistic, and Duhemian, and explicitly anti-foundationalist; there is no privileged, ostensive basis, for meanings and sentences are "interanimated" and connected within a holistic whole. So Quine is actually quite close to the kind of coherence conception of truth and knowledge that Russell criticized in Hempel in Chapter 10 of the *Inquiry*. Last but not least, Quine's analysis is a sort of *reductio* of the whole enterprise of giving an empiricist account of meaning, at least if a theory of meaning based on experience is supposed to give us a completely specified account of the meanings of the sentences of a given language in the sense of a theory answering the schema [M] above. For meaning, according to Quine's famous thesis, is indeterminate, in the sense that two translation manuals that would equally fit the evidence could diverge in the meaning that they would attribute to the sentences of a given language. Indeed, given the thesis that Quine calls the "inscrutability of reference", the very idea that types of sentences could have their specific verifiers or truthmakers is a view that Quine strongly rejects; given that reference as well as meaning is indeterminate, there is no such thing as an ontological counterpart of our sentences in reality.

Quine's and Wittgenstein's view of meaning come, in the end, quite close to the priority thesis, which has very strong similarities with the thesis that no genuine theory of meaning can be given at all. A theory of meaning, on such a view, can only, at best, be an exercise in linguistic paraphrase of words the meaning of which we already know. They agree more or less on the idea that at best what a theory of meaning can do is to give us specifications of the form "P" is true iff p, where p is a translation of "P" or P itself, and where our knowledge of the meaning of this sentence is already secured. Although they reach this disenchanted conclusion about meaning (and often about truth) through distinct arguments, such views have been developed under the names "scepticism about meaning" and "deflationary", "modest" or "nihilistic" conceptions of meaning.[17] In other words, we would be more or less bound to end up on the right-hand side of the diagram above.

Disenchantment with the project of a substantive theory of meaning, however, may well be premature. Even if we subscribe to the priority thesis and accept the idea that there is always a kind of circle in an account of language learning, the circle has to be broken, for even the most convinced defendant of the innateness hypothesis has to recognize that language is learnt and that the child has to start from somewhere. Wittgenstein himself held that signs can convey meaning only if at some point there is a natural, non-linguistic, uptake of how they are being used. He took this uptake to come through a drill (*ein Abrichten*; Wittgenstein 1958: §5). Russell took the uptake to reside in association, conditioning and habit. Quine took it to reside in a set of dispositions. Contemporary innatists take it to reside in some structures of the brain. So in a sense there are all sorts of plausible ways to break the circle and to reject the priority thesis. But its proponents do not deny that we learn a language, and that there can be empirically plausible theories about this. What they object to at a more fundamental level is the claim that one could give a *philosophical account* of content or meaning without using, in one way or another, the very concepts that we intend to define. In other words, they are sceptical that a reductive account of meaning in terms of things that are not meanings (physical entities, Platonic entities or whatever) can ever be given. Now even if we grant them this, it does not follow that nothing can be said of meaning within a kind of enquiry inspired by Russell's own.

I have already mentioned the fact that Russell's account of egocentric particulars was in large part pioneering with respect to contemporary work on the semantics of demonstratives and other indexicals. Now in this respect, in order to find the true heritage of Russell's *Inquiry* within contemporary philosophy, we have to turn to the work on singular reference and demonstrative thoughts that has emerged during the past twenty years along the lines laid down by writers such as Gareth Evans and John Perry. One of Evans's main theses in his *The Varieties of Reference* (1982) is that a number of linguistic expressions are

149

"Russellian" in approximately the sense in which Russell talked of "logically proper names": that is, expressions that are such that they essentially make a reference to their bearer. He argues that proper names, demonstratives and a number of pronouns are Russellian in this sense. He defends, with respect to singular thoughts, the very principle that Russell defended in his *Problems of Philosophy*: the "principle of acquaintance". "Every proposition which we understand must be composed wholly of constituents with which we are acquainted" (Russell 1967: ch. 5), or, in other terms, a subject cannot make a judgement about something unless he knows which object the judgement is about. The specification of the kind of knowledge necessary for acquaintance with objects leads Evans to specify the kind of information possessed by a subject, especially in the case of demonstrative identification with words such as "this" and other indexicals. Evans's account of singular thought is much more sophisticated than Russell's, and it does not rest on any behaviouristic premises, but it is equally psychological in that it accepts the idea that there is a "fundamental level of thought" that is *prior* to language, and on the basis of which the relation of reference is built. Unlike Russell, however, Evans grounds demonstrative thought in basic thought structures of self-identification. If Evans is right, there *is*, contrary to Quine's verdict, a fact of the matter as to what our thoughts about objects are *about*.

Another line of development of ideas from Russell's legacy has already been mentioned. A striking feature of the *Inquiry* is Russell's refusal to set apart epistemological, semantic and ontological matters. He does not intend simply to tell us what psychological states are responsible for our thinking, but also what there is in the world for our thoughts to be about. This is why he cares so much for what sentences "indicate" and their "verifiers". As recent work on the relation of truthmaking and on the kinds of entities that have to exist if our sentences are true shows that even if it encounters difficulties of its own, this kind of project is not completely bound for failure.[18] In other words, contrary to what the partisans of various deflationary, minimalist or modest theories of meaning have argued, there is room for a substantive epistemic, and truth-conditional conception of meaning. In many ways the construction of such a theory is still to come, but it owes much of its inspiration to Russell's *Inquiry*.

Notes

1. Actually the phrase "theory of meaning" often has the technical sense of a set of axioms from which one could derive knowledge of meaning. I leave this sense aside here. For a recent account of this tradition, see, for instance, *A Companion to the Philosophy of Language*, B. Hale & C. Wright (eds) (Oxford: Blackwell, 1997). My presentation is much inspired by J. Skorupski, "Meaning, Use, and Verification", 29–59 in that volume.

2. Frege: "It is determined through and through under what conditions any sentence stands for the True. The sense of this name (of a truth value) that is the thought, is the sense or thought that these conditions are fulfilled" (*The Basic Laws of Arithmetic*, partial translation, M. Furth (trans.) (Berkeley, CA: University of California Press, 1964), I, 32); and Wittgenstein, *Tractatus Logico-Philosophicus*, D. Pears (ed.) (London: Routledge, 1960 [1922]), 4.024. To understand a sentence in use means to know what is the case if it is true.

3. For a clear statement of this view see D. Kaplan, "What is Russell's Theory of Descriptions?", in *Bertrand Russell: A Collection of Critical Essays*, D. Pears (ed.), 227–44 (New York: Doubleday, 1972).

4. This is, notably, why there are no rules to interpret rules, one of the morals of Wittgenstein's rule-following considerations.

5. J. McDowell, "In Defense of Modesty", in *Mind, Meaning and Reality: Collected Papers, II* (Cambridge, MA: Harvard University Press, 1988) and P. Horwich, *Meaning* (Oxford: Oxford University Press, 1998), and a number of views inspired by the late Wittgenstein have been of this "deflationary" kind.

6. Actually the early Russell took the sentences of logic and mathematics as describing the world in its most general features, hence as synthetic, unlike the positivists, who took them to express merely linguistic conventions. But the later Russell came close to the logical positivist view that they are tautologies (see Russell, *My Philosophical Development* (London: Allen & Unwin, 1959), ch. XVII).

7. Russell had already defended such a view in *The Analysis of Mind* (London: Allen & Unwin, 1921). The analogy with the functionalist conception has been observed by T. Baldwin in "Introduction", in B. Russell, *The Analysis of Mind* (London: Allen & Unwin, 1992). It is also present in Ramsey's elaboration on Russell's definition in "Facts and Propositions", in *Philosophical Papers*, D. H. Mellor (ed.), 34–51 (Cambridge: Cambridge University Press, 1990 [1926]) (see also Dokic & Engel 2002: 24–5).

8. See K. Mulligan, B. Smith & P. Simons, "Truth Makers", *Philosophy and Phenomenological Research* **44** (1984), 287–321, and D. M. Armstrong, *Truth and Truthmakers* (Cambridge, Cambridge University Press, 2003). Armstrong, *Truth and Truthmakers*, 5, explicitly credits Russell for having anticipated the notion of a truthmaker in the *Inquiry*.

9. Wittgenstein did not accept such negative and general facts. See Wittgenstein, *Tractatus*.

10. In Armstrong's terminology, Russell tended to be, in his logical atomist period, a "truthmaker maximalist", that is, he accepted (almost) the view that every truth has a truthmaker, which Armstrong calls "truthmaker-maximalism".

11. H. Reichenbach, *Elements of Symbolic Logic* (New York: Macmillan, 1947) is mentioned in a note at the end of Chapter 7.

12. The point has been rediscovered and argued for by J. Perry, "The Problem of the Essential Indexical", *Noûs* **13**(1) (1979), 1–29.

13. R. Chisholm (1944) raises the objection about the elimination of egocentric particulars. On the bundle theory of universals, see J. Van Cleve, "Three Versions of the Bundle Theory", *Philosophical Studies* **47** (1985), 95–107.

14. Although it cannot be done here, it would be interesting to compare Russell's view here with those of Frank Ramsey, who discussed Russell on logical, epistemological and ontological matters. Russell himself reviewed Ramsey's posthumous book *The Foundations of Mathematics* (1931, in Russell 1931). His rejection of the dualism of universals and particulars may well have its origins in Ramsey's paper "Universals". Ramsey also had an account of general propositions that probably attracted Russell's attention. He took them

to be "variable hypotheticals", expressing inferences that we are prepared to make. Thus to believe that "All men are mortal" is for Ramsey to be prepared, when one encounters a man, to infer that he is mortal. Hence general propositions are based on habits (see Dokic and Engel 2002). Russell, however, in his review of Ramsey's book, finds this circular, for the notion of habit already contains, according to him, the very notion of generality. Russell was also in strong disagreement with the anti-realist implications of Ramsey's conception of truth (Ramsey was attracted by intuitionism at the end of his life).

15. Russell 1948, 537.
16. Wittgenstein, *Philosophical Investigations*, 5, 6, 27–36.
17. Although they are in many ways quite distinct, works such as S. Kripke, *Wittgenstein on Rules and Private Language* (Oxford: Blackwell, 1981), D. Davidson, *Inquiries into Truth and Interpretation* (Oxford: Oxford University Press, 1985), McDowell, *Mind, Meaning and Reality: Collected Papers, II*, S. Schiffer, *Remnants of Meaning* (Cambridge, MA: MIT Press, 1987) and Horwich, *Meaning*, can be said to belong to this family.
18. Stephen Mumford, *Russell on Metaphysics* (London: Routledge, 2002), a recent collection of texts by Russell, is very much a reading of his work along these lines.

References

Armstrong, D. M. 2003 *Truth and Truthmakers*. Cambridge: Cambridge University Press.

Baldwin, T. 1992. "Introduction". In B. Russell, *The Analysis of Mind*. London: Allen & Unwin [1921].

Baldwin, T. 2003 "Knowledge by Acquaintance and Knowledge by Causation". In *The Cambridge Companion to Bertrand Russell*, N. Griffin (ed.). Cambridge: Cambridge University Press.

Carnap, R. 1934. *Die logische Syntax der Spache*, Vienna. Translated as *The Logical Syntax of Language* (London: Routledge, 1937).

Chisholm, R. 1944. "Russell on the Foundations of Empirical Knowledge". In *The Philosophy of Bertrand Russell*, P. A. Schilpp (ed.), 419–44. Evanston, IL: Northwestern University Press.

Davidson, D. 1985. *Inquiries into Truth and Interpretation*. Oxford: Oxford University Press.

Dokic, J. & P. Engel 2002. *Frank Ramsey, Truth and Success*. London: Routledge.

Dummett, M. 1975 "What is a Theory of Meaning? (I)". In *Mind and Language*, S. Guttenplan (ed.). Oxford: Oxford University Press.

Evans, G. 1982. *The Varieties of Reference*, J. McDowell (ed.). Oxford: Oxford University Press.

Frege, G. 1964. *The Basic Laws of Arithmetic*, partial translation, M. Furth (trans.). Berkeley, CA: University of California Press. Originally published in 1893 as *Grundegezetze der Arithmetik*.

Griffin, N. (ed.) 2003. *The Cambridge Companion to Bertrand Russell*. Cambridge: Cambridge University Press.

Hale, B. & C. Wright (eds) 1997. *A Companion to the Philosophy of Language*. Oxford: Blackwell.

Horwich, P. 1998. *Meaning*. Oxford: Oxford University Press.

Kaplan, D. 1972. "What is Russell's Theory of Descriptions?". In *Bertrand Russell: A Collection of Critical Essays*, D. Pears (ed.), 227–44. New York: Doubleday. Originally published 1966.

Kripke, S. 1981. *Wittgenstein on Rules and Private Language*. Oxford: Blackwell.

McDowell, J. 1987. "In Defense of Modesty". In *Michael Dummett: Contributions to Philosophy*, B. Taylor (ed.), 59–80. The Hague: Nijhoff. Reprinted in *Mind, Meaning and Reality: Collected Papers, II* (Cambridge, MA: Harvard University Press, 1998).

Mulligan, K., B. Smith & P. Simons 1984. "Truth Makers". *Philosophy and Phenomenological Research* **44**, 287–321.

Mumford, S. (ed.) 2002. *Russell on Metaphysics*. London: Routledge.

Pears, D. 1967. *Bertrand Russell and the British Tradition in Philosophy*. New York: Random House.

Pears, D. (ed.) 1972. *Bertrand Russell: A Collection of Critical Essays*. New York: Doubleday.

Perry, J. 1979 "The Problem of the Essential Indexical". *Noûs* **13**(1), 1–29. Reprinted in his *The Problem of the Essential Indexical* (Oxford: Oxford University Press, 1993).

Quine W. V. O. 1960. *Word and Object*. Cambridge, MA: MIT Press.

Quine W. V. O. 1973. *The Roots of Reference*. LaSalle, IL: Open Court.

Ramsey, F. P. 1990 [1926]. "Facts and Propositions". In *Philosophical Papers*, D. H. Mellor (ed.), 34–51. Cambridge: Cambridge University Press.

Reichenbach, H. 1947. *Elements of Symbolic Logic*. New York: Macmillan.

Russell, B. 1903. *The Principles of Mathematics*. London: Allen & Unwin.

Russell, B. 1905. "On Denoting", *Mind* **14**, 479–93. Reprinted in Russell (1950), 39–56.

Russell, B. 1910. *Philosophical Essays*. London: Longmans and Green.

Russell, B. 1912. "On the Relation between Universals and Particulars". *Proceedings of the Aristotelian Society* **12**, 1–24. Reprinted in Russell (1950), 103–24.

Russell, B. 1914. "The Relations of Sense Data to Physics". In *Mysticism and Logic*, 145–79. London: Allen & Unwin.

Russell, B. 1918. "The Philosophy of Logical Atomism". *The Monist* **28**, **29**. Reprinted in Russell (1950), 175–282.

Russell, B. 1919. "On Propositions: What they Are, and How they Mean". *Proceedings of the Aristotelian Society*" supp. II, 1–43. Reprinted in Russell (1950), 283–320.

Russell, B. 1921. *The Analysis of Mind*. London: Allen & Unwin.

Russell, B. 1927a. *An Outline of Philosophy*. London: Allen & Unwin.

Russell, B. 1927b. *The Analysis of Matter*. London: Routledge.

Russell, B. 1931. "Critical Notice of F. P. Ramsey: *The Foundations of Mathematics*", *Mind* **41**, 476–82.

Russell, B. 1948. *Human Knowledge*. London: Allen & Unwin.

Russell, B. 1950. *Logic and Knowledge*, R. C. Marsh (ed.). London: Allen & Unwin.

Russell, B. 1959. *My Philosophical Development*. London: Allen & Unwin.

Russell, B. 1967 [1912]. *Problems of Philosophy*. Oxford: Oxford University Press.

Russell, B. 1970 [1940]. *An Inquiry into Meaning and Truth*. London: Penguin.

Russell, B. 1984 [1913]. *Theory of Knowledge*, E. R. Eames (ed.). London: Allen & Unwin.

Russell, B. & A. N. Whitehead 1910. *Principia Mathematica*. Cambridge: Cambridge University Press.

Schiffer, S. 1987. *Remnants of Meaning*. Cambridge, MA: MIT Press.

Skorupski, J. 1997. "Meaning, Use, and Verification". In *A Companion to the Philosophy of Language*, B. Hale & C. Wright (eds), 29–59.

Tarski, A. 1933. "The Concept of Truth in Formalized Languages" [Polish], *Prace Towarzystwa Naukowego Warszawskiego, Wydzial III Nauk Matematyczno-Fizycznych* **34**. Published in English in *Logic, Semantics, Metamathematics*, J. H. Woodger (trans.), 152–278 (Oxford: Oxford University Press, 1956). Second English edition, J. Corcoran (ed.) (Indianapolis, IN: Hackett, 1983).

Van Cleve, J. 1985. "Three Versions of the Bundle Theory". *Philosophical Studies* **47**, 95–107.

Wittgenstein, L. 1960 [1922]. *Tractatus Logico-Philosophicus*, D. Pears (ed.). London: Routledge.

Wittgenstein, L. 1958. *Philosophical Investigations*. Oxford: Blackwell.

Wittgenstein, L. 1975. *Philosophical Remarks*. Oxford: Blackwell.

8

Jean-Paul Sartre
Being and Nothingness

William R. Schroeder

Jean-Paul Sartre (1905–80) ranks among the leading thinkers of the twentieth century. His philosophical treatises developed and defended an original picture of human nature. He also wrote successful novels and plays that dramatized his important philosophical insights. While editing a leading popular journal of ideas, he addressed many contested political issues of his era with acumen and commitment. In addition, he published several literary biographies (and a partial autobiography) to demonstrate his approach to comprehending individuals in their historical contexts. His works stimulated responses from many of his most important contemporaries, for example, Merleau-Ponty, Levinas, de Beauvoir and Camus.

Being and Nothingness is subtitled *An Essay on Phenomenological Ontology*. Phenomenology is the systematic study of types of consciousness (or structures of human being) and their relationships to their objects. Sartre is an *existential* phenomenologist; he believes that lived experience can be described directly in a way that will yield important philosophical results. His approach is opposed to Edmund Husserl's *transcendental* phenomenology, the aim of which is to produce *certain* truths by withdrawing from the existential commitments of pre-reflective, lived experience. Husserl believed that all mental states emanate from an indubitable ego. Sartre argues that this ego appears only in the self-observational, reflective attitude Husserl presupposed and claims that no such ego exists in pre-reflective life.[1] To the extent that people experience a continuant self, it derives from the defining gaze of others. Like Husserl, Sartre seeks to clarify the structures of consciousness, but he wants to clarify pre-reflective, lived experience that is practically engaged with the world.

"Ontology", the analysis of being, had been resurrected in philosophy by Martin Heidegger, who also challenged Husserl's disengaged, contemplative standpoint and whose treatise, *Being and Time*, sought to clarify essential structures of human being. Heidegger's *hermeneutic* phenomenology assumes that traditional philosophical frameworks and assumptions prevent a direct elucidation of experience. He insists that philosophy must challenge its tradition as it rebuilds it. Sartre refashions traditional assumptions too, but he is more confident than Heidegger that fundamental structures of human life can be described directly. Sartre learned much from Heidegger's analysis of human being, but he offers a different analysis of the nature of being, tools, death, authenticity and other people. Sartre's project in *Being and Nothingness* is thus to elucidate the types of being (with a special focus on human being) and their relationships through a descriptive analysis of lived experience.

Overview

I shall begin by surveying the key claims of the book, and then I shall clarify some of the more difficult assertions in each chapter.

Sartre argues that consciousness cannot be isolated or self-sufficient; it depends on some distinct, independent being in order to experience itself. It is parasitic on this independent realm, which is fundamentally indifferent to consciousness (Introduction, iii–v). In this respect Sartre reverses Descartes's claim that consciousness can survive a sceptical annihilation of the perceived world and can function independently. Sartre's "being" differs from everyday objects; so it will eventually require some clarification (Introduction, i–ii, iv, vi). Sartre calls this independent, self-sufficient realm "being-in-itself". His term for consciousness is "being-for-itself".

For Sartre, the being of consciousness exhausts itself in negating being-in-itself, defining itself in relationship to its object. This "negation" is quite complex and requires Sartre's entire book to explain; so my clarification will proceed gradually. Initially it means *transcend* or go beyond: refusing to be limited by the objective being of which it is aware. It imagines other ways in which this being might be organized and new ways in which consciousness might transcend it. In effect, consciousness initially says "No!" to things as they are, even if in the end it may choose to maintain them. Consciousness can never just passively "fit in" with world; it either *actively* sustains it or *actively* strives to change it. This negation means that consciousness cannot simply lie inert – as if in a womb – merely an outgrowth of being-in-itself (Part One, Ch. 1). This sense of being pure reactivity – without any justification or support except what consciousness provides itself – produces an *anguish* that is the heart of Sartrean freedom. Individuals must create their own destinies and identities through their actions.

Consciousness exhausts itself in negating the in-itself, but it registers the form its negation takes and the specific object it negates. For example, consciousness is aware that it is now reading a book or imagining a sexy scene. Simultaneously and implicitly, consciousness is non-directedly (peripherally) aware (of) this focal awareness so that every state of consciousness is two-dimensional: at once directed towards its object and non-directly aware (of) being so directed (Introduction, iii). So consciousness has a distinctive self-relation, but this does not mean that its self-knowledge is always perfect because translating the content of non-directed awareness into language is often imperfect. Yet it does imply that consciousness has the capacity to correct self-misunderstandings, if it can access its non-positional dimension. Sartre calls such self-illumination "purified reflection".

Nonetheless, people often deceive themselves. Sartre begins to explain how this is possible by introducing another important dichotomy bisecting persons: facticity and transcendence (Part One, Ch. 2). He insists that people always exist in both dimensions at once. "Facticity" is that aspect of human life that resembles being-in-itself: that is fixed, inescapable, and need *not* be sustained by consciousness, for example, one's past, embodiment and death. "Transcendence" includes those aspects of human life that must be consciously sustained in order to continue to exist, for example, one's future goals, current commitments and *attitudes* towards death and the past. Human beings exist in these two dimensions in entirely different ways; the word "are" means something different in the phrases "people *are* their pasts" and "people *are* their futures". Both are true, but people's relationships to their facticity and their transcendence are easily confused with each other, or the distinctiveness of these dimensions is easily ignored. These structures allow Sartre to provide an initial analysis of self-deception: self-deceivers deny one of their dimensions by interpreting their lives entirely in terms of the other (e.g. they see themselves as entirely fixed and finished, like the past; or they see themselves as entirely open and malleable, like the future), or they intentionally misconstrue the nature of one by interpreting it in terms of the other (they want to see a past shameful deed as still alterable, or they want to see an open future as foreclosed). Human existence is ambiguous, and that ambiguity must be acknowledged in order to avoid self-deception.

The negation that defines the relation of consciousness to being-in-itself also affects every aspect of one's own existence. The division within consciousness of a directed aspect (*towards* an object) and a non-directed aspect (peripherally aware [of] itself) is the first manifestation of this negative or non-identical relation *to itself*. This self-division helps clarify one of Sartre's key tenets: that being-in-itself just is itself, is what it is, and thus is self-identical, whereas consciousness is never identical to itself, never is what it is, but always both "is what it is not" (is its future goals even though they are not yet realized) and "is not what it is" (is never reducible to its past even though partially defined by it). Although this lack of self-identity may initially seem paradoxical, it is the heart of Sartre's understanding of human existence, and it played an important role in the philosophies of his successors, Foucault, Derrida and Deleuze. The next sections (Parts Two and Three) take this negative self-relation several steps further.

Sartre takes human action to be purposive or goal-directed (Part Two, Ch. 1). People find themselves in specific situations and negate them. This means that they transcend the situation towards a *possibility*, a way the situation might be (which includes the possibility of maintaining it as it is); they do this through a chosen *value*, which determines which possibility is chosen. Action then strives to realize this possibility over time; the distance (which includes the resistance exerted by the world as well as the effort required to realize the goal) between the present situation and future success Sartre calls "the circuit of selfness". It is a second way, beyond the division at the heart of consciousness (being directed and non-directed at once), in which consciousness is self-divided. It is always in process, seeking to achieve a future goal, but never completely coincident with its goals. Some goals, such as being a good lover, require whole lifetimes to achieve; others, such as finishing a course paper, can be completed, but new goals emerge immediately afterwards, often responding to the perceived weaknesses in the previous "success" (e.g. to write an even better paper next time). Human life is a constant process of defining and realizing goals.

This existence-in-process suggests that human life is always temporal – distended in time – unifying past, present and future in one movement. People *escape* the pasts that were, reaching *towards* futures that may emerge, *in relation to* present situations that must be reshaped (or consciously maintained) (Part Two, Ch. 2). These are three inseparable dimensions of a single dynamic, which continues refashioning past actions and reassessing possible future actions. Sartre calls this unified flow "*ontic* temporality". In addition, people sometimes experience temporal speed: some months whizz by; others flow like molasses; or sometimes time "stands still". This is "*psychic* temporality", and Sartre contends that it requires a reflection that he calls "impure" because it falsely unifies discrete phases of consciousness into extended temporal wholes. When we feel engulfed by a mood (e.g. depression, anxiety), we experience a *psychic state*: a reflective synthesis of various discrete experiences. Impure reflection creates these temporally extended psychic "states" and invites us to believe that they have causal influence on our actions. Sartre denies that this is possible. These psychic states (including the experience of an ego initiating actions and being qualified by them) are themselves *effects* of *reflective* consciousness, a consciousness directed towards itself. One goal of *purifying* reflection is to break through these psychic illusions, which we induce in ourselves by submitting to them. For example, we often nurture potentially foul moods by incorporating tangentially related phenomena into them. My favourite team loses, and this adds to *my* depression. Reflection then is a *third* self-division of consciousness (although not a necessary one); it is one act of consciousness trying to turn back on and objectify itself, which is impossible. The effort produces illusory psychic unities that are assumed to inhabit and influence pre-reflective consciousness. Careful attunement to pre-reflective life shows that such states do not exist at that level.

Finally, consciousness, in directing itself towards being-in-itself, experiences a world, a specific set of qualities to which one typically attends and an arrangement of tools on which one typically relies. Sartre discusses the kinds of knowledge we have of this world and the ways in which we are responsible for much of its structure (Part Two, Ch. 3).

Impure reflection often experiences consciousness as necessary and fixed, as if seen from the outside (e.g. "I am a lazy person", "I am an intense person"). In effect, impure reflection emulates the viewpoint that other people typically adopt in making their judgements ("You are evil", "You are beautiful"). This sense of being objectified, when contrasted with a condition of pure subjectivity (which therefore objectifies everything), reveals that other people have the power to *objectify*, to create a dimension of one's existence of which one is not the author. Sartre calls this new dimension a person's "being-for-others" (Part Three, Ch. 1). It is created by others, but borne by the person objectified. It is a third form of being, which exists only because we co-inhabit the world with other people. Moreover, it conditions our attitudes towards other people because it is unsettling, rendering us temporarily impotent. We therefore struggle to recover control over our self-definition. Either we seek to prevent others from objectifying us at all (thus, always dominating them), which is ultimately impossible, or we seek to seduce or coerce others into objectifying us in a way that we can control (which is also ultimately impossible). Elaborating these two basic strategies, Sartre skilfully derives many other attitudes to people: love, sexual desire, indifference, sadism, masochism and hatred (Part Three, Ch. 3). This division between the self-for-itself and the self-for-others also cuts across the body, and thus people experience a body-subject – a point of view and instrument for dealing with the world – and also a body-object, which can become broken, diseased, aged or dysfunctional (Part Three, Ch. 2). Thus, other people condition one's experience of one's body and one's sense of identity. Indeed the social self is probably the first and most pervasive experience of selfhood, one on which the psychic self (produced by impure reflection) is parasitic.

Sartre is famous for claiming that human beings are always free, and therefore responsible. But his exact meaning needs clarification. He does *not* mean that people are omnipotent, able to achieve anything they want. Instead he means they have the ability to *try to achieve* anything they *value* and, more importantly, they necessarily have the power to *transcend* any situation towards some alternative (Part Four, Ch. 1). No situation is so dire that a person's choices are eliminated. Even when facing the threat of a loaded pistol, one can choose to fight back heroically. Indeed in response to *any* apparent limit to freedom (being located in space and time, being defined in a certain way by others, facing the inevitability of death), Sartre insists that there are always various possible *attitudes* we can take to the situation, and thus no apparent limit ever eliminates our freedom (and *necessity*) to choose. Sartre's freedom thus consists of two elements: the power to imagine alternatives and the power to *attempt* to realize them. Nothing guarantees success, but nothing can eliminate this power of negation. This suggests that people are essentially purposive: seeking goals that embody values to which they are committed.

Sartre sometimes calls persons "spontaneities", but in fact they typically live regular, routinized lives that seem anything but spontaneous. Does this fact disprove Sartrean freedom? He argues that the routinized element of life derives from *higher-order choices*. I prepare for my classes each day because I have chosen to be a philosophy professor. This choice organizes all of my teaching and research routines. But there are even *higher-order* choices than this, which organize other basic choices (e.g. one's chosen attitude to other people, to living and to nature); these Sartre calls our "fundamental projects". The task of understanding a person – whether oneself or another – is to identify this fundamental project (Part Four, Ch. 2). Sartre thinks we have a vague, ancillary apprehension of this project so that we can assess the correctness of hypotheses about it, if they are made explicit. Two differences thus distinguish Sartre's manner of understanding people from Freud's: Sartre sees human beings as purposive, organizing their lives through their choices, and he thinks they have some access to their fundamental projects, enabling them to legitimately dispute hypotheses about them. Freud, on the other hand, would claim that human actions are caused by unconscious forces and would insist he is close to the truth if the patient persistently denies his interpretations.

The overall interpretation of *Being and Nothingness* depends on the analysis of two crucial footnotes in which Sartre *denies* what seem to be *his own* universal claims (the necessity of falling into self-deception and the inevitability of the domination–seduction dynamic in relation to other persons). He allows the possibility of an alternative form of human existence, which he calls "authenticity". It involves overcoming our fundamental aspiration to be "God" (a synthesis of the being of the in-itself and consciousness, a synthesis that cannot be achieved). The authentic person abandons this aspiration, accepts both dimensions of facticity and transcendence, and adopts an orientation to other people that enables reciprocity and recognition. All three conditions are related to "purifying reflection", which makes them possible. Thus, readers should realize that some elements of human existence described in the book are common (but *not inevitable*) – defining only the inauthentic state of human existence – whereas others *are* necessary, elucidating the human condition in all its forms. Discovering which is which is an important interpretive task.

Additional highlights

Since Sartre's Introduction and Part One are the most difficult parts of the book, I shall provide a closer analysis of them. For the other parts, I shall indicate his central arguments and identify pertinent questions, but shall not attempt a thorough exposition.

In the Introduction, Sartre explores a fundamental question in philosophy: the nature of being. He uses several unfamiliar Latin terms (*percipere* = act of perception; *percipi* = perceived object; *percipiens* = perceiver-subject) as well as some German and Greek terms from his phenomenological predecessors (*Wesenshau* = intuition of essence; *Abschattung* = profile; *Erlebnis* = experience; *Selbständigkeit* = independence, self-sufficiency; *noesis* = act of consciousness; *noema* = meaning or concept through which an object is grasped), and some of his own technical terms (transphenomenal = not exhausted by the phenomenon; non-positional = non-directed, not taking a position or asserting a thesis; pre-reflective = directed towards something other than consciousness).[2] Sartre's main goal here is to clarify the being of any phenomenon and of consciousness (and to show that they are distinct). (A "phenomenon" is simply anything given, just as it offers itself to consciousness.) He also elaborates these two types of being, and the rest of the book explores their relationships.

His "ontological proof" is intended to show that consciousness requires an object to target; it cannot exist without such an object. Yet the object's being is not reducible to consciousness, and consciousness's being is not reducible to the object. So Sartre rejects both idealism and materialism. The being of consciousness is its non-positional dimension (Sartre argues that consciousness must always exist in two dimensions [positional and non-positional] in just the way that material objects must always exist in three spatial dimensions), whereas the being of the phenomenon is its *condition* of appearing, what makes any phenomenon possible. He also concludes that the principle of identity (i.e. *x* is identical to itself) is true only for material objects, not consciousness, whose existence is always questioned or challenged by the self-sufficient being of objects. Human beings must *sustain* their existence moment to moment in a way that material objects do not: they must *create* their continuing identity; they are not self-identical of necessity.

In Section i of the Introduction, Sartre argues that some progress on dissolving various dichotomies that have plagued traditional philosophy (e.g. being–appearance, essence–appearance, act–potential) has been made by appealing to the finite–infinite distinction. For example, the being of an object is simply the series of all its possible appearances, which is infinite and never fully revealed by any one appearance. Being is not forever beyond appearances, never to be accessed; it is revealed in each appearance even if it is not reducible to any one. Moreover, the *principle* of the series (an object's essence) is not reducible to anyone's whims, but is independent, requiring investigation and discovery. The being of objects thus *transcends* consciousness. Still Sartre wonders whether this appeal to an infinite series of appearances is sufficient to clarify the object's being and whether it really overcomes traditional dichotomies, for the object's being is both wholly within the series of appearances (in each one) yet wholly outside it (not fully manifest in any one). Because being still seems inadequately clarified, further analysis is necessary.[3]

In Section ii, Sartre suggests that being itself can appear and thus can become a phenomenon; this is "the phenomenon of being", which he thinks is revealed in special conscious states, such as boredom and nausea. He describes this phenomenon vividly in his novel *Nausea*, in the encounter with the tree root late in the book.[4] When it appears, being exhibits a bald, insistent even domineering presence that challenges all the social rituals, psychological manoeuvres, instrumental manipulations and intellectual categories with which people try to conceal and control it. Thus, the raw being of a root, when fully experienced, resists and shatters any human categories, uses and rituals. Any phenomenon, however, is related to other phenomena (those forming its series); but all are supported by their being – their *condition of revelation* – which is transphenomenal (beyond any single revelation). Being is not a *quality* of the object, nor a *meaning* given to it by consciousness; it is the condition of the object's revelation. It does not appear as such, but is necessary for all the object's appearances. Although helpful, these Sartrean suggestions still could be further developed.

In Section iii, Sartre shows that non-positional consciousness is the condition of revelation for any positional (or directed) act of consciousness, and thus is the being of consciousness. (Thus, the same *analysis* of being applies both to consciousness and to objects; what satisfies this analysis in each case differs.) Moreover, all consciousness is exhausted in its revelation of its object; it contains no other content or representations or mediations. It is pure relatedness to its object while remaining self-translucent. This non-positional dimension of consciousness is not *reflective* (*directed* consciousness *of* consciousness); this is what prevents non-positional consciousness (of) consciousness from generating an infinite regress. Non-positional consciousness does not judge – take a position on – what it reveals and thus does not yield knowledge. It is the ever-present condition of positional consciousness: an unmediated, non-cognitive relation of consciousness to itself. Non-positional consciousness unifies awareness, retaining its immediate past and projecting its oncoming future. It is a tacit awareness, but it reaches beyond the directed aspect of consciousness (and thus is transphenomenal). It sustains the existence of the directed dimension of consciousness while in turn being sustained by it. Consciousness is thus self-generating and self-determining.

In Sections iv–vi, Sartre argues that being-in-itself is independent of consciousness and supports it. He defends this by pointing to the directedness of consciousness and to consciousness's lack of intermediaries. He also suggests that the object's being is beyond any appearance consciousness may reveal at a given time. Sartre takes consciousness to be essentially relational; it *requires* an object to reveal if it is to exist, but because its being is distinct from the object's being, it is not *relative* to being-in-itself. For this reason, he calls consciousness a "non-substantial absolute"; it is non-substantial because it requires an object (it is pure relation), but it is an absolute because its being is not relative to or reducible to the object's being. Sartre concludes his Introduction by suggesting that being-in-itself is full and complete in a way that consciousness can never be, but that it is also simply there – contingent and superfluous – rather than necessary. It is undifferentiated, massive and everywhere. The being of consciousness is always questioned by the self-sufficiency of being-in-itself and by the fact that it requires a being beyond itself. Consciousness can cast new meanings on to being-in-itself, but it cannot touch or affect its raw, insistent reality. It can rearrange it, but cannot destroy it without destroying itself. It can discover the object's essence, but never create its being. Finally, being-in-itself is self-identical in a way consciousness never can be because consciousness is always split, divided within itself (positional and non-positional at once). This internal fission or gap (nothingness) within consciousness becomes exacerbated as Sartre's analysis of consciousness continues.

The experiential factors to which Sartre appeals in the Introduction are the weight of raw being (experienced in the brute thereness of things, not their properties, uses or classifications, which often conceal their naked harshness) and the translucency of pre-reflective (world-directed) consciousness. People do seem able to report their current conscious states (Sartre's example is counting), and this fact supports his two-dimensional analysis of consciousness. In addition, Sartre articulates a deep philosophical point in passing: that metaphysics and epistemology are mutually interdependent; one cannot answer questions about knowledge without facing questions about fundamental reality (and vice versa).

One might wonder, here, whether consciousness is *always* directed. While walking in pitch-black darkness, for example, one is not aware of anything in particular, but rather one seems to float in darkness. Similarly, when absorbed in a sexual caress, one may not focus on anything in particular, simply the surrounding warmth or softness/hardness. One might also wonder whether all consciousness is non-positionally aware of itself. Dreaming and absorption in mechanical tasks have been offered as counter-examples.[5] Certainly the presence of non-positional consciousness in these cases is arguable, but to that extent they may lose their status as examples of consciousness, which atrophies in these cases. Recovering from both conditions involves a recovery of non-positional consciousness, as well as focal, positional consciousness. Such cases may reinforce Sartre's claim, rather than undermine it. The main premises from which Sartre's system emerges are highlighted here. Some defence is given, but additional evidence comes from showing that his resulting analysis of human existence rings true. Reviewing Sartre's Introduction after completing the book will show how many of his key claims flow from these premises.

Part One further clarifies the nature of being and consciousness by examining negation (one of consciousness's fundamental features) and non-being, which Sartre believes has a kind of objective status. I recommend skipping the discussion of Hegel and Heidegger on negation because Sartre's interpretation of those figures is questionable. Sartre argues that negative judgements are rooted in an apprehension of objective non-being. Further, as an existential stance towards the world, questioning remains open to the *possibility* of negative answers and is aware of many *alternative* possible answers. So questioning the world is haunted by various kinds of non-being. Sartre calls this revelation of non-being "nihilation", and he thinks all consciousness effectively introduces vortices, alternatives, possibilities, voids and distances into being-in-itself. These "négatités" support negative judgements and make them possible. Négatités emerge with consciousness itself (which is the primary nothingness), but being-in-itself remains prior to nothingness (since non-being itself has a kind of objective existence status). Consciousness is capable of refusing, negating or reshaping being-in-itself even though its existence is dependent on it.

Consider Sartre's illuminating example: arriving late, you look for a friend in a café. You look *everywhere*: the *non-presence* of your friend leaps out at you at every turn. Completing your sweep of the room, you realize your friend is not there. Sartre insists that your friend's non-being (not-being-there) dominates your experience, virtually eradicating the presence of all the strangers there. It allows you to assert, "My friend is not here." There must be something to search or interrogate, but consciousness's basic impact on being is to transcend, neutralize, withdraw from or negate it. In doing so, Sartre adds, it transcends its own past. Thus, as consciousness negates being-in-itself, it negates itself (at least its own facticity) as well. Anguish reveals this ever-present power of consciousness to escape even itself (its past glories; its future plans); only by deadening itself to this open future does consciousness conceal its anguish. In effect, consciousness surges anew in each situation, forced to define itself and "make itself be". It sustains past projects only by reanimating them and sustaining them in the present. The past *cannot* determine the present; this is the heart of Sartrean freedom. Humans thus create themselves through their actions; they do not have a predefined essence to which they must conform. They also choose the values that organize their long-term projects and are thus responsible for their lives.

Some critical questions might arise here:

(i)   Are there objective forms of non-being that do not depend on consciousness (e.g. black holes; antimatter)?

(ii) Would a third-person, scientific observer accept the reality of an open future so readily? Must Sartre simply assert the primacy of the first-person viewpoint, or can he reconcile his position with the third-person stance?

(iii) If we examined the experience of touch, would the results of clarifying the relation of consciousness to being-in-itself differ?; perhaps touch involves a mutual contact and intertwining that sight does not?

(iv) Does the consciousness that exists in animals, children and brain-damaged human beings contain the same powers of nihilation as normal, adult, human consciousness? If any of these cases lacks the full nihilating power of consciousness, then Sartre needs to better elaborate the genesis of this power of consciousness in human development.

Sartre's discussion of the paradoxes of self-deception in Chapter 2 stimulated an extensive literature, especially in Anglo-American philosophy. One paradox is that self-deception seems to involve both believing x (the truth to be concealed) and not-believing x (the truth successfully hidden) at once. Another emerges because self-deception seems impossible if Sartre's claim about non-positional consciousness is correct, since the intention to deceive oneself would have to be aware of itself, thus undermining its chance of success. Sartre's best response to these paradoxes emerges in section iii of Chapter 2, "The Faith of Bad Faith". Consider ironic statements. The ironist seems both to assert y and deny y at once.

(One might well say he *seems* to assert *y in order to* deny it.) Also, if one keeps enough company with ironists, the very possibility of making assertions evaporates. Sartre thinks that belief (especially in contexts where belief involves *faith*) operates similarly, and then he suggests that nearly every human orientation to the world is similarly ambiguous.

In acknowledged belief, one is aware that one *merely* believes (and thus does not *really know*), and this seems to undermine the belief. Sartre contends that the self-deceiver, in order to sustain her belief, abandons rational evidence entirely, thus interpreting *all* belief to be insufficient. Such a believer only *half-believes*. To overcome this condition would require taking evidence for one's beliefs seriously: adopting only the degree of belief that the evidence supports and living in a way that ensures one's beliefs always track the evidence for them. The self-deceiver adopts a quasi-sceptical stance towards all belief so that he can retain the belief that matters to him. Its shortcomings simply exhibit the general inadequacies of all beliefs. Sartre argues that this requires a transformation of the self-deceiver's existence, similar to falling asleep. Once she succeeds, waking up is exceptionally difficult because she cannot acknowledge her condition. She lives in a benumbed dream-state. No evidence – no revelation or truth – is sufficient to overcome it; only a complete reawakening, which Sartre calls "authenticity", can do this.

Human beings are readily susceptible to self-deception because the nature of consciousness invites it: the non-positional dimension of consciousness threatens its positional or directed dimension in the way that the implicit consciousness of faith's shortcomings threatens the resulting faith. Moreover, Sartre notes that human beings always exist between facticity and transcendence. Each threatens the other, and denying one of them involves the same duality – one remains focally conscious of one, while only peripherally conscious of the other. Sartre's examples illustrate this. Recall that he describes a woman who is enjoying a man's sexual interest in her without explicitly acknowledging this, a waiter who is overzealously fulfilling his role, and a champion of sincerity who is insisting that a homosexual own up to his desires. The woman wants to deny the transcendent meanings of her suitor's actions (their sexual implications), and she also wants to deny the larger meanings of her own choice (of leaving her hand in his, suggesting sexual interest). The waiter takes his role as fixed, playing at *being* a waiter (the way a desk *is* a desk), refusing to acknowledge both that he *chooses* the role and *defines* it. The homosexual refuses to see that his past actions have an undeniable factual aspect, even though his future remains open, but the champion of sincerity refuses to see that people can always rethink their past patterns and choose differently in the future. Indeed, for Sartre, the ideal of sincerity (being what one is) is incoherent because it presupposes a conception of being (static self-sufficiency) that cannot apply to human beings.

Two other features of this chapter are important. Sartre's main point against Freud can be generalized to nearly every attempt to personify some "internal element" of persons (here, the censor, but equally often the self). The problem is that whatever problem the internal element is alleged to solve nearly always recurs in the internal element itself. Here, the censor, introduced to explain how self-deception is possible, itself must be self-deceived in order to provide an explanation; so there is no theoretical gain. Often the self, introduced to show how people make choices, exhibits the same vacillations and dilemmas that people do. Postulating a personified internal figure rarely solves the philosophical problem; it merely replicates it. A second point concerns emotions. Sartre argues that even emotions are *chosen* responses to situations; other, more effective responses are often possible. Emotions are not psychic forces that overwhelm people, but intentional responses that express their purposes.[6] People are as responsible for their emotions as for their actions. Moreover, the inveterate human tendency towards self-deception also extends to people's emotions; many apparent loves are false, and many actions express no genuine desire.

What then would an authentic person be like? Although Sartre is less explicit about this than he should be, such a person would (i) acknowledge her ambiguous nature and refuse to deny or misinterpret it; (ii) see the situation's many possibilities as real (thus refusing to deaden herself to any of them) (e.g. I could *choose* a different profession any time; I do not *have* to continue teaching philosophy); (iii) realize that her values are supported solely by her choices (and are not *external* imperatives that demand a specific response) (e.g. I must *choose* to remain faithful to my partner; marriage does not *force* me to); (iv) accept the temporal split within consciousness, which implies that her past cannot determine her future, but nonetheless must be acknowledged as real (e.g. although I have always cared about teaching well in the past, I may cease to do so at any time); (v) insist that her beliefs track the evidence and respond to its changes; (vi) accept the necessary limitations of commitments concerning the future – they may be reconsidered at any time.[7]

Part Two elaborates the negating relation consciousness has to being-in-itself, which is experienced in action, lived time and knowledge. Chapter 1 concerns the structures informing human action. Action is motivated by a perceived lack in the situation introduced by consciousness as it transcends situational givens and its own past. This lack indicates a direction in which the situation can be improved, and thus lack presupposes an experience of value. Sartre suggests that people typically seek a static self-sufficiency (emulating being-in-itself), despite (perhaps even *because* of) their sense of dividedness and ambiguity. One value haunts every human action: a condition that would synthesize the in-itself and for-itself – a god-like state (wholly self-sufficient yet self-transcending) – but which is contradictory. In addition, other values are infinite series of perfect realizations; hence values typically make unsatisfiable demands. So, for Sartre, unless people undergo a conversion to authenticity, their lives constantly seem inadequate, their values never fully realized. Thus, not only are emotions experienced as insufficiently genuine, actions always seem inadequate even if successful because one must triumph again in future situations. The essentially temporal nature of consciousness derives from its perpetual escape from the given situation toward future possibilities.

Chapter 2 analyses lived time. For Sartre consciousness is essentially temporal, and its temporality is holistic. All three temporal dimensions exist at once, mutually defining each other: as consciousness negates being, it negates its own past, in favour of a future possibility, in relation to a present situation. Sartre says human life is "ek-static" because it *stands out* in all three temporal dimensions at once. The in-itself has no temporal relations of its own. Static temporality maintains these tri-dimensional temporal relations. Dynamic temporality transforms what was a future possibility into a present situation to be negated, what was a present into a past, and what was a past into something surpassed. This flow is rarely explicitly experienced; it correlates with the forward thrust of human action as it realizes its goals and chooses values. When time is explicitly experienced, it becomes what Sartre calls "psychic temporality", which is a product of *impure* reflection. Impure reflection creates temporally extended emotional states (e.g. anger, boredom), which seem to have a life of their own that dominates consciousness. For Sartre, such psychic states are illusions created when reflective consciousness attempts to objectify itself, to take an external viewpoint on itself. At such times an apparent self that seems to "possess" and unify these various psychic states emerges; it too is illusory. Impure reflection induces impotence; psychic states seem to casually influence behaviour in a way Sartre thinks is impossible. What really happens is the reflective act *projects* its own synthetic activity into these states, pretending that they exist in pre-reflective life. However, careful examination of pre-reflective experience shows that they are absent.

Crucial here is Sartre's discussion of *purifying* reflection, which gives his readers a way to confirm his experiential claims. This requires purifying our own reflective acts. A moment of impure reflection suddenly becomes lucid, revealing pre-reflective consciousness just as it is: its nihilation, transcendence, temporality, ambiguity and contingency. Purifying reflection does not yield knowledge because knowing objectifies the known, and this happens only in impure reflection. *Nausea* describes several processes by which its anti-hero achieves this purified state. It involves rejecting many traditional categories and ingrained forms of perception, overcoming habituated, customary behaviours, and sudden insight into one's contingency and freedom. Purified reflection is a path out of self-deception, and Sartre certainly could have more adequately clarified how it is achieved. He says it requires a catharsis, and later uses "conversion" to describe it; he also relates it to Husserl's *epochē*, which neutralizes the assumption that *perceptual* objects exist. For Sartre, purifying reflection seems to neutralize the assumption that *psychic* objects exist, and this allows one to grasp pre-reflective consciousness accurately, in effect making the implicit grasp of non-positional consciousness suddenly explicit. It is cathartic because many psychic structures simply dissolve because their illusory status is acknowledged.

Chapter 3 explores some features of the experienced world and tries to explain them. This is probably the most counterintuitive chapter in the book. The basic idea is that many common aspects of the perceived world are bizarre refractions of the structures of consciousness on to being-in-itself. Recall that being-in-itself is a compressed, self-sufficient, raw blankness, but in fact we perceive individual things (thises) with properties (qualities) and functional relations (instrumentality), which are countable (quantity), exhibit potentials and even embody their own time (geological time, for example). Sartre tries to explain many of these features as shadow-like projections of the essential temporality of consciousness; yet he also wants to claim that consciousness adds nothing to the in-itself. Very briefly, consciousness seizes a particular thing in negating the in-itself as a whole, but it also negates the thing in the same movement, and in doing so it apprehends only external relations among particulars (thises), relations that contrast sharply with its own internal, temporal self-relatedness. This purely *external* relatedness is experienced space and also explains countability (quantity). Each thing exhibits several qualities, all of which interpenetrate each other (thus the blackness of the desk differs from the blackness of the book because the desk's other properties infuse its blackness). In negating a particular thing, consciousness focuses on a particular quality, which implies or suggests all the others. Every particular is given as part of a series of revelations that indicate potential developments that are organized by its essence (the principle of the series of appearances of the thing). Again Sartre suggests that this "potentiality" is just a shadow-projection of consciousness's lived temporality. Finally, particulars are given as continuing unless consciousness intervenes to change them; this already-thereness (givenness) constitutes the time of the world, and motion is also possible only because particulars are externally related to each other.

Sartre struggles with many different issues in this section. Many of his theories need further elaboration. Merleau-Ponty, for example, better defends the interanimation of perceptual qualities of a perceived object. Also, Sartre could better explain exactly how the various features human beings overlay on to the in-itself really are refractions of features of consciousness. Sartre asserts this, but he needs to better defend and explain his stance.

In Parts Three and Four, Sartre reconnects with lived experience. Part Three concerns other people. Traditional philosophy actually attempts to *prove* the existence of other minds, but Sartre believes that its method ensures its failure. The other's subjectivity cannot be revealed while his objectified body is being examined for signs of mental activity; the power of the other's subjectivity is revealed only when it transforms one into an object. This happens through the other's "look" (*le regard*): any judgement or action that defines, transgresses or objectifies one.[8] This look produces a radical transformation of one's existence, as anyone can confirm by recalling the experience of shame or fear. Instead of being in control, transcending the situation towards one's own goals, one loses control and becomes located, defined and imprinted by the other's judgement. This mode of the other – their transforming subjectivity – provides the basis for our *lived certainty* that other people really exist, making solipsism a purely theoretical hypothesis. It also means that people are *internally* related to each other; the mode in which they exist (object or subject) depends on the mode in which others exist (subject or object). One dimension of our existence (our social selves) exists *only because* others exist and *must* exist given that they do exist. Sartre explicates this lived certainty of others by showing that this self-objectification cannot occur in any other way except through another consciousness. Nature alone cannot produce this change; it can only offer resistance to one's efforts. One cannot fully objectify oneself; at best impure reflection provides a pale approximation of such a self-definition, which remains ethereal and unconvincing. Only other subjects have the power to create this change. This is Sartre's transcendental argument for the existence of others: they constitute a *factually necessary* condition for this common social experience.

But what of the objection that sometimes we feel ourselves objectified (we hear a noise in the dark and freeze, sensing danger), but no one is there? Sartre responds that although this may show that a particular other is not *present* in person, it does not show that the other-as-subject is absent. Sartre even suggests that "the other" is pre-numerical and can be instantiated in many different kinds of events (the wind, a slap, voice or look). So he avoids the objection, but the "other" now becomes a more generalized structure that the looks of many different persons and events can embody. Sartre also describes some additional features of the looking–looked at relationship: these two modes *exclude* one another, *exhaust* all possibilities and are *asymmetrical* with each other. These claims are suggestive and allow Sartre to develop some important ramifications, but they are debatable. Some examples: two shy people can experience themselves looked at by each other at once (symmetrical); there may be a mutual recognition that supersedes Sartrean antagonism (not exhaustive); and in a tennis match, each player typically experiences himself as subject and object simultaneously (not exclusive).

Since the social self renders people impotent, they strive to recover some kind of control over it by adopting various attitudes towards others. Sartre discusses six of these "attitudes" – love, masochism, indifference, sexual desire, sadism and hatred – claiming that all other orientations can be derived from them. Since he believes that the function of these attitudes is to recover control of the social self and that at best this can be achieved only temporarily, he thinks all interpersonal relationships fail, and fail of their own accord.[9] The other remains transcendent, ultimately beyond one's seductions and dominations. To see how this works, consider love and sexual desire.

Love is an assimilation attitude; it invites the other person to define you in a reassuring way. Indeed the beloved[10] seeks to become the entire world and absolute value for the lover, to fascinate him, enticing him to freely sacrifice his own freedom to her. If this works, the lover will see the beloved as infinitely wonderful, and this vision will sustain her social identity over time. But three things happen: (i) the beloved can be judged by an outsider (a third person), thus shattering her image of perfection; (ii) the beloved may ask the lover to avow his love, and this can cause him to assess his real feelings, thus breaking the fascination; and (iii) the lover may seek a reciprocal commitment from the beloved, which, if she were to provide it, would force her to become a subject, thus abandoning her secure position as a perfect object. Sartre may have captured something important about the fascination of love, but there may well be more to the story. In later works, Sartre acknowledges that reciprocity is possible, which qualifies the analysis he offers here.

In sexual encounter, one partner seeks to prevent the other from objectifying him by inviting her to lose herself in her own lived body (through caresses). He also allows himself to dissolve into his lived body in order to provoke this loss of subjectivity in her. Sartre carefully describes the loss of lucid, focused consciousness that occurs during sexual caressing and suggests that this loss is the *goal* of intercourse, not pleasure or orgasm. Indeed, for Sartre, orgasm is the *failure* of sexual desire because it releases both parties from their lived embodiment, allowing each to return to full subjectivity and thus to their power to objectify. Sartre also suggests that sexual partners easily become confused about the aim of sex during intercourse, and this leads to blindly manipulating the other's body rather than caressing it, and this too can motivate a return to lucid subjectivity. Sexual intercourse thus cannot sustain its goal of neutralizing the other-as-subject. Some might find this analysis of sexual encounter far-fetched, but not only do Sartre's descriptions of the experience ring true, the function of intercourse may well emerge more fully in its process than in its completion. And certainly Sartre is right that any neutralization of the other-as-subject is temporary (often one's performance is *judged* immediately thereafter).

171

The experience of sexual caressing compromises one's experience of the body-as-subject, merging it with experiences of the body-as-object. Sartre discusses these modes of the body in Chapter 2. He identifies the body-subject with the for-itself. The body-subject insures that consciousness sees the world from a view-point and acts on the world from a particular location. Just as we become philosophically confused about others when we confuse their two modes of appearance (object and subject), we also become confused about the body when we confuse its two dimensions. Too easily our rich experience of embodiment – including habits and skills – becomes lost in physiological analyses of the body-as-object. For example, Sartre argues that there are no physical "sensations" mediating perception, only a perceptual grasp of actual objects from a perspective. He also argues that the body has non-positional consciousness of itself that allows it to adapt to the relationships among tools in the environment. In addition, the pre-reflective experience of pain involves a feeling of disorientation and difficulty in performing tasks, but the reflective experience of pain attends to the pain, unifies its effects into a single condition, and treats it as a cause of other experiences. The experience of illness organizes various pains into a broader psychic condition to which the person submits.[11] Sartre's main point about the body-as-object is that it is fully expressive; a person's experiences are accessible through his bodily orientations towards the world; this is because a person's fundamental project is expressed in all his actions. This view explains why one often comprehends so much (inarticulately at first) about someone in just one encounter. The third dimension of the body is the body objectified by others (e.g. a doctor), an experience that estranges one's relationships to the lived body, inviting capitulation to the other's viewpoint.

Part Four concerns Sartrean freedom. Since I have already analysed his conception, here I will summarize his arguments for it. People are free because they necessarily escape their past and the limits of their situation through their capacity to negate/transcend them. In addition, they must determine the *means* to achieve their goals. Sartre adds that *resistance* emerges in part because we pursue chosen ends; the ends make an existing state of the world refractory. Also, persons choose the manner in which they respond to the various obstacles and resistances they face: as challenges, defeats or burdens. Freedom is meaningful only because there is resistance; omnipotent beings are not really free, but magical. The goal of the action defines it; only if one knows the goal can one even imagine possible causes and motives; this is one reason Sartre believes they are ineffective at the pre-reflective level and only assume (illusory) power in impure reflection. Experience suggests, however, that people do not explicitly choose their goals in every situation. Sartre agrees and argues that this is because such actions sustain *higher-order* projects that have been chosen in the past. Such higher-order projects may be abandoned or revised at any time – even the fundamental project – but often they are simply maintained and enriched. Since fundamental projects can be amplified in a variety of ways, most human actions remain unpredictable. Some examples of fundamental projects are: to attempt to merge with being-in-itself; to be pure negation – abandoning facticity altogether; and to slide thoughtlessly between them. Sartre argues that self-command and rational deliberation are merely *means* to achieve an already posited end; they are not what they seem. The real choice has already been made when they enter the scene. For example, if one pretends to deliberate between two possible life-partners, the real choice already has been made; deliberation merely ratifies it.

Sartre identifies at least five components of one's "situation": place, past, tools, fellowman and death. Each of these is a mixture of objective and subjective factors – meanings which are overlaid on the objective conditions and objective conditions that fuse with personal meanings. Thus, though death is unavoidable, one's attitude toward death is chosen. Though the meanings others impose on one's race, ethnicity or gender are given (yet sustained by the choices of those who impose them), one's response to those meanings (acceptance, rejection, or struggle) is chosen. Indeed the situation as a whole reveals the hierarchy of one's choices through its specific resistances. The order of importance of one's projects is indicated by the situational elements that demand immediate attention. Sartre also claims that his freedom is sufficient for ethical responsibility. Human beings cannot avoid being responsible for their lives because they cannot escape their freedom. Every action is chosen in some sense, and every action contributes to one's self-definition. If one fails to change a troubling aspect of one's situation, then one is responsible for sustaining it. Sartrean freedom can thus become a heavy burden because of the many institutions and practices which people support indirectly by neglecting to alter them.

Sartre establishes the reality and significance of choices (though he could be clearer about exactly when and how the choice of one's fundamental project is made), but his notion of choice may be insufficient for ethical or legal responsibility. Sartre needs to consider this issue more critically. Moreover, he ignores two alternative conceptions of freedom that may be more meaningful. Merleau-Ponty argues that we are free only if we have sufficient means to realize our goals. Sartre's analysis sidesteps this issue by promising only the opportunity to try to realize them. Also, some would argue that freedom requires a more complete self-expression or coming alive in a course of action. Even if all actions are chosen, not all are self-expressive in this way. On this view freedom is rarer, but far more valuable than Sartrean choices.[12]

In Chapter 2, Sartre offers an alternative model of understanding human action, given his teleological analysis. Instead of seeing actions as causal results of antecedent conditions (often, postulated psychic givens like pleasure, survival or aggression), he argues that one must understand an action by clarifying how it expresses and modifies an ongoing higher-order project. Understanding the whole range of a person's projects – their developments and transformations – is what Sartre means by "existential psychoanalysis". Sartre thinks every action ultimately expresses one's most basic response to being-in-itself (merging, rejection, shifting between them), though the agent realizes this only implicitly. Still this non-positional awareness of the fundamental project is sufficient to force interpreters to take a person's assessment of their hypotheses seriously. Sartre also strives to understand the individual specificity of each person by understanding the ways people enrich their fundamental project in specific historical contexts.[13] But his psychoanalysis fails to offer any kind of therapy; at best it makes a person's fundamental project explicit so that it can be examined and altered, should the person choose, and then work, to do so.

Sartre also explores several different attitudes toward the world that seek to "appropriate" it: knowing, desiring and creating. These attitudes attempt to incorporate the world without destroying it: investing the world with one's own meanings while allowing it to remain independent. Sartre also explores universal meanings for certain qualities of the world: viscosity versus solidity, for example. Here he provides an analysis of general qualities similar to Freud's discussion of dream symbols or Jung's study of archetypes. He grounds these symbolic meanings in his ontological analyses.

In his Conclusions, Sartre explores some metaphysical questions about the relationships between consciousness and being-in-itself, the most important of which is why consciousness came to exist at all, and some ethical issues that follow from his analysis, mainly what an authentic person might look like.

Perhaps Sartre's best critic is his friend and fellow-phenomenologist Maurice Merleau-Ponty. Merleau-Ponty suggests that Sartre is insufficiently attentive to the ways in which the body-subject and the body-object are two sides of the same unified whole, rather than two dimensions that are only contingently related to one another. He also stresses the importance of habits and skills in understanding humanity's interaction with tools and argues that perception is more primary than negation as a basic orientation towards being. He shows that perception has both passive and active elements (and thus that perceived being has some degree of antecedent structure), drawing on neurological research to defend his position. He also claims that self-knowledge is a function of the practical unity that the person's fundamental project brings to the rest of her life. Self-knowledge degenerates to the extent that this unity is compromised. Space does not allow full discussion of these objections, but careful consideration of Sartre's replies may show that his positions are stronger than many scholars have believed.[14]

While providing a remarkably coherent analysis of the basic structures of human life, *Being and Nothingness* makes many creative contributions to a variety of philosophical issues: being, negation, self-deception, action, temporality, knowledge, other subjects, the body, freedom, authenticity, self-knowledge, and the understanding of others. Sartre's contribution to these issues equals those of Heidegger and Merleau-Ponty, two other central figures in existential phenomenology. In his other early works, Sartre further discusses the contrasts between perception, imagination and cognition; ethics; art and literature; and political commitment.[15] Sartre provided the intellectual foundations for French existentialism in this book and demonstrated concretely how phenomenology could be used to clarify the pre-reflective level of lived experience, thus broadening its appeal. Although he supplemented and revised some of his key claims in later works, he remained remarkably faithful to the book's core intuitions throughout his life.

Sartre's central intuition that human life is not self-identical was taken up and generalized in the philosophies of his successors: Foucault, Derrida, Deleuze and some French feminists. His way of interpreting people as unified fundamental projects contributed importantly to hermeneutics and to non-Freudian forms of psychoanalysis, especially to the theories of R. D. Laing and Rollo May. And his later treatise, *Critique of Dialectical Reason*[16], showed how the existential phenomenological insights explored above could redefine and reshape the Hegelian–Marxian dialectical interpretation of society, history and the world. He thus made substantial contributions to the dialectical tradition as well.

Notes

1. Sartre's discussion appears in his short, but difficult, essay *The Transcendence of the Ego* (New York: Noonday Press, 1962).

2. Sartre's translator, Hazel Barnes, provides a brief but serviceable guide to many of Sartre's technical terms at the end of the book. When key terms are introduced, you might compare Sartre's full discussion with this glossary.

3. Sartre is reacting both to Husserl and Heidegger in this section. Husserl believes existence can simply be bracketed and that this would provide greater certainty to the analysis of consciousness, but Sartre insists that being resists such an intellectual procedure. Being always threatens to explode one's neutral stance. Moreover Heidegger argues that being is most vividly revealed in humanity's relationship to tools. Sartre challenges this by claiming that tools presuppose the more indifferent, undifferentiated being-in-itself.

4. Reading *Nausea* (New York: New Directions, 1949) before reading *Being and Nothingness* (New York: Philosophical Library, 1956) may illuminate some of Sartre's more abstract claims. It shows a person gradually achieving purified reflection and encounter-

ing being just as it is, without the mediating structures of thought, narrative and society.

5. See Kathleen Wider, *The Bodily Nature of Consciousness* (Ithaca, NY: Cornell University Press, 1997), 94–9.

6. Sartre also has already provided a complex analysis of emotions, as opposed to feelings, in his essay, *The Emotions: Outline of a Theory* (New York: Philosophical Library, 1948).

7. In his play *The Flies* (in *No Exit and Three Other Plays* (New York: Vintage, 1949)), Sartre adds two other conditions: facing one's situation (rather than ignoring it) and bearing responsibility (rather than denying it).

8. Sartre offers interesting discussions of Husserl's, Hegel's and Heidegger's theories of intersubjectivity, but they are too complex to summarize here. A thorough treatment of those sections is provided in my book *Sartre and His Predecessors: The Self and the Other* (London: Routledge & Kegan Paul, 1984). I also examine a variety of objections to Sartre's own theory and elucidate it in more detail.

9. Sartre's play *No Exit* (in *No Exit and Three Other Plays* (New York: Vintage, 1949)) provides a dramatic depiction of these analyses.

10. I am reversing Sartre's use of "beloved" and "lover" here; *we* typically think of the beloved as the one who receives love, not the one who offers it, as Sartre's phrasing suggests.

11. Being dominated by the psychic objects that are created by impure reflection is another affinity it has with other people's judgements.

12. For a fuller elaboration of this view of freedom, see Frithjof Bergmann, *On Being Free* (South Bend, IN: Notre Dame University Press, 1977).

13. Sartre shows in detail how to provide such an understanding in his biographies of Mallarmé, Baudelaire, Genet and Flaubert.

14. For a fuller discussion of these issues consult the essays collected in Jon Stewart, *The Debate Between Sartre and Merleau-Ponty* (Evanston, IL: Northwestern University Press, 1998).

15. See especially *The Imagination* (New York: Philosophical Library, 1948), *Notebooks for an Ethics* (Chicago, IL: University of Chicago Press, 1992) and *What is Literature?* (New York: Philosophical Library, 1949). *The War Diaries* (New York: Pantheon, 1984) contains sketches of ideas given further elaboration in *Being and Nothingness*.

16. Jean-Paul Sartre, *Critique of Dialectical Reason* (London: New Left Books, 1976).

9

Maurice Merleau-Ponty
Phenomenology of Perception

Eric Matthews

Introduction

Maurice Merleau-Ponty (1908–1961) would be generally agreed to be the most distinguished French phenomenologist, and his book *Phenomenology of Perception*, first published in French by Gallimard in 1945 and in English by Routledge & Kegan Paul in 1962, is certainly his major work. In it, he first outlines what he means by "phenomenology", namely, the description of our direct, pre-reflective contact with the world around us in perception. The rest of the book consists in developing a phenomenological account of the various elements in our perceptual experience, such as our awareness of our own bodies, the social world of other people, time and space as they are "lived", history, freedom and action, and the *cogito*. This account enables him to make distinctively original and illuminating contributions to the discussion of such traditional philosophical topics as the mind–body problem, the relation of consciousness to the unconscious, the explanation of human behaviour, the freedom of the will, the relation of the individual to society and the meaning of history and its relevance to politics. What emerges from these discussions is a particular view of our humanity, as embodied beings participating actively in the world and finding meaning in it as a result.

If we want a guide that will help us to find our way about a book such as this, it is probably best not to attempt a chapter-by-chapter commentary, following the order of topics as they appear in the work. That will not help us to grasp the underlying connections between its various themes. Instead, I shall try to present

Merleau-Ponty's central concerns in a way that shows how they develop out of each other. This may sometimes involve a certain amount of repetition, in which themes already considered take on a new significance in a different context, but this repetition will be kept to a minimum.[1]

Subjects and objects

The best place to begin such a presentation is where Merleau-Ponty himself begins, in the Preface to the book, in which he tries to answer the question "What is phenomenology?". Any answer to that question must make some reference, as Merleau-Ponty's does, to Edmund Husserl, who was to all intents and purposes the founder of modern phenomenology, in the relevant sense of that word. But Husserl's thinking developed in the course of his life, partly in response to the ideas of his greatest and most original student, Martin Heidegger, and the version of Husserlian phenomenology that most influenced Merleau-Ponty was the one that Husserl was developing in the last years of his life, in works that were only published after his death. Even this version was given a fairly free interpretation by Merleau-Ponty. What we should aim for, he says (PP: viii) is not fidelity to the texts, but a "phenomenology for ourselves", "a manner or style of thinking". Phenomenology, in Merleau-Ponty's eyes (and it is his version, rather than Husserl's, which concerns us here), is more of a method than a doctrine or system.

So what does this method involve? First of all, it sees philosophy as a matter of *describing*, rather than *explaining* or *analysing* (PP: ix). Phenomenological philosophy does not, in the manner of traditional metaphysics, aim to construct a general theory that will explain the world that we experience. Nor does it, in the style of empiricist or positivist opponents of metaphysics, take for granted the scientific explanation of our experience and attempt to analyse experience on that basis. Rather, it seeks simply to describe, without metaphysical or scientific presuppositions, our human experience itself, which is, after all, what gives to all our metaphysical and scientific constructions whatever meaning they can have for us.

A phenomenological description of experience, as has just been said, must be without presuppositions; in particular, one assumption made in modern philosophy since Descartes must be set aside. This is what Merleau-Ponty calls "objective thinking": the view that there is an objective world, in the sense of a world totally detached from our experience of it. This means that our experience of it must be purely contemplative: we, as it were, observe the world (including our own bodies) from a position outside it, much like the way in which a cinema audience looks on from the outside at the "world" depicted on the screen (cf. PP: 408). A subjectivity that is not part of the world is what was called by Kant a "transcendental" subjectivity. From this assumption flow two ways of explaining our experience, which seem at first sight utterly opposed to each other, but that are united at least by their common source. One is the world as seen by science: a set of objects with fully determinate qualities, which have only spatial and causal relationships with each other. One of these objects is ourselves as physical beings (any reference to "transcendental", or non-physical aspects of ourselves is ignored by science, which is concerned only with what is "objective" or measurable). The objective world is free of value and meaning, and any value or meaning we think we find in it is not part of objective reality, but is "subjective", projected on to the world by us (for example, it expresses our emotional reactions to things).

Empiricist philosophies try to take over this scientific objectivism to explain experience itself, as the effect of the causal influence of external objects and their qualities on another kind of object, namely, ourselves. But there is clearly a problem here: for it is surely necessary, if we are to speak of "experience", to include some reference to *someone who experiences*, a "subject" of experience, and there seems no room for subjectivity in this kind of account. Furthermore, the world as we actually experience it does not seem to consist in a collection of meaningless sensory data, or "sensations" as Merleau-Ponty calls them, but in meaningful patterns. For instance, as Hume points out, we naturally see one thing as causally related to another, and science itself would be impossible if we did not. So paradoxically, empiricism seems to make it hard to make sense of the scientific view of the world from which it is supposed to derive. (Merleau-Ponty's discussion of empiricism can mainly be found in Chapter 1 of the Introduction).

This leads to the other way of explaining experience referred to above, namely idealism or what Merleau-Ponty sometimes calls "intellectualism" (one example would be Kant's transcendental idealism). On this view, the "objective" world of science and common sense is not really objective at all, but is constituted by the transcendental subject out of the materials supplied by the senses. This explains the meaningfulness of our experience: the meaningful patterns, such as causality, are created by our own transcendental subjectivity as part of its constitution of an objective world. The scientific view of the world, as a set of perfectly determinate objects linked by space and causality, can thus be explained by intellectualism, although only at the cost of reducing the objectivity and independence of reality to a mere projection of our own subjective patterns of thinking. Intellectualist idealism and empiricist realism are like mirror images of each other: empiricism tries to have experience, as we have seen, without genuine subjectivity (by treating the experiencer as one more object in the world), whereas intellectualism tries to have experience without a genuine object (by treating the objective world as the creation of our subjectivity). But anything that could meaningfully be called "experience" is a relation between a person who experiences (a subject) and

179

something experienced (an object) that is not part of the subject. (Merleau-Ponty's discussion of intellectualism, and of its relation to empiricism, is mainly to be found in Chapter 3 of the Introduction.)

Both empiricism and intellectualism ultimately fail because they start from the wrong end: they are premature attempts to construct abstract theories to explain experience, before first describing what it is that they are trying to explain. Phenomenology starts from the other end: it reflects on experience itself, without bringing into its description any assumptions derived from such explanatory theories. In a sense that must not be misunderstood, it is a return to the subjective. This is a dangerous way of expressing the point, since it might suggest either that phenomenology is itself a form of intellectualist subjectivism or that it is an example of introspective psychology in the empiricist framework. Phenomenology is neither; it is a return to the subjective, not in the sense that it holds that the objective can be explained in terms of what is subjective, but in the rather more subtle sense that it is a return to a point before we make any distinction between the subjective and the objective. Phenomenology recognizes that any concepts used in general theories of science or philosophy, including the distinc-tion between "subjects" and "objects", are human constructs, which must derive their meaning from a more basic level, from our actual engagement as human beings with our surroundings. True philosophy, Merleau-Ponty says, "consists in relearning to look at the world" (PP: xxiii): to look at the world straight, without the general preconception of modern culture that only a "scientific" or objective approach can give us the ultimate truth about things, including ourselves.

The word that Merleau-Ponty uses more often than "experience" is "perception" (hence the title of his book). Perception, for him, is not what it is for "objective thinking": a kind of pure detached contemplation of things by a subject distinct from them. Nor is it, as in intellectualism, an "absorption" of objects into our own subjectivity. The very meaning of the word "perception" (or "experience") implies, as we have seen, a *relation* between subjects and objects, each of which has a degree of independence from the other. Subjectivity is not something purely inner, detached from its objects, but something that can exist only in so far as it is in communication with the world of objects. The phenomenological concept of the intentionality of consciousness, embodied in the slogan that "all consciousness is consciousness *of* something", encapsulates this idea. But it is important, Merleau-Ponty emphasizes, to stress that the intentionality of consciousness is not some kind of purely cognitive relation to objects, of the kind that Kant speaks of. Rather, it is a relation of active engagement with objects: "The world is not what I think, but what I live through" (PP: xviii). Merleau-Ponty is happy to agree with Descartes that we have to start from the *cogito*, the

"I think": but only if we recognize that the *cogito* is the basis only because all thought necessarily transcends itself to the whole world, and that the certainty of thought therefore extends to what is thought about.

Just as subjects cannot exist without objects to be conscious of, so objects cannot form part of anything that we could regard as "the world" unless they were objects *for* some consciousness or other. What we mean by an object is an object of experience. And the character of the objective world as we perceive it reflects the nature of our active involvement with it, as a phenomenological description of experience makes clear. Even the simplest perceptions are seen, as was said above, as meaningful patterns. But this does not, in idealist fashion, reduce objects to mere correlates, or even contents, of subjective experience: to experience something *as an object* is to experience it as something that always transcends my (or anyone's) experience of it. There is always something more to be learned about real objects; they are, to use one of Merleau-Ponty's favourite words, "inexhaustible". The objective world retains its independence of subjectivity, while still inseparably related to it.

Being-in-the-world

A phenomenological description of perception is thus not an account of an inner world of subjectivity, nor a causal scientific account of the way in which one kind of objects, the things we perceive, affect another kind of object, ourselves and our sense organs. Rather, it is an account of how the world presents itself to subjects who are "permanently rooted" in it (cf. PP: 240), and actively involved with it (living it rather than just thinking about it). In the term that Merleau-Ponty borrowed from Heidegger, it is a description of our existence as perceiving subjects as "being-in-the-world" (the hyphens are necessary in English and French, although not in German, to indicate that this expression is in effect a single compound word, not simply a collection of related words). For when we set aside the attempt to explain perception and simply describe our perceptual experience as we live it, we find that we do not infer the existence of a world from data that are immediately presented to our minds, but that we experience it directly from a point of view that is within the world, from "here" and "now". My perception of the world is different from yours, because I necessarily have a different location in space and time from you, and so a different perspective. But the world that we both experience is there before either of us begins to experience it, and extends far beyond the limits of what is perceptible to either of us. In this sense, Merleau-Ponty is a realist: the existence of what we perceive does not depend on our perceiving it, rather "the world ceaselessly assails and beleaguers subjectivity" (PP: 240). (Indeed, it is this that makes it so easy to adopt the "objective thinking" spoken of earlier.)

Nevertheless, we do not perceive the world as something entirely detached from ourselves and our concerns. Being in the world in the way we are entails that our perception of things is not detached thought about them, but active involvement with them. Things are therefore perceived as *meaningful*. For example, I perceive the laptop on which I am writing these words as a *laptop*, a type of computer on which I can do such things as word-processing, preparing spreadsheets, creating slide presentations and so on; in other words, the way I perceive it is related to my own purposes in using it. In a different way, I perceive other people as friends, relatives, enemies, business partners and so on; in other words, they have a meaning for me based on the nature of my relationship with them. These meanings are experienced as being as much part of what is "given" to perception as, say, the size and shape of the laptop, or my friend's height and waist measurement. In this sense, the world is always a world *for me* (or rather, for us, since we can communicate with each other about the world and the meanings we find in it). This sounds like a form of idealism, but it is not, since even on this view the world is the place in which we live, and so which exists independently of us, not a system of representations that we construct. (The meanings that objects in the world have for me are likewise there to be *discovered*, not something that I arbitrarily *impose* on the objects).

Thus, to say that our being is being-in-the-world is to say that our subjectivity is always located in space and time, engaging with the world from a particular perspective determined both by that spatiotemporal location and by our own needs, which motivate us to engage with the world. The perceptions that we have from this point of view are the only possible basis for any knowledge that we can achieve about the world: but, because they are always *from a particular point of view*, they can never give us the kind of absolute clarity and certainty to which rationalist philosophies aspire. The world that we actually experience can never be fully determinate; for that, we should need to be able to adopt a "God's-eye view", a view from outside the world altogether, where we could observe things non-perspectivally and so form an absolute conception of their properties. But we cannot of course do that; indeed, it seems logically impossible for any being to do so, since it would mean adopting a perspective that was yet not a perspective. So the conception of the world as a set of objects with perfectly determinate properties and relations, which is characteristic of the objective thinking of modern science, is not after all the final truth about reality, but only an abstract picture formed by human beings, useful for certain purposes but not necessarily for all.

At any particular time in the development of human thought, therefore, our grasp of truth is incomplete. Nevertheless, the nature of human experience is such that we must pursue a greater completeness of knowledge. For, just because we live in the world, and experience it as inexhaustible, we are driven to seek more knowledge and understanding. The world is perceived as independent of our subjectivity, so that inherent in our very attachment to the world is our power to deny that attachment, as we do when we engage in objective thinking (PP: 381). But although this gives sense to the ideal of perfect objectivity, which inspires our quest to transcend our present perspectives, such complete detachment is in fact impossible for beings like ourselves, who are located within the world.

To be-in-the-world is necessarily to be embodied: it is our bodies that give us our place within the world, the place that defines our point of view; and it is our bodies that make our engagement with the world a matter of active involvement rather than passive contemplation. We see with our eyes, and hear with our ears; we move about the world, seeing it from different perspectives; we handle objects, turning them around and looking at them from different points of view. We respond to objects emotionally and sensually, and our concepts of what they are and how they relate to each other are as much affected by these emotional and sensual responses as by their more "objective" or measurable properties. It is this interaction with objects around us that "condemns us", as Merleau-Ponty puts it, "to meaning" (PP: xxii), so that our embodiment is crucial to the meaningfulness of the world as we perceive it.

At the same time, the fact that our bodily interactions with things are meaningful in this way (and not just causal) implies that our bodies are not to be regarded only as biological organisms, but also as the vehicle for our subjectivity. The point of view of scientific biology, which sees human bodies as one kind of object in the world, is perfectly valid in its own context. But it is not the only valid point of view; our bodies are also, for us, part of ourselves as subjects, which we experience from the inside, and which make possible our experience of the objective world. This idea is often expressed by saying that Merleau-Ponty regards human beings as "body-subjects", and this is a useful term, even though he himself never seems to have used precisely that expression. The conception of human beings as body-subjects is to be contrasted both with the Cartesian dualist view of them as disembodied subjects loosely attached, in this life at least, to mindless lumps of matter called "bodies"; and with its polar opposite, the materialist "identity-theory", which sees human beings as nothing more than complex objects of a certain kind, namely, biological organisms. Instead, as the hyphen implies, it regards their subjectivity as inseparable from their embodiment. Human sense-perception takes the form it does because the human senses have the character that they have. Human responses to objects are what they are because of the structure of the human brain and central nervous system.

But our own bodies, as we experience them, are not mere objects for scientific (biological) study for us. My eyes are what I see through, my legs are my means of walking, my hands are what I pick things up with and so on. For some purposes, for instance those of biological study or medical treatment, it is a useful abstraction to regard human bodies, even one's own, in a detached spirit, as simple pieces of living machinery operating purely in accordance with the laws of physics and chemistry; but this is not how we regard our own bodies (or indeed other people's bodies; see below) when we are engaged in living, rather than in scientific theorizing. Our bodies are ourselves, as subjects of experience, and we have our being-in-the-world through our embodiment (PP: 239).

The emphasis on embodied subjectivity is thus itself part of the rejection of the objective thinking that predominates in a modern science-based culture. Cartesian mind–body dualism is an integral part of Descartes's whole project of finding a sure foundation for science, which provides the philosophical basis for objective thinking (and in this sense, Descartes can be seen as the founding father of the classical scientific or "objectivist" view of the world). But how did Descartes come to accept this dualism? Indeed, why should anyone do so if the whole of our experience seems to contradict it? Descartes sought for certainty by doubting whatever could be doubted (however bizarre the reasons for doubting), and ended with only one indubitable truth: that of his own existence as a thinking thing, or, putting it more generally, that of the existence of a thinking subject. The existence and nature of anything that might be an *object* of thought was still doubtful, and so, Descartes argued, must be distinct from that of the subject. But this included the thinker's own body, not to mention other possible subjects of experience. In this way, Descartes arrived at the characteristic position of objective thought: that the objective world as a whole is arrayed before a thinking subject who is not part of it. And the understanding of that objective world must therefore not be the same as the way in which we understand subjectivity: I understand my thoughts as the product of reasoning, in which each thought stands in a rationally intelligible relation to the thoughts that precede and succeed it. But objects cannot be understood in this way; all that we can do by way of explaining their behaviour is to see one state of an object as regularly associated in space and time with another state of the same object, or with a state of another object, just as we understand the behaviour of a simple mechanism, like a clock, in terms of the regular connections of the motion of one part through space with those of another, adjacent, part. The objective world, in short, is like a kind of great machine, proceeding on its way without any purpose or meaning of its own: meaning belongs only within ourselves, in our subjective or "inner" world of thought. Intentionality, to use that term again, is supposed by dualists to apply only to what is mental.

One of the familiar objections to Cartesian dualism can be expressed in terms of this contrast. Critics point out how difficult it is for the dualist to account for the familiar fact of interaction between the mental and the physical. We could express this criticism by saying that dualism implies that we can explain the mental in one way, and the physical in a different, and incompatible, way: but what it cannot account for is the possibility of explaining some mental activities in terms of physical processes, and vice versa. Examples might be explaining the role of brain biochemistry in the generation of certain moods, or conversely the way in which a desire for food (say) may motivate certain bodily movements. Brain biochemistry, according to the dualist, is a purely mechanical process, in which one event follows another with no purpose or meaning; the same is true of the movements of my arm in reaching out to pluck an apple and eat it. On the other hand, moods, such as depression or elation, and desires, such as the wish to eat the apple, are supposed to be purely mental; we have reasons to be depressed (perhaps we have failed an important exam, or have ended a love affair), and we have reasons to want to eat the apple (perhaps we have not eaten for quite a time, and this apple looks so juicy and tasty). It is difficult, to say the least, to see, within the dualist framework, how chemical processes in the brain could constitute a reason for feeling depressed, or how the thought that this apple looks very tasty could cause someone to salivate or make their arms and hands move in an appropriate way. But we all know that precisely this kind of thing happens all the time.

Body-subjects

Merleau-Ponty's conception of human beings (and indeed other animals) as "body-subjects", who have their being in the world, is an essentially non-dualist view of ourselves, and so avoids this kind of objection. To say that we are embodied subjectivities is to reject the view that we are fundamentally disembodied minds, loosely attached to bodies that are totally different in character from anything mental. In a way, it is taking more seriously than Descartes himself seems to have done the significance of the remark in Descartes's *Sixth Meditation* that we are not lodged in our bodies like a pilot in his ship, but are more intimately related to our own bodies than that. As was said above, Merleau-Ponty differs from Descartes in that he accepts that there is a sense in which we *are* our bodies, and nothing other than our bodies; but he differs from the identity-theorist in his interpretation of that sense. The bodies with which we are to be identified are not biological organisms, objects whose behaviour can be completely explained mechanically in terms of the laws of physics and chemistry. If I am my body, it

185

follows that my body is me; in other words, we should not be entrapped by the false dichotomy of "me" and "my body", but think in terms of me, a unified person, who exists as an embodied part of the physical world. I am my body-for-me, which is me myself, as physically engaged with my world, and as experienced by me "from the inside".

The biochemical and other processes that go on in my body, from this perspective, are part of my intentional response to objects outside myself, and an *essential* part, given that I am a physical being. It is *I* who feels depressed at the end of the affair, not my brain, or the serotonin levels in my neurons; but for me to feel depressed at the end of the affair entails that my brain should be in an appropriate state (the details of what that state is are to be discovered by empirical investigation). Human depression takes the form it does because the human body, including the human brain and nervous system, is structured as it is. Similarly, we respond as we do to particular sorts of apples because our bodies are structured as they are; thus to feel hungry at the sight of that kind of apple involves certain characteristic bodily responses. If we are concerned to understand why someone feels depressed, in the context of our normal human dealings with each other, then the appropriate answer to our question will be something like "Because he has just broken up with his lover". But that will also be the answer in that context to the question, "Why is his brain in that state?". Brain processes, as essential parts of a human response to a situation, in short require just as much of an "intentional", or "reason"-explanation as other aspects of that response. But when we are investigating human behaviour in a more detached and scientific spirit, we are not concerned with it in the context of our ordinary human dealings with each other, but simply as part of a mechanistic system of human relationships. In that scientific context, we are concerned with brain processes simply as physical changes in a particular sort of object, requiring a purely mechanical or causal explanation.

Merleau-Ponty's opposition to Descartes's mind–body dualism depends ultimately on his critique of the argument by which Descartes arrived at that conclusion, which has already been briefly summarized. Descartes, as we saw, sought a foundation for all real knowledge in what could not possibly be doubted, and concluded that only our own, purely "inner", thought was absolutely indubitable in that sense. But this implies, Merleau-Ponty argues, that we could somehow have a thought that was purely inner, a thought that did not refer beyond itself. Thought, however, necessarily "outruns itself" (PP: 452): it is always a thought *about* something, a thought that therefore points beyond what is purely inner to the world. If we cannot doubt our perception, then equally we cannot doubt what we perceive (PP: 436). (Interestingly, similar points are made by Wittgenstein and Austin.) Doubting the existence of one thing only makes sense against the background of certainty of the existence of other things: I can be uncertain whether what I presently seem to be seeing is an illusion only because I am certain that other things are not; there is implicit in the very meaning of the word "illusion" a contrast with what is not illusory.

The conclusion that is drawn from this argument is that we cannot ultimately separate the "thought" element of perception, which is purely within us, purely "subjective", from the "objective" world that we perceive. Perception is a direct contact with the world, to be understood only as part of our active engagement with objects as embodied beings; and, by the same token, the world is what we directly engage with in perception, not something apart from ourselves, related to us only causally. It might be objected that this conclusion does not follow from the argument. There is surely, it might be said, a sense in which our own thoughts are "inside" us, in that they are directly accessible only to us ourselves, and this is not affected by the fact that we can only distinguish some thoughts as "illusions" because we also have some thoughts that are not illusory. It is not clear how Merleau-Ponty could cope with this kind of objection, which depends ultimately on something that he himself would accept, namely, the separation of one subject of experience from others, of "me" from "you".

Other people, time and freedom

One important consequence of Cartesian dualism and the objective thinking (or alternatively the intellectualist idealism) that derives from it is their implications for our relations with other people. For objective thinking, other people must be seen as simply another set of objects in the world; for the intellectualist, they are reduced to our constructions out of our subjective experience of them. Either view is profoundly unsatisfactory, for obvious reasons, and wildly at variance with our actual experience of others. For we do, clearly, distinguish other people, the beings with whom we can communicate and have meaningful relationships, from mere objects such as sticks and stones, or chairs and tables. And we are aware of them (sometimes painfully so) as subjects who are *independent* of our experience of them, of ourselves, and the world as perceived by us, as part of *their* world. (Merleau-Ponty's friend Sartre constructs a whole dramatic scenario on this basis, in which our relations with others inevitably consist in unending conflict, in which each seeks in vain to reduce the other to a mere object in her world.)

Merleau-Ponty acknowledges that, even if one abandons objective thinking, there is a problem of "other minds", and that it is possible to see the force of what is called "solipsism", in the sense of the doctrine that I am, or at least might be, the only conscious being in existence. (The word "solipsism" is sometimes used to refer to the even more radical doctrine that I and my thoughts might be the only things in existence at all: that even the material world might not really exist. But this is not the form of solipsism with which Merleau-Ponty is here concerned.) The question is, as he puts it, "how can the word 'I' be put into the plural?" (PP: 406). The first-person pronoun, by its very meaning, refers in direct speech only to the person who is making the utterance. For each of us, "I" is only one person, ourselves, so how can there be more than one "I"? Putting it differently, our experience of others is always "from the outside". We do not feel their emotions, or think their thoughts, as we do our own, but observe their consequences in their outward behaviour. So how can we know that they have emotions or thoughts as we do? Perhaps they are indeed just mindless automata that go through the motions of being human. Once one has reached this point, solipsism begins to seem plausible.

But solipsism is impossible. I could not even speak of myself as conscious unless I was aware of other conscious beings: I could not meaningfully think of myself as "alone in the universe" unless I had the experience of other people (PP: 419). There must be some way, therefore, in which we can indeed make sense of a multiplicity of "I"s. Phenomenologically speaking, it must be built into our basic experience of ourselves as having being-in-the-world. We are *essentially*, as we have seen, *embodied* subjects; we could not be what we are unless we were embodied. Our subjectivity is thus not something "inner", to which we alone have access, but opens on to a world that exists *independently* of ourselves. That world includes other embodied beings, other people (and indeed other, non-human, animals). "If my consciousness has a body," Merleau-Ponty asks, "why should other bodies not 'have' consciousness?" (PP: 409). Our basic experience of the world, if we describe it without objectivist assumptions, is not of a set of objects arranged merely spatiotemporally before us, but of a *world* in which what we experience has a meaning for us. And crucial to that world are those beings we experience as "other people", beings like ourselves who also find meaning in what they experience from their own point of view. We and they can *share* meanings: we use the same concepts, see the same things as streets, houses, buses, churches, books, computers and so on. These shared meanings constitute a *cultural world*, which emerges from the natural world in which we inevitably find ourselves as biological beings, but which also helps to determine how we see nature itself. Our being-in-the-world is in this way being in a cultural or social world, a world that we share with other human beings, and to a lesser extent with other living creatures, whose separate individuality and interests we have to acknowledge as potentially conflicting with our own. Our membership of a society is in this way an essential part of what defines us as the individuals we are.

These other human beings (and animals) are experienced as mere objects, to be understood in terms of physicochemical laws, only when we are engaged in the abstract (although perfectly proper) ways of thinking characteristic of scientific investigation. Our normal, pre-scientific and more basic experience of them is as beings with whom we can enter into relationships (which may of course be competitive as well as cooperative), in which we communicate with them, not only by means of spoken and written language, but in those non-verbal forms with which we are all familiar. In this context, we can make sense of their behaviour, not by giving causal explanations as in science, but in terms of the concepts that we share with them. For instance, we can make sense (to use one of Merleau-Ponty's own examples) of the way in which many Russian peasants in 1917 joined in a common revolutionary struggle with the factory workers of Petrograd and Moscow by realizing that they felt that their fate was entwined in that situation with that of the industrial workers (PP: 422). We can understand their behaviour because we share a concept of a sense of common destiny as leading to joint action.

This example is drawn from history, from a time other than our own, but yet connected with the one in which we live; our world is what it is in part because of the events of 1917 in Russia and their consequences. This illustrates another important theme in Merleau-Ponty's thought: that of the importance of *time* and *history* both in our understanding of our own and other people's behaviour and social structures, and in the very constitution of individual and social identity. The Cartesian doctrine of a disembodied thinking subject necessarily leads, Merleau-Ponty argues, to a conception of the timelessness of mind (PP: 433). For if we as subjects are not *in* the world, we can give no sense to being "here" rather than "there" or to existing "now" rather than "then". We are, in effect, in the same position as God: eternal expressions of pure reason. Of course, since the things we experience are in time, we can in a way locate our experience of one as "earlier than" or "later than" our experience of another. But this is not what might be called "lived time"; we do not *experience* time as part of the actual fabric of our existence.

From a phenomenological point of view, however, this is clearly mistaken, for our experience *does* pass from the past through the present to the future. To exist in the world is to be at a specific place and time, and the world is experienced as "incomplete" (PP: 387): that is as continuing to exist into the future, beyond the stage that it has reached now. The same applies to ourselves as subjects; the subject, he says, "is time itself, and ... we can say with Hegel that time is the existence of mind" (PP: 280). To experience an object is to experience it as present, but the very idea of presence carries with it a reference to the past from which that present emerged and to a future in which what we plan in the present will hopefully be brought to fruition. It is thus not only the world that we experience that is "incomplete", but also ourselves who experience it. We are never fully constituted as the self that we are as long as we exist. In this sense, both the world and ourselves are (to use one of Merleau-Ponty's most characteristic terms) "ambiguous". What exists is ambiguous in that it is never completed, and so never fully determinate.

Merleau-Ponty distinguishes between "natural" and "historical" time, although he does not completely separate them. The time of nature is the time of simple succession, of one event being objectively earlier than or later than another. Historical time is that of past, present and future, which carries an inescapable reference to subjectivity; what is present is present *for someone*, and what is past and future is defined by their relation to what is present. These are clearly distinct concepts, but equally clearly they cannot be isolated from each other. Even historical time is not *constituted* by subjects; what is present for me now is not a matter for me to choose, but is what is happening in this objective place where I am and at this objective time. Equally, however, the objective time of nature is not entirely independent of historical time, since we could not have even a conception of objective time unless we could relate it to the historical time we "live" (PP: 388).

What does it mean for us to exist in historical time? It means, first of all, that the time of our lives does not consist in a succession of unrelated moments. Indeed, the whole idea of a "moment", as a unit of time, is an abstraction, which may have some utility in certain contexts (as in science, where time has to be measured), but which corresponds to nothing in our actual experience. Each present, as said before, is inseparably connected to the past from which it has emerged, and to the future by which it will be superseded. There is, and can be, no sharp dividing line between past, present and future. Merleau-Ponty compares time to a fountain, in which the form is preserved amid the change of the water, "because each successive wave takes over the functions of its predecessor" (PP: 489). But it is important to this simile that the water *does* change. Neither the past nor the future exists *in* the present (otherwise they would *be* present): the past no longer exists, the future does not yet exist, but both have a bearing on the character of the present.

This has profound implications for what it is to be an individual human being, or a human society, or the human species. Our thoughts and experiences are not timeless, but temporally dispersed, and can be properly understood only if that is taken into account. Merleau-Ponty quotes the novelist Proust, who declared that we are "perched on a pyramid of past life" (PP: 457). What we are now is determined not only by those things that we can expressly remember, but by all that we have experienced in the past. This, for Merleau-Ponty, is the element of truth in Freudian psychoanalysis. Freud himself had still been in the grip of objective thinking; he had thought of psychoanalysis as a natural science of human behaviour, exposing the causes of deviant behaviour in adults in the process of imposing social control on natural biological, above all sexual, urges.

But Merleau-Ponty argues that we need to see human sexuality as something more than a set of biological mechanisms. Because human beings are embodied subjects, sexuality cannot be separated from its human *meaning*. Sexuality is part of the very structure of an embodied human life, expressed in contrasting poles of autonomy and dependence; it is present in the whole of human life "like an atmosphere" (PP: 195), sometimes made explicit and conscious, sometimes simply giving a not-fully-conscious tone to our relations with each other. In neither case is it an object for scientific knowledge, but rather part of the colour-ation of our experience of the world and each other. To say this is, to repeat the point made earlier, not to say that we *project* some purely inner experience of sexuality on to a neutral world; rather, sexuality is as much a part of the world as we experience it as, say, the colours or shapes of things.

As we develop from infancy to adulthood, the attempted solutions to the problems thrown up by our sexually toned relations with others, especially in the first instance with our parents, may become "sedimented" (to use Merleau-Ponty's term) in our bodily habits of behaviour, and in this way our past may come into conflict with the needs of our present, adult, selves (needs of which we are largely conscious). It is this conflict that gives rise to what are called "neuro-ses". Psychoanalytic treatment for such neuroses does not take the form, as objective thinking might lead one to suppose, of giving scientific assent to a par-ticular theory about the causes of our peculiar behaviour, but of "binding the sub-ject to the doctor through new existential relationships" (PP: 529). The patient has to relive the past experience, which he sees "in the perspective of his coexist-ence with the doctor". The problem can then be, not dissolved, but replaced by a new set of relations to others and to the world.

The result of successful psychoanalytic treatment is thus an increase in the patient's freedom, to control his or her contacts with things and people in the light of conscious, adult, purposes and motives. In this way, the interpretation of psychoanalysis forms part of Merleau-Ponty's general account of human free-dom. Like Sartre, Merleau-Ponty accepted that human beings, in virtue of being conscious subjects, were always able to step back from their situation and so could not be determined by it. Also like Sartre, he held nevertheless that freedom was always "in a situation": that is, that the choices that are really open to us at any given time are necessarily constrained by the situation in which we find ourselves at that time. To take an excessively simple example, if I am sitting at my desk in Aberdeen writing this chapter, I do not have a real possibility of choosing to address the United Nations in New York this afternoon. But Merleau-Ponty takes this necessary "situatedness" of freedom much more seriously than Sartre does, and recognizes its full implications. Part of my situation is constituted by my body, with its physical limitations; part is constituted by my past, and by the ingrained habits of behaviour that I have inherited from it. Both these factors impose constraints that make human freedom much less absolute than Sartre is tempted to make it.

Using an example derived from Sartre's *Being and Nothingness*, Merleau-Ponty speaks of the way in which, at the end of a long day's walking, someone may feel so utterly fatigued that they simply cannot walk another step. Sartre would see this denial of one's own freedom as in "bad faith". But Merleau-Ponty, while accepting that there is an element of choice about the refusal to walk any further, nevertheless argues that we must recognize the element of "sedimentation"; the habit of feeling that there are certain limits to how far one is willing to exert oneself may be so ingrained that it "acquires a favoured status for us" (PP: 513). In another example, Merleau-Ponty argues that our social position, as a member of the "working class" or the "middle class", has a certain objectivity to it. Someone can, of course, as a middle-class intellectual of a leftist persuasion, still choose to identify with the working class, even perhaps to the extent of taking a job as a labourer and living in a working-class district. But such a person still cannot escape the influence of his or her origins entirely; an intellectual-turned-worker is a different sort of person from someone who is born and bred in the working class (PP: 514–15).

What is true of individuals is equally true of societies, as one might expect, given that societies are expressions of the shared meanings of many individuals. A society exists historically; what it is now is shaped by, and must be understood in terms of, what it has been in the past. History is thus something more than, and prior to, the scientific study of an objective past: it is primarily a fundamental structure of the social world, which is itself, as we have seen, an essential dimension of my existence as an individual. The Athenian Republic or the Roman Empire, Merleau-Ponty argues (PP: 421–2), are, without being consciously studied, there at the boundaries of my existence as an individual. In other words, in order to understand myself and the meaning of my life, I need to see myself in the context of the society and culture in which I live; and in order to understand that context properly, I need to see it as emerging from its particular past, facing problems bequeathed it by the past, and having to find solutions to those problems that will shape its future. The role played by Freudianism in relation to the individual as such is played in relation to society by a "humanistic" interpretation of Marxism. According to this interpretation, Marxism is, briefly, the view that human beings face problems inherited from their history, particularly problems of economic organization, which they need to resolve in order to continue to exist as a society. How they solve them is to some extent a matter of choice, so that the course of history is not pre-determined as it is in some versions of Marxism; but freedom here, as elsewhere, is constrained by the situation, so that it is not absolute.

Like individuals and societies, humanity as a whole exists in historical time, so that what it is to be human is always open to further change; our humanity is never complete. "Man", Merleau-Ponty says, "is a historical idea and not a natural species" (PP: 198). Human beings do, of course, belong to a certain biological species, but what we mean by "humanity" is defined by what members of that species have made of themselves in the course of their history. There is, in that sense, no pre-given essence of humanity that determines what human beings are or may become. At the same time, to say that human beings are historical is to say that their particular past (and indeed their biological make-up) constitute constraints on what they can make of themselves, just as they do on what individuals and societies can make of themselves. The world has what Merleau-Ponty calls an "autochthonous significance" (a significance that is part of its very "soil" or constitution), which it derives from the way in which we human beings, because of our own biological structure and history, deal with it, and this "autochthonous" significance provides the background to every attempt that we make to give it a meaning by our own choice (PP: 512).

This is the essence of Merleau-Ponty's philosophy as a whole, as expressed in *Phenomenology of Perception*. Human beings are objects in a world that extends far beyond their experience of it; but they are not only objects, they are subjects, interacting purposively with that world. Because they interact *purposively* with it, meaning is given to the world, and so to their own existence as human beings. But these meanings are not a matter for absolutely free choice; they are constrained by what human beings already are, biologically and historically, and by the independence of the world. And because human existence is open to the future, the definition of the meaning of that existence is always incomplete and ambiguous.

Note

1. To help in relating this presentation to the text of the book itself, I shall give page references in *Phenomenology of Perception* (PP), C. Smith (trans.) (London: Routledge, 2002).

Further reading

Langer, M. M. 1989. *Merleau-Ponty's Phenomenology of Perception: A Guide and Commentary*. Basingstoke: Macmillan.

Madison, G. B. 1981. *The Phenomenology of Merleau-Ponty: A Search for the Limits of Consciousness*. Athens, OH: Ohio University Press.

Matthews, E. 2002. *The Philosophy of Merleau-Ponty*. Chesham: Acumen.

Merleau-Ponty, M. 2004. *The World of Perception*, O. Davis (trans.). London: Routledge.
Priest, S. 1998. *Merleau-Ponty*. London: Routledge.

10

A. J. Ayer

Language, Truth and Logic

Barry Gower

Introduction

"Short, sharp and shocking" was the verdict of those who read *Language, Truth and Logic* when it was first published in January 1936. And it has retained much of its impact. It remains the best short introduction to an influential, if controversial, version of ideas associated with logical positivism in the first half of the twentieth century; its arguments have a cutting edge and they still challenge the book's readers; and although the passage of time has blunted its power to shock and disturb, it still reads like the provocative manifesto for a revolution intended to sweep away what its author saw as the over-ambitious exercises in thinking that characterized much of academic philosophy at that time. It was clearly intended to unsettle complacent readers, and it still provokes vigorous reactions, both positive and negative. Few are left unmoved. Some think its conclusions totally untenable and judge that the arguments leading to those conclusions must be faulty because no respectable arguments could lead to such conclusions. There have been, as a consequence, some sharp criticisms of some of those arguments. Others find its conclusions refreshing and agreeable, and think that the arguments used to establish them must be broadly sound. They have urged that most of its claims and conclusions are, with the help of some qualifications, correct and the arguments establishing them are sound, or can be made so by greater attention to some details.

The book's author, Alfred (Freddie) Jules Ayer, was not yet twenty-five when he finished writing it. It was his first book. The idea for it came from his friend

195

and colleague Isaiah Berlin, with whom he had enthusiastically discussed the ideas of the logical positivists. He had met many of the prominent philosophers, scientists and mathematicians associated with logical positivism when, shortly after graduating from the University of Oxford in 1932, he had spent some time in Vienna and had been invited to attend meetings of the *Wiener Kreis* – the Vienna Circle – by its director, Moritz Schlick. Ayer began writing his book early in 1934, soon after returning from Vienna in order to start a teaching job at the University of Oxford, and by the middle of the following year he had completed it. When it was published, and especially when a new edition was produced after the Second World War, it made Ayer's name as a philosopher and is still widely read. It may not be his best book – Ayer later expressed the hope that it would not be so regarded – but it is probably the one by which he is most widely known, both by philosophers and by the general public. It has been described as the most influential single book written by a philosopher in the twentieth century.

Although *Language, Truth and Logic* has a distinctive style, Ayer never claimed originality for the ideas it expressed and explored. It was, he said, a synthesis of Vienna Circle positivism, the reductive empiricism of David Hume and Bertrand Russell, and the analytical approach of G. E. Moore, with an element of pragmatism reflecting his admiration for the Cambridge philosopher Frank Ramsey. Ayer made a strong connection between the logical positivism of the Vienna Circle and Wittgenstein, whose work he had first encountered as an undergraduate. His tutor, Gilbert Ryle, introduced him to Wittgenstein on a post-graduation visit to Cambridge. Although, by this time, Wittgenstein had turned against some of his earlier ideas, including those that were closest to the most characteristic of the views of the logical positivists, for Ayer the Wittgenstein that he knew and met was the author of the *Tractatus*. He has said that his discovery of the *Tractatus* was the impulse that set his book in train.

Formulating the verifiability criterion

The first chapter of *Language, Truth and Logic*, entitled "The Elimination of Metaphysics", begins in a characteristically combative manner: "The traditional disputes of philosophers are, for the most part, as unwarranted as they are unfruitful." These traditional disputes are, he claims, metaphysical, by which he means that they purport to concern the most comprehensive structural characteristics of reality, described in a way that relies on *a priori* reflection and is independent of empirical investigations such as those used in science. In some respects Ayer's aim in trying to "eliminate" metaphysics, or show that it is "impossible", was not at all new. Since at least the seventeenth century philosophers have claimed that their subject is, or contains, nonsense of one kind or another. What was new about the position Ayer wished to defend was the reason given for the impossibility of metaphysics. Consider, for example, that part of metaphysics that proposes to provide information about reality that transcends, or goes beyond, what is available to our senses and can be observed, counted, measured or experimented upon. Ayer's claim was that the statements used to try to convey such information do not satisfy conditions that any statement must satisfy if it is to be meaningful, and so they convey no factual information. They are, in other words, nonsensical and we can eliminate them from consideration. It is no good our trying to find out whether they are true or false because, just like an ungrammatical sequence of words, they are neither. The conditions he refers to are those imposed by a criterion that any statement must meet if it is "literally significant". Statements that lack this kind of significance, although they may be grammatically correct, and may have other kinds of significance, fail to express a genuine thought.

The criterion Ayer proposed is known as the verifiability criterion. It says that genuinely meaningful statements are either analytic, and therefore true or false by virtue of decisions we have taken about how words and symbols are to be used, or alternatively synthetic, and therefore true or false by virtue of facts about the way the empirical world is. Leaving analytic statements to one side for the moment, the criterion requires of a synthetic statement that we are able to use our experience to verify it if we want to count it as factually meaningful and as telling us something, true or false, about the world. So, we will have to eliminate claims about fundamental reality whose truth or falsity is supposed to depend on facts about "the absolute" if we cannot verify the statements reporting those facts. For if we cannot verify such claims then, contrary to appearances, they do not tell us anything, true or false, about the world, because the verifiability criterion implies that there are no factually meaningful statements reporting facts that go beyond, or "transcend", our capacity to ascertain empirically whether the facts obtain or not. This does not of course mean that we must verify statements as true, or as false, before we can count them as meaningful; it means that it must be possible, in some sense, for us to verify them.

Why, though, is empirical verifiability a suitable criterion to use in deciding on the meaningfulness of a statement about the way the empirical world is? It is here that Ayer's empiricism has a role. For learning how to use statements to describe the world is a matter of recognizing what verifies the statements, and the basis of that recognition is our experience of the world. What else would we recognize as verifying a statement about the world, other than the actual or possible experiences relevant to deciding whether it is true or false? We must, of course, interpret experience broadly in this context. It is not just my experience I turn to when I recognize what verifies a statement; I can also refer to the experience of others.

For many of the statements that I know how to use, it is a matter of recognizing what, in the experience of others, verifies the statements. Most scientific statements are, for most of us, like this. What we must understand – if we understand a factually meaningful statement – is the distinction between being in a position to reasonably believe the statement, or its negation, and not being in that position. And when we are in a position to reasonably believe the statement, or its negation, there must be evidence enabling someone to verify it, or its negation.

But although we might for these general reasons accept that the meaningfulness of an empirical statement is connected with its verifiability, much depends on what we understand by "verifiable". It has proved extremely difficult to give an account of this concept that is not subject to strong objections. In the first place we have to acknowledge that if we were to require that factually meaningful statements are now verifiable by me or others, in practical terms, then we would have to eliminate many if not most of the statements we regard as acceptable. Thus, nobody can now personally verify any statement that is about the future, but there are many such statements that are certainly not metaphysical and that we cannot, and should not, eliminate. We need, then, a less rigorous concept of verifiability. What matters is not our practical ability to verify a statement, but our ability in principle to do so. The example Ayer gave was of the claim that there are mountains on the far side of the moon. Recall that at the time the example was given, there was no practical way in which anyone could decide the matter by observation, so the claim was practically unverifiable. But it was verifiable in principle because, given the prospect, however remote and unlikely, of a spacecraft in which to make the necessary expedition, it was "theoretically conceivable" for a person to be in a position to decide the matter by observation. Similarly with statements about the future; we cannot in practice verify them now, but in principle they are verifiable so long as we can rely on what is now in the future eventually becoming available to us in the present.

We also need to recognize a distinction between conclusive verification, which establishes truths or falsehoods beyond doubt, and a weaker version of the concept, which requires that experience makes truths or falsehoods probable. For example, we cannot, even in principle, conclusively verify the truth or falsity of universal generalizations of science and everyday life. We can only ever have a finite number of observations of, say, metals expanding when they are heated, and that evidence cannot conclusively prove the truth of the universal generalization that all metals expand when heated. Conclusive proof of its falsity is also beyond our reach, for whenever we think we have encountered a metal that fails to expand however much we heat it, and are tempted to conclude that we have thereby established beyond doubt the falsity of the generalization, we will find ourselves confronted with the task of proving, beyond doubt, that what we think is a metal really is one. Yet such generalizations are undoubtedly factually meaningful. Ayer argued, indeed, that all factual statements are, like universal generalizations, hypotheses whose truth or falsity we cannot conclusively prove. So the use of the strong version of the verifiability concept would lead to the "self-stultifying" conclusion that no factual statement is significant. Much depended, therefore, on whether the weaker version requiring the verification of statements as probable truth or falsehoods would deliver the right verdict for universal generalizations.

The criterion of meaningfulness, when used with this weaker concept of verification, requires that there be observations, actual or possible, that are relevant to the truth or falsity of the statement whose factual meaningfulness is being judged. What, though, does "relevant" mean in this context? Ayer explained that what he had in mind was logical, rather than causal, historical or psychological, relevance. This implies that the essential characteristic of a factually meaningful statement is that we can deduce other statements recording actual or possible observations from it when it is conjoined with certain other premises, without the deduced statements being deducible from those other premises alone. For example, the statement recording the observation that a metal has expanded is deducible from the generalization "heated metals expand" in conjunction with the statement that the observed metal was heated, but is not deducible from the latter statement alone. So, according to the verifiability criterion, the generalization "heated metals expand" counts as meaningful, as indeed it should. By contrast, a metaphysical claim such as that which maintains that the world we experience is a world of appearances rather than the real world, is not meaningful because there is no premise with which we can conjoin it so that a statement recording an actual or possible observation is deducible.

That was what Ayer thought and expressed in the first edition of his book. By the time he came to write his Introduction to the second edition he had realized that this understanding of weak verification was just as useless as strong verification. The difference was that whereas strong verification allowed nothing, or hardly anything, to count as meaningful, weak verification allowed everything to count as meaningful, including every metaphysical claim. To see why we only need to notice that no restriction is placed on the premise conjoined with the statement under scrutiny. In every case, we just have to make the conjoined premise say that if the statement under scrutiny is true then some statement recording an actual or possible observation – we can choose whatever statement we wish – is also true. We do not even have to believe that this conjoined premise is true; it is sufficient that it enables us to deduce a statement recording an observation from the statement we are testing for significance. The result of our test will of course always be that the statement is significant, simply because this conjoined premise enables us to deduce a statement recording an observation from it. And this is the case no matter what the statement we are testing says. Thus, the metaphysical claim that the world we experience is not the real world will, after all, have to count as meaningful because we can conjoin it to the premise "if the world we experience is not the real world then my cat is sitting on the mat" and so deduce the statement recording the observation that my cat is sitting on the mat, thereby satisfying the requirement of the criterion of factual meaningfulness.

In the Introduction to the second edition Ayer tried to repair the deficiency he had identified. What he suggested was that we distinguish between direct and indirect verifiability. A statement is "directly" verifiable if it is either a report of an actual or possible observation, or if such a report can be deduced from it when it is conjoined with one or more reports of actual or possible observations, without the original report being deducible from those further reports alone. And a statement is "indirectly" verifiable if we can deduce a state-ment that is directly verifiable from it when it is conjoined with other statements that are not themselves sufficient for deducing the directly verifiable statement, provided that those other statements are either directly or indirectly verifiable. In effect, Ayer tried to repair the deficiency by imposing restrictions on what we can use as conjoined statements when, with the help of such statements, we derive consequences from the statement we are testing for meaningfulness. The restrictions require, reasonably enough, that any conjoined statement is itself verifiable.

Hope that the repair would suffice was short lived, and critics were able to show that the proposed revision would still allow any arbitrary statement to count as factually meaningful. Subsequently, yet further modifications have been suggested, most of which have been shown to suffer from a similar defect. This outcome might have been expected, for the principle behind the verifiability criterion requires that we recognize all statements involved in using it as having a truth-value, that is, as being either true or false, including the statement whose factual meaningfulness we are testing using the criterion. But if a statement has a truth-value then it must be meaningful, and if it is about matters of fact then it is factually meaningful. It is hardly surprising, therefore, if the use of the criterion yields the result that the statement is factually meaningful. For suppose the statement that interests us does really lack factual meaningfulness and is nonsensical. It cannot report an actual or possible observation, and we cannot conjoin it with other statements without producing a nonsensical conjunction from which there is nothing we can legitimately deduce. So we cannot apply the verification criterion. If we know that the statement does not have factual meaning, then the criterion has no application; if we do not know this, then we can apply the criterion only if we implicitly assume the statement is factually significant, in which case we are bound to generate the conclusion that it is factually meaningful.

The only way of avoiding the difficulty is to retreat to the original vague formulation of the verification criterion. But the price for so doing is high. For the vagueness of a criterion that simply requires that reports of actual or possible observations are "relevant" to any statement that we can count as factually meaningful means that we may have no way of settling disputes about whether such observations are relevant or not. For example, some might say that familiar observations about how our senses can mislead us are relevant to the claim that the world we experience is not the real world but a world of appearances, and therefore this claim is factually meaningful and not, as Ayer said, metaphysical nonsense. Others will say that such observations are not relevant to the claim because they do not enable us to distinguish between the truth of this claim and the truth of its negation, that the world we experience is the real world and what are called appearances are simply different ways in which that real world looks to us. So neither the claim itself, nor this negation of it, is factually meaningful; both are metaphysical nonsense.

However, despite the technical difficulties in finding a foolproof way of stating precisely what the verification criterion requires of factually meaningful statements, we might well think that fundamentally there is something right about a principle that insists that we must anchor what we say about the world in experience of the world. Ayer's view was that metaphysical talk is not constrained in this way; it floats free of experience of the world and is not answerable to anything that that experience teaches us. What understanding could we have of such talk, given that the meaning of the words we use, even in metaphysics, must be learned and fixed by such experience?

The prospects of sustaining this view, however, are not good. To see why, we need to consider whether the statement expressing the criterion of verifiability is itself significant. Some early critics thought it could not be, for they supposed, with justification, that no reports of observations would be relevant to it. Ayer responded by claiming that we should regard the criterion as a conventional stipulation, or definition, of what it is for a statement to be meaningful. It would therefore count as analytically true and would satisfy the requirements of the criterion. It is not, though, an arbitrarily chosen conventional definition of meaningfulness, for it successfully captures the sense in which we understand scientific hypotheses and common-sense statements as meaningful. Even so, it would be open for metaphysicians to claim that the sense in which they understand metaphysical statements as meaningful is different, but no less legitimate. The use of the verifiability criterion to condemn all of metaphysics might therefore need to give way to a more piecemeal approach requiring, Ayer confessed, the "detailed analyses of particular metaphysical arguments" (Ayer 1946: 16).

Ayer's concession reveals a weakness in the verifiability criterion; no metaphysician need accept the verifiability criterion as providing a test for the meaningfulness of his or her claims. But the concession also shows that if we nevertheless accept it then implicitly we are relying on some important assumptions. For in defending his criterion Ayer has clearly demonstrated his commitment to science and common sense as embodying not only factual meaningfulness but genuine knowledge. This could be regarded as no more than a justified pragmatic judgement; science and common sense are indeed important sources of knowledge for us. But there is a natural link between that judgement and an empiricist approach to language and knowledge. As we have seen, empiricism has a role in motivating the verifiability criterion, and now we see a further connection with the background assumptions on which the criterion rests. For consider what would happen to our use of the criterion if we were to abandon empiricism. A central and essential component of empiricism is the claim that it is only by use of observation, experiment, measurement and whatever we can derive from them, that we can attain knowledge of matters of fact. By giving up empiricism we allow for the possibility that we can have knowledge of matters of fact by other means, a possibility we can express by saying that we can use rational insight, or "intellectual intuition", to obtain such knowledge. Of course, we will need to say something about how this rational insight is supposed to work, and about the kind of matters of fact that it is supposed to provide information about. But for our purposes it is sufficient that anti-empiricism should incorporate acknowledgement of this means of obtaining some knowledge of matters of fact. If we now turn to the verifiability criterion we can see that even apart from difficulties in formulating it so as to avoid the conclusion that every grammatically correct statement is meaningful, anti-empiricism will enable us to verify metaphysical statements. All that is needed is a declaration that rational insight enables us to know about matters of fact that we cannot know by means of observation, experiment and measurement, and this includes the matters of fact reported on in metaphysical statements. Such statements are therefore verifiable, just as scientific statements are verifiable. Our anti-empiricism has therefore led to the conclusion that we cannot use the verifiability criterion in the way Ayer intended: to eliminate metaphysics as nonsense. Clearly, his view relies on our willingness to adopt empiricist principles, and to reject the suggestion that rational insight provides us with a source of information about the empirical world.

In fact, though, Ayer's position was stronger than this indicates. It is not just that human beings do not have rational insight providing knowledge of the world, for that would imply that our verdict that metaphysical statements are meaningless is a contingent feature of our cognitive powers, whereas Ayer wished to claim that the verdict stands no matter what is true about human beings and their abili-

202

ties. Rational insight, if we were to possess it, would be idle simply because there are no facts beyond the reach of observation, experiment and measurement that it might be used to access. Thus, he believed that it is nonsense to claim that the world we experience is not the real world, because that claim depends on the thought that there is a world – the "real" world – lying beyond, behind, or above the "appearances" that our experience makes familiar to us. But there is no such world and therefore even if we were to have rational insight it would be of no use to us in verifying the truth or falsity of statements about it; we cannot verify statements about something that does not exist. The real world, if we wish to use such an expression, is the world of appearances.

What is striking about this position is that it requires a commitment to a bold and contentious metaphysical claim about what the world is like: the world does not contain some of the things that people commonly think it does. We suppose, for example, that even if it is impossible, in principle, for me to tell whether I am awake and really writing this sentence, or whether I am asleep and dreaming that I am awake and writing this sentence, there is a fact of the matter as to which of these very different states of affairs holds in the real world. But Ayer's verifiability criterion presupposes that if it really is impossible, in principle, to tell the difference between these two states of affairs, then there is no fact of the matter eluding the grasp of our senses, but perhaps accessible to rational insight. When we are tempted to say that in reality things must be one way rather than the other, even though we cannot tell, even in principle, which way they are, we are talking about something that does not exist. It is not surprising, therefore, that the verifiability criterion delivers the verdict that we are talking nonsense when we succumb to the temptation. But the commitment that leads to this conclusion is itself a metaphysical commitment. If the verification criterion leads us to dismiss it as meaningless then the criterion itself fails to eliminate metaphysics; no matter how we formulate it, it is self stultifying.

Defending the verification criterion

One might expect that, having satisfied himself that the verifiability criterion embodies a reasonable approach to philosophical issues, Ayer's strategy would have been to show how we can apply it to eliminate the "traditional disputes" of philosophers as meaningless nonsense. But that is not what he did. What he did instead was to consider challenges to his criterion that arise because we need to take seriously just those statements that it eliminates as nonsensical. According to these challenges, some of the eliminated statements are required because otherwise we cannot make good sense of matters that are indispensable to our understanding of the world and of our place in it. In each case, Ayer tried to show that the statements in question are either not needed, or are, when properly analysed, verifiable and therefore legitimate. We can, therefore, make good sense of these matters without having to abandon the verifiability criterion.

Ayer's approach to the statements of logic and mathematics illustrates this strategy. Potentially, such statements constitute a problem for empiricism and for the verifiability criterion. We might think that there is no problem because we can understand these statements as generalizations that are particularly well established as true or false by our observations of the empirical world. They report matters of empirical fact, and their truth or falsity only seems certain and necessary because our empirical evidence establishes them so conclusively. We might indeed wish to claim that their truth or falsity is conclusively verifiable, but in any case there can be no doubt about their meaningfulness. Ayer could not, though, adopt this view of logic and mathematics. His empiricism entailed that no generalization, however well established by observation, could count as certain and necessary, and it was precisely because the truths of logic and mathematics did count as certain and necessary that we could not regard them as empirical generalizations. But how, in that case, do we justify our knowledge of the truths of logic and mathematics, and how are we to account for their meaningfulness if they are not verifiable by observation? The challenge to empiricism, and to the verifiability criterion, arises because the prospect of appealing to rational insight as the means by which we justify logical and mathematical knowledge, and as the faculty enabling us to "see" and thereby verify the truths and falsehoods of logic and mathematics, is not available. No empiricist can countenance such a prospect. But no one, whatever they think about empiricism, can accept the conclusion that the statements of logic and mathematics are meaningless because they are unverifiable. Rather than accept that conclusion we would, and should, abandon the verifiability criterion of meaningfulness.

To maintain his criterion, Ayer had to argue that the statements of logic and mathematics are meaningful even though they are not verifiable. And he had to do this in a way that did not allow metaphysicians to claim that their statements too are meaningful even though they are unverifiable. He took as his starting-point the acknowledgment that we hold logical and mathematical statements as true or as false whatever we observe, however unusual or bizarre. This, he claimed, can only be because they are not about the empirical world, and so are not made true or false by facts about the world. In other words they are not synthetically true, or synthetically false. They are, instead, analytic statements. But they are, still, either true or false and Ayer must find an answer to the question as to what makes them true or false, if not facts about the world.

His answer was that they are made true by decisions we have taken about how the words and symbols we use to express statements in logic and mathematics are to be used. For example, the principle of logic expressed in statements of the form "either *p* is true or *p* is not true", where *p* is a statement, is an analytic truth because anyone who knows how to use the words "either", "or" and "not" will agree that it is true without having to refer to experience of the world. Indeed, statements of this form provide no information about any matter of fact and so we cannot verify or refute them by referring to facts. They "say nothing" but they are not meaningless because they record, correctly or incorrectly, the ways in which we have decided to use words and symbols. Thus, the arithmetical claim "3 + 5 = 9" says nothing about matters of fact because it is neither verifiable nor refutable by experience of any matters of fact. But it is not nonsense. Rather, it is false because it signifies an incorrect understanding of the way we have decided to use the symbols used to express the claim. We use the symbols "3", "+", "5", "=" and "9" in such a way that "3 + 5 = 9" is certainly and necessarily false. There are, of course, plenty of examples of logical and mathematical claims that are not so straightforwardly true or false. It is easy enough to work out that "23 × 156 = 3588" is true, but most of us do have to work it out using principles that record the ways we have decided to use symbols. So instead of saying that this arithmetical truth itself signifies a correct understanding of the symbols used to express the truth, it would be more accurate to say that it is a consequence of our understanding of those symbols. Similarly, there are truths of logic that are better described as consequences of principles that directly record decisions about how we should use words and symbols and that we can therefore understand as certain and necessary. In both mathematics and logic, statements are true only because of decisions we have taken about what words and symbols mean, and if we deny their truth we are in effect contradicting ourselves because we will be both accepting and rejecting those decisions. The claim that "3 + 5 = 8" will be false because we deny its truth, and will also be true because the claim we are denying is made true by our decisions about what the symbols it uses mean. This is why the truth of the claim is certain and necessary.

We should treat geometry, according to Ayer, in the same manner. The axioms of geometry are definitions recording decisions about how we use words and symbols expressing geometrical concepts. The decisions are conventions in the sense that we could take other decisions and thereby generate alternative geometries. The theorems of a geometry are simply the logical consequences of the decisions made for that geometry about which axioms, or definitions, we should adopt. Accordingly, geometry is not – as many have supposed – about physical space, although given some facts about physical space we can use a geometry that best fits those facts to derive further facts about physical space. Whether we can use a geometry in this fashion is indeed an empirical question whose answer depends on facts about the world, but because geometrical statements are either records of conventional decisions, or are derived from those decisions, they do not say anything about empirical facts and their truth or falsity does not depend on empirical facts. To deny that the parallel straight lines of Euclidean geometry never meet is not to contradict, controversially, the facts about physical space; it is, rather, to assert that this axiom of Euclidean geometry is false, and also to assert that it is true because the meaning we have given to the geometrical terms we use to express the axiom make it true. Our denial therefore leads to self-contradiction, and we must concede that the axiom is a certain and necessary truth.

In the Introduction to the second edition Ayer considered and answered some of the difficulties that his position on logic and mathematics was thought to entail. He did not, however, address the major problem facing any view that requires that some statements are true "by convention". The problem is that it is not just those statements that directly record decisions about how words and symbols are used, and what they mean, that are true by convention. The statement "3 + 5 = 8" may be said to be true by convention because its truth follows directly from conventional decisions about what the symbols it uses mean. But that cannot be said of most other mathematical and logical statements; for even if they are, for example, straightforwardly arithmetical they will nevertheless be beyond our direct apprehension. For example, "23 × 156 = 3588" is true but our understanding of the symbols it employs does not enable us to apprehend directly that it is true; we have to do some calculation. We have to say, that is, that the truth of "23 × 156 = 3588" follows from conventional decisions we have made about the use and meaning of arithmetical symbols. The same is true of almost all the statements of logic and mathematics. But of course it is only with the aid of principles or rules of logic and mathematics that "23 × 156 = 3588" follows from those decisions. So it is not just conventional decisions that we rely on when we assert the analyticity of logic and mathematics; we rely also on these principles or rules. Ayer would claim, no doubt, that since the principles or rules are those of logic and mathematics, we can represent them as expressing the consequences of conventional decisions about the words and symbols they employ. This, though, will not do because we are still making use of the idea of some things following other things with the aid of logic and mathematics. The argument can be repeated indefinitely, and it would seem that the only way to stop the repetition is to declare that we can just "see" that such-and-such follows from so-and-so without having to identify any principles or rules enabling the inference, and without therefore having to acknowledge that those principles or rules would have to follow from conventional decisions. To stop the indefinite repetition of the argument, we have to invoke a capacity tantamount to rational insight.

We can see the same difficulty occurring if we return to the idea that we cannot deny the truths of logic and mathematics without contradicting ourselves. To show that this is the case we had to use logical reasoning, which is nothing other than reasoning in accordance with logical rules. We rely on the reasonableness of these rules when we derive a self-contradiction from the denial of an analytic truth. But the reasonableness of the rules is determined by, and follows from, conventional decisions about the use and meaning of words and symbols. If we do not accept the rules, then no self-contradiction follows from our denial of an analytic truth, so they are essential. We need, though, further rules if we are to accept them, and the acceptance of these further rules will require yet further rules, and so on indefinitely. At each stage we can claim that the reliability of the rules we need follows from conventional decisions, but that will not stop the argument from repeating indefinitely. Once again we can only stop it by declaring that rules are not needed; we can just "see", using rational insight, that what we need follows from what we are given. In either case, Ayer's contention that the truths of logic and mathematics are guaranteed not by rational insight but by conventional decisions about the use and meaning of words and symbols is undermined. The contention played a key part in the broader picture presented in *Language, Truth and Logic*, for if we allow rational insight a place in logic and mathematics the case against the meaningfulness of metaphysics would collapse; there would be little or nothing to prevent metaphysicians from claiming that they, like logicians and mathematicians, need recourse to rational insight in establishing the truth or falsity, and thus the meaningfulness, of metaphysical statements.

Ayer's aim was to show that the statements of logic and mathematics can, and indeed must, be regarded as meaningful only if we understand them in a certain kind of way. As we have seen, regarding them in the way he suggested – as conventions – is problematic, but even if we cannot say that these statements are true, or false, by convention, it does not follow that the verifiability criterion must be abandoned. What, though, is the consequence of using Ayer's strategy in the case of other kinds of statements that are thought to present difficulties for the criterion?

Statements about material objects, such as those describing the shape or colour of a table, are certainly meaningful, and yet an attractive way of understanding how we are able to verify them leads to difficulties with the criterion. For when we look at a material object, such as a table, our senses provide us with data about its shape, colour, size and so on. Ayer called these data "sense contents". Sense contents are not to be identified with the table, if only because we do not want to make the existence of the table depend on the existence of these sense contents, but it seems reasonable to say that they represent the table to us. And we might claim that the sense contents are able to represent the table because the table is causally responsible for their occurrence, when they occur. In terms of the verifiability criterion, we can directly verify statements about sense content, but what of statements about material objects? It would seem that we have a difficulty because we can only verify such a statement if we can conjoin it to a verifiable statement and thereby derive a statement about sense contents, and although we would wish to use as the conjoined statement a claim about the material object being the cause of the occurrence of sense contents, we cannot verify such a statement on the basis of our experience of sense contents. The data provided by our experience when we look at a table are confined to sense contents; they cannot tell us that the occurrence of these data is caused by something other than sense contents, and any claim that they are so caused will be unverifiable. So, in order to sustain the meaningfulness of statements about material objects, we must either concede that, after all, we should identify material objects with the sense contents we experience, or we should abandon the verifiability criterion on the grounds that it delivers a verdict about these statements that we cannot accept.

Ayer responded to this challenge by proposing a phemomenalist analysis of statements about material objects that avoids the objection – and indeed the metaphysical claim – that the existence of material objects is somehow dependent on the existence of sense contents. His linguistic phenomenalism said that material objects are "logical constructions" out of sense contents, and he meant by this that we should analyse a statement about a material object as a statement about the sense experiences we have when we observe the material object, or would have if we were to observe it. So a statement about a material object does not have any content over and above the content of the statements we use to report our sense experiences when we observe it, or would use to report our experiences if we were to observe it. To say that material objects are "logical constructions" out of sense contents does not mean that objects are in some sense "composed" of sense contents and that there is nothing more to material objects than sense contents. It is, rather, to make a claim about the meaning of statements about material objects. Analogously, when statisticians make statements about what the average consumer, or the average family, has or does, what they say is equivalent to statements about what actual consumers and actual families have or do. In this sense, the average consumer, and the average family, is a logical construction out of actual consumers and actual families. Statements about material objects are, then, verifiable because material objects are logical constructions out of actual and possible sense contents. There is no more difficulty about verifying statements about material objects than there is about verifying statements about sense contents.

But are material objects, understood as logical constructions, real things? Ayer no doubt considered the question metaphysical, and therefore eliminable, but he did insist that logical constructions are not fictitious, in the way that fictional characters in a myth, novel or play are fictitious. But, as the analogous examples indicate, this does not answer the question; the average consumer is neither a real person nor a fiction. The question arises quite naturally from Ayer's commitment to phenomenalism. If he simply refused to acknowledge it because any answer he gave to it would be metaphysical and therefore, by the verifiability criterion, meaningless, he will not have carried through his strategy successfully. For his phenomenalism was developed in order to answer the challenge that statements about material objects are only meaningful if we reject the verifiability criterion. Ayer's claim was that a correct analysis of these statements shows that we do not have to reject the criterion in order to understand them as meaningful. But this analysis depends on phenomenalism, which is itself a metaphysical doctrine. To make use of it is to reopen the challenge: how can we adopt a version of phenomenalism, and treat it as a meaningful doctrine without implicitly rejecting the verification criterion? Ayer claimed that the only legitimate philosophical question is how statements about material objects should be analysed, and his answer was the phenomenalist answer that they are to be analysed as statements about logical constructions. The metaphysical issue about the reality of material objects, understood as logical constructions, was rejected as senseless because that was the verdict of the verifiability criterion. He was, in effect, making use of the criterion in order to show that his phenomenalistic analysis of statements about material objects provided a good way of demonstrating that the challenge to the criterion can be met. His strategy assumed the cogency of what it was intended to establish.

As a final example of Ayer's strategy we can turn to one of the more striking features of *Language, Truth and Logic*, namely the account he gives of moral judgements. Once again, Ayer found that an apparently straightforward way of dealing with these judgements was unacceptable even though its adoption would not present problems for the verifiability criterion. Alternatives, however, seem to require us to exercise rational insight, or intellectual intuition, in ascertaining whether a moral judgement is true or false. Such judgements could, perhaps, be verified, but not in the way required by the verifiability criterion. To avoid the difficulties Ayer proposed and defended a distinctively different kind of analysis of moral statements, which required that we understand them as expressions of attitudes, feelings and emotions we have towards facts and states of affairs, rather than as true or false descriptions of facts or states of affairs. He proposed and defended what has come to be known as the emotive theory of ethics.

From an empiricist point of view, the straightforward way of analysing moral judgements is as statements that, when they are true, satisfy an empirically determined requirement, and, when they are false, fail to satisfy that requirement. For example, if we analyse the moral statement that stealing is wrong as a statement about the feelings of disapproval that a person, or a group of people, have towards stealing, then the statement is true or false depending on whether the person, or group of people, have in fact those feelings of disapproval. Similarly, if we analyse the statement as a statement about the tendency of stealing to promote unhappiness, or displeasure, or dissatisfaction, then again the moral statement is true or false depending on whether stealing does in fact have those tendencies. A consequence of these "naturalistic" analyses is that moral statements are verifiable by observation and experience of the empirical world. They will therefore count, as indeed they should, as meaningful.

Nevertheless, Ayer rejected naturalistic analyses of moral statements. In doing so he relied on a contentious form of argument. Consider, for instance, the utilitarian analysis that claims that when we say that an action is morally right or good we are saying that it promotes well-being. If this analysis were correct then we would be contradicting ourselves if we said that an action is morally right or good but it does not promote well-being, or if we said that although an action promotes well-being it is not morally right or good. But, Ayer claimed, we are not contradicting ourselves when we say such things, and there are contexts in which this kind of thing is exactly what we want to say. Telling the truth is morally right, but there are circumstances in which it does not promote well-being. We may all agree that stealing is wrong, but that does not mean that we all agree that stealing is something that promotes unhappiness, or displeasure, or dissatisfaction. For it could be the case that no one is actually made unhappy, or is displeased, or is dissatisfied, by a theft, and yet we are still entitled to claim, and might want to claim, that the theft is morally wrong.

The reason why this form of argument – sometimes known as the "open question" argument because it supposes that the question whether an action is morally right is still open even though we agree that the action does have the empirical characteristics identified in the analysis of the statement that the action is right – is contentious is that in arguing that a proposed naturalistic analysis is mistaken, it seems to assume that the proposed analysis is mistaken. If, for example, we propose to analyse the moral statement that telling the truth is right as a statement saying that telling the truth promotes well-being, then it follows from our proposal that it is not an open question whether when someone tells the truth they have done the right thing, provided that their telling the truth promoted well-being. If we say that the question is open then we are simply denying that the proposed analysis is correct, without producing any argument for our denial. In other words, we only avoid contradicting ourselves when we say that telling the truth is right but it does not promote well-being, if we reject the proposed analysis. There may, of course, be good reasons for not analysing moral statements in the way that naturalists suggest, but the "open question" argument does not provide them.

For Ayer, however, his rejection of a naturalistic analysis of moral statements threatened to undermine his verifiability criterion. If moral statements are not answerable to empirical facts about what promotes people's well-being, or about what leads to some other observable state of affairs, then it seems we must conclude that they are answerable to non-empirical facts. We are obliged, that is, to countenance the real existence of non-observable states of moral affairs, and the only way we could verify statements answerable to these states of moral affairs would be to acknowledge our possession of rational insight, or of moral intuition, enabling us to discern them. But then we would, once again, be abandoning the verifiability criterion, at least in the form Ayer presented it. If we refuse to go down this path, and persevere with the verifiability criterion, then we must draw the unpalatable conclusion that moral statements are meaningless.

The way out of the difficulty, Ayer claimed, was to identify and defend an analysis of moral statements that would avoid the dilemma. Moral statements, according to this analysis, are not statements at all, despite their grammatically misleading form. They are, instead, expressions of our feelings, attitudes and emotions. So, when we say that stealing is wrong we are not attributing, truly or falsely, a moral character to a certain kind of behaviour; we are, rather, expressing or evincing our feeling of disapproval towards that kind of behaviour. This means that when we say "stealing is wrong", our statement has no factual content and there is therefore no question of verifying it. It is indeed unverifiable, but not because it tries to say things that cannot legitimately be said, but because it does not say anything at all. Moral statements are not genuine statements, and do not come within the scope of the verifiability criterion. They do not have factual meaning, but they do have what we might call expressive or emotive meaning. When someone steps on my toe and I say "Ouch!", what I say is not appropriately described as true or false. But it is not meaningless; it has an entirely legitimate expressive meaning. Similarly, when I say "stealing is wrong" what I say is not appropriately described as true or false, despite appearances to the contrary. The statement is not, however, meaningless; it has, according to Ayer's analysis, an expressive or emotive meaning.

The emotive theory of value is, as Ayer acknowledged, a radically subjective theory. It is, therefore, open to the objection that if moral judgements simply express their authors' feelings, then it is impossible to argue about moral questions. This follows, indeed, from their analysis as sentences that are neither true nor false. So, if you say that chastity is a virtue, and I say that it is not, we are not disagreeing with each other. You are evincing or expressing your feelings of approval towards chastity, and I am declining to express those feelings towards chastity. Many would claim that it is wrong to rule out the possibility of disagreement about moral questions, but Ayer was prepared to defend his view that such disputes never do take place. He did not deny that we disagree when we consider questions about what is the morally right thing to do, but in every case, he claimed, we are not disputing questions of value but only questions of fact. So, when I argue with you about the virtuousness of chastity, I might try to get you to agree with me about the facts regarding the consequences of chastity and thereby persuade you to change your attitude, so that it coincides with mine. If, however, you were to agree with me about those facts, but you did not change your attitude, then there is nothing I could do to get you to change your mind. Your values, I might say, are quite different from mine. I can deplore your values, and you can deplore mine, but in doing so we are simply expressing our feelings, our attitudes and our emotions. There is no room for persuasive argument.

Much of what is ordinarily counted as ethics goes by the board if we accept Ayer's emotive theory of value. For example, we must reject the view that there must be some characteristic of an action, or kind of action, that makes it morally right, if it is morally right, because there are no moral facts about actions for us to discern when we make such claims. Ayer developed his theory because he thought that naturalistic theories were mistaken, and because he could not accept the alternative view that moral statements refer to non-natural properties of actions whose truth or falsity we can know by rational insight or moral intuition. He could, of course, have concluded, in accordance with his verifiability criterion, that moral statements are, like metaphysical statements, meaningless and we should take no notice of them. The question is whether his emotive theory represents a position that is clearly distinct from this conclusion. Like metaphysical statements, moral statements are cognitively meaningless; they do not say anything about matters of fact, and they are not analytic. But metaphysical statements, unlike moral statements, should be eliminated. What, we might ask, justifies the difference? When we make moral judgements we think that what we say is either true or false, and that there are facts about the world that make what we say true or false. Ayer proposed an analysis of moral statements that implies we are wrong when we so think. But we could, and perhaps should, respond by rejecting his analysis precisely because it fails to take into account the fact-stating role of moral statements, just as Ayer himself rejected naturalistic analyses of these statements on the grounds that they fail to take into account their normative role. The emotive theory of value depends on a radical and distinctive analysis of moral statements; the debate that it has fostered raised core issues about whether this analysis is sufficiently responsive to the character of these statements and the way we use them. The arguments Ayer gave for his adoption of the theory are less than conclusive, but the theory itself has retained its interest and much of its power.

Conclusion

Towards the end of his life, Ayer took part in a television interview and was asked what he considered to be the main defects of *Language, Truth and Logic*. He replied that all of it was false. This is, of course, an exaggeration and Ayer commented that the remark was not entirely sincere. Nevertheless, the most distinctive features of the book – his conventionalism about logic and mathematics, his linguistic phenomenalism, his emotive theory of value, and above all his verifiability criterion – have all been subject to scrutiny and criticism, and have all been found wanting. It is, perhaps, because so much of that scrutiny and criticism is linked to prominent themes in contemporary analytic philosophy that the book has retained its interest and its reputation. We continue to struggle with many of the issues Ayer addressed, and although we may not accept his conclusions, the reasons we give for our dissent help to illuminate the alternatives we prefer. We should not mind that it is all false, if that is the case, provided we can use it to help us to identify theories and views that are true, or at least less false. Other philosophy books published in the twentieth century may have sustained their central themes in a more detailed and sophisticated manner, but few, if any, can match the confidence, vitality and ingenuity that are evident on almost every one of its pages. Students invariably read it with pleasure, and when they later return to it with a scepticism born of considering what has been achieved in philosophy since it was published, they find that its arguments still stimulate thought and that its author's youthful enthusiasm still provides pleasure.

Bibliography

Ayer, A. J. 1946. *Language, Truth and Logic*, 2nd edn. London: Victor Gollancz.

Foster, J. 1985. *Ayer*. London: Routledge & Kegan Paul.

Gower, B. (ed.) 1987. *Logical Positivism in Perspective: Essays on Language, Truth and Logic*. London: Croom Helm.

Hahn, L. E. (ed.) 1991. *The Philosophy of A.J. Ayer*. La Salle, IL: Open Court.

Macdonald, G. & C. Wright (eds) 1986. *Fact, Science and Morality: Essays on A.J. Ayer's Language, Truth and Logic*. Oxford: Blackwell, 1986.

11

Gilbert Ryle
The Concept of Mind

Rom Harré

The man behind the philosopher

Gilbert Ryle was born in Brighton in 1900. He read first Classics and Philosophy and then Philosophy, Politics and Economics at The Queen's College, Oxford. He was appointed to a lectureship at Christ Church, Oxford, in 1924. After war service in Intelligence, he was elected to the Wayneflete Professorship in Metaphysical Philosophy in 1945. He died in 1976, still active in philosophy. Apart from his service during the Second World War, and occasional although extensive travels, he spent the whole of his life in Oxford.

In later life he was an impressive, somewhat "military" figure. Through the editorship of *Mind* and his dominant role in developing the philosophy graduate school in Oxford, he exercised an almost worldwide influence on how philosophy developed in the 1950s and 1960s, and who occupied teaching positions over a large part of the globe. He was an indefatigable traveller, willing to go to the ends of the earth to present his ideas. His lectures were animated versions of his writings, with the same charm and the same method of presentation. Surprisingly, he had little talent for informal discussion. If challenged he would fall back on the points he had made in a lecture.

Ryle had very high standards for the conduct proper to members of the academic profession. Strong argument was not to be confused with personal abuse. As editor of *Mind*, he caused a stir by refusing to review Ernest Gellner's attack on Oxford philosophy, on the grounds that it was *ad hominem* rather than argumentative.

Ryle had already revealed the existence of a new voice in philosophy with his "Systematically Misleading Expressions" published in 1931. Nevertheless, the appearance of *The Concept of Mind* in 1949 was a landmark. It was the first widely read work in the style that was soon to become "Oxford philosophy". In this book the marriage of linguistic analysis and philosophical argument is set out in a major study of one of the most difficult topics in philosophy: what is the nature of the human mind? All our troubles with understanding the mind, he argues, come from the tendency to illegitimately bring together diverse and conflicting conceptual schemes in trying to set up one comprehensive account of what it is to be a human being.

However, the problem of the nature of the human mind was not the only philosophical conundrum to which he applied the idea of resolving seemingly intractable problems with what one might almost describe as the Rylean technique. All sorts of diverse puzzles could be shown to be artifacts of the tendency to falsely unify distinctive conceptual frames. The puzzles disappeared once this tendency was unmasked. In *Dilemmas* (1954), Ryle exploited the technique to great advantage.

The Concept of Mind

The plot of the book is straightforward. Philosophy of mind has been mired in a persistent pattern of gross philosophical errors. With some historical licence, Ryle claims that these errors lead from different directions to Descartes and his two-substance account of personhood. According to this account, the body is made of one substance, matter, and the mind of another substance, an immaterial stuff. This is an ontological error that has had all sorts of unwelcome consequences. However, as we shall see, it is remediable by attention to the way the words we use to describe thinking, feeling and acting are actually used.

Attention to language shows that there is no ground for the presupposition of a hidden realm of mental states and activities "behind" those we actively produce and experience in thinking, feeling and acting as we do. It shows this by tracking the erroneous path along which philosophers have led us towards the mentalistic illusion through misunderstandings of the way key words are used. What exactly is the illusion? It is that there is an unobservable immaterial "machine" the workings of which are responsible for all the phenomena, be they the public behaviour or the private thoughts and feelings that make up the domain of common experience. Material substance makes up the body as a physical machine and a second, immaterial substance makes up the mind as a mental machine.

215

It is not quite clear in which direction the finger of blame points. Is the root of our linguistic muddle an uncritical acceptance of the idea of "the ghost in the machine"? Or, is it these very misunderstandings that lead inexorably to the two-substance picture of what it is to be a human being?

There are key words in our psychological vocabulary that are thought to refer to hidden states of mind. Attention to how they are actually used shows instead that they are used to ascribe to a person certain dispositions to behave in various and particular ways. For example, intelligence is a real attribute of some people, but is mis-assigned as a mental property to the immaterial "ghost" inhabiting the human bodily machine. If we are convinced that there is no such machine, the temptation to misinterpret words such as "intelligent" is more easily resisted.

Often the discussion in *The Concept of Mind* seems to move in the opposite direction. The prime mover to error is presented as our tendency to slip into mistakes about the meanings and uses of words. If "intelligence" is a mental state, to what is it to be ascribed? The obvious subject for an immaterial property is an immaterial mental substance invented for just this purpose. For example, Ryle insists that it is a mistake to suppose that there is any such thing as an "act of will" that brings about a deliberate human action. This gratuitous invention is the result of a misunderstanding of the everyday distinction between voluntary and involuntary acts. There is no hidden realm of acts of will behind the deliberate voluntary acts we all carry out. However, if we were to mistakenly think that there are acts of volition, their only possible site is in an immaterial mental machine.

Ryle's book can be read as a kind of philosophical medicine that will free us from an ancient and longstanding metaphysical mistake. At the same time, it presents a quasi-historical diagnosis of the route by which philosophers, for example Descartes, have been led to make that mistake. The intersection of these lines of argument in disposing of any vestige of Cartesianism is the source of the strength of the whole enterprise.

The Concept of Mind was widely read. At the time of its publication, only an inner circle of devotees knew the later writings of Wittgenstein, although Ryle may have had some acquaintance with them. The close link between the Rylean method of analysis and Wittgenstein's technique of undertaking a surview of the relevant language games was visible to most people only in hindsight.

It must also be said that the fact that Ryle's studies were devoted to the uses of everyday English words was responsible for a widespread misunderstanding of the Oxford philosophical style. It came to be called "ordinary language philosophy", as if the rules for the use of everyday expressions in the vernacular were to be the touchstone of all wisdom, the repository of philosophical truth. On the contrary, the temptations to misunderstand the uses of words were not thought to be confined to the language of everyday life. The use of linguistic analysis to reveal philosophical confusions had an equal place in studies of even the most recondite vocabularies. The "ordinary language of quantum mechanics" tempted one to misunderstand the import of the "uncertainty" principle, just as the "ordinary language of the law" tempted one to misunderstand the legal concept of causation (Hart & Honoré 1985).

The "Cartesian" category mistake

Ryle's target in accusing philosophers of a profound mistake in the interpretation of our mentalistic vocabulary was the misassignment of all mental phenomena to an immaterial substance. Mental activities were treated as properties of that substance. The mistake lay in treating the mind as a being of the same category as the body, namely a substance. Ryle calls the two-substance account of persons the "official doctrine". The person is thought of as a conjunction of a mental substance with a material substance. This doctrine is the result of a category mistake.

The argument proper of *The Concept of Mind* begins with an explanation of this fallacy. Ryle examines several examples of common category mistakes (Ryle 1949: 16–17) to illustrate the structure and force of the fallacy. A visitor's quest for the university among the buildings of the city of Oxford is an illusory project because it is based on a category mistake: taking the university to be of the same category as the colleges. Colleges are spatiotemporally locatable institutions. The university is not another such institution. It is, in a certain sense, the aggregate of the colleges. It has no spatiotemporal location. Having visited the colleges one has visited the university.

Then there is the child who, having seen the battalions of a military division march by, asks when the division is to appear. Moreover, more to the point of the book, there is a third example. A foreign visitor, having watched a cricket match and seen the various players batting, bowling, fielding and so on, asks which person is responsible for the *esprit de corps*. However, displaying team spirit is not another cricketing activity of the same category as batting, bowling and fielding. Importantly for the later argument, Ryle remarks that we cannot say that the bowler bowls *and* displays team spirit, because displaying team spirit is not the same kind of thing as bowling or batting or fielding.

A category mistake arises, declares Ryle, because the person who makes it does not have a clear and explicit grasp of how the *words* "university", "division" and "team spirit" are used. In general, people manage their vocabularies very well, until they begin to reflect on them in some abstract way: in short, until they start to philosophize. Then they tend to misinterpret the pertinent words, removing them from the everyday contexts of use. Why should that lead to error? Because the fact that a word is a noun, for example, and so likely to be the name of some thing or substance, becomes the dominant feature of its meaning, when it has been abstracted from context. Thus, to take another of Ryle's illustrations, a political philosopher might come to believe that in addition to the organs and activities of government there was another entity, the British Constitution, as if it were of the same ontological type, the same sort of existent, as the readily observed governmental institutions scattered up and down Whitehall.

Substantival mind as a category mistake

Adopting the mentalistic myth of mind-as-substance, either because of mis-assignments of word-kinds, or as a longstanding error seemingly supported by Cartesian arguments, leads to several consequential errors. First of all, there is the idea that people live in two worlds. There is the physical world of bodily states and happenings, the world of material substance. There is also the mental world of cognitive and emotional events. The mistake is to construe the mental world as consisting of a mental substance, paralleling the material substance of the body. The one is said to be "outer" and publicly visible to all. The other is said to be "inner" and its properties are known, wholly or in part, only to the person to whom such events as forming a thought, recollecting a past experience, suffering a pang of hunger and so on, are occurring. Physical being is in space and time, whereas mental being is only in time. Thus, there are two realms or "insulated fields": the physical realm and the mental realm.

An important and seemingly intractable problem stems from this way of thinking: that is, treating the difference between the material and the mental aspects of a person's life as grounded in a radical difference between substances. The way that events as pairs of states, one from each of the two incommensurable substances, can influence one another then becomes a seemingly irresolvable mystery. How is it possible for a state or process occurring in a mental substance to affect the state or condition of a material or physical substance, if the substances of which they are properties have nothing in common? How could a thought influence the making of a sound? How could a sound influence what someone thinks or feels? Yet it must be admitted that people can influence one another's thoughts and feelings only via the mediation of some process in the physical realm. This is an important aspect of the traditional *mind–body problem*.

Ryle's diagnosis is that this traditional philosophical problem is not a problem at all. It appears so only because of the root category mistake that segregates the mental and physical as attributes of distinct and diverse substances.

218

What exactly is Ryle denying in rejecting the idea of the "ghost in the machine"? He is not denying that there is a domain of personal and private experience. He is denying that there is a realm of cognitive *entities* and *processes* beyond the realm of experience, be it private or public, the behaviour of which explains the psychological phenomena of which we are witnesses. He argues, mostly by piling up examples on examples, that the concepts appropriate to the private and personal domain of experience are continuous with and subject to the same logical grammar, that is the same general rules of use, as those that are displayed publicly and socially.

In a curious way, Ryle's target was an approach to psychology that had not yet been born. Many of the theses the fatal flaws of which he diagnoses are the very principles on which a certain strand of so-called "cognitive science" has been built. (See particularly Fodor (1975) for the idea of a cognitive realm unknown to those who think, feel and act intentionally, and yet determining what those thoughts, feelings and actions will be.) Ryle's argument would seem to show that there is no "language of thought", no mind behind the mind. Although Ryle never says so, it surely follows that the only domain "behind the mind" is the domain of neural activity. Psychology terminates in the public and private activities in which people engage.

Consistently with his general line, Ryle also denies that our private experiences are processes in and properties of that same immaterial mental substance. In this vein, he seems to be saying that the contents of our mental lives are *acts* we perform, things we *do*, rather than static properties of something mysterious. Imagining something privately, that is "in the mind's eye", is just as much a matter of something someone does as drawing something publicly on a sheet of paper. According to this line of argument, the concept of a mental substance is intelligible, but as it happens there is no such thing. We do not need to invoke that hypothesis to explain all that needs to be accounted for in our thoughts, feelings and actions.

Ryle sometimes seems to suggest that the hypothesis of the mind behind the mind is arrived at by faulty reasoning. On this reading, it would be a matter of fact that the hypothesis of a hidden mental realm, a mind behind the mind, is false. It is false in the same way that the hypothesis of a luminiferous aether is false. That hypothesis, central to nineteenth-century physics, was arrived at by faulty reasoning, based on the mistaken principle that light waves required a medium. It turned out that the hypothesis, although meaningful, was false as a matter of fact. There is no such thing.

Sometimes Ryle seems to be suggesting that the very concept of a substantival but hidden mental realm is incoherent, and so meaningless. The conclusion from this reading would be that there *could be* no such thing. There are no round squares because the concept is incoherent. Ryle's primary intention was surely to promote the latter view in order to show that there could be no place for the former view.

Historical origins of the idea of "ghost in the machine"

How did the dual substance account of personhood come to be dominant in Western thought, a dominance that ran for at least three hundred years? Ryle locates the substantialization of the mind firmly in the seventeenth century (Ryle 1949: 18–24). The physicists, exemplified by Galileo, had made a splendid start on creating a mechanistic picture of the physical world. According to this way of looking at material reality, the hypothesis of unobservable material corpuscles as the constituents of material things, and the laws of mechanics describing how everything material behaves, were adequate to account for every material phenomenon. By parity of reasoning, if the mental was not to be reduced to the material, nor "mental-conduct words construed as signifying the occurrence of mechanical processes, they must be construed as signifying the occurrence of non-mechanical processes" (Ryle 1949: 19). Some human behaviours will have mechanical causes, and others non-mechanical causes. This is a different but contributing source of the idea of an immaterial mind behind the mental lives of human beings.

Now comes Ryle's most innovative step, a move that links these historical considerations to the diagnosis that the hypothesis of the ghost in the machine is a category mistake. The Cartesian way of preserving the mind from a mechanistic reduction is grounded in the treatment of the differences between the physical and the mental "as differences within a common framework of the categories of 'thing', 'stuff' [and so on]" (Ryle 1949: 19). What is mental is treated as a subcategory of the category of substance, the other subcategory being matter. This is just like the error of the visitor who treats the concept of "the university" as a subcategory of the category to which the colleges belong: spatiotemporally locatable institutions housed in appropriate buildings.

Having disposed of one alleged seventeenth-century legacy, the Cartesian "ghost in the machine", we are not yet home free. There is another bogy: the threat of mechanism. The Galilean project was to find the laws of mechanics, which reflected the motions and structures of material things. These laws were to be naturally necessary and the processes they described deterministic. From time to time Ryle makes small-scale and not very well-informed forays into history and philosophy of science, mainly to identify the alleged sources of the bogy of mechanism. In his review, Stuart Hampshire (1950) drew attention to Ryle's often cursory and sometimes shallow historical asides.

According to Ryle the very idea of a mental "mechanism" is yet another facet of the Cartesian point of view that has proven both influential and mischievous. What sorts of entities are these mental substances of which each person possesses a unique exemplar? Belonging to the same category as bodies, the scientific project will show, it was hoped, that minds too will be found to obey a parallel set of laws to the laws of mechanics that describe material phenomena. Not only is there a ghost in the machine, but the mind is itself a ghostly machine. This links back to the supposed parallel between the ambitions for an actual science of material phenomena, and those for a possible science of mental phenomena.

This brings us to the final step in Ryle's analysis, a step that has been one of the driving forces behind the social constructionist psychologies of the late twentieth century. The treatment of mental processes on the model of the physics of matter entails a deeply disturbing consequence. There is no place in such a scheme for moral concepts in the assessment of the mental life. The intuition that this was an unacceptable consequence of Cartesianism led to heroic efforts to solve another pseudo-problem that the Cartesian mental mechanism account of mind throws up. If the body and the mind are both deterministic machines, obeying strict causal laws, how could there be human agency? This is the traditional problem of the freedom of the will. It looked as if in a universe in which there was both material and mental causation, there could be no room for the application of the idea of human freedom. Without freedom, there is no place for the concept of personal responsibility and so no place at all for moral concepts.

Ryle argues that abandoning the Cartesian project, now seen to be rooted in a category mistake, removes the most persistent problems of philosophy of mind in the modern era at a stroke. How could mind and body interact if each was a substance with no properties in common with its counterpart? How could there be free action when causal laws dominated both the material and the mental worlds? These questions do not present problems to be solved; they are consequences of a misunderstanding of the grammar of our language. Psychological words are not used in such a way as to imply the existence of a hidden mental realm, the domain of an immaterial substance.

Having diagnosed the roots of the "disease" of mentalism, and explained how a right understanding of the words of our mental vocabulary relieves us of paradoxes and problems, Ryle then sets about a detailed demonstration of the logical grammar, that is of the rules of correct – that is, the current received – use of a wide range of the relevant words.

The mentalistic vocabulary and its uses

The notion of a disposition, along with other linked concepts such as skill and ability, makes its appearance piecemeal in Chapters 2, 3 and 4. These chapters follow the traditional division of psychology into three main topics: cognition, conation and affection – knowing, willing and feeling. The detailed analysis of the difference between dispositions and occurrences, expressed in dispositional and episodic words respectively, is tackled only in Chapter 5. I believe the clarity of the argument will benefit from the explicit introduction of the distinction between dispositions and occurrences before the three traditional topics are given the Rylean treatment!

Let me introduce this distinction with a simple non-psychological example. To say solubility is a *dispositional property* of sugar is to so say that if it is placed in any warm watery liquid it will dissolve. To say that a teacup is full is to ascribe an *occurrent property* to the cup. "Being soluble" is a disposition, whereas "being full" is an occurrence.

In several places, Ryle lists some of the professions members of which use mentalistic words. Among them are judges, teachers, novelists, psychologists, sportsmen and "the man in the street". They use words from two main groups. There are dispositional words such as "knowing", "believing", "aspiring", "clever" and "greedy", and episodic words such as "seeing", "hearing", "running", "paying attention to" and the like. Already it is easy to see that these lists are not homogeneous. Each group of words falls into diverse kinds.

At the root of the category mistakes that disfigure the philosophy of mind Ryle finds a tendency to treat mental disposition words as if they referred to mental states. Expressed in linguistic terms the mistake is to treat dispositional words as if they were a special group of episodic words. Since dispositions are not observable occurrent states of persons or things, the temptation into which "many epistemologists"[1] fall is to treat disposition words as referring to unobservable or occult occurrences and states. Hence, we come to believe that there is a hidden mental realm.

The vocabulary that is used to describe human activities includes dispositional terms such as "know", "aspire" and "habit". In contrast there are episodic words, such as "run" and "tingle". What distinguishes dispositions? The answer will come from a close look at the logic of dispositional attributions. It is a mistake to construe dispositional words as episodic words. Dispositions are described in conditional statements, but descriptions of episodes are categorical.

Listing adverbs that are appropriate to qualify the members of one group, but not the other brings out the distinction between these classes of words.

The overall argument is very simple. Realizing that dispositional words do not refer to anything observable other than the behaviour they describe, and slipping into treating them as if they were episodic words, it seems natural to suppose that they refer to unobservable states of affairs. To what then do they refer? Since there are no other observable phenomena to competences, tendencies, capabilities and skills than the conditions under which they are displayed in the appropriate kind of performance, people are tempted to suppose that there must be occult or unobservable states, conditions and processes as their referents. However, Ryle argues, these words do not have a descriptive function at all. They are used to license the drawing of inferences. Conditionals are rules for predicting and explaining happenings by reference to certain antecedent happenings. Dispositions, as condensed expressions of rules that license certain inferences, are no exception. To say that someone is clever is to say, among other things, that if this person is presented with a problem, he or she will readily solve it. With this conditional in hand, one can infer that this person, when presented with a problem, will quickly solve it. Cleverness is not a hidden mental attribute that makes the problem-solving behaviour possible.

Tendencies, for example, are attributed to material and organic beings, including people, in statements of the conditional or "if … then …" form. Their role is to serve as licences for drawing inferences as to a person's likely behaviour in specific circumstances referred to in the antecedent clause of the conditional statements with which we unpack the meaning of dispositional terms. We might say that Joe has a tendency to get annoyed when frustrated by bureaucratic red tape. Analysed as the conditional "if Joe is frustrated by red tape then he is likely to get annoyed", the statement serves to support predictions as to what Joe will do when he is asked to fill in yet another form! "Sentences embodying these dispositional words have been interpreted as being categorical reports of particular but unwitnessable matters of fact [occult causes and effects] instead of being testable, open hypothetical … statements" (Ryle 1949: 117).

To bear out this important thesis the first step will be to show that the logic of dispositional attributions requires that dispositional statements take the form of conditionals, that is that dispositions are indeed ascribed by the use of open hypotheticals, which take the "if … then …" form. However, there is an episodic aspect to dispositions. Someone who is properly said to be touchy may not be displaying irritation at this moment. The person so described has a tendency to take offence too readily. However, if that individual never took offence it would surely be improper to describe him or her as touchy. In general, a disposition must have been or will be displayed. Could there be personal dispositions that are never displayed? A person may feel a strong urge to jump off a high place, but has always managed to resist it. What is it about the person that persists even when the disposition is not being displayed?

There is an obvious objection to admitting the conditional analysis to be exhaustive of the meaning of words of this kind. How is one to explain the grammatical fact that dispositions are ascribed to someone (or something) when the relevant behaviour is not being displayed there and then? In short, in contemporary terminology, how are dispositions grounded? What persists, according to Ryle, is that the relevant inference licence continues to be able to be used to make valid inferences about the person or thing to which the disposition is ascribed. Its occurrent truth amounts to no more than the presumption that we are licensed now to infer what Joe might do later, or probably did do before. No continuing *mental* state need be implied. Of course, this is compatible with there being a persisting *material* state of the person's brain and nervous system.

Ryle has been often accused of being a closet behaviourist. Except in so far as there are certain general similarities between his views and those of B. F. Skinner, the accusation is wide of the mark if Watsonian behaviourism is what we have in mind. He never denied the reality of private conscious experience. However, his account of dispositional hypotheticals as law-like and so as expressing inference licences takes him very close to repeating Hume's notorious dismissal of real causal efficacy. A law-like statement in its overt "if … then …" format licenses one to infer from one matter of fact to another. According to Ryle, knowing a law is not the same as knowing any particular matters of fact. It does not require belief in the efficacy of any particular state of affairs to engender another.

The cloven hoof of Hume is at last revealed (Ryle 1949: 24). To the suggestion that dispositional statements not only license inferences but describe usually "hidden goings on" Ryle responds with three highly tendentious comments:

- We know that a being has a certain disposition without knowing of any "hidden goings on".
- The utility of this occult knowledge would consist in supporting what we already know we can do, namely draw matter of fact inferences.
- We can know of such "goings on" only by inferring them from the fact that we can use the dispositional statement as an inference licence.

Ryle uses "conducts electricity" as a non-psychological example to illustrate the irrelevance of "hidden goings on" to the inference-licensing power of the disposition. He is surely quite mistaken in using this example to reject "occult goings on". In the case of electrical conductivity, these "goings on" would be the well-established but unobservable passage of electrons through the conductor. However, in the case of mental dispositions the "no occult goings on" principle looks a good deal more defensible, if the alleged grounding is presented as mental.

Of course, statements asserting capacities, tendencies, propensities and liabilities are not laws. Nevertheless they are used in a partly similar way, namely to support our expectations of what someone is likely to do in this or that circumstance. Is there a necessity about these expectations? Not necessarily. "If" does seem to suggest "can", although this word is itself used in rather diverse ways. Ability to do something does not guarantee that it will be done.

The last general point in this famous analysis is the emphasis on standards of correctness. "Abilities", "capacities", "capabilities" and "skills" suggest mastery of the performances in which they are realized. The use of words such as "spell", "solve" and "persuade" involve performances to be gone through and something that is brought off or not brought off. Along with competences go liabilities to get things wrong "to perform inadequately". In contemporary terminology, Ryle's dispositions are normative.

Kinds of mental dispositions

Ryle's first major distinction among kinds of dispositions is between those that can be displayed in many different ways (determinable) and those that can be displayed in only one way (determinate). This distinction is of major importance for Ryle's argument since he insists that such central words as "know", "clever" and so on are determinable dispositional words. "They signify abilities, tendencies or pronesses to do … things of lots of different kinds" (Ryle 1949: 118), without any assumption that there are also corresponding mental acts.

Tendencies carry the implication of "likely to perform or display" the relevant behaviour. "Habits", "interests", "jobs" and "occupations" are all higher-level tendencies. They are self-imposed and in many cases require adherence to codes and customs.

In contrast to tendencies are capacities. "Knowing" is a capacity word, and requires correct performances, be they cognitive or practical. The distinction between knowing and believing is not between two sorts of mental states or conditions. "Believe" is a tendency verb. Knowing and believing differ as capacities and tendencies differ. Knowing is not, therefore, a superior degree of believing.

Kinds of mental episodes and occurrences

The mark that distinguishes mental occurrences from mental dispositions implicit in much that Ryle has to say is grammatical. The former are described with episodic verbs the use of which is categorical in the indicative mood. The latter are ascribed with dispositional verbs, the use of which is conditional, often in the subjunctive mood. "Something" is occurrent if it is fully realized in the here and now. Digging a ditch is a here and now activity. "Something" is dispositional if it is manifested only occasionally in appropriate contexts, and perhaps in special cases never manifested at all. Being a gymnast is manifested only occasionally in gymnasia and on horses, rings, mats and the like. Having a tendency to make a violent physical response to a minor personal slight might be lifelong but never displayed.

Both occurrences and dispositions are dateable, many taking time, having beginnings and endings. "Paying heed to what one is doing" is one of Ryle's most telling examples of an episodic verb, whereas "performing a task" is another. Although to be disposed to or to tend to do something is not, in general, an occurrence, it makes sense to date the acquisition and loss of an ability. The temporal dimension simply covers the time during which it would be correct to use that inference licence to make predictions about what the person or thing might do. So there is no clear temporal criterion for distinguishing dispositional words from those for episodes and occurrences. Yet, for Ryle, the temporal dimension of dispositional words does not reflect anything that is both permanent *and psychological* about the being to which the disposition is ascribed.

Semi-hypotheticals and mongrel categoricals

Ryle's analysis has the immediate effect of forcing dispositions and occurrences apart. Yet, there is a very important class of statements that seem in some respects like statements of fact, and in other respects like inference licences. "Heed" words are often used to qualify how one is performing an activity. One can drive a car carefully, paying attention to what one is doing. Notoriously, one can drive a car inattentively, thinking of something else. What is the difference between the two occasions? One negotiates the curves and stop signs correctly and arrives at one's destination safely. The analyst faces a dilemma. Either the distinction refers to a hidden concomitant of the operation, or it serves to make an open hypothetical statement about the actor. If the second horn is grasped, on the plausible grounds that being attentive and being inattentive are private and personal states of mind that one might come to attend to, it is also clear that certain predictions can be made on the basis of the distinction. If we believe the driver to have been attending to what he or she was doing, we would expect ready answers to such questions as how long it took for a traffic light to change. So "attentive" is at the heart of an inference licence.

Ryle remarks that "the description of [someone] … as minding what he is doing is just as much an explanatory report of an actual occurrence [how he was able to avoid the maverick cyclist] as a conditional prediction of further occurrences" (Ryle 1949: 141). These examples bring to light an important category of words and the statements they can be used to make that fits neatly under neither the dispositional nor the episodic. Because of their ubiquity and importance, they deserve a special name. Ryle calls them "semi-hypotheticals" or "mongrel categoricals". These statements are in some respects like descriptions and in some respects like inference licences. Critics have been bothered by the way the ubiquity of mongrel categoricals seems to undermine the sharp contrast between dispositional verbs and episodic verbs on which the diagnosis of the root category mistake seems to depend.

Tasks and achievements

Ryle's task–achievement distinction has become so embedded in the way we reflect about people's ways of thinking and acting that it now seems entirely obvious. Making use of everyone's grasp of everyday activities by listing all sorts of examples, Ryle points out that there are two broad kinds of occurrences. Running a race is a task and takes time. Winning a race is an achievement that, although dateable, does not take time. This common-sense distinction appears in the grammatical distinction between task verbs and achievement verbs. At the same time, it lays bare yet another source of grammatical confusion, another kind of category mistake to which theoreticians of perception are particularly prone.

Our intuitions are mobilized with the help of a list of commonplace, everyday instances of the distinction between performing a task and achieving an appropriate outcome. The list includes "kicking and scoring", "treating and healing", "hunting and finding", "clutching and holding fast", "listening and hearing", "looking and seeing" and "traveling and arriving" (Ryle 1949: 149). Ryle's argumentative technique is quite evident. The psychological words are sandwiched between instances from football, medicine, searching, playing cricket or some other ball game and journeys. So bracketed, how can we fail to agree that perception displays the same kind of distinction between task and achievement as do the commonplace and unproblematic activities of gardening, playing games, taking tours and the like?

Refinements come quickly in the text (Ryle 1949: 150–51). The use of an achievement verb asserts that some state of affairs obtains over and above the task performance. There can be achievements without task activities preceding them. We can see something without first having looked for it. All this underlines the point that an achievement is not an occurrence of the same type as a task. It is not separately perceptible, for example. Winning is the result of racing, not a separable activity engaged in by the champion alone.

The application of the distinction between tasks and achievements to the problems of perception is continued by offering another list. This is an extensive list of adverbs that can be applied to search verbs but not to perception verbs. For example, these include "successfully", "in vain", "methodically", "inefficiently", "laboriously", "lazily", "rapidly", "carefully", "reluctantly", "zealously", "obediently", "deliberately" or "confidently". Grasping the point of the list helps us to see that perception words are not "process words". "They do not stand for perplexingly undetectable actions or reactions" (Ryle 1949: 152). So I cannot answer the question "What are you doing?" by saying that I am seeing. Looking for something is a task, while seeing it is an achievement. The same holds for "knowing", "proving" and so on. Such verbs cannot be qualified by such adverbs as "erroneously". This does not show that some people are infallible or that some cognitive states are incorrigible. It is just a grammatical remark about how we use the verbs "to know" and so on.

Cognition

There are two main themes in Ryle's treatment of cognition. By piling up examples he sets out to demonstrate that our cognitive vocabulary has as good a use for discussing bodily actions as it does for discussing mental operations. The second theme is the exorcism of the pervasive illusion that behind our overt cognitive doings there is another hidden realm invoked to explain these doings. This is just another case of the malign influence of the idea of the ghost in the machine.

Knowing how and knowing that

To know how to do something, say to make the tea, is a practical skill that usually does not call for the consultation of a recipe or a set of rules. The test of whether someone knows how to do something is consistent and successful performance. To know that something is the case or that something happened is to be able to produce the relevant proposition on demand. Ryle uses this general distinction to draw attention to a disparity between being intelligent and possessing knowledge. The former is dispositional, the latter episodic. Intelligence is not defined as the apprehension of truths. How do we know? Let us look at how the intelligence-ascribing words are used. Ryle gives several lists of such words, including "shrewd", "silly", "prudent" and "imprudent". Plainly, these words do not impute knowledge to someone. They qualify what that person does, and at the same time ascribe dispositions, abilities and liabilities to act in certain ways.

Furthermore, the dispositions of the people whose performances merit such epithets are tendencies or capacities to do things correctly, properly and successfully. Failures attract the corresponding epithets of demerit. Just being successful is not enough to justify calling someone's actions intelligent. The person must be paying attention to what he or she is doing, monitoring and correcting the action. Misconstrued, this commonplace observation gives rise to the intellectualist legend on another dimension. We are tempted to explain successful performances as the result of inwardly consulting and then following rules and maxims of correct practice. Knowing how would depend, if we took the intellectualist account seriously, on knowing that. Cooks would need to recite recipes, heroes to consult moral imperatives and chess players to run over strategic maxims, before they could act skilfully, competently, bravely or successfully. But they do not! Or not often.

Ryle deploys two lines of argument, as well as the above assertion. The first involves not only Aristotle inventing logic but Isaac Walton reflecting on fishing. Efficient practice preceded the theory. It follows that people were able to reason correctly and to fish successfully before the principles of correct reasoning and skilful fishing were enunciated. The second argument points to the regress of rule consultations that easily opens up. Selecting the right or best maxim to apply is itself an intelligent action. However, if intelligence is adverting to maxims, knowledge of what it is right to infer is the result of another cognitive performance, which must itself be conducted according to a maxim. If the intellectualist legend is right, yet another maxim will be required in selecting that maxim and so on. At each point, the choice can be made stupidly or intelligently. Abandon the intellectualist legend and the regress cannot begin.

The cleverness of clowns

How does the intellectualist legend arise? Since parrots can make sounds that match human remarks as far as muscular movements go, and a lout might be tactful by accident, wit and tact are not just behaviour. There is a temptation to suppose that there must be a counterpart mental act that is the real exercise of wit, tact, skill and so on. When people admire the cleverness of a clown, it is the skill exhibited in the visible performance they admire. The skill cannot be recorded separately from the performance. However, this is not because it is a hidden counterpart performance. It is not something that happens to accompany the performance. This is because it is not of the logical type to be a happening, since it is a disposition. "The clown's trippings and tumblings are the workings of his mind, for they are his jokes" (Ryle 1949: 33). The mistake is to suppose that there must be "unwitnessable mental causes and their witnessable physical effects" (*ibid.*).

Ryle concedes that some propositional competence is necessary to acquire practical skills. However, it does not follow that the mature exercise of practical skills requires a parallel process of the exercising of propositional competences. One can be bad at practising what one preaches.

Conation

The second member of the traditional triad of thinking, willing and feeling, is conation, or the "executive faculty". By this is meant the power an individual has (or lacks) to put into practice his or her intentions and decisions as to what to do. In this context, according to Ryle, the malign influence of the mentalistic myth leads to a misunderstanding of the distinction between voluntary and involuntary actions. Philosophers have been tempted to insert an *act of will*, a volition, between a person's intention to do something and the execution of that intention. I decide to weed the cabbage patch, but to get the weeding started there seems to be something else needed to propel me into action. The existence of this executive act, so it is supposed, is what distinguishes acting voluntarily from acting out of habit, or merely responding automatically to some influence or stimulus.

What is wrong with this account? Not surprisingly, Ryle begins his attack by an argument based on a list of attributes these alleged acts would need to possess were they to be real. People do not report being occupied in willing, performing a certain number of acts of volitions in a certain episode. Juries do not ask whether a volition preceded a criminal act. In true Rylean style there then comes a long list of adjectives, participles and so on that are used to qualify both real conscious processes and overt actions, but that, Ryle presumes, we would agree do not characterize volitions. Here is a selection: "weak", "difficult", "enjoyable", "accelerated", "interrupted", "inefficient", "learned", "habitual", "forgotten", together with such expressions as "being mistaken about" and "moment of performance" and so on. The belief in the existence of these acts is an empty hypothesis, based on a mistake.

What is the mistake? The diagnosis begins with the observation that we use the concept pair voluntary–involuntary in situations in which the action under scrutiny ought not to have been done. "In this ordinary use", says Ryle, "it is absurd to discuss whether satisfactory, correct or admirable performances are voluntary or involuntary" (Ryle 1949: 69). "Philosophers", Ryle's vaguely specified villains, misuse the distinction by applying it to meritorious and correct performances as well. To blame someone for doing something implies that the actor knew what was right or correct but did not do it. To decide whether someone who failed in some task should be blamed, we need to enquire not into whether a certain "occult episode" had occurred, but into whether the individual knew what to do, although he or she failed to do it correctly or at all.

Strength of will is not a feature of a mental organ, the will. It is used, along with many other expressions, to refer to the resolution that someone displays in doing things. "It is a propensity, the exercise of which consists of sticking to tasks" (Ryle 1949: 73).

How did it come about that "philosophers" had slipped into the error of expanding the voluntary–involuntary distinction to cover both meritorious and incorrect actions? If the mechanistic account of human action had been correct, then there would have been no room for moral appraisals of what someone did. We need to be able to distinguish between those actions that can be praised or blamed and those to which neither comment is appropriate. The "inner world" could serve as the location of volitions, while mechanistic causes resided in the material world. This is a live issue to this day. In its current form, the take-over bid comes from the science of genetics. If everything one is and does is the result of one's genetic endowment, where is there a place for moral and political appraisal?

Ryle has another line of argument against the threat of scientific determinism. The pattern is familiar. People dread the possibility of it turning out that everything people do is explicable ultimately by the inexorable laws of physics. However, this is not a contingency that might or might not happen. This is because it makes no sense to suppose that it might. In short, there is a philosophical or conceptual argument against this kind of super-determinism. Since the issue is still very much on the agenda for the third millennium, Ryle's argument deserves to be spelled out in some detail.

The analogy of playing a game to living one's life in general is the key move in the argument. Games involve rules to which the players are committed. A game is bounded by and managed in accordance with rules of various kinds. But games also involve people, who, in Ryle's analogy, choose from varieties of moves, placements of kicks, sweeps or off drives and so on. However, once the move is underway then it *must* accord with the rules of the game. A bishop necessarily moves on a diagonal, but not necessarily two, three, or four squares. An off drive of sufficient power and direction penetrates the covers necessarily going for four according to the laws of mechanics and the rules of cricket. The people in the analogy have radical freedom to initiate moves the development of which is necessitated by the rules.

This is really a very bad argument to issue from the pen of the Wayneflete Professor of Metaphysical Philosophy. It presupposes what is to be proved. That someone chooses a certain move is, the determinist alleges, fixed from some prior conditions that obtained before the game started. Moreover, those conditions could be argued to have been the result of lawful evolution of the world from states that existed from before the appearance of *Homo sapiens*, and even before the invention of cricket. For the strict Laplacian determinist the initial conditions of the world were set at the Creation!

There is a little subsidiary argument that is not much better. To ask for the cause of a happening in the material domain a "chain-argument" is proper. The initiating cause is linked to the relevant effect by a chain of intermediate causes and effects. However, if we ask "How does my decision lead to my squeezing the trigger?", we can be puzzled by how difficult it seems to be to offer a chain-argument. The right answer, according to Ryle, is to assign radical causal powers to persons, in such phrases as "Lee Harvey Oswald did it", perhaps in response to yet another conspiracy theory about the death of President Kennedy. In effect Ryle wants to distinguish "Who was responsible?" questions from "What caused it?" questions. However, it seems to me obvious that we cannot even begin to answer the former without having at hand a tentative answer to the latter.

Affection

The third province of psychology has traditionally been the emotions and the feelings with which they are intimately involved. Ryle highlights the alleged role of emotions in the explanation of what someone did. Motives such as ambition and moods such as depression are contrasted with emotions such as anger. All three are to be distinguished from bodily feelings. Here is a list of some of them: "thrills", "twinges", "pangs", "throbs", "wrenches", "itches", "prickings", "chills", "glows", "loads", "qualms", "hankerings", "curdlings", "sinkings", "tensions", "gnawings" and "shocks". We could add many more (Ryle 1949: 83).

There are, Ryle acknowledges, "throbs of compassion". However, the compassion is "not to be equated with the throbs". There are throbs of pain and pleasure too. The difference between these various uses of such words as "twinges" is to be put down to how we believe they are caused. A twinge of guilt is a feeling induced by a belief that we have behaved badly. A twinge of indigestion is a feeling induced by overindulgence at the table. Unlike his social constructionist descendents Ryle does not pursue this line of analysis very far. A discussion of the moral surroundings of emotions is the next step.

Motives come on the scene through one of Ryle's enigmatic attributions to an unspecified group of muddle-headed folk: the "theorists". They have fallen into the category mistake of thinking that when we explain what someone has done by the use of motive words such as "vain", "considerate", "avaricious", "patriotic" or "indolent" these words refer to motives, and thence to feelings. "Vanity" and "indolence" are dispositional properties having the usual sense of "whenever X is in situation Y he or she is likely to do or not do Z". Of course, there must be occasions on which a person displays vanity in order for the attribution "vain" to be apposite. These words denote not only motives, but also traits of character and personality. The point is that feelings of patriotism are occurrences, and it is absurd to suggest that a person's lifelong patriotism consists in a sequence of such incidents. Rather his or her tendency to have such feelings is yet another consequence of the inclination, as is tying the national flag to the car radio aerial.

Moods such as "depression" or "joyfulness" compare with feelings of despair and ecstasy as inclinations and dispositions do to occurrences. Moods are lasting and dateable, although, like the weather, they are changeable. They affect everything a person does. One of the most powerful and important of Wittgenstein's distinctions is that between "avowals" and "descriptions" (Wittgenstein 1953: §§244–6). Ryle presents it explicitly. "If a person says 'I feel bored' or 'I feel depressed,' we do not ask him for his evidence" (Ryle 1949: 102). Part of what it is to be bored is to be inclined to say such things as "I feel bored", to yawn, fidget and so on. It follows that such a remark does not call for such judgements as "true or false", but rather "sincere or simulated".

One of the most widely discussed parts of this analysis of the emotional life is the section devoted to "pleasure" and "pain" (Ryle 1949: 107–10). Ryle's concern is to bring out some of the differences between the supposed logic of the use of these words and their actual use. There are feelings *of pleasure*. So it denotes of a certain kind of mood, such as elation. Thus, a flutter, glow or thrill is a pleasurable one. "Pleasure" and "enjoyment" are also used for describing activities in which someone is wholly absorbed, thinking of nothing else, doing it effortlessly and so on. It might be the pleasure someone gets from playing his or her clarinet in a Mozart divertimento. However, there are not two things going on: the performance and the pleasure. Once again, the members of anonymous opposition, "theorists", are so misguided as to treat delight and enjoyment as feelings. Does one enjoy the joke or the ripple of laughter? Pains, on the other hand, are or can be stand-alone aversive bodily feelings. It follows that the words "pain" and "pleasure" do not denote the poles of a fundamental affective dimension.

Personal identity

Personal identity is expressed for the most part by the use of the word "I". Is it the name of the ghost in my machine? The nature of selfhood comes up in several places, but is highlighted by Ryle's robust rejection of the thesis that knowing myself is observing a spate of mental happenings. It is thus that it is supposed that I know non-dispositionally what I am experiencing. This cannot be right because there are no such happenings to get to know, this for the somewhat recondite reason that what follows the verb "to know" is that something is the case. That Ryle should have failed to make use of the difference between *"conocer"* (*"connaitre"*, "to be acquainted with") and *"saber"* (*"savoir"*, "to know intellectually") is a surprise.

The question of the uses of "I" first comes up in Ryle's emphasis on unstudied talk, on avowals. A lorry driver who asks "Which is the way to London?" avows or discloses his anxiety about the route rather than reporting or describing his state of mind. If someone says "I wonder if the shop has any aubergines in today", he or she is not offering a snippet of autobiography. Reflection on the first person soon engenders the intellectual vertigo of a cluster of philosophical problems. Here are some: "Could I be you?", "What is it that for a religious person is saved or damned?", "Who am I really?" and so on. "Philosophers [who?] have speculated whether 'I' denotes a peculiar or separate substance and in what consists my indivisible and continuing identity" (Ryle 1949: 186).

Anticipating the concept of indexicality, a formulation of the 1970s, Ryle points out that "I" is not a name of anything, but a word such as "today" or "here". It is, he says, "systematically elusive". "I" indicates from which person the vocable "I" issues. "You" indicates to you which person I am addressing, namely you.

However, in some contexts some first-person expressions, for example, "myself" could be replaced by "my body". Ever good for a startling example, Ryle asks us to reflect on the first-person pronouns in "Cremate me after I am gone". However, there are plenty of uses where such a substitution makes no sense. In "I caught myself daydreaming", "my body" could not replace the reflexive first-person pronoun. For example, when "I" is used to commit the speaker to a course of action, and sometimes to avow or express how I feel or what I am thinking the substitution of "my body" makes no sense.

In a final point, reminiscent of G. H. Mead's "I" and "me" distinction (Mead 1934), Ryle remarks that "self-commentary, self-ridicule and self-admonition are logically condemned to perpetual penultimacy" (Ryle 1949: 195). Once I have picked up from the surrounding conversation the practice of commenting on or ridiculing the performance of others, I can apply the skill thus acquired to my own thoughts and acts, but only after I have done them.

The possibility of psychology

The Concept of Mind ends with a short but deeply incisive reflection on the possibility of a science of psychology. Again, one is struck by the way that the Ryle of the 1940s anticipates so much of the new paradigm psychology of the past twenty years. Between 1949 and 2002 lie more than fifty years of much misplaced endeavour, if Ryle is right.

Ryle's first point is terminological, but of paramount importance. Psychologists and lay people alike use "the concepts of learning, practice, trying, heeding, pretending, wanting, pondering, arguing, shirking, watching, seeing and being perturbed" (Ryle 1949: 319) in the same way. Ryle omits to add the really telling point: that when psychologists seem to be using a technical vocabulary, specific to their supposed science, it consists largely of synonyms for words from the above list and others of the same provenance. "Visual perception" appears for "seeing", "chronic fatigue syndrome" for a range of personal states, such as "feeling exhausted" and even sometimes "shirking", and so on.

The alleged parallel between a Newtonian science of material stuff and a Cartesian science of mental stuff is a leitmotif throughout the book. Ryle presents it as a legacy of the "'two-worlds legend", a rather dubious historical judgement. Even when this programme was riding high, psychological researchers studied

what people said and did, thought and felt, not the non-existent happenings behind these actions.

He distinguishes between what psychologists declare to be their project and
what they do in their actual studies. In experimenting on visual perception, they
"analyse the reactions and verbal responses of the subjects of their experiments"
(Ryle 1949: 321). Memory is studied "by recording their successes and failures in
recitations [of stimulus material] after the lapse of different periods of time". But
surely the mind behind the mind is not the realm of private thoughts and feelings
that lies behind the public world of actions. We thought the dual world was a
generally unobservable but hypothetical world of mental states and processes.

One is led to surmise that Ryle has slipped up badly here by reflecting on his
account of the way chemists turned to the phenomena of combustion after abandoning the search for the hidden substance phlogiston. Some knowledge of the
history of science would have helped. What Lavoisier actually did was establish the
existence of a different occult substance, oxygen, as an alternative to the nonex-
istent phlogiston.

Nevertheless, Ryle's positive suggestion has merit. There are many domains
and methods of enquiry into "men's minds" Here is a Rylean list: practising
psychologists, economists, criminologists, anthropologists, political scientists
and sociologists, teachers, strategists, statesmen, employers, confessors, parents,
lovers and novelists. There seems to be no difference between what these people
do and what psychologists purport to do. Ryle's advice is that we give up "the
notion that 'psychology' is the name of a unitary enquiry or tree of enquiries"
(Ryle 1949: 323). "Medicine" could serve as an analogy for a similarly loosely
connected cluster of enquiries and techniques.

Some might retort that psychology offers to provide *causal* explanations of
human conduct. Ryle has already shown the folly of that proposal in the bulk of
the book. We know very well what caused this or that human performance, say
the farmer bringing back the pigs from the market. The price was too low.
Furthermore, although there are phenomena for which one does not have an
explanation, for the most part the idea that a psychologist could arrive at an
ulterior and disparate kind of explanation from the one we already have is absurd.
To the objection that there is a question as to why the price being too low led to
the farmer abandoning the sale, Ryle's response is to argue that, in the end, there
are simple correlations and that is it.

There is one strand of behaviourism that resembles the Rylean account of
mind. It is the "radical behaviourism" of B. F. Skinner. Despite the crudeness of
the Skinnerian terminology and his simplistic account of the developmental process, both authors hold to the continuity of the private and public domains, while
denying that there is any good ground for the hypothesis of a hidden realm of

235

cognition with which the mental dispositions and occurrences of human life are to be explained. According to Ryle, behaviourists (and that must mean J. B. Watson) neglected the meaning of public performances, asserting that thinking consisted in making complex movements and noises. Others held that the "inner mental life processes" were inaccessible to scientific, that is public, study, and should be excluded from science. The merit of the behaviourist programme, according to Ryle, was in showing how shadowy were the inner life processes. Mechanists and para-mechanists have both mislocated the phenomena of the mental life.

Private and public activities are alike in almost every respect. Neither is in need of an extra explanatory dimension of mental mechanisms that parallel the hidden explanatory dimensions of the physical sciences. That does not seem to be quite the right exegesis of the line in *The Concept of Mind* either. If it were, why did Ryle so conspicuously neglect to mention oxygen in his discussion of combustion? Sometimes Ryle writes as if he were a positivist, rejecting the reality of a theoretically supported domain in the physical sciences as in psychology.

Ryle's method

There are three striking features of the method Ryle uses in *The Concept of Mind*. The reader is immediately struck by the way Ryle uses comparisons between the meanings of problematic psychological words, and the meanings of everyday expressions about which no one is likely to be mistaken or misled. For example to *show* that "seeing" does not refer to a special cognitive activity in the way that "looking" does, Ryle offers the distinction between "fishing and catching" and "walking and humming". Catching is the upshot of fishing, whereas humming is a different activity from the walking with which it is accompanied. The comparisons serve to throw the problematic uses into a clear light. Our grammatical intuitions are readied for the philosophical task of coming to see something recondite about perception and cognition by attending to something mundane about fishing. The relation between "looking" and "seeing" is like that between "fishing and catching", but unlike that between "walking and humming". In case we have not grasped the point Ryle makes his other characteristic methodological move: the presentation of a list of similar words. Thus, "searching and finding", "fighting and winning", "journeying and arriving" are offered as well (Ryle 1949: 150–51).

Lists have another role. For instance, in the discussion of emotion Ryle offers a list of words doing duty for one of the generic uses of the word "pleasure". His list includes "delight", "transport", "rapture", "exultation" and "joy" (Ryle 1949:

236

108). The point of the list is to highlight the cases in which there are feelings associated with such moods. Although there are thrills of pleasure, Ryle declares that it is not pleasure that courses through our bodies. Neither delight nor enjoyment are themselves feelings. They are moods, "signifying agitations". Why should we accept Ryle's assertion? Well, we know how to use the words in the list. All we need are reminders. What, then, is pleasure? It is neither a feeling nor a mood. In this it is unlike its presumed complement, pain.

The third innovation could be called "argument by adverbs". In several places Ryle sets about establishing a distinction between two kinds of expressions, for example task-verbs and achievement-verbs, by presenting a list of adverbs that can be used to qualify one sort of verb but not the other. While we can say he ran quickly, we cannot say, so Ryle claims, he won quickly. We can say he looked assiduously, but not that he noticed assiduously.

These moves are indeed innovatory as the texture of philosophical argument. They rest in the end on *reductiones ad absurdum*, but the full text of the arguments is rarely spelled out. There is no need to spell out formal contradictions stemming from the views Ryle attributes to that mysterious company "some epistemologists". Anyone can see from running through the relevant list that delight is a mood *expressed* in various feelings, but is not itself a feeling.

Part of the pleasure in reading *The Concept of Mind* comes from the extraordinary wealth of observations and comparisons that the Rylean method requires. Quite unlike the often boring abstractions of academic philosophy, Ryle's world is rich in people fishing, gardening, soldiering, playing golf, planning to redecorate the sitting room and so on. Every page opens a window on to the activities of everyday life. There are no abstract persons denoted by letters of the alphabet, nor are their doings expressed algebraically. The concreteness of the illustrations is an essential part of the argument. How can we fail to assent to suggestions that draw on comparisons with that which we know intimately in our own homes, gardens, jobs and pastimes?

Ryle's legacy

In the relatively recent development of discursive psychology one finds many Rylean themes and concepts. Yet, I think it is true to say that *The Concept of Mind* was not the vehicle by which these ideas came into psychology. The direct influence of Ryle's great book has been overshadowed by the floodtide of Wittgenstein's writings and commentaries thereon, through which this approach to psychology has been fostered. However, there are some Rylean phrases that are now part of the common currency of philosophy of mind. For example, the distinctions between "dispositions and occurrences", "knowing how and knowing that" and "tasks and achievements" are ubiquitous.

In philosophy, at least for a while, it was a different story. The analysis of the family of dispositional concepts has become a long-standing field of philosophical study. The technique of argument by lists has been used to good effect by many writers of the second half of the twentieth century, for example by A. R. White, in a study of "attention" (White 1964). The publication of a new edition of *The Concept of Mind* in 2000 with an important introduction by Daniel Dennett will, no doubt, bring the book back to the influential position it deserves.

Notes

1. Throughout *The Concept of Mind*, Ryle identifies his philosophical adversaries in the vaguest terms. The use of the phrase "some [many] epistemologists" is typical.

References and further reading

Armstrong, D. M. 1968. *A Materialist Theory of the Mind*. London: Routledge & Kegan Paul.

Fodor, J. A. 1975. *The Language of Thought*. New York: Crowell.

Hampshire, S. 1950. "Review of *The Concept of Mind*, by Gilbert Ryle". *Mind* **59**, 237–55.

Hart, H. L. A. & T. Honoré 1985. *Causation in the Law*, 2nd edn. Oxford: Clarendon Press.

Hofstadter, A. 1951. "Professor Ryle's Category Mistake". *Journal of Philosophy* **48**, 257–70.

Mumford, S. 1998. *Dispositions*. Oxford: Clarendon Press.

Passmore, J. 1957. *A Hundred Years of Philosophy*. London: Duckworth.

Ryle, G. 1931. "Systematically Misleading Expressions". *Proceedings of the Aristotelian Society, NS* **32**, 139–70. Reprinted in A. G. N. Flew (ed.) *Logic and Language, Series 1* (Oxford: Blackwell, 1978), 11–36.

Ryle, G. 1949. *The Concept of Mind*. London: Hutchinson. New edition with an introduction by D. C. Dennett (Harmondsworth: Penguin, 2000).

Ryle, G. 1954. *Dilemmas*. Cambridge: Cambridge University Press.

Weldon, T. J. 1950. "Review of *The Concept of Mind*". *Philosophy* **25**, 266–70.

White, A. R. 1964. *Attention*. Oxford: Blackwell.

Wittgenstein, L. 1953. *Philosophical Investigations*, G. E. M, Anscombe (trans.), (3rd edn 1989). Oxford: Blackwell.

12

Ludwig Wittgenstein

Philosophical Investigations

Robert L. Arrington

In this chapter[1] I want to suggest an approach to Wittgenstein's *Philosophical Investigations* that I believe will make this profound book more accessible to readers not already familiar with it. The *Investigations* is considered Wittgenstein's second masterpiece; it was published posthumously in 1953 many years after the appearance of his first masterpiece, *Tractatus Logico-Philosophicus*. Whereas the *Tractatus* was the force behind the development of logical analysis and logical positivism, the *Investigations* gave rise to new forms of conceptual analysis and ordinary language philosophy. Arguably, both works were misinterpreted by many of their readers and disciples. Together, the two books are responsible for Wittgenstein's being considered the foremost linguistic, analytic philosopher of the twentieth century.

Ludwig Wittgenstein was born in Vienna, Austria in 1889.[2] He was the son of a domineering and immensely wealthy Viennese steel magnate, and he possessed the highly cultivated, and psychologically tortured, personality one would expect from his family background. After studying engineering and aeronautics in England, he moved on to study logic and philosophy with Bertrand Russell at the University of Cambridge. He was associated with Cambridge for much of his professional career as a philosopher. Wittgenstein was a complex and difficult person, and stories about his life are a staple of intellectual legends of the twentieth century.

Despite its conversational tone and its relative lack of technical terms, *Philosophical Investigations* (PI) is a work that most new readers find immensely puzzling. It consists of two parts, Part I being considerably longer than Part II. Part I consists of many numbered sections (some 693 in all). Frequently these sections do not appear to be systematically connected to one another, and even the various remarks within a section often seem unrelated. Certainly, we can identify topics to which a group of sections is devoted, although where the discussion of a topic begins and where it ends is seldom clear. And it is often difficult to see the *point* of the various remarks made in talking about or investigating a topic, and often very difficult to grasp the transitions from remark to remark or topic to topic.

My suggestion for reading a number of the seemingly disparate sections in Part I will indicate similarities of argument found therein. I propose that we view these passages through the lenses of comments Wittgenstein makes in his earlier *Philosophical Remarks* and *Philosophical Grammar* about the autonomy of language. More specifically, the reading of the *Investigations* that I recommend will highlight the autonomy of the *use* of language. This strategy will connect many apparently unrelated sections by showing them to be various ways of insisting on the autonomy of use. Throughout Part I, the use of language is contrasted with other notions that philosophers have considered basic to understanding language, notions such as meaning, reference, objects, simples, rules, logical form, essence as "something in common", thought and experience. Time and again Wittgenstein shows that these proposed items will not do the job required of them and that we must fall back on use. *Use* – and the human practices embodying it – is bedrock; there is no more ultimate foundation of language.[3]

In the *Investigations* we do not find Wittgenstein talking explicitly about the autonomy of language, or of the autonomy of grammar or use.[4] There are, certainly, passages in the book that can be viewed as invoking the notion of autonomy, but they can be seen in this light most easily if we look first at the explicit references to the autonomy of language in the earlier *Philosophical Remarks* (PR) and *Philosophical Grammar* (PG).[5]

Language, Wittgenstein tells us, is "self-contained and autonomous" (PG: 97). The grammatical rules that create language (PG: 143) are not accountable to any reality (PG: 184). The grammatical rules are those that give meaning to terms of language. They are the rules for the proper uses of these terms.[6] It is these grammatical rules that establish the connection between language and reality (PG: 97) whereby the former represents and conveys information about the latter. "Language must speak for itself", (PG: 40, 63) and "It is in language that it is all done" (PG: 143). Such are the gnomic and cryptic utterances that Wittgenstein uses to convey his theme of the autonomy of language. What do they mean?

They mean no one thing, since there are various ways of arguing that language is *not* self-contained but on the contrary built on a foundation of something else. One of the things meant is that the rules of grammar do not reflect some language-independent logical form or set of essences; these rules are, on the contrary, arbitrary. Wittgenstein makes this point in the context of rejecting the idea that the rules of grammar can be *verified*. In *Zettel* (Z) he writes:

> One is tempted to justify rules of grammar by sentences like "But there really are four primary colours." And the saying that the rules of grammar are arbitrary is directed against the possibility of this justification, which is constructed on the model of justifying a sentence by pointing to what verifies it. (Z: §331)

Any such attempt to verify the rules of grammar, Wittgenstein points out in *Philosophical Remarks*, is circular:

> Grammatical conventions cannot be justified by describing what is represented. Any such description already presupposes the grammatical rules. That is to say, if anything is to count as nonsense in the grammar which is to be justified, then it cannot at the same time pass for sense in the grammar of the propositions that justify it. (PR: 55)

Grammatical rules define the senses of the terms they govern. To falsify or disconfirm these rules, one would have to show that the terms they govern are in fact senseless (or have some other sense.) To do this, one might try to describe certain facts in the world that render these terms senseless. But these descriptions must incorporate or utilize the grammar of the very terms at issue, and if the descriptions are to make sense, so too must the terms governed by these rules of grammar. So the attempted refutation is internally incoherent. Likewise, if the facts described were alleged to verify the grammatical rules, the descriptions of these facts would again rest on the grammatical rules governing their constituent terms. Such descriptions would therefore beg the question as to the validity of these rules; the effort to justify the rules would be circular. So it is impossible to describe or point to facts in the world that justify or invalidate the rules of grammar. To the question Wittgenstein asks in *Zettel*, "Yet can't it after all be said that in some sense or other the grammar of colour-words characterizes the world as it actually is?" (Z: §331), his answer is "No". His claim is not, of course, that "as a matter of fact" (as a matter of limited human ability) one cannot do this. The very effort is question-begging and hence logically unsound.

It is important to note that the attempt to justify grammar by describing facts in the world that verify grammatical rules is not the only way to attempt a validation of grammar. In the middle-period works (written after the *Tractatus* but before the *Investigations*) *and* in the *Investigations*, Wittgenstein also discusses a pragmatic effort to underwrite grammar by showing that grammatical rules "work" or lead to desirable results. This attempt construes grammar as helping us to achieve certain goals we have. If we think of the use of language as a form of action, with ends in view and words and concepts as instruments, it is easy to form a picture of grammar as a set of instrumental guidelines for achieving the goals of our speech-acts. Wittgenstein himself, the pragmatically inclined reader will note, compares language to a set of tools (PG: 67; PI: §11) and tells us that language and its concepts are instruments (PI: §§421, 569).

But in the *Investigations* Wittgenstein rejects any pragmatic validation of grammar. "Grammar," he writes, "does not tell us how language must be constructed in order to fulfill its purposes, in order to have such-and-such an effect on human beings" (§496), and for this reason he concludes (§497) that the rules of grammar are arbitrary. Earlier (§492) he had distinguished between inventing a language (or a part of language) as an instrument for a particular purpose, on the one hand, and inventing a language as a game, on the other. Clearly, while granting that there may be linguistic innovations that are justified in terms of their practical effects, he wants to stress the idea of language as being comparable to a game. This is certainly the focus of his attention in *Philosophical Grammar*, where he categorically states that "Language is not defined for us as an arrangement fulfilling a definite purpose" (PG: 190). In *Philosophical Grammar*, he distinguishes between rules of grammar and rules of cookery. The latter are susceptible of a pragmatic justification, since any cooking rule can be tested to see if it produces tasty food: a recipe-independent fact. If you do not follow these rules, you perhaps cook badly, but for all that you are still cooking. But if you do not follow the rules of a game (like chess), you do not play the game badly: you do not play *this* game at all. If you do not follow the rules of grammar, "that does not mean you say something wrong, no, you are speaking of something else" (Z: §320, PG: 184). And so Wittgenstein concludes, "That is why the use of language is in a certain sense autonomous, as cooking and washing are not" (Z: §320). Language is autonomous because its rules of grammar are not susceptible to pragmatic validation by reference to some language-independent goal or purpose.

The comments considered above show us two ways in which language does not rest on an exterior foundation: the rules of grammar are "arbitrary" because they cannot be seen as justified or supported by ("accountable to") (a) any "facts in the world" or (b) their instrumental value in achieving some given human purposes. The arbitrariness of these rules leads Wittgenstein to speak of the autonomy of language. As arbitrary, the rules of grammar are contained within language (as are the rules of a game) and are part of its "self-contained" nature. With this idea of autonomy in mind, let us turn to the *Investigations* and begin to examine some of its early sections.

The book begins with a quotation from Augustine's *Confessions*, which is immediately followed by Wittgenstein's remark that Augustine gives us one particular picture of the essence of language: words name the objects that are their meanings. The third paragraph of §1 (1c) alerts us to the idea that not all parts of language work like its nouns and proper names, which do seem to be words that name objects. In the fourth paragraph (1d), we are asked to imagine a particular use of language, the famous shopkeeper example. This example, Wittgenstein suggests, indicates "ways that one operates with words": in this case in order to buy and sell five red apples. But the interlocutor (the hypothetical, unnamed philosopher Wittgenstein wants to engage in dialogue and debate with) desires to know how the shopkeeper would know "where and how he is to look up the word 'red' or would know what he is to do with the word 'five'", to which Wittgenstein's answer is blunt but not altogether clear: "Well, I assume that he *acts* as I have described. Explanations come to an end somewhere." And to the interlocutor's next question, "But what is the meaning of the word 'five'?", Wittgenstein's response is equally short: "No such thing was in question here, only how the word 'five' is used."

I take this opening set of remarks to be an admirable introduction to the book as a whole. Right off the bat it introduces one of the leading motifs of the work: the primacy of use and the wisdom of *stopping* with use when we are thinking philosophically about language. At the foundation of language are certain actions, what one does, for example, in using a word such as 'red' or 'five'. Questions about mental states or conditions, questions, for instance, about possessing a certain kind of knowledge – such as how one knows where and how to look up a word on a colour chart or in a book of samples, or how one knows what to do with 'five' – these questions are not basic. That the shopkeeper understands 'red' and 'five' is demonstrated by his actions, not by some inner state of "knowledge". It is with his actions that "explanations come to an end". If we are dissatisfied with this end-point and think that to understand language we must at a minimum grasp the crucial and basic notion of *meaning*, Wittgenstein remains obstinate: "But what is the meaning of the word 'five'? – No such thing was in question here, only how the word 'five' is used." Not *meaning*, not *knowledge*, but *use* is the fundamental philosophical category to be employed in a philosophical discussion of language.

In the sections immediately following §1, Wittgenstein juxtaposes the notion of use to a particular kind of meaning, referential meaning, the kind that names are often thought to have. The famous example in §2 of a language-game in which all the terms are names, what commentators refer to simply as language-game 2 – the builders' language-game – allows us to see that possessing referential meaning is neither necessary nor sufficient for something to be a part of language. It is not necessary, because, Wittgenstein tells us in §3, not all languages need be like the one containing only terms such as 'block' and 'slab'. Here he begins to stress the indefinite number of uses we find in various language-games, for example, the use of 'Wow!' or 'or'. But neither is referential use sufficient for language. Section 4 gives us an example of language (a script) in which words (or letters) stand for sounds but "also as signs of emphasis and punctuation". If one interpreted these letters as simply standing for the sounds, one would have "an over-simple conception of the script". Surely the same applies to the "script" in language-game 2: the terms 'block' and 'slab' can be used not only to designate objects but also as sounds of emphasis; just imagine 'block!' with an exclamation point. Moreover, in uttering the word 'block', the builder is not just *designating* a block, he is also asking that one be brought to him, that is, the term 'block' is used to request a block. So even for language-game 2, the words are not used just to stand for certain objects; rather the words function as part of a language-game in which orders are made and fulfilled and building or construction takes place. Likewise in §1, the customer and grocer are not just using words as names: the customer uses 'apples' to make an order, and the grocer fills the order. *Naming*, *designation*, *reference* are not necessary or sufficient to explain *any* language-game. Language does not depend on the name-relation and the *alleged* connection to the world (to objects in the world) that this relation is supposed to supply.

Wittgenstein tells us in §5 that the notion of meaning and the construal of the meaning of a word as an object creates a haze: what, in the *Big Typescript*,[7] he calls in wonderful fashion a "thoughtfog". One way to penetrate this haze is to look at primitive language-games "in which one can command a clear view of the *aim and functioning* of the words" (§5, emphasis added). In other words, the simple language-games allow us to see how *use* is the critical factor and to see the variety of uses to be found in language. We will also come to see that an expression such as "the word 'slab' signifies a slab" or "the word 'slab' refers to this object" does not instantiate the canonical form of meaning-explanation but rather has a use within a language-game only in specific circumstances, for example, when someone already knows the *kind of use* of the term being defined, namely its use as the name of some building material, but has mistakenly taken the word 'slab' to refer, say, to a block instead of a slab (§10). Underlying and presupposed by the "signification" statement is an understanding of the grammatical use of the name defined. Even names have different kinds of use, so equating all meaning with naming gets us nowhere. To know that both colour terms and numerals refer to something is not to know anything that comes close to being sufficient for understanding these terms, since the way numbers are used is very unlike the way colour terms are used. "Every word signifies something" says nothing (§13), unless it is just a way of contrasting a certain set of words that have a use with words that do not, such as nonsense syllables. Far from being the underlying, basic way of explaining language, appeal to meaning, reference, signification and the like are not sufficient to explain *any* part of language.[8]

If reference is not at the heart of language, then language – and the meanings and appropriate uses of its terms – cannot be derived from, or dependent on, the objects in the world that are the referents of words. Words can have meaning – use – even though they signify nothing, and even in the case of words that do signify objects, one cannot derive the use of one of these terms simply from an acquaintance with or knowledge of the object denoted.

Sections 18 and 19 introduce us to another line of philosophical thought that has aimed at establishing a language-independent entity as something we must appeal to in order to understand language. Here the focus is not on what a word designates but on what the *speaker* means when she speaks, or, put differently, on what she *thinks* as she uses her words. What a person thinks when she speaks is suggested by the interlocutor to be the determinant of what form of words is canonical and best expresses the thought, that is, the meaning of the expression. The builder who says "Slab!" surely thinks "Bring me a slab!", so, it might be argued, the utterance "Slab!" really means "Bring me a slab!" Speaker's-meaning is thus proposed as the basic reference for understanding and explaining the meaning of expressions in a language.

Against this notion Wittgenstein brings a host of considerations. How does one mean "Bring me a slab!" when one says "Slab!", Wittgenstein asks, opening up one of the richest veins in his later thought: the grammatical investigation of the notions of thinking, meaning, and understanding. Clearly one does not mean by "Slab!" the unshortened "Bring me a slab!" simply by virtue of saying this unshortened sentence to oneself, since one might very well *not* say it. What if the person merely thinks or says the word 'slab' to herself? Does she thereby mean "Slab!" by 'Slab!'? What a person "says to herself" as she utters a sentence may vary enormously; in fact, more often than not she probably says nothing at all to herself. In the latter case, is her utterance therefore without meaning? And why should not 'Bring me a slab!' be an *expanded* version of the canonical 'Slab!', so that on hearing "Bring me a slab!" one has to grasp that the speaker thinks (says to herself) 'Slab!' in order to understand "Bring me a slab!"? Clearly, it is completely arbitrary whether we take 'Slab!' or 'Bring me a slab!' to be the canonical form that truly expresses meaning, and the entire attempt to understand the meaning of an utterance in terms of what the speaker means or thinks in saying it cannot get off the ground. After all, what is important is that 'Slab!' and 'Bring me a slab!' have the same use; that is all we really need to know.

Here we have a pattern of argumentation often found in the later Wittgenstein. "What *constitutes* meaning something by a phrase?" he asks, and he proceeds to show that a proposed answer – in this case an accompanying thought – does not identify an entity that always is and must be present for someone to mean something. When the "thing to be constituted" is *meaning*, the argument instantiates the autonomy theme: the meaning of word w, let us call it m, cannot depend on or be a function of a non-linguistic item t, a thought or idea, because t is not always present when m is.

Sections 23–5 constitute a sort of recapitulation in which Wittgenstein stresses the multiplicity of kinds of sentence and their uses in our language and notes in his characterization of the notion of a language-game that the speaking of language is "part of an activity, or of a form of life". The stress on use, and multiple uses, sums up much of what he has already said. In particular he singles out as particularly wrong-headed the idea that descriptions are the basis of all language: that they have the correct (or *general*) propositional form. Even descriptions, he warns, have different uses. Thus the idea of description *qua* description – and what it might entail about the relationship of language and reality – is too impoverished to yield a picture of how language might be modelled on something outside language.

Section 26 begins a lengthy discussion of "objects" and ostensive definition. On the topic of "objects", more later. Wittgenstein's discussion of ostensive definition is, in my opinion, one of the most important ways in which the autonomy theme surfaces in the *Investigations*. Ostensive definition has been seen by many philosophers as the means whereby language is connected to reality, and connected in such a way that language can be used to convey information about the world. It is the basis, empiricists think, of all intentionality, of the fact that we can think and talk *about* things, that we can *mean* them. According to this view, words have to be connected to more than other words, since otherwise we would be in a linguistic circle, meaning by any one word nothing more than other words, and by them still other words and so on. Without ostensive definition, the thinking goes, we could never break out of this linguistic circle and use our words to mean *things* and *facts*, that is, the world. Unless words mean objects, and unless they come to mean these objects by being attached to them through the process of ostensive definition, we could only move around among words and would not know, in using these words, anything about reality itself. It is ostensive definition that connects words, and us, to reality. What words mean, then, is what objects they are attached to as a result of ostensive definitions having the form "Word 'w' means object o."

If "it's all done in language", if language is free-floating and self-contained, if it must "speak for itself", then this traditional theory of ostensive definition must be wrong. The theory tells us that it is the object referred to in the definition, the referent of the demonstrative 'this' (or 'that') and the gesture accompanying it, that gives meaning to the word defined, that is, in fact, itself the meaning of this word. Thus meaning is thought to come from outside language. We give meaning to words by pinning them on specific objects through the use of ostensive definitions; subsequently we can use these words to talk about *these* objects. The meanings of our words are dependent on, indeed derived from, the nature of these objects. Far from being autonomous, the theory has it, language depends entirely on the nature of the language-independent world for what its terms mean. Ostensive definition, in the hands of traditional philosophers, entails a repudiation of the autonomy of language.

Wittgenstein does not reject ostensive definition.[9] It provides, he grants, many of the rules we use to determine correct language use (PG: 60, 153). What he rejects is the understanding of ostensive definition incorporated in the above picture of it as the means whereby linguistic terms come to have meaning, the picture that sees this meaning as bestowed by something outside language. His "critique" of ostensive definition will show that, here too, language is autonomous. Once again, "use" is what must be presupposed; use cannot be derived from an ostensive definition, at least not from such a definition as it has been traditionally understood.

Philosophers usually think of ostensive definition as a technique for giving names to objects. If we accomplish this, it is like attaching a label to an object. But, Wittgenstein warns us, attaching the label is not the final goal of our activity; we define the term or label in order to be able to use it later on. But use it *how*? There are many possible uses of words, and the fact that a word is ostensively defined – attached as a label to a thing – does not tell us which of these many uses is intended. An ostensive definition may be a preparation for the use of a word, "But *what*", Wittgenstein asks, "is it a preparation *for*?" (§26). This matter is left undecided by the ostensive definition, which, according to the traditional theory, only attaches a name to an object. Examining the referent of the demonstrative 'this' will not show one the use of the word defined. Understood simply as attaching a name to an object, an ostensive definition is not sufficient to instruct someone in the use, the meaning, of a word.[10]

A traditionalist might reply that the ostensive definition prepares one to use the word defined, the *definiendum*, to refer to the object pointed to in the definition and hence to talk about it. Wittgenstein's rejoinder to this suggestion focuses on the contrast between mere naming and use: "'We name things and then we can talk about them: can refer to them in talk'. – As if what we did next were given with the mere act of naming" (§27). After establishing a term such as 'water' as a name, we might use it in many ways: to refer to this particular volume of liquid, to refer to *any* instance of the same kind of stuff, to call out for water, to express disgust at water, to express delight at it, to ask whether there is any water, to ponder the essential nature of water and so on. Surely none of these activities are given by the naming that allegedly occurs in the ostensive definition "This is called 'water'." What has been left out by the ostensive definition, conceived simply as attaching a name to an object, is the use – the uses – of that name.

Wittgenstein goes on to point out the ambiguity of any ostensive definition: it can be understood in many different ways. If one wishes to define the number two by pointing to two nuts and saying "That is called 'two'", the definition *could* be understood to assign the name to *this* group of nuts, in which case the word 'two' would be taken as a proper name and not as signifying a number at all. Equally, of course, it could be taken as a general term to be used to designate any pair of items. The ostensive definition alone does not convey which of these two uses is intended; looking at the nuts does not tell one if the word 'two' is to be used as their proper name or as a general term. One might try to improve on the ostensive definition so as to remove the ambiguity. One way of doing this would be to introduce a grammatical category into it: "This *number* is called 'two'." Likewise we might say "This *colour* is called 'red'" to make sure our audience takes the term to be used as a colour term and not one, say, that applies to the *shape* of the colour sample. Wittgenstein warns us, however, that this expansion of the ostensive definition may not work; it may not do the job of revealing what use the *definiendum* is to be put to. This is because "This number is called 'two'" *itself* remains ambiguous and could be understood in various ways. There are many ways in which we could use 'number': to refer to individual groups of objects, to refer to shareable quantities; indeed, to refer to shapes, colours, individuals and so on. *If* our audience knows what use we have in mind, then she will understand the ostensive definition. At some point, the audience must bring to the ostensive definition this knowledge of use. "So one might say: the ostensive definition explains the use – the meaning – of the word when the overall role of the word in language is clear" (§30).

Even if someone comes to pick up the use of the *definiendum* through repeated instances of the ostensive definition – as surely does happen – Wittgenstein's point remains valid. Critics of Wittgenstein have argued that repeated instances of ostension can do what Wittgenstein claimed cannot be done – bring about an understanding of use – but this is to miss the point. Any array of ostensive definitions – defining 'two', for instance, by pointing to two nuts, two books, two people, two triangles and so on – will remain ambiguous in the sense that the same array could be used to define 'two' as meaning several different things or having several different uses, for example, to describe something as a pair of things or to describe something as, for instance, a set of objects in space – note that all the objects referred to in the above array of ostensive definitions are "objects in space" – as well as "objects on the planet earth," and they might all be dark in colour, or less than one mile high and so on. But for the learner to recognize one or all of these possible uses of 'two', this person must already grasp the notion of describing something numerically, or describing something spatially, or describing something as coloured. One must already be a "master" of a language – or this part of a language – in order to understand an ostensive definition (§33). Which is to say, one must know a particular linguistic use and be able to engage in it if one is to benefit from the ostensive definition that introduces a new term having this use. If I know how to use a word as a number, and know that the use of the number being defined is the "number-use", then I can understand "This is called 'two'"; that is to say, I can proceed to use 'two' as a number.

What is the lesson conveyed in Wittgenstein's critique of ostensive definition? Part of it, at least, is this: even if an ostensive definition links up a word and an object, the object does not reveal the use of the word. This is so because the same object could be described differently; it does not uniquely determine *one and only one* way to use the *definiendum*. Hence mere awareness of the object does not dictate, entail or reveal any one use of the word being ostensively defined. The meaning of the word, then, is not derived from the nature of the object observed. Acknowledging this is to acknowledge the autonomy of use.

How does an ostensive definition, *correctly understood*, serve as a rule of language that reveals the meaning, that is, *use*, of a word? As we have seen, to know what object a word refers to we already must have mastered a part of language that can be used to refer to this thing. If, for example, in providing an ostensive definition of 'red' I say "This is called 'red'" or "This colour is called 'red'", I am *using* the word 'this' or the phrase 'this colour' to refer to *the colour red* (PG: 88), and I go on to say that this word 'red' can be used in the same way. In giving the ostensive definition to someone, I am assuming that she can use 'this colour', or understand its being used, in a certain way – to refer to the colour red – and can therefore, as a result of the ostensive definition, use the word 'red' instead of the more cumbersome 'this colour'. Only if someone already knows (that is, has mastered) a certain use can she understand and benefit from an ostensive definition. Properly understood, then, an ostensive definition conveys or manifests a use. It is understood only when this use is grasped. Thus ostensive definitions can serve as a means, along with verbal definitions, of explaining the meanings of words. The analysis I have just suggested also shows how, in giving an ostensive definition, I remain purely within language and do not violate the autonomy requirement. An ostensive definition is not unlike a verbal definition: in both we pass from one verbal expression to another. In both cases one of these verbal expressions is being used; the other is said to have the same use.

In the rest of this chapter I shall point more briefly to passages in which Wittgenstein tries to establish the crucial importance of use and to show that other proposed language-independent foundations of language do not work. Section 39, for instance, considers the age-old claim that names ought to signify simples. Complexes can be broken apart and thereby disappear, and if names referred to these complexes and they gave these names their meanings, then the destruction of a complex object would result in the meaninglessness of the name referring to it. But then, of course, we could not meaningfully use the name to say that the complex does not exist, for the name would no longer have any meaning.

Wittgenstein responds to this argument by pointing out that we do not use the term 'meaning of a name' as we use the term 'bearer of a name' (we do not say, for example, that the meaning dies when the bearer does; §40), and he also points to various ways in which a name might continue to have a use (and meaning) when its bearer ceases to exist (§41). Even in language-game 2, a word such as 'slab' might continue to have a use if the workers ran out of slabs; when called out it might be used, for example, as a joke. A name would fail to have a meaning only when, for whatever reason, it could no longer be used in *any way*. There could be, Wittgenstein admits, a language-game in which a name is used only in the presence of its bearer (which must, therefore, exist), but this, he urges, is not our usual language-game with names.

In response to the claim that objects or individuals (the bearers of names) must be simple so as to avoid destruction and generate the meaninglessness of the names they bear, Wittgenstein launches in §47 into his famous critique of simplicity. The crux of this critique is that what 'simple' and 'complex' mean is relative to the language-games in which they are employed, and that what is simple in one language-game may be complex in another. There is no such thing as absolute simplicity that could be the metaphysical underpinning of language. Whether something is simple depends on how we are *using* the term 'simple'. In §48 Wittgenstein draws our attention to an arrangement of coloured squares or boxes. It would be natural, he says, to take the individual squares as the simple parts of this arrangement. But we might, Wittgenstein points out, think of one of these monochrome squares as being a composite "consisting of two rectangles, or of the elements colour and shape". The figure itself, or the picture of this figure, does not itself determine if it is simple or complex. Whether it is the one or the other depends on the use of 'simple' and 'complex' in these circumstances. We cannot appeal to the simples found in reality to give us the meanings of our names, since whether something *is* a simple is a matter of how these names are used. Use is autonomous.

And in response to the claim that we can attribute neither being nor non-being to the supposedly indestructible elements, Wittgenstein shows that there are in fact some things in our ordinary world that have similar properties: we can say of the metre rod in Paris neither that it is one metre long nor that it is not one metre long. But the reason for this prohibition is not some metaphysical property of this rod but rather the special role or function it has: its role as a standard. If it did not exist, we could not use it in this fashion, but it does not follow that the term 'one metre' would become meaningless. We could always turn, as in fact we have done, to some other thing or process and use it as the standard for something being one metre long.

Certainly, there are many objects that function as *paradigms* in our language: we point to them in defining our terms – colour samples, for example (§50). If they did not exist, we would have to resort to other paradigms, if we continue to want or need paradigms! But paradigms, like colour samples, may fade, as in a particular case we might judge from memory (§56). However, a memory image of a colour may *also* change its colour! If we had to depend on objects in the world remaining the same, or activities in the mind remaining constant, in order to sustain meaning, we would be "at the mercy" of these things (*ibid.*). *But we are not at their mercy!* Nothing in the world, or in the mind, guarantees that a word has meaning, or the same meaning. We could decide that *red* is whatever colour is possessed by our memory-image of red, whether it has faded or not; or we could decide that *red* is the colour of *this* object here-now, whether it is the same colour we remember as red or not. In our language-games we are not at the mercy of anything independent of language, in the world or in the mind, because use is not logically dependent on any such thing.

I turn now to Wittgenstein's discussion of family resemblances in §§65 and following. Philosophers have often suggested that language requires "something in common" among the various particular things to which we apply the same term. Otherwise, the argument goes, what could be the reason for applying this term again? If there were not something in common among the things to which we apply the word 'chair' or 'red' or 'democracy', then the uses of these terms would be completely arbitrary. 'Chair' might mean just anything if it could be applied to objects having nothing in common. Meaning, communication, and rationality all require that there be universals that *justify* the application of language. There *must* be something in common among the items to which we apply a word if this word is to have meaning.

I take Wittgenstein's comments on family resemblances to be a challenge to this type of argument. On the contrary, he argues, we apply terms to various items that simply have similarities or resemblances – "family resemblances" – among them. And these similarities need not always be the same. All games (Wittgenstein's example) resemble one another, as do all chairs, but not always in the same way. Universals – for instance, the universal *game* or *chair* – are not required.

The argument for "something in common" would undermine the autonomy of language by basing language on something independent of it: real universals.

Wittgenstein is not arguing, or interested in arguing, that all terms, or even most, are family resemblance terms. If it turned out that there were some common property to all *games*, one finally turned up by an industrious and ingenious critic of Wittgenstein, this would in no way invalidate Wittgenstein's observations about the term 'game'. *I*, and I dare say *you*, do not know what this common property is, but we nevertheless have no trouble at all using the term and using it correctly, and *that's* the basic point Wittgenstein wishes to make. A grasp of a universal, or a general definition, is not required for the correct use of a term. Correct use does not depend on such a universal or definition.

Certainly, Wittgenstein often points out that if asked why we call a particular activity a game, we would probably point to some resemblances, perhaps even vague ones, that this activity has to other things we call games. But in saying that resemblances are all we need, Wittgenstein is not, I think, supporting the philosophy of resemblances embraced by H. H. Price.[11] Resemblances, too, are 'things in the world' (at least Price thought so), and if they were required for a rational or meaningful use of language, autonomy would once again be threatened.

I take the crux of Wittgenstein's discussion of family resemblances to be §68 and §69. In §68 someone is trying to force him to accept a definition of 'number' in terms of a logical sum of arithmetic kinds, and he will not buy it: "It need not be so", he rejoins. He goes on to say that we can give the concept 'number' rigid limits if we wish, but that we can use this term so that its extension "is *not* closed by a frontier". One can always draw a boundary, but one has not so far been drawn. With regard to the term 'game', the fact that no boundary for its use has been drawn "never troubled you before when you used the word 'game'".

In §69 he goes on to say that if we were to explain to someone what a game is, we might describe examples and then add: "This *and similar things* are called 'games'." And in §71 he remarks, "Here giving examples is not an *indirect* means of explaining – in default of a better. For any general definition can be misunderstood too." A general definition, in other words, can be interpreted – applied – in different ways, and hence it can be misunderstood by being applied in the wrong way. So having a general definition helps me understand a word only if I know how to apply the definition, and hence only if I know how to use the term defined. By itself, the definition is of no value. Examples, too, can be misunderstood. If we give examples to someone else, we intend these examples to be taken in a certain way. This means "that he is now to *employ* those examples in a certain way" (§71); he must employ or use them in the way we do in playing the language-game with the term. As Wittgenstein says about the proper use of 'game': "The point is that *this* is how we play the game. (I mean the language-game with the word 'game'.)" (§71). We play the language-game a certain way, including or excluding a particular activity as a game – and that is what, in general, is basic about meaning and language. The proper employment of words is not *derived from* or *dependent on* or *validated by* something in common among the items in the world to which they are applied, be this a universal or a resemblance. Proper employment is manifested in the way the language-game is played, in how words are used.

Wittgenstein's focus on use comes out clearly in his discussion of what has traditionally been called the conceptualist view of universals: that they are, and are no more than, general ideas (images) in the mind. The theory is that we apply a word to a particular thing because the general idea applies to it, that is, resembles it. Take the general idea of a leaf, or of the colour green. Do we not call things leaves because they match up with our general idea of a leaf? Do we not call those colours green that resemble our general idea of green? One might want to ask, à la Berkeley, what shape the general idea of a leaf shows us, or what shade the general idea of green exhibits. But this is not Wittgenstein's problem with the theory. He admits that there might be a schematic leaf, or a sample of pure green. Such a thing, however, is not the foundation of our talk of leaves and green things for the following reason:

> [F]or such a schema to be understood as a *schema*, and not as the shape of a particular leaf, and for a slip of pure green to be understood as a sample of all that is greenish and not as a sample of pure green – this in turn resides in the way the samples are used. (§73)

Nothing prevents us, for example, from using the schema of a leaf as a picture of a particular kind of leaf having precisely this irregular shape, just as we may take the sample of green as a sample of a particular green colour (pure green) and not as a sample of all things greenish (*ibid.*). We might think of all general ideas as schemas, in which case Wittgenstein's argument shows that a mental idea itself does not dictate how the word it defines is to be used. In order for the latter to occur, the idea itself must be used, understood, *as a schema*, but, of course, it need not be used this way. Thus ideas do not dictate how we take them or ought to take them. In fact, only the practice or language-game of taking them a certain way determines what ideas these *are*, for example, schematic ones or particular ones. This practice is autonomous.

Here we have another pattern of argumentation often found in the later Wittgenstein. Let us try to identify some thing in the mind or in the world as the basis of a linguistic practice. Whatever the item – a mental image, a sample, a correlation chart, an arrow, a sign-post – it could be interpreted or seen in different ways and thereby give rise to different uses. So in positing it as the meaning of a word, one must presupposes a particular use of the item, which use is therefore not grounded in the nature of this thing. Use is autonomous.

There are a number of other topics in the early sections of the *Investigations* that are subjected to similar treatment by Wittgenstein. For instance, there is the case of rules. Do we always have to have, or appeal to, rules in order to use language? Must a language be like a game with rules or like a calculus? No, we cannot say "that someone who is using language *must* be playing such a game" (§81). Moreover, what it means to say that someone is following a rule may vary from case to case (§82), and there may be cases where there is no rule at all that is being followed, or no rule that applies (§80). We may even make up the rules as we go along, or alter them as we please.

What if the rules of a game are vague? Does this mean that the game cannot be played (§100)? Is an indefinite boundary not really a boundary at all (§99)? Certainly not. If someone says "Stand roughly there" we have no difficult understanding this order and following it, that is, playing this game. Definite, clear-cut rules are not necessary for the use of language to occur.

And what if we give someone a rule in the form of a table (§86)? Does the table itself show how it is to be followed? Are there not different ways in which it could be followed? The table, the rule-vehicle out there in the world, does not dictate its own application. Our pupil must learn how to use it.

A rule, we are told in §85, "stands there like a sign-post". Does the sign-post – the object itself with its pointed end – "leave no doubt about the way I have to go?" Well, I probably will follow it in the direction of the pointed end, but I *could* follow it in the direction of the blunt end; some *strange* human being, or a Martian, might do so. There is nothing about the sign-post itself that rules out the latter use of it. Only the practice of using sign-posts, the practice of following them by going in the direction of the pointed end, rules out the strange use as incorrect *and* reveals what I am to do in order to follow one of them. This practice is a standard, repeatable manner of acting: a *use* of a sign-post, like the use of a word. The use, the practice, is what is basic and autonomous.

In his discussion of the nature of philosophy (the way philosophy *ought* to be practised according to him), Wittgenstein writes, "We must do away with all *explanation*, and description alone must take its place" (§109). We must stop trying to explain how language is possible and satisfy ourselves with describing language as it is. We must stop trying to explain how language requires, or is built up upon, a set of rigid rules, or a set of universals, or a set of simple objects in the world, or a set of objects in the world with their given natures. We are, rather, to describe the activities we engage in by using language. Philosophy cannot give these actual uses of words any foundation (§124).

But surely, Wittgenstein acknowledges, there is such a thing as understanding a word, knowing what it means, and this phenomenon may give us a clue as to conditions for the intelligibility of language (§139). We can even understand a word in a flash. What comes before our mind, perhaps suddenly, when we understand a word such as 'cube'? Is it not an image or picture of a cube? Certainly such an image might suddenly pop into the mind, indeed in a flash. So, must it not be the case that to be intelligible, our words must attach themselves to images, which, presumably, are in the mind as the result of its empirical intercourse with the world? These images or pictures, the theory goes, then dictate certain uses of the word, and the uses must fit, be consistent with, the pictures.

Suppose, Wittgenstein responds, that an image of a cube comes before my mind when I hear the word 'cube'. If I then point to a triangular prism and call it a cube, does my use of the word *not* fit the picture? "But doesn't it fit?" Wittgenstein asks. "I have purposely so chosen the example that it is quite easy to imagine a *method of projection* according to which the picture does fit after all./ The picture of the cube did indeed *suggest* a certain use to us, but it was possible for me to use it differently" (§139). Just as in geometry one can construct a method of projection that maps a cube onto a triangular prism, so we can imagine a use of 'cube' that is such that a picture of what (*we* would call) a cube leads one to apply the word 'cube' to a triangular prism. The image does not dictate its own application. Many uses may be considered consistent with it. Thus the image does not in any way restrict use or chart its direction. "There are other processes, besides the one we originally thought of, which we should sometimes be prepared to call 'applying the picture of a cube'" (§140). And so Wittgenstein concludes, "What is essential is to see that the same thing can come before our minds when we hear the word and the application still be different. Has it the *same* meaning both times? I think we shall say not" (*ibid.*). The meaning of a word is not defined by the image it is associated with, because we can have the same image, different applications (uses) of it, and thus different meanings. Even if one thinks of the method of projection as something that can come before the mind – like lines of projection one might find on a blueprint or other schema – this does not really get one any further. "Can't I now imagine different applications of this schema too?" (§141). No mental conditions, states or occurrences can be postulated as the determinants of meaning and intelligibility.

Wittgenstein's discussion of *reading* (PI: §§156–78) and the notion of *being guided* can provide additional examples of autonomy. What is reading? Is it not a particular kind of conscious mental experience or mental process? Is it not in fact the experience of being guided by the words on a page, a piece of paper, or the like? But what is this distinctive experience? What am I aware of when I read? It does not seem to be any particular sensation; any sensation I might mention could occur and I still not be reading, or, on the contrary, I might be reading and feel no sensation whatsoever. Is there a special experience of deriving spoken words from written ones? It is not even clear that reading ought to be thought of as a matter of deriving one thing from another; do I not, at least frequently, just *see* the written words and, perhaps, read them out loud? Of course I could say these words without actually reading them (I may guess the words or simply have them memorized), so saying them out loud is no proof of reading. If there are characteristics in experience of being guided by written words, what exactly are these characteristics? Do I feel some sort of influence of the letters I am reading? It may be the case that the words look familiar, or that the eye passes easily over them, but none of this is necessary. Do the words cause something to happen or occur in us? Wittgenstein suggests that reading the words may be accompanied by all sorts of experience, but equally need not be accompanied by any particular experience. Look to the experience of reading and we shall not find anything that is essential, distinctive in it. On the contrary, he tells us, we think of ourselves as being guided by the letters in reading because we bring to bear the concept of *because* or *causation* in describing the experience. We do not obtain the distinctive language of reading from the experience of reading; we use the language to tell us what reading *is.* And crucial to how we use the verb 'to read' is the set of situations in which it is appropriate to say of someone that he is reading: situations such as his having been taught to read, his having read before, his being able to answer certain questions after reading, and the like. There is no *one* situation or set of such that is required, but it is to an "external" set of conditions and not an "internal" one that we look if we want to say that someone is reading. And we ourselves do not *find out* (by introspection) that we are reading; we just … read. But I would not (should not) *say* that I was reading if the situation were entirely inappropriate, for example, I had never learned to read, and could not answer questions on the basis of my activity and so on. For after all, we learn how to talk about reading, which involves grasping the situations in which reading occurs, or does not. Reading is a particular form of human activity, one that we learn to master and talk about. It is a language-game, not derived from any alleged experience but antecedent to any description of an activity as one of reading.

Let me pass now to the important rule-following considerations in §185ff. We are to imagine a pupil being given instruction in developing an arithmetic series, let us say the series $n + 2$. The teacher's examples include the members of the series 2, 4, 6, 8, 10, 12 … 996, 998, 1000. Our pupil masters all these steps, but then he proceeds to write 1,004 after 1,000, 1,008 after 1,004 and so on. The teacher says he has made a mistake; the recalcitrant pupil denies this, saying that he went on in the same way, that he has done exactly what he and the teacher were doing before the number 1,000. Well, Wittgenstein asks, "How is it decided what is the right step to take at any particular stage?" (§186). Does the earlier series of examples, given first by the teacher and then repeated by the pupil, dictate that 1,002 is to follow 1,000, that 1,002 is the right step to take after 1,000? The answer must be "no", since the series of examples is consistent with an order to add 2 up to 1,000, 4 up to 2,000, and 6 up to 3,000 (§185). We might say that the series of examples can be interpreted differently or taken in different ways, so the examples themselves do not dictate or determine what number is to follow 1,000. Is, then, the right step determined by what is *meant* by the order "add two"? In a way the answer to this question is "yes", but we must first ask how we ascertain what is meant by the order. Is it what occurred in the mind of the teacher when he gave the order "add two"? Is the right step somehow determined by this state of mind? Wittgenstein points out that this "state of mind" could be exceedingly variable. The teacher might not have, probably *did not* have, the thought "go from 1,000 to 1,002", and he surely did not (could not) have thoughts corresponding to each of the infinite steps in the series $n + 2$. But 1,002 is the right step to take after 1,000 even if the teacher did not have this thought, and it might have been the wrong step even if the teacher did have the thought "1,002 after 1,000", since the teacher *himself* might have made a mistake in thinking this. Thus the right step cannot be determined by considering the state of mind of the teacher. Of course the teacher did *mean* for the pupil to go from 1,000 to 1,002, but what his meaning this amounts to cannot be equated with some state of affairs in his mind. He meant it in the sense that he *would* have responded "Go from 1,000 to 1,002" *if* asked what to do at that stage. Neither a state of mind nor a series of real examples in the world determines what the correct step after 1,000 is.

Wittgenstein asks, "what is the criterion for the way the formula $[n + 2]$ is meant?" (§190), and his answer is: "the kind of way we are taught to use it". The way we are taught to use it is later characterized as a *practice*, a standard way of proceeding, standard both in the sense of a uniform, regularly repeated mode of behaviour and in the sense of a standard of correctness, since the regularly repeated mode of behaviour *is* the criterion of correctness. Obeying a rule, following an order, these are *customs* (uses, institutions) (§199) and hence obeying the order or rule $n + 2$ is a *practice* (§202). This practice is autonomous, since nothing in the natural world (the previous examples) or in the mental world determines its nature or acts as a standard for whether or not an application of it is correct. The practice itself – the institutionalized use itself – is the criterion of correctness.

Are there reasons for engaging in a practice in the way we do? In one sense, yes, of course there are. If asked why I wrote 1,002 after 1,000 in developing the series $n + 2$, I will surely say "because the previous number was 1000", and if asked why 1,002 follows 1,000 I will say that it bears the same relationship to 1,000 as all of the other previous steps in the series bear to one another. In saying these things I am giving reasons for what I do. But at some point my reasons give out. Why do I think that 1,000 and 1,002 are related in the same way as 998 and 1,000? Here I might say: "well, they just *are*", which is only a way of confessing that I am out of reasons. I might answer, of course, by saying that they are both two digits apart, but then what reason do I have for saying they are both two digits apart? Once again, I may have to say that they just are. So, Wittgenstein tells us, "my reasons will soon give out. And then I shall act, without reasons" (§211). The practice I and others engage in is not in the end buttressed by reasons; it is simply the way we act, the way we use numbers, like the way we use words. In the end there are no reasons for this use – it is autonomous. "If I have exhausted the justifications I have reached bedrock, and my spade is turned. Then I am inclined to say: 'This is simply what I do'" (§217).

We are now close to the sections of the *Investigations* in which private experience and private language are discussed. Once again the idea of the autonomy of use comes to our aid. It might appear, and certainly has appeared to many empiricist-minded philosophers, that we learn the part of language referring to our inner experiences by associating a name with a particular experience and then using the name to refer to and talk about this experience. Take the case of pain, surely an inner experience if anything is. Do we not learn the meaning of the word 'pain' by first experiencing pain and then giving this experience the name 'pain'? Is what the name means not something learned from the experience itself? Since no one else can have *my* experience of pain, just as I cannot have anyone else's pain, it follows that no one else understands (*can* understand) what I mean by 'pain'. This term is part of a private language I have developed to talk about my inner experiences. Perhaps others guess what I mean by 'pain' by inferring that I have the same experience they have when I behave in ways analogous to the ways they behave when they have what *they* call pain. But this would only be a conjecture on their part. No one else can really know that I am in pain. Only I can know that I have this inner experience.

The pattern of reasoning here on the part of the empiricist is by now a familiar one. Words denote or designate things in the world, in this case inner things such as pain. We learn the meaning of a word by having the appropriate experience. What is the appropriate experience? In this case only I can tell, since only I can experience what the name 'pain' names. Hence at least this part of my language must be a private one.

Wittgenstein's argument against this empiricist dogma is immensely complex, but one strain of it is similar to his previous critique of the traditional theory of ostensive definition. He paraphrases the empiricist's position as follows: "Once you know *what* the word stands for, you understand it, you know its whole use" (§264). Supposedly I know this use by concentrating my attention on the thing designated by the word, for example, the experience of pain, and then calling it 'pain', associating the word with the experience. Subsequently I use the word to refer to this experience and say things about it. But where or how did I learn how to use it? The use of 'pain' cannot be derived just from the experience of pain. The latter does not show, for example, that anything similar is also pain, or that having this experience is something others are expected to sympathize and commiserate with. It does not reveal that I am to cry out for help by saying, for instance, "I am in pain." The experience does not reveal that hurting is one of the properties of the pain. The hurting might be an irrelevant accompaniment. How can I learn that the hurting is one of pain's essential properties? How I understand all these things from the experience itself and the experience alone is a mystery. In so far as the naming of pain with the word 'pain' does not teach anyone the use of the name, then the alleged process of associating the name with the experience of pain is only a "ceremony" (§258), an idle one at that. If we are to understand the word 'pain' we must grasp how to use it, how to talk about pain (*my* pain and *others'*), how to express it, how to interact with others when I am in pain or they are. But all of these activities are public ones, and they are unavailable to someone who restricts the meaning of a name to private experiences.

The empiricist thinks that things such as the colour red are similar to pains: only the person experiencing red can know what it is like and hence know what the meaning of the word 'red' is. Wittgenstein replies: "Of course, saying that the word 'red' 'refers to' … something private does not help us in the least to grasp its function" (§274). This function, this use, is not conveyed by the inner experience; it can only be taught in a public way. Only in this way can the "practical consequences" of using the word 'red' come to be grasped. The use, the function, the practical consequences of talk about red, and talk about the quintessential inner experience of pain, these are matters of the *grammar* of the words 'red' and 'pain', and this grammar is part of the stage-setting that must be in place if a person is to understand the terms. This stage-setting is *presupposed* by designating something a pain, or by concentrating on the sensation of red. The proper use of 'pain' or 'red' is independent of the experience itself. Or, put otherwise, we do not even know what the experience of pain, or of red, *is* until we have mastered the language of pains or colours.

Do I have reasons for saying that I am in pain? Does the experience I am having, the sensation itself, somehow inform me that it is a pain? Are there present in this particular case the essential aspects of an experience of pain, that is, the *criteria* of the sensation pain, that lead me to call *this* sensation a pain? Wittgenstein's answer: "What I do is not, of course, to identify my sensation by criteria: but to repeat an expression. But this is not the *end* of the language-game: it is the beginning" (§290). In the beginning, we are always reminded, is the deed. In the beginning there is the activity, indeed the public practice, of repeating an expression and then mastering its proper use: to talk about my pains and yours, and about red and non-red objects. Use could not be more fundamental.

And, finally, "it shews a fundamental misunderstanding, if I am inclined to study the headache I have now in order to get clear about the philosophical problem of sensation" (§314). What a sensation is, what the sensation of headache is, what the experience of red is, none of these questions are to be answered by consulting sensations such as headaches or experiences such as seeing red. Similarly, we are not to get clear about the meaning of the word 'think' by watching ourselves while we think (§316). What we are to consult are the language-games in which we use the words 'sensation', 'headache', 'red' and 'think'. These language-games are what is basic; they and the forms of life in which they are embedded are the *given*.

I hope I have produced enough examples to allow you yourself to go on and identify other passages in *Philosophical Investigations* as instances of one of its basic messages: the autonomy of use.

Notes

1. In memory of the late Dean Spencer, dedicated student of the philosophy of Wittgenstein.
2. For an excellent and vivid account of Wittgenstein's life, see Ray Monk's *Ludwig Wittgenstein: The Duty of Genius* (New York: Free Press, 1990).
3. In treating the early sections of the *Investigations* as instantiating the autonomy theme in various ways, I am not, of course, following what is often regarded as the standard model of interpretation of these passages, namely, the view of them as stages in the development of a critique of the Augustinian theory of language (see G. P. Baker & P. M. S. Hacker, *An Analytical Commentary on the Philosophical Investigations*: *Volume I, Wittgenstein: Understanding and Meaning* (Oxford: Blackwell, 1980–96)). It is not my intention to suggest that this other model is incorrect; the richness of Wittgenstein's thought will surely bear more than one strand of significance. It does appear to me, however, that the Augustinian model is just *one* way of rejecting the autonomy of language and attempting to ground language in something more basic than use. Moreover, in the early sections of the *Invesitgations* we find examinations of notions that do not fit clearly within the theory embedded in the initial quotation from Augustine, for example, rules and schematic ideas. But these notions are central to other philosophical efforts to get behind or below use. For these reasons I see the autonomy theme as incorporating the critique of the Augustinian theory of meaning and having the additional advantage of illuminating passages that do not fit neatly into the critique.
4. But he certainly continues to talk about the issue, for example: "Is there some reality lying behind the notion, which shapes the grammar?" (PI: §562). There are also the remarks in §496 and §497, which I shall discuss shortly.
5. References to these works will be by page numbers.
6. Wittgenstein's concept of grammar is much broader than and different from the idea of school grammar, the classification of words (as nouns, verbs, adjectives, etc.) and the rules for the syntactically proper ways to put them together in sentences. A grammatical rule

for Wittgenstein defines the type of *activity* one is engaged in in using a word. For him, school grammar can give a very misleading picture of use-grammar. For instance, all *nouns* do not have the same use-grammar, since different nouns have very different uses.

7. *The Big Typescript* consists of a dictation of a collection of Wittgenstein's writings from 1929 to 1933, extensively revised by him.

8. The famous tool-box analogy (§11) and the locomotive analogy (§12) are ways in which Wittgenstein drives home the point that it is the different uses or functions of words with which we need to concern ourselves if we are to understand a language or language-game.

9. See my essay "'*Mechanism and Calculus*': Wittgenstein on Augustine's Theory of Ostension", in *Wittgenstein: Sources and Perspectives*, C. G. Luckhardt (ed.), 303–38 (Ithaca, NY: Cornell University Press, 1979).

10. It must be stressed that this is true of an ostensive definition only as it is interpreted by the traditional account. I believe that, for Wittgenstein, a full account of the grammar of an ostensive definition does show it to convey the grammatical use of the *definiendum*, although this use may not be grasped or understood by the person to whom one gives the definition.

11. See H. H. Price, *Thinking and Experience*, 2nd edn (London: Hutchinson, 1962).

Further reading

Baker, G. P. & P. M. S. Hacker 1980–96. *An Analytical Commentary on the Philosophical Investigations*, four volumes, volumes III and IV by P. M. S. Hacker. Oxford: Blackwell.

Brenner, W. H. 1999. *Wittgenstein's Philosophical Investigations*. Albany, NY: SUNY Press.

Glock, H.-J. 1996. *A Wittgenstein Dictionary*. Oxford: Blackwell.

Glock, H.-J. (ed.) 2001. *Wittgenstein: A Critical Reader*. Oxford: Blackwell.

Hacker, P. M. S. 1996. *Wittgenstein's Place in Twentieth-Century Analytic Philosophy*. Oxford: Blackwell.

McGinn, M. 1997. *Wittgenstein and the Philosophical Investigations*. London: Routledge.

Monk, R. 1990. *Ludwig Wittgenstein: The Duty of Genius*. New York: Free Press.

Sluga, H. & D. G. Stern (eds) 1996. *The Cambridge Companion to Wittgenstein*. Cambridge: Cambridge University Press.

Wittgenstein, L. 1953. *Philosophical Investigations*, 3rd edn, G. E. M. Anscombe (trans.). Oxford: Blackwell.

Wittgenstein, L. 1970. *Zettel*, G. E. M. Anscombe & G. H. von Wright (eds), G. E. M. Anscombe (trans.). Berkeley, CA: University of California Press.

Wittgenstein, L. 1974. *Philosophical Grammar*, R. Rhees (ed.), A. Kenny (trans.). Oxford: Blackwell.

Wittgenstein, L. 1975. *Philosophical Remarks*, R. Rhees (ed.), R. Hargreaves & R. White (trans). Oxford: Blackwell.

Wittgenstein, L. 1994. *The Wittgenstein Reader*, A. Kenny (ed.). Oxford: Blackwell.

13

Karl Popper

The Logic of Scientific Discovery

Jeremy Shearmur

Some of the ideas that Karl Popper set out in his *Logic of Scientific Discovery* may be familiar to those with an interest in philosophy. Thus, people may readily identify him with the idea of falsifiability as the mark of science and of the fallibility of even our best scientific knowledge. They may know of his emphasis on the logical asymmetry between verification and falsification, and his thesis that a single counter-example may show that a general theory is false while confirmations cannot show that it is true. They may also know that falsifiability was offered as a theory of demarcation – of what marks the difference between science and non-science – rather than as a theory of what is meaningful. They may also be aware of the fact that Popper offers a solution to the problem of induction by way of offering a rational but non-inductive account of the growth of knowledge, through a process of conjecture and refutation.

However, what is perhaps most distinctive about Popper's approach to epistemology and the philosophy of science in *The Logic of Scientific Discovery* may be unfamiliar. This unfamiliarity is, I suspect, in part of a product of people's initially reading works of Popper's other than *The Logic of Scientific Discovery*, and in part of their looking at *The Logic of Scientific Discovery* in a piecemeal manner, and with expectations shaped by the empiricist tradition in epistemology and the philosophy of science. However, there is something genuinely distinctive about his work. Popper, while he gives an account of empirical science, is not an empiricist in any usual sense. Further, while there are important Kantian influences on his work, he is not a Kantian either. In addition, many of what might seem to be the obvious objections to his work – for example, that falsifications can be avoided – were not only anticipated by Popper, but some of the most distinctive features of his epistemology consist in the kind of response that he made to these problems.

In the rest of this chapter, I shall discuss some of the main features of Popper's book. But first, I shall say something about its background. In part, this story explains some of the complications associated with the publication of Popper's work that may be useful to the reader when he or she turns to Popper's text. But in part they say something about the intellectual pedigree of Popper's views that may be of help to the reader in understanding what makes his approach distinctive.

Background

Karl Popper's *Logic of Scientific Discovery* (LScD) was first published in German in 1934 with a 1935 imprint. It appeared in a series associated with the Vienna Circle, and received a good measure of attention (see Hacohen 2000; O'Hear 2003). After various attempts by others to translate the work into English ran into difficulties, Popper was himself involved with the revision of a translation that was planned to appear in 1954 and that in the end was published in 1959. To this edition Popper added a number of footnotes and appendices (what is new is usually indicated as such). These additions are interesting, but they complicate matters for the reader as Popper's views changed in some significant ways between the writing of the original text and the publication of the translation. Material intended to form further appendices and a postscript took on a life of its own, and it was eventually decided to bring it out as a supplementary volume, in 1954 (as *Postscript: After Twenty Years*). The *Postscript* was set up in proofs, but Popper made extensive revisions, and then ran into problems with his eyesight. Publication plans were postponed and the *Postscript* remained in proofs for many years. Some material from the *Postscript* was subsequently published independently (e.g. Popper 1957a/1972: ch. 5, 1958/1963: ch. 8.2, 1957b). (In addition, Popper 1961/1994: ch. 5, 1957c, 1959b draw on material from the *Postscript*.) The *Postscript* itself, with added material, was finally published in three volumes in 1982–3 under the editorship of W. W. Bartley III (Popper 1982a, 1982b, 1983). In the final section of this chapter I briefly discuss changes in Popper's views since the publication of the original text of *The Logic of Scientific Discovery*.

The Logic of Scientific Discovery was not the first book that Popper wrote. He had, before this, written the two-volume work *Die beiden Grundprobleme der Erkenntnistheorie* [*The Two Fundamental Problems of the Theory of Knowledge*]. The first volume, on the problem of induction, was eventually published (together with some associated material) under the editorship of Troels Eggers Hansen (Popper 1979a). Popper refers to a second volume – a treatment of the history of the problem of demarcation – in a footnote to *The Logic of Scientific Discovery* (LScD: §11, n.3); however, there has been some controversy about just how much of the second volume was written (see Hacohen 2000: 220–39). Be this as it may, it seems that the second volume has been lost, other than a few fragments that were published in the Hansen edition of *Die beiden Grundprobleme*. An English translation of *Die beiden Grundprobleme* has existed for some years, and it is to be hoped that a revised version will be published in due course (see Zahar (1983) for some useful discussion of the book). I shall not, in this chapter, discuss the relation between the two works.

Popper tells us in his *Unended Quest* that he initially wrote a long version of *The Logic of Scientific Discovery*, but, to meet the space requirements of the publisher, it was drastically cut by his uncle, Walter Schiff (Popper 1976: §16). This cut-down volume became *The Logic of Scientific Discovery*.

Popper has given us an interesting account of his intellectual development (e.g. Popper 1963: ch. 3, 1976). The account that Popper gives us there and in other places is of the context in which particular ideas occurred to him; but what he says presents his views as broadly continuous with those of *The Logic of Scientific Discovery*. However, some recent work has drawn our attention to a problem concerning his account (see Hacohen 2000; Hansen 2002; ter Hark 2002). It relates to the text of an unpublished thesis *"Gewohnheit" und "Gesetzerlebnis" in der Erziehung* ["Habit" and the "Experience of Laws" in Education] (Popper 1927). This includes a theory of the demarcation between science and non-science, but one that is inductivist in character. This means that the reconstruction of Popper's early ideas is a little more difficult than it had previously seemed. In the light of all this, I shall confine myself to some rather general remarks.

Popper has told us that he was influenced by his early involvement with Marxism, and his subsequent disillusionment with its claims to scientific status, and by concerns about the status of psychoanalysis and of the ideas of Alfred Adler, with whom he worked. He was also strongly impressed by Einstein's correction to well-established Newtonian theory, and by the fact that Einstein's revision was open to a (challenging) empirical test.

In terms of Popper's substantive ideas, two currents of thought seem to have been particularly important. In order to obtain a teaching qualification, Popper had to attend the Pedagogic Institute in Vienna, where Karl Bühler was a professor. Popper became interested in psychology, and was sympathetic to the approach of Bühler, of Otto Selz and of the Würzburg School, who were critics of associationist psychology (for a brief discussion, see Popper 1976; Popper & Eccles 1977). These ideas left their mark on Popper's own psychological work; and Otto Selz seems to have been a particularly important influence (see Berkson & Wettersten 1984; ter Hark 1993a, 1993b, 2004; Wettersten 1992). Popper interpreted Kantian themes psychologically, as predispositions to interpret the world in particular ways (cf. Popper 1972: add. 1 and 1963: ch. 1); in addition, in line with Selz's ideas, these psychological ideas were understood in biological terms.

A second influence stems from a distinctive and unorthodox interpretation of Kant. Popper had himself read Kant (being led to his work by an earlier reading of Schopenhauer). Of particular importance was the fact that he engaged in an extensive discussion of epistemological issues with Julius Kraft (see Popper 1962), who was himself strongly influenced by Leonard Nelson's revival of Jacob Fries's earlier "anthropological" reinterpretation of Kant. Popper was himself not a Kantian or a follower of Fries, but he was sympathetic to Kant, and Kant was a significant influence upon him. He indicates at one point in *The Logic of Scientific Discovery* that he is closer to the "critical" Kantian approach, than he is to positivism (LScD: §29, n.3; see also Popper 1976: §16). *Die beiden Grundprobleme* contains, *inter alia*, an extensive critical discussion of Kant and of Fries, while its systematic approach towards the assessment of different alternative answers to the problem of induction was influenced by Nelson. In *The Logic of Scientific Discovery*, all this leaves its mark on Popper's discussion; notably, of "Fries's trilemma" in the context of the problem of justification, and on his theory of the empirical basis, and it serves, more generally, to distance him from the positivism of the Vienna Circle.

These two themes – from his work on psychology and his engagement with the Nelson School – fit together neatly in Popper's thought, in the sense that they led him to stress what might be called a Kantian epistemological activism – a view of us as attempting to impose interpretations on to the world, rather than our being passively instructed by it – whereas our propensity to behave in this way was understood in terms of biological predispositions. What Popper stressed also, however, is that while all this provides an important alternative to an empiricist view that sees us as being instructed by what comes passively to our senses, what we project onto the world in this manner may well turn out to be false. That is, as distinct from a Kantian view, these interpretative predispositions are on Popper's account *not a priori valid*. It thus becomes important to put them to the test.

Popper was very much interested in science, in the theory of probability, and in contemporary problems of the interpretation of scientific theories. He was interested also in and enthusiastic about recent developments in formal logic. He had a distaste for pretentious metaphysics, and for pontification about ethics. Philosophically, he was not in agreement with the Vienna Circle; but he shared substantive interests with some members, and he shared with them and with Bertrand Russell an enthusiasm for science in the context of a broad identification with the spirit of the Enlightenment. (Popper's early review of Russell's *History of Western Philosophy* is published in English in Grattan-Guinness (1992).)

Introduction

In his book, Popper sets out "the logic of scientific discovery". This, on his account, is a theory about *method*. What methods – what methodological rules – we follow is a matter of choice, decision or convention. In this respect, Popper stresses that his theory is not a naturalistic one. Indeed, while he sees some value in naturalistic or sociological approaches to the study of science, he argues that what counts as science must itself be a matter of convention or decision. What is to count as experience must also, in his view, be understood as a product of convention or decision, rather than something that can be settled naturalistically (for an explanation of this, see the section "The empirical basis", below). On these grounds, while Popper is dealing with natural science, he distinguishes his views from those in the empiricist or "positivist" tradition just because they do not share his view of the centrality of decision or convention.

What does this emphasis on decision or convention in Popper amount to? Some writers who have noted its prominence take it as if Popper were concerned with arbitrary decisions, or as if he simply stipulated a number of conventional rules that we should follow (cf. Johansson 1975). But in fact, his conventional rules have a systematic character; he is offering a theory, rather than just a collection of rules. He also has something specific and important to say about the choice of such conventions; namely, that they depend on our view about what should be the aim of science. In *The Logic of Scientific Discovery*, Popper discusses contrasting views as to what we might take the aim of science to be: for example, a body of fixed truths, or, alternatively, a body of falsifiable knowledge that is for ever open to revision. In his view, it is open to people to adopt one or another such view. However, Popper favours the latter view; he expresses the hope that it fits the intuitions of scientists, and he develops his account of scientific method with this particular view of the aim of science in mind. Accordingly, when Popper is talking about decisions or conventions, these are to be understood not as arbitrary, but as things to be adopted on the basis of a particular view of the aim of science (so that, say, a conventionalist such as Henri Poincaré, who has a different view from Popper about the aim of science, would be expected to develop a very different epistemology).

Given all this, what kind of an account of science – and, indeed, of epistemology – does Popper offer? He starts with a statement of the problem of induction, in terms of asking whether inductive inferences are justified. He asks further whether a principle of induction that could justify such inferences could be established, and then offers a version of Hume's criticism of induction as a response: that such a principle is not a logical truth, but if its truth is to be known from experience, then we would need to apply the same inductive inferences that we wished to justify in the first place (LScD: §1). Faced with this, Popper sets out to offer an account of scientific knowledge that does not make use of induction. It has five main building blocks.

First, there are Popper's ideas about the aim of science. What he says about this in *The Logic of Scientific Discovery* is somewhat limited. But it includes statements expressing his disagreement with those who see the aim of science as certainty. With this aim he contrasts his own view, as involving "logical rigour [and] also freedom from dogmatism; ... practical applicability ... but ... even more the adventure of science, ... and discoveries which again and again confront us with new and unexpected questions, challenging us to try out new and hitherto un-dreamed-of answers" (LScD: §4). He favours the view that:

> the distinguishing characteristic of empirical statements [lies] in their susceptibility to revision – in the fact that they can be criticized, and superseded by better ones; and [he aligns himself with those] who see it as their task to analyse the characteristic ability of science to advance.
> (LScD: §9)

Popper further writes that:

> We and those who share our attitude will hope to make new discoveries; and we shall hope to be helped in this by a newly erected scientific system. Thus we shall take the greatest interest in the falsifying experiment. We shall hail it as a success, for it has opened up new vistas into a world of new experiences. And we shall hail it even if these new experiences should furnish us with new arguments against our own most recent theories.
> (LScD: §19)

Popper concludes his book with a stirring and inspirational presentation of science as he sees it. Such ideas Popper again contrasts with those of the conventionalists (and those of inductivists). But at the same time, in *The Logic of Scientific Discovery* he holds the view that the choice between these views of the aim of science "must, of course, be ultimately a matter of decision, going beyond rational argument", a view that he was later to revise by developing ideas about how such issues could be approached rationally (LScD: §4, n.*5).

Secondly, Popper displays a resolute anti-psychologism. For him, the validity of knowledge claims can be no more a matter of our subjective conviction than is the validity of a deductive inference or the correctness of a mathematical proof. Popper does not deny that we have subjective experiences, and that these motivate us to make claims about the world. But – in a move that he suggests is close to an idea of Kant's in the *Critique of Pure Reason* – he places emphasis on inter-subjective scrutiny rather than private conviction. This plays a key role in his work, notably in what he says about the "empirical basis" (which I discuss below).

Thirdly, as is well-known, Popper points to falsifiability as the distinguishing characteristic of empirical statements (he does not distinguish systematically between statements, sentences and propositions), and of science. It is worth stressing that although Popper is offering a theory of the growth of scientific knowledge, he also sees himself as addressing key problems in epistemology more generally. For Popper, falsifiability is in the first instance a characteristic of statements. Empirical knowledge is seen as consisting of universal statements, which can in principle clash with basic statements, which report on what is the case. Suitably restricted existential statements are also empirical (i.e. "there is now a regular-sized elephant in my room" is falsifiable, whereas "there is now an ant in my room" probably is not, because the room is large, and full of books and papers; my failure to find an ant would not establish that one was not there). It is at once important to mention further that, for Popper: (a) falsifications are fallible (they depend on basic statements being inter-subjectively accepted, with a suitable background hypothesis to hand as to how others could test them); (b) they serve (tentatively) to falsify a *system* of statements – a theory or theories and various statements of initial conditions, such that it will be a matter of conjecture as to what stands in need of modification, as I explain further, below.

Fourthly, Popper went out of his way in *The Logic of Scientific Discovery* to stress that it was possible to save any *prima facie* empirical statement from falsification, by way of making modifications to its scope, or by making changes to other parts of one's theoretical system (or, indeed, to the meaning of ones terms). He was both well aware of, and appreciative of, the critical contributions here of conventionalist writers including Poincaré and Pierre Duhem. Popper's response to this issue – which he discussed extensively – was to argue that a purely logical theory of the character of empirical statements was insufficient, and that what was needed, instead, was a theory of method: indeed, what he called a "logic of scientific discovery" (LScD: §11). This was concerned with spelling out the methodological rules that should guide us fallibly towards the achievement of our chosen aims. Fifthly, there is Popper's theory of the "empirical basis" (discussed below).

At the heart of Popper's approach there is thus the choice of methodological rules; he often refers to this in terms of "decisions", but it is clear that the decisions are being made with regard to a particular conception of the aims of science. These then play a key role in relation to his views about how we should react in the face of the falsification of our theories, and also in the development of his views about experience and basic statements. Although it is not the way in which Popper himself put the matter, I think that Ian Jarvie is correct in his emphasis, in his *Republic of Science* (2001), on the result being that Popper's theory of knowledge has a social character. To bring out the conflict with a naturalistic view, one could describe Popper's approach as involving the idea that we impose a set of disciplines upon ourselves, with an eye to attaining a particular chosen aim or goal.

Given the prominence of these ideas in Popper's book – and the clarity with which they are developed – it is strange to discover the extent to which they have not been appreciated by many of those who have discussed Popper's ideas. In particular, it is striking the degree to which problems that Popper himself pointed out and then subsequently addressed in *The Logic of Scientific Discovery*, by way of his methodological "logic of scientific discovery", are treated as if they were knock-down objections to his views. This is not to make a claim about the viability of Popper's response, or otherwise, but rather to point out that many critics do not seem to have looked very carefully at the structure of his argument, or to have appreciated what they need to engage with if they are to criticize his ideas (cf. the first part of Popper 1974).

One other general theme is worth noting. It is that Popper, in *The Logic of Scientific Discovery*, adopts a general strategy of avoiding metaphysical commitments and the discussion of metaphysical issues, and that he was critical of the way in which some people were drawing metaphysical lessons from quantum theory. Popper was aware that he held metaphysical views (e.g. realism, and an attachment to a simple correspondence theory of truth). He also argued that some metaphysical ideas had had a positive influence on the development of science, and that discovery might not be possible without a psychological inspiration from such views (LScD: §4). However, he did not have to hand a theory of the rational defensibility of his ideas about truth or of his views in metaphysics. He dealt with this problem in part by way of simply seeing us as faced with decisions (e.g. with regard to different, equally coherent, views about the aims of science), in part by treating metaphysical ideas as hypostatizations of methodological rules. Accordingly, a metaphysical principle of causality was treated as a hypostatization of the methodological rule: continue to search for explanations (LScD: §§12, 78). The point of this was that, for Popper, the adoption of particular methodological rules in the light of the aim of science that he favoured seemed to be a procedure for which one *could* provide a rationale, of a kind that he was not able to provide for his ideas about metaphysics. In *The Logic of Scientific Discovery*, Popper showed considerable ingenuity in his use of this approach. For example, he was able to offer a reading of simplicity (as in the context of theory choice), which made it neither an arbitrary metaphysical assumption about the world, nor something that rendered, after the fashion of conventionalism, the simplicity of the world a product of our decision. Instead, a methodological rationale was offered for the choice of (in one sense) a more simple theory over something more complex, and for the preferability of theories of the highest universality and precision; it became a facet of the most effective use of experience in learning about the correctness or otherwise of our ideas (see LScD: chs VI, VII, notably §43; Popper links testability with high logical improbability and this in turn with simplicity). His approach also serves to address – from a non-inductivist perspective – the problem sometimes referred to as the under-determination of theory choice by experience. For Popper, there was a prior methodological selection of theories on the basis of their testability. In addition, in writing about probability (of which more below), he was able to propose a methodological rule that served to render falsifiable, probabilistic statements that, strictly regarded, are unfalsifiable (LScD: §§65, 68).

The mention of probability leads me to a further – and important – theme in Popper's work. Popper devoted a fair proportion of the text of *The Logic of Scientific Discovery* to discussion of the interpretation of probability, and to the application of some of his ideas about this to problems in the interpretation of quantum theory. This work of Popper's is technical and, despite the fact that he writes clearly, its appeal is likely to be confined to those with a prior interest in the problems with which he is dealing. In his writings in this sphere, he has three broad concerns, concerns that, in one form or another, preoccupied him through much of his life.

The first of these was an exploration of different interpretations of probability. One of his contributions here was to admit a "logical" interpretation of probability alongside various physical interpretations. (Most previous writers held that probability was invariably logical or invariably physical.) This was to play an important role in some of his later work, in which he set out to investigate whether probability, so interpreted, could serve as a theory of confirmation or of probabilistic induction. He argued that it could not, and was inspired by this idea, over many years, to suggest that other logical theories of confirmation or of induction (e.g. that of Carnap; cf. Michalos 1971; Lakatos 1978), were problematic for this reason. *The Logic of Scientific Discovery* also contains, in Chapter X, a discussion of his own ideas about the non-inductive "corroboration" of theories, and a critique of probabilistic theories of induction, including that of Reichenbach.

Secondly, as Popper mentions in the introduction to the new appendices added to *The Logic of Scientific Discovery* in the 1959 translation, his claim that the degree of corroboration or confirmation of a hypothesis does not satisfy the rules of the calculus of probability led some proponents of probabilistic theories of confirmation to claim that they meant something different by "probability".

This, in turn, led Popper into much technical work, over many years, on the topic of how the calculus of probability should be axiomatized.

Thirdly, in *The Logic of Scientific Discovery* Popper defends a form of the frequency theory of probability. This interprets probability as an objective feature of the world, rather than a feature of our judgements or attitudes, or of degrees of rational belief. He deals with many technical problems concerning this view, including the substantive difficulty (especially from his own point of view, according to which the empirical character of a statement is characterized by its falsifiability) that probability statements understood as statements about limiting frequencies are "impervious to strict falsification" (LScD: ch. VIII, introduction). The problem here is that, so understood, probability statements – for example, that the probability of a particular tossed coin coming up heads is 0.5 – are compatible with any actual occurrence: any actual sequence of heads (i.e. any deviation from a uniform distribution) may possibly be compensated for by throws later in the sequence. As I indicated above, Popper suggested that we could render probability statements, so understood, falsifiable by way of a methodological decision to disregard certain possible but highly unlikely events.[1]

Despite the fact that Popper discusses these ideas extensively, I shall not say more about them here. This is in part because the material is technical, and in part because Popper himself later developed a different view of probability: understanding it in terms of propensities or dispositions that could be tested in terms of empirical frequencies. This he set out in various parts of the *Postscript*; it was interesting both as a technical development in the interpretation of probability (cf. Gillies 2000), and also because it related to wider cosmological views that he came to favour. (See Popper (1982b: 159–77, 1997) and, for a general appraisal of Popper's formal work on probability, Leblanc (1989).) There was also an additional theme concerning Popper's views about probability in *The Logic of Scientific Discovery*, which relates to the interpretation of quantum theory.

Popper had a longstanding interest in the interpretation of quantum theory. In *The Logic of Scientific Discovery* he argues against Heisenberg's interpretation, suggesting that what had been seen as puzzling features of the theory, such as supposed limits on the attainable precision of measurement, and the reduction of the wave packet, are simply consequences of the fact that it is a statistical theory. Popper thus championed an objective, inter-subjectively testable, statistical interpretation of the theory. He was also led to develop some ideas about a possible thought experiment, about which he had correspondence with Einstein (Einstein's letter discussing Popper's suggested thought experiment is reproduced as Popper (LScD: app. *xii)), who convinced Popper that his specific suggestion was untenable. Although Popper subsequently changed his views about quantum theory, he indicated that, in 1959, he still regarded his earlier discussion

– with the exception of the defect in his thought experiment – as significant (LScD: "Introduction to Chapter IX", n.*1).

These issues of probability, its interconnection with the interpretation of quantum theory, and more general issues in the interpretation of quantum theory, continued to be a major interest of Popper's. However, what he wrote subsequent to *The Logic of Scientific Discovery* was strongly influenced by the change from a frequency to a propensity theory of probability. In the light of its technical character, and because in Popper's own view the approach in *The Logic of Scientific Discovery* was superseded by his own later work, I shall not discuss it further. Instead, I shall turn back to the more purely philosophical themes that I have introduced above, and discuss in more detail two important issues: the complex of falsifiability, falsification and methodological rules, and Popper's theory of the "empirical basis".

In what follows, I shall thus concentrate on philosophical rather than technical aspects of Popper's book. This is in part a matter of my personal preference and competence, in part because it seems to me that the distinctive philosophical character of Popper's approach has been unduly neglected. I should however commend strongly the more technical aspects of Popper's work to those with an interest in these matters, notably in terms of what he was able to accomplish by way of interrelating testability, content (not least the identification of the empirical content of a theory and the class of its potential falsifiers), improbability and simplicity, and also by the technical (and historical) interest of his work on the frequency theory of probability and quantum theory.

Falsifiability, falsification and methodological rules

As I indicated in the previous section, a key role is played in Popper's work by his conception of the aim of science. I quoted some of Popper's statements from *The Logic of Scientific Discovery* about the aim of science, which contrasted with the views of the conventionalists, and which put a premium on the growth, adventure and open-endedness of scientific knowledge. Popper offers an account of science as a non-inductive endeavour, in which our activities target this aim.

We start, for Popper, from a problem-situation given to us by the state of play of our previous theories. We then come up with attempts to resolve this problem. From his perspective, it does not matter where our ideas come from. He does not think that there is a rational procedure for the generation of successful theories, and refers to the idea that every discovery contains what Henri Bergson called "a creative intuition" (LScD: §2). Such a view places Popper alongside Whewell (in his controversy with Mill) in holding the view that we bring theoretical ideas to our material, rather than extracting them from it (cf. Whewell 1849; but see also Snyder 2004); an idea that Popper expressed many years later in his "The Rationality of Scientific Revolutions" (1975), where he quoted Sir Ernst Gombrich as saying "making comes before matching".

Such ideas need then to be assessed: they should be consistent; they should be synthetic (rather than tautological); and also empirical statements of the kind that could conflict with basic statements. The theory should also be compared with other theories to tell us if it would constitute an advance in our knowledge if it were to pass tests, and then it should actually be tested (LScD: §3). What we further require of a theory is that it is daring: ideally, that it clashes with what we would normally expect, or would be led to expect by our best current theories.

All this leads Popper to his ideas about falsifiability and demarcation. What we should be after, on his account, is a theory that is open to testing, and that is as testable as possible: a theory that is highly falsifiable. Such theories are open to appraisal on the basis of empirical tests, a procedure that does not involve us in inductive procedures, just by virtue of the fact that there is an asymmetry between confirmation and falsification. Whereas a confirmation of a theory does not show that it is true, if a theory is falsified, this shows that it is false. (Although, of course, falsification is tentative, and there are many issues about what we should actually conclude from a test turning out other than we had expected, which I shall discuss below.) Openness to falsification also serves to distinguish between a scientific theory and a theory that is not scientific, for example, a metaphysical theory (or a pseudoscientific theory that pretends to scientific status). Falsifiability, for Popper, is not a theory of meaning; he is highly critical of approaches that stipulate some notion of meaningfulness, and then rule out various perfectly understandable claims as "meaningless", as if in the light of some kind of natural property of language. As we have seen, although he wishes to avoid making his theory depend on metaphysical assumptions, he does not hold that metaphysics is meaningless.

Popper also argues that only theories that are genuinely testable may be taken to be confirmed or corroborated. As he was to discuss elsewhere, one feature of unscientific theories is that their proponents may claim that they are confirmed where, in fact, there was no serious test involved; such "confirmations" Popper argues, are worthless (cf. his discussion of Adler in Popper (1963: ch. 1), and his discussion of science and pseudoscience in Popper (1976: §9)). Further, on Popper's account corroboration does not itself tell us that the theory will be successful in the future. There has been a great deal of controversy about Popper's views concerning corroboration, the understanding of which has not been aided by slightly ambiguous formulations in some of his later writings. But the situation seems to be as follows (cf. LScD: §§82–4). For Popper, the best that we can say for a theory is that it has passed the kinds of assessment indicated in the previous paragraphs, and has been corroborated. He does not think that this tells us that it is true, or that it is made probable, in some objective sense. Indeed, we know perfectly well that some of our most highly corroborated theories have turned out not to be true (in that some predictions subsequently made on the basis of them have been false), while any corroborated theory is open to Hume's more "metaphysical" objection that the laws of nature might suddenly change. From Popper's perspective, all of our evidence is negative, in the sense that we shall have picked out the most interesting and testable theories and – at any one time – all that we know is that some of them seem to be alright, so far.[2] Clearly, Popper expected the continuation of various regularities with which we are familiar but, and this is the mark of a robust realism, this would be the case if we had grasped the truth, or theories near to the truth. Yet how the world is does not depend on our knowledge or subjective certainty, so that we could well be wrong.

Let me now turn from these ideas – which took us some way beyond *The Logic of Scientific Discovery* – back to the main themes of this section. As I explained in the Introduction, for Popper, if our theories are falsified not only is that falsification itself tentative, but it serves to call into question the system of ideas with which we were working, rather than any one specific component of that system. As Popper writes:

> we falsify the whole system (the theory as well as the initial conditions) which was required for the deduction of the statement [which was falsified] ... Thus it cannot be asserted of any one statement of the system that it is, or is not, specifically upset by the falsification.
>
> (LScD: §18)

Let me offer a simple illustration. A chemist might be testing a theory, and discover that the experiment undertaken to test it does not come out as one would expect if the theory were true. Can he or she conclude that the theory is false? That is one possibility. But it could be the case that something else was responsible for the problematic outcome: a reagent on the bench might have been incorrectly labelled; a known impurity might have produced a previously undetected effect; or a piece of apparatus might have been contaminated. Alternatively, various pieces of technical apparatus might have been used in the course of undertaking the test, but the design of these assumes the correctness of various chemical or physical theories, which might themselves be problematic. In addition, various kinds of human error might have been responsible for the problem. We know – if the effect can be reproduced – that *something* is wrong. But just what has given rise to the problem? How, then, should we proceed?

First, it may be possible for us to work out some way of testing, independently, which item of our system of knowledge is at fault: to construct a "crucial experiment" (LScD: §22, n.1; see also §19, n.1 and the reference there to Popper (1963: ch. 3)). In *The Logic of Scientific Discovery* Popper offers some suggestions, in a similar vein, about the way in which we may be able to attribute responsibility for a problem to some newly introduced and independently testable hypothesis (LScD: §18).

There is, however, also a deeper issue involved here, which relates to Popper's discussion of the role of methodological rules. It concerns the fact that the possibility of blaming other things than our pet theory may lead us to behave in such a way that our theory is rendered immune to criticism. Popper introduced his discussion of these ideas by considering the views of conventionalist philosophers of science such as Poincaré, Duhem and Hugo Dingler. He noted that conventionalists were correct in their claim that we can attain certain knowledge by such means, for example, "because it is possible to interpret any given scientific system as a system of implicit definitions" (LScD: §19). Various "conventionalist stratagems", as Popper calls them, can be adopted towards our theories that will render them immune to falsification. These may include such moves as "blaming our inadequate mastery of the system" or "suggesting *ad hoc* the adoption of certain auxiliary hypotheses, or perhaps of certain corrections to our measuring instruments" (LScD: §19). Also:

> we may introduce *ad hoc* hypotheses, or we may modify … so-called "ostensive definitions" … [or] we may adopt a sceptical attitude as to the reliability of the experimenter whose observations, which threaten our system, we may exclude from science on the ground that they are insufficiently supported, unscientific, or not objective, or even on the ground that the experimenter was a liar … In the last resort we can always cast doubt on the acumen of the theoretician … (LScD: §19)

Popper states explicitly that "it is impossible to decide, by analysing its logical form, whether a system of statements is a conventional system of irrefutable, implicit definitions, or whether it is a system which is empirical in [his] sense" (LScD: §20), but he concludes from this that "Only with reference to the methods applied to a theoretical system is it at all possible to ask whether we are dealing with a conventionalist or an empirical theory". This brings us back to the centrality, for Popper's approach, of the methodological rules that we choose to adopt (in the light of our desired aim for science). The approach that Popper favours is usefully illustrated by what he has to say about the treatment of auxiliary hypotheses (LScD: §20; this will obviously require the modification of some aspect of our initial hypotheses, rather than just the adding of auxiliary hypotheses). For although the use of auxiliary hypotheses would seem problematic if it serves to render some theory beyond criticism, it would equally – as my example suggests – seem to be a perfectly legitimate response for us sometimes to make. It might, indeed, have been some other assumption that was at fault, and that needs to be revised. Popper's response to this problem is as follows. He mentions that: "Our methodological rule may be qualified by the remark that we need not reject, as conventionalistic, every auxiliary hypothesis that fails to satisfy these standards" (LScD: §20). He goes on to discuss some examples of exceptions:

> As regards auxiliary hypotheses we propose to lay down the rule that only those are acceptable whose introduction does not diminish the degree of falsifiability or testability of the system in question, but, on the contrary, increases it … If the degree of falsifiability is increased, the introducing of the hypothesis has actually strengthened the theory: the system now rules out more than it did previously: it prohibits more. We can also put it like this. The construction of an auxiliary hypothesis should always be regarded as an attempt to construct a new system; and this new system should then always be judged on the issue of whether it would, if adopted, constitute a real advance in our knowledge of the world. (LScD: §20)

All this serves to illustrate a distinctive feature of Popper's approach to which I have already drawn attention. As he himself explained, his view of science is not naturalistic in the sense of being a descriptive account of how scientists behave. But it is also non-naturalistic in another sense, too. Popper's approach involves the view that we need to adopt distinctive procedures and ways of behaving in the light of what we are aiming at. One might even say that it involves a will to truth (albeit not in Nietzsche's sense), or to the growth of knowledge, although what is involved may, clearly, be a matter of habit or tradition rather than of conscious decision.

The empirical basis

Popper's theory of the "empirical basis" constitutes another point of significant difference between his views and more traditional forms of empiricism. It also bears a distinctive mark from his dialogue with the Friesian development of the Kantian tradition. It is, however, an aspect of his views that has received considerable criticism even from scholars who in other respects were sympathetic towards his work (see Watkins 1984; Zahar 1989, 1995; also Shearmur (forthcoming) for a defence of Popper).

Popper's starting-point is, on the one hand, a disagreement with positivism. Positivists, Popper claims, dislike "the idea that there should be meaningful problems outside the field of 'positive' empirical science". He further comments that "time and again do the despised defenders of 'traditional philosophy' try to explain to the leaders of the latest positivistic assault that the main problem of philosophy is the critical analysis of the appeal to the authority of 'experience'" (LScD: §10; citing Gomperz (1905: 35)).[3] Popper's own response to this problem, his "own attempts to analyse 'experience'", amount to his account of "the method of empirical science" (LScD: §10) and thus in part to the ideas that we have already analysed, notably his ideas about methodological rules. But they also relate to his ideas about the "empirical basis".

The other starting-point relates to a concern for the objectivity of scientific knowledge. Popper tells us that his use of the terms "'objective' and 'subjective' is not unlike Kant's" (LScD: §8[4]). Popper draws here on Kant's idea about understanding objectivity in terms of inter-subjectivity, and says, more particularly, that "the objectivity of scientific statements lies in the fact that they can be inter-subjectively tested" (LScD: §8). He refers further to Kant with the remark that "the objectivity of scientific statements is closely connected with the construction of theories – with the use of hypotheses and universal statements" (LScD: §8). From this Popper draws the idea that "only when certain events recur in accordance with rules or regularities, as is the case with repeatable experiments, can our observations be tested – in principle – by anyone" (LScD: §8). This, in turn, leads him to the view that "stray" observation statements and unrepeatable observations, so-called "occult effects", can play no role in our empirical knowledge.

Popper contrasts objectivity in this sense with personal conviction, and argues that however strong a person's feeling of conviction may be about some experience or about the truth of some statement, this cannot serve to justify it. Although such feelings of conviction may motivate us to make statements, what is crucial is not our subjective conviction about them, but their inter-subjective acceptability. This leads Popper to the view that "those statements which belong to the empirical basis of science" must also be objective, and thus inter-subjectively testable. From this he draws the further conclusion that "there can be no ultimate statements in science: there can be no statements in science that cannot be tested, and therefore none which cannot in principle be refuted, by falsifying some of the conclusions which can be deduced from them" (LScD: §8).[5]

One further theme is worth spelling out. Popper refers to the way in which it was once the case that:

logic was [held to be] a science dealing with mental processes and their laws – the laws of our thought … A logical inference seemed to be justified because it was experienced as a necessity of thought, as a feeling of being compelled to think along certain lines.   (LScD: §27)

He then comments, however:

In the field of logic, this kind of psychologism is now perhaps a thing of the past. Nobody would dream of justifying the validity of a logical inference, or of defending it against doubts, by writing beside it in the margin the following protocol sentence. "Protocol: In checking this chain of inferences today, I experienced an acute feeling of conviction."
(LScD: §27)

With this, he then goes on to contrast the situation in epistemology. And he concludes that, just as in logic:

There is only one way to make sure of the validity of a chain of logical reasoning. This is to put it in the form in which it is most easily testable: we break it up into many small steps, each easy to check by anybody who has learnt the mathematical or logical technique of transforming sentences.   (LScD: §27)

So, he argues, empirical claims should be presented in a form that makes them open to inter-subjective testing. Thus:

In the case of the empirical sciences, the situation is much the same. Any empirical scientific statement can be presented (by describing experimental arrangements, etc.) in such a way that anyone who has learned the relevant technique can test it. If, as a result, he rejects the statement, then it will not satisfy us if he tells us about his feelings of doubt or about his feelings of conviction as to his perceptions. What he must do is to formulate an assertion that contradicts our own, and give us instructions for testing it. If he fails to do this we can only ask him to take another and perhaps more careful look at our experiment, and think again.   (LScD: §27)

What does Popper's theory of the empirical basis then actually amount to? Popper introduces his discussion with what he termed "Fries's trilemma".[6] This is the idea that claims to justification face the (problematic) options of either:

dogmatic assertion that something is true or, if statements can only be justified by statements, a regress of justification; or psychologism, the claim that statements can be justified by perceptual experience. Popper rejected psychologism, but also justification, arguing that Fries's trilemma could be resolved by way of the admission of an "innocuous" dogmatism (LScD: §29): that is, that at a certain point we accept a basic statement, but that the dogmatism is innocuous precisely because it is always open to us to undertake further tests, should we wish to do so. The basic statements themselves consist of statements about the behaviour of observable macro-level objects, made on the occasion of our performing the appropriate tests. These statements are themselves inter-subjectively testable, on the basis of a theory that we offer as to how such tests are to be reproduced: in effect, instructions for its replication.

For Popper, we undertake a test, and this leads to our issuing such a basic statement; other people may repeat the test, and either concur or call the earlier report into question. If they accept it (with or without testing it) then it is for the time being used for the purposes of corroborating or falsifying theories. If, however, it is called into question, then we repeat the test, or draw further consequences from what the other people claim took place, and test them. We stop this process – for the time being – when we reach inter-subjective agreement, although it will always be possible in principle for the testing to be re-opened, either if someone is led to question our results, or if, say, a new theory is put forward that leads to these results being questioned. Popper commented that "experiences can motivate a decision, and hence an acceptance or a rejection of a statement"; but he also stressed that "a basic statement cannot be justified by them – no more than by thumping the table" (LScD: §29). All this follows fairly simply from Popper's stress on objectivity as being a matter of inter-subjective acceptability. Yet, as I have indicated, it has been an aspect of his work that – alongside his most fundamental claim, to have solved the problem of induction (and his later theory of verisimilitude, which has generated a technical growth industry of its own) – seems to have been most widely rejected, even by those who one would have expected to be sympathetic towards it (cf. Watkins 1984; Zahar 1989, 1995).

One other feature of Popper's account is worth bringing out explicitly. It is that, as Popper puts it: "we can utter no scientific statement that does not go far beyond what can be known with certainty 'on the basis of immediate experience'" (LScD: §25). Every statement, Popper suggests, "has the character of a theory, of a hypothesis". He develops this idea, by way of arguing that a statement such as "Here is a glass of water" cannot be verified by any specific sense-experience, for "By the word 'glass' … we denote physical bodies which exhibit a certain law-like behaviour, and the same holds for the word 'water'" (LScD: §25). Popper is not here arguing that we experience sense data; by contrast, his view is that interpretation is involved in all perception. His point, however, is that that perception involves the conjectural attribution to what we perceive of properties that transcend the occasion on which we do the perceiving. If we see a glass of water, this means that what we are taking ourselves to be seeing is something that will behave in various ways in the future, and that – if we are right – would also behave in countless different ways (e.g. in relation to different chemical reagents), should we choose to test it.

The result is a striking fallibilist, non-foundationalist yet non-arbitrary theory of knowledge. It is non-arbitrary because of its inter-subjectivity, and because of the constraints imposed upon the moves that we make, by methodological rules. I have described it as a theory of knowledge, because Popper saw himself as contributing to epistemology, and indeed to philosophy more generally, rather than just to the philosophy of science. In his "Preface, 1959" to the first English edition of *The Logic of Scientific Discovery*, Popper brought out some of the differences between his approach and then-contemporary approaches to philosophy. He stressed his own view that an interest in the growth of knowledge – something that he thought was illuminated particularly by the development of science – is vital for the theory of knowledge more generally, and he defended his approach against the contrasting claims of ordinary language philosophy, and of formalist approaches to the philosophy of science.

There is much more to *The Logic of Scientific Discovery* than I have been able to bring out here. One striking theme – which is worth pursuing by way of what he says in both the text and footnotes[7] – is his critical engagement with Wittgenstein's *Tractatus*.[8] But this and many other topics, such as his allusions to parallels between his epistemology and evolutionary theory, cannot be discussed further here, for reasons of space.

How things changed

Popper's *Logic of Scientific Discovery* offers a distinctive approach to the problems of empirical knowledge. Because it deals with science, and because it is not Kantian in an orthodox sense, it has typically been read in a manner that assimilates it to, and finds it wanting against what would be expected of, work in the British empiricist tradition. However, as I have suggested, Popper is offering a *distinctive* approach to epistemology, and in my view his work merits more systematic attention than it has received.

It is, however, important also to note that there are various respects in which *The Logic of Scientific Discovery* differs from views that Popper was to develop later. This is not always a matter of their being deeply at odds. But it is I think important to point them out, just because Popper himself tended to view – and to present – his work as a whole, and because he also annotated and appended material to *The Logic of Scientific Discovery* that reflected later developments, and that may make differences over time tricky for the reader to discern. I shall discuss several points here.

The first is truth. In *The Logic of Scientific Discovery*, Popper comments that "In the logic of science here outlined it is possible to avoid using the concepts 'true' and 'false'" (LScD: §84). Instead, he suggests, one could talk about derivability and conventional decisions to accept or reject statements. He also writes, however, "This certainly does not mean that we are forbidden to use the concepts 'true' and 'false', or that their use creates any particular difficulty" (LScD: §84).

In his later work, Popper has no hesitation about speaking about truth and falsity, and in linking his views about science – as set out in *The Logic of Scientific Discovery* – to a fallibilist search for truth. The situation was as follows (cf. Popper's (1974) reply to Lakatos). When he was writing *The Logic of Scientific Discovery*, Popper appears to have favoured what one might call an "Aristotelian" or classical correspondence theory of truth: a view that says that a statement is true if what it asserts is, as a matter of fact, the case, but that does not espouse any particular theory as to how such "correspondence" is to be understood. At the time, however, there existed criticisms of the correspondence theory, in particular the semantic paradoxes, that Popper was not able to answer, and so he was happy to write in such a way that his work did not depend on an idea whose cogency he was not able to defend. As he has recounted on several occasions (e.g. Popper 1976: §20), after he had completed his book he met the Polish logician Alfred Tarski, who explained to him his semantic conception of truth.

As Tarski himself indicated, this could be read as a way of rehabilitating the correspondence theory of truth (see Popper 1979b), and this, certainly, is what Popper took from Tarski's approach. Popper was able to make use of facets of Tarski's approach to avoid the problems that had hitherto given him pause about freely using the idea of truth. What Popper did with this seems to me to stand independently of the issue of how, in the end, one might best interpret Tarski's own theory. It is, though, crucial to note that in Popper's work truth is used objectively, and without any suggestion that we will necessarily be able to recognize it if we have, in fact, grasped it. (The same is, in fact, also the case for his idea of "verisimilitude" or "truthlikeness", which has often also been misunderstood as an epistemic idea.)

Secondly, when writing *The Logic of Scientific Discovery* Popper was not always unfriendly to metaphysical ideas. He noted their sometimes benign influence on the development of science, and their heuristic role in scientific discovery; it is also pretty clear that he was himself a realist (Popper 1972: ch. 2). At the time, he did not have to hand a theory of the rational assessability of metaphysical ideas, or of how one could assess progress in this sphere (cf. his critique of Whitehead along these lines (1945: ch. 24, §v)). In *The Logic of Scientific Discovery*, he develops the theme – which I have already mentioned briefly – that one might see certain philosophical theories as hypostatizations of methodological rules (where the thrust of Popper's approach was that, if seen as methodological rules, they could be assessed rationally relative to some aim), and he was also quite critical of views that tried to read a metaphysical significance into quantum theory (LScD: ch. IX, Introduction).

Popper was later, in his *Postscript*, to develop a theory of the rational assessability of philosophical theories (relative to a problem-situation). He was also led to generalize his ideas about falsifiability, to emphasize the significance also of inter-subjective criticism. He became more ready to endorse metaphysical theories explicitly; not only did he develop, in the *Postscript*, a theory about the role in the growth of science of what he called metaphysical research programmes, but he also offered a specific cosmological theory of his own about the role of indeterministic probabilistic propensities.

This, in turn, was related to two significant respects in which Popper revised the ideas of *The Logic of Scientific Discovery*. The first of these was that he shifted from a frequency to a propensity theory of probability, a theory that is set out in various parts of the *Postscript*. This he further thought to be of significance in the interpretation of quantum theory, and he wrote several other papers on this theme. Secondly, Popper became a resolute defender of objective but indeterministic metaphysical realism. Here it is worth looking at *The Logic of Scientific Discovery* (§§69, 71, 76), for he there dismisses the very kind of theory that he later came to champion, an issue upon which he comments, clearly with some amusement, in footnotes added to the English translation of 1959.

Conclusion

In this brief chapter[9] I have offered an introduction to Popper's *Logic of Scientific Discovery*. If I have been successful, I will have thrown some light upon the text and, more generally, upon the general character of Popper's views. What I have not done here is offer any critical assessment of Popper's ideas, but that is a task in which I hope that readers of this chapter may subsequently join me.

Notes

1. For Popper's more sophisticated summary of his proposal, see the end of §68 of *The Logic of Scientific Discovery*. There is also an approach to the problem by way of the introduc-

tion of finite random sequences. D. Miller, *Out of Error* (Aldershot: Ashgate, 2005) not only provides an excellent overview of Popper's views, but gives a particularly useful account of Popper's work on probability, including of this idea.

2. The adequacy of such an approach is perhaps best pursued by way of David Miller's defence of his interpretation of Popper (in *Critical Rationalism: A Restatement and Defence* (La Salle, IL: Open Court, 1994), "Induction: A Problem Solved", in *Karl Poppers kritischer Rationalismus heute*, J. M. Böhm, H. Holweg, & C. Hoock (eds), 81–106 (Tübingen: Mohr Siebeck, 2002) and *Out of Error*), which documents and attempts to answer the views of many critics. For other perspectives from those broadly sympathetic to Popper's work see J. Watkins, *Science and Scepticism* (Princeton, NJ: Princeton University Press, 1984) and A. Musgrave, *Essays on Realism and Rationalism* (Amsterdam: Rodopi, 1999).

3. In *Unended Quest* (London: Fontana, 1976) he refers to the significance for him of Gomperz's encouragement. For some recent discussion of Gomperz see F. Stadler & M. Seiler (eds), *Heinrich Gomperz, Karl Popper und die "österreichische Philosophie"*, *Beiträge zum internationalen Forschungsgespräch aus Anlaß des 50, Todestages von Heinrich Gomperz (1873–1942) und des 90, Geburtstages von Karl R. Popper (1902–)* (Amsterdam: Rodopi, 1994).

4. Note 1 refers to Immanuel Kant, *Critique of Pure Reason*, cf. N. Kemp Smith (trans.) (London: Macmillan, 1933), Transcendental Doctrine of Method, ch. 2, §3.

5. He qualifies this in his new note *4 in §78, where he writes that "a falsifiable statement may have all kinds of logically weak consequences, including non-falsifiable ones".

6. Jakob Friedrich Fries was the philosopher upon whose work Leonard Nelson had drawn the inspiration for his own ideas. In developing his argument, Popper (LScD: §25) refers to Fries's *Neue oder anthropologische Kritik der Vernunft* (Heidelberg: Christian Friedrich Winter, 1828–31).

7. And also in notes to his *The Open Society and its Enemies* (London: Routledge, 1945) and in the text of his *Die beiden Grundprobleme der Erkenntnistheorie*, T. Eggers Hansen (ed.) (Tübingen: J. C. B. Mohr (Paul Siebeck), 1979).

8. In the early 1950s Paul Feyerabend put together a paper-length critique of Wittgenstein, based on Popper's discussion in *The Open Society and its Enemies* and *Die beiden Grundprobleme*, and wrote it up as a paper that Popper might publish. A copy is held in the Popper Archive at The Hoover Institution Archive (no. 537-1).

9. I should like to thank, Brian Garrett, Peter Roeper, David Wall and especially Joseph Agassi, John Shand and above all David Miller for most useful comments and suggestions on an earlier version. They are of course not responsible for the chapter's remaining deficiencies.

References

Berkson, W. & J. Wettersten 1984. *Learning from Error: Karl Popper's Psychology of Learning*. La Salle, IL: Open Court.

Fries, J. F. 1828–31. *Neue oder anthropologische Kritik der Vernuft*. Heidelberg: Christian Friedrich Winter.

Gillies, D. 2000. *Philosophical Theories of Probability*. London: Routledge.

Gombrich, E. 1960. *Art and Illusion*. London: Phaidon.

Gomperz, H. 1905. *Weltanschauungslehre I*. Jena: E. Diederichs.

Grattan-Guinness, I. 1992. "Russell and Karl Popper: Their Personal Contacts", *Russell* **12**(1), 3–18.

Hacohen, M. 2000. *Karl Popper: The Formative Years*. Cambridge: Cambridge University Press.

Hansen, T. E. 2002. "Which Came First, the Problem of Induction or the Problem of Demarcation?" Paper presented at *Popper 2002* conference, 3–7 July 2002, Vienna.

Jarvie, I. 2001. *The Republic of Science: The Emergence of Popper's Social View of Science 1935–1945*. Amsterdam: Rodopi.

Johansson, I. 1975. *A Critique of Karl Popper's Methodology*. Gothenburg: Akademiförlaget.

Kant, I. 1933. *Critique of Pure Reason*, N. Kemp Smith (trans.). London: Macmillan.

Lakatos, I. 1978. "Changes in the Problem of Inductive Logic". In *Mathematics, Science and Epistemology, Philosophical Papers 2*, J. Worrall & G. Currie (eds), 128–200. Cambridge: Cambridge University Press.

Leblanc, H. 1989. "Popper's Formal Contributions to Probability Theory". In *Perspectives on Psychologism*, M. Notturno (ed.), 341–67. Leiden: Brill.

Michalos, A. 1971. *The Popper–Carnap Controversy*. The Hague: Nijhoff.

Miller, D. 1994. *Critical Rationalism: A Restatement and Defence*. La Salle, IL: Open Court.

Miller, D. 1997. "Sir Karl Raimund Popper, CH, FBA". *Biographical Memoirs of Fellows of The Royal Society of London* **43**, 367–409.

Miller, D. 2002. "Induction: A Problem Solved". In *Karl Poppers kritischer Rationalismus heute*, J. M. Böhm, H. Holweg, & C. Hoock (eds), 81–106. Tübingen: Mohr Siebeck.

Miller, D. 2005. *Out of Error*. Aldershot: Ashgate.

Musgrave, A. 1999. *Essays on Realism and Rationalism*. Amsterdam: Rodopi.

O'Hear, A. 2003. *Karl Popper: Critical Assessments of Leading Philosophers*. London: Routledge.

Popper, K. 1927 *"Gewohnheit" und "Gesetzerlebnis" in der Erziehung* ["Habit" and the "Experience of Laws" in Education]. Thesis, Pedagogic Institute of the City of Vienna.

Popper, K. 1934. *Logik der Forschung*. Vienna: Julius Springer.

Popper, K. 1943. Popper to Fritz Hellin 29 June 1943; Popper Archive 28–7. Hoover Institution Archive, Stanford University.

Popper, K. 1945. *The Open Society and its Enemies*. London: Routledge.

Popper, K. 1957a. "Aim of Science". *Ratio* **1**, 24–35.

Popper, K. 1957b. "Probability Magic or Knowledge out of Ignorance". *Dialectica* **11**, 354–72.

Popper, K. 1957c. "The Propensity Interpretation of the Calculus of Probability, and the Quantum Theory". In *Observation and Interpretation*, S. Körner (ed.), 65–70, 88–9. London: Butterworth.

Popper, K. 1958. "On the Status of Science and of Metaphysics II: The Problem of the Irrefutability of Philosophical Theories". *Ratio* **1**, 97–115.

Popper, K. 1959a. *The Logic of Scientific Discovery* (LScD). London: Hutchinson.

Popper, K. 1959b. "The Propensity Interpretation of Probability". *British Journal for the Philosophy of Science* **10**, 25–42.

Popper, K. 1961. "Philosophy and Physics: The Influence on Physics of Some Metaphysical Speculations on the Structure of Matter". *Atti del XII Congresso Internazionale di Filosofia (Venezia, 12–18 Settembre 1958)*, **2**, 367–74. Florence: G. C. Sansoni Editore.

Popper, K. 1962. "Julius Kraft 1898–1960". *Ratio* **4**, 2–12.

Popper, K. 1963. *Conjectures and Refutations*. London: Routledge.

Popper, K. 1972. *Objective Knowledge*. Oxford: Clarendon Press.

Popper, K. 1974. "Replies to my Critics". In *The Philosophy of Karl Popper*, P. Schilpp (ed.), 961–1197. La Salle, IL: Open Court.

Popper, K. 1975. "The Rationality of Scientific Revolutions". In *Problems of Scientific Revolution*, R. Harré (ed.), 72–101. Oxford: Clarendon Press.

Popper, K. 1976. *Unended Quest*. London: Fontana.

Popper, K. & J. Eccles 1977. *The Self and Its Brain*. New York: Springer International.

Popper, K. 1979a. *Die beiden Grundprobleme der Erkenntnistheorie*, T. Eggers Hansen (ed.). Tübingen: J. C. B. Mohr (Paul Siebeck).

Popper, K. 1979b. "Is it True what She Says about Tarski?". *Philosophy* **54**(207), 98.

Popper, K. 1982a. *The Open Universe: An Argument for Indeterminism*, W. W. Bartley III (ed.). London: Hutchinson.

Popper, K. 1982b. *Quantum Theory and the Schism in Physics*, W. W. Bartley III (ed.). London: Hutchinson.

Popper, K. 1983. *Realism and the Aim of Science*, W. W. Bartley III (ed.). London: Hutchinson.

Popper, K. 1994. *The Myth of the Framework*, M. Notturno (ed.). London: Routledge.

Popper, K. 1997. *A World of Propensities*. Bristol: Thoemmes.

Shearmur, J. forthcoming. "Karl Popper and the Empirical Basis". In *Karl Popper: A Centenary Assessment*, I. Jarvie, K. Milford & D. Miller (eds). Aldershot: Ashgate.

Snyder, L. 2004. "William Whewell". In *Stanford Encyclopedia of Philosophy* (http://setis.library.usyd.edu.au/stanford/contents.html, accessed 15 September 2005).

Stadler F. & M. Seiler (eds) 1994. *Heinrich Gomperz, Karl Popper und die "österreichische Philosophie". Beiträge zum internationalen Forschungsgespräch aus Anlaß des 50. Todestages von Heinrich Gomperz (1873–1942) und des 90. Geburtstages von Karl R. Popper (1902–)*. Amsterdam: Rodopi.

ter Hark, M. 1993a. "Problems and Psychologism: Popper as the Heir to Otto Selz". *Studies in History and Philosophy of Science* **24**, 585–609.

ter Hark, M. 1993b. "Searching for the Searchlight Theory: From Karl Popper to Otto Selz". *Journal of the History of Ideas* **64**(3), 465–87.

ter Hark, M. 2002. "Between Autobiography and Reality: Popper's Inductive Years". *Studies in the History and Philosophy of Science* **33**A(1), 79–103.

ter Hark, M. 2004. *Popper, Otto Selz and the Rise of Evolutionary Epistemology*. Cambridge: Cambridge University Press.

Watkins, J. 1984. *Science and Scepticism*. Princeton, NJ: Princeton University Press.

Wettersten, J. 1992. *The Roots of Critical Rationalism*. Amsterdam: Rodopi.

Whewell, W. 1849. *Of Induction, With Especial Reference to Mr. J. Stuart Mill's System of Logic*. London: J. W. Parker.

Zahar, E. 1983. "The Popper–Lakatos Controversy in the Light of *Die beiden Grundprobleme der Erkenntnistheorie*". *British Journal for the Philosophy of Science* **34**, 149–71.

Zahar, E. 1989. "John Watkins on the Empirical Basis and the Corroboration of Scientific Theories". In *Freedom and Rationality: Essays in Honor of John Watkins*, F. D'Agostino & I. C. Jarvie (eds), 325–41. Dordrecht: Kluwer.

Zahar, E. 1995. "The Problem of the Empirical Basis". In *Karl Popper: Philosophy and Problems*, A. O'Hear (ed.), 45–74. Cambridge: Cambridge University Press.

Further reading

Popper's writings

The Logic of Scientific Discovery (London: Hutchinson, 1959) is the best way into Popper's work, but chapters VI–IX contain technical material. The book is currently published by Routledge (1995). *Popper Selections*, D. Miller (ed.) (Princeton, NJ: Princeton University Press, 1985) provides a useful overview of Popper's work as a whole. *The Myth of the Framework*, M. Notturno (ed.) (London: Routledge, 1995) is a lively and accessible selection of talks and articles by Popper on a range of topics. *Conjectures and Refutations* (London: Routledge, 1963) is an important collection of Popper's papers, which takes further some of the themes in *The Logic of Scientific Discovery*. *Objective Knowledge* (Oxford: Clarendon Press, 1972) is a further collection of Popper's papers. Popper's *Postscript* to *The Logic of Scientific Discovery*, together with some related papers, has been published in parts in *Realism and the Aim of Science; The Open Universe: An Argument for Indeterminism* and *Quantum Theory and the Schism in Physics*, W. W. Bartley III (ed.) (London: Routledge, 1982–83). *Die beiden Grundprobleme der Erkenntnistheorie*, T. E. Hansen (ed.) (Tübingen: J. C. B. Mohr (Paul Siebeck), 1979) is Popper's first book, only published in 1979, and not yet available in English. In *The Self and Its Brain* (with J. Eccles) (New York: Springer International, 1977), Popper and Eccles each have (separate) sections on aspects of the mind–body problem; there is also a third section of discussion between them. The book is now published by Routledge.

Writings by others

Alan Chalmers, *What is This Thing Called Science?*, 3rd edn (Milton Keynes: Open University Press, 1999) is a general introduction to the philosophy of science, broadly sympathetic to a Popperian perspective, but which includes criticism and an account of competing views. Malachi Hacohen, *Karl Popper: The Formative Years* (Cambridge: Cambridge University Press, 2000) is a superlative intellectual biography of the younger Popper. Ian Jarvie, *The Republic of Science: The Emergence of Popper's Social View of Science, 1935–1945* (Amsterdam: Rodopi, 2001) is a striking interpretation of Popper's philosophy of science, bringing out its social aspects. Bryan Magee, *Karl Popper* (London: Fontana, 1985) provides a useful introductory overview of Popper's work. David Miller, *Critical Rationalism: Restatement and Defence* (La Salle, IL: Open Court, 1994) is a powerful defence of a Popperian approach to the theory of knowledge. Anthony O'Hear, *Karl Popper* (London: Routledge, 1980) is a useful overview that takes a critical approach to Popper's work. P. A. Schilpp (ed.), *The Philosophy of Karl Popper* (La Salle, IL: Open Court, 1974) contains Popper's "Intellectual Autobiography" (= *Unended Quest*), critical engagements with his work by a variety of figures, and Popper's "Replies to My Critics". Geoffrey Stokes, *Popper: Philosophy, Politics and Scientific Method* (Cambridge: Polity, 1998) is a more recent overview which, again, is critical of Popper. Jeremy Shearmur, *The Political Thought of Karl Popper* (London: Routledge, 1996) discusses Popper's political and social thought and its links with his theory of knowledge. John W. N. Wakins, *Science and Scepticism* (Princeton, NJ: Princeton University Press, 1984) is a critical engagement with issues raised by Popper's work by a former colleague.

Index